KESSELRING: A SOLDIER'S RECORD

ALBERT KESSELRING

GENERALFELDMARSCHALL A.D.

KESSELRING
A SOLDIER'S RECORD

With an Introduction by

S. L. A. MARSHALL
Chief Historian of European Theater

GREENWOOD PRESS, PUBLISHERS
WESTPORT, CONNECTICUT

Introduction

My personal view of Field Marshal Kesselring is perhaps different from that of any other American for reasons which are readily explained.

When the fighting ended in Europe in May, 1945, it seemed to me as Chief Historian of the European Theater to be clear as a pikestaff that, if the work of my division was ever to become complete, it would be necessary gradually to absorb the majority of the enemy commanders and their staffs into our operation. The reasoning was self-evident. Most of the German records had been captured by our forces and would not be returned. Germany, as a captive nation, would never be permitted to write its own operational history. Therefore if the enemy battlefield operations were ever to be profiled against our own, so that we might know the why, when and where of what had happened to our own forces, the reconstruction of the enemy effort would have to become a mutual undertaking, under my direction.

My superiors were at first skeptical of this approach and tended either to laugh it off or oppose it directly; there was, however, a deep understanding of the need among my opposite numbers at the War Department. I could well understand why the idea was little favored on our own side of the fence. It was radical. Nothing of the sort had ever been done before. There were no regulations to cover it. Nor was the fact that we were confronted with a wholly new situation requiring original methods enough to combat normal administrative prejudice successfully.

In perplexity of mind, I went then to certain of the enemy commanders to get their views about whether the requisite measure of co-operation would be forthcoming. Von Rundstedt was weary, aloof and scarcely interested, but he expressed his confidence that the majority of his military colleagues would respond at any time to a problem which aroused their professional concern.

Maj. Kenneth W. Hechler, one of my staff officers, was my right bower in the pioneer explorations. From General Walter Warlimont, who had been chief of operations of the Wehrmacht, he brought the word that the idea was so thoroughly workable that he (Warlimont) would volunteer as our first recruit, if we would have him. When the fact was reported at a General Staff council, it prompted louder laughter than would a jest from the commanding general.

Still, we went ahead. When doors will not open, a bulldozer is sometimes effective. The rigors to which the enemy commanders were being subjected in several of our prison camps were appalling to any American who believed that his nation should always do things decently and in order and according to the spirit of law. I officially protested, pointing out that the treatment was wrong *per se* and that we were in effect destroying knowledge which could prove as useful to us as the brains of the German scientists whom we were already embracing. On that point I was sustained by higher command, which needed only to have the situation called to its attention. Gradually, and by devious steps, we cleared our own right of way. An initial group of ten enemy high commanders was put in our temporary custody. It was thereafter steadily expanded. We got along with these officers because, while we treated them as prisoners, we also recognized that they were fellow members of the human race in heavy tribulation. To afford them minimum creature comforts, so that they could settle to their work in relative peace of mind, my people bought them such things as tobacco, sweets and shaving soap with their own pocket money. We also tried to get word to their families that they were still alive, a boon which had been previously denied them.

To these simple measures, combined with the absolute loyalty, zeal and purposefulness of five young American officers—the above-mentioned Major Hechler, Major Howard Hudson,

Captain Francis P. Halas, Captain Frank C. Mahin, and Captain James Scoggins—who became dedicated to this project, must be credited its ultimate phenomenal success. All five had the quality of compassion; it has rarely paid a larger dividend.

We found these new "colleagues" as various in character, spirit and response as any other collection of humanity. Some were so eager to please that they seemed almost servile. Their work therefore required extra watching. Others were as methodically efficient and as normally courteous as if they were doing routine staff work in freedom. This was the best type; even more than we, they gave direction to the work of the others. And there was a small minority which remained sullen, resentful and uncommunicative. We could do little with them and it occurred to us that they had perhaps been problems to their own families and neighbors.

It is a vivid recollection. Reflecting upon that experience, I find appropriate the words which Donald Hankey said of the battlefield: "I have seen the naked souls of men stripped of circumstance . . . I saw who were slaves and who were free; who were beasts and who were men; who were contemptible and who were honourable." As rank and reputation became leveled, and fear of the war crimes tribunal mounted, it was a trial of manhood in which the real general became distinguishable from the others who had merely attained the rank. Perhaps this is leadership in its vital essence; subconsciously, we acknowledge the superiority of the individual who in any circumstance commands himself.

Albert Kesselring is a multiple person. No other great German commander had such a variety of major tasks within one war. None other may claim as many curiously conflicting public reputations. Supreme Commander! Convicted war criminal! Hitler henchman! Objective soldier! Depending on the point of view, Kesselring is an inspired leader, a military meddler, a felon, an honourable opponent, a genius at military organization, a confused operator, a horse for work, a weak vessel—all these things and a few more.

Since the facts of a matter are incontrovertible, my opinion as to where truth lies is of no moment, though it should be clear that if I did not respect Kesselring, and above all, respect him as a *man*, I would not be writing. Moreover, I feel that the story herewith presented in which he reflects upon his own life is a more valid basis for judgment of him than the partial verdicts of the courts and critics. He has told the story as he sees it, in plain words, without shading, without apology. The performance is consistent with his character. From what he says, it would be possible to dismiss him as a pliant and useful military tool of Hitlerism and thereby to deny him all virtue. But I should not consider that a proper exercise.

"Smiling Al," as he came to be known to the people in our operation, was not of the group of German generals who worked with us through the latter months of 1945. He had taken command in the West very late in the game and our initial effort was directed toward the true crises of operation. Months later, he was pried out of Nürnberg and taken to the historical camp at Allendorf by the two young West Pointers in our show, Captains Mahin and Scoggins. By then the Germans had chilled toward the work. Their withdrawal of co-operation was due to the flood of vilification spilling from Nürnberg. Having just left that cauldron of calumny, Kesselring was in position either to harden the others permanently against the project or to guide them in the light of reason.

He didn't fall to our side; he stepped right over the fence. From the moment of his arrival—smiling, dignified, unembittered—the scales tipped our way. More important than his own significant contributions to the histories of the Italian and Western Front campaigns was his influence on the conscience-searchers and pouters. This was exerted by the force of his example on the one hand and a combination of bland persuasion and iron logic on the other. Whenever one of the more recalcitrant tried to throw a block against the operation, the problem was given to Smiling Al. Invariably he brought the other man around.

The crucial test of his influence arose when the imminence of his trial by the British in Italy became public knowledge. Large segments of the Allendorf population went on strike and quit their writing because of what they considered the grave injustice done him. By some process which the Americans in the camp never quite understood, Kesselring persuaded them to get back to the jerry-built work tables. He had that special power and dignity which appear ever to attend the man who comes to think of his own fate as being relatively unimportant.

By the hour of his trial and conviction, I was back in this country and had resumed editorial work. My view of the judgment was published in *The Detroit News*, May 10, 1947:

"The verdict would appear to be that Kesselring, in taking reprisal, overstepped the bounds. But what are the bounds? They are not defined by law. He did his duty, and a soldier's duty is ever hard and sometimes brutal.

"A poorer soldier would have quit, or let himself be overrun. And it is conceivable that a wiser one might have better judged what measure of reprisals would be militarily justified later in the presence of an enemy court. But this, I doubt. Rather, I believe that Kesselring was the victim of unavoidable circumstance and that any competent commander put in the same position would have found it impossible to come through with clean hands."

Many other men felt these same assailing doubts that this enemy commander was receiving that essential fair play which is the mainspring of goodwill in the world. There were vigorous protests from several leaders of influence. But the person least disturbed was Kesselring. He faced death and public disgrace in full serenity of spirit. To one of my associates who had written him a note of regret, he replied: "It is as if this were a battle. There comes a time when a commander has heard the best advice of all others. All factors have been weighed and turned slowly in the hand. One step remains—to look deeply into one's own heart."

Much that he says in this book—his summing-up—has that same clarion tone. Lofty phrases are not uncommon to generalship; frequently they reflect the inner philosophy of the author not at all. It is enough to say that Kesselring, as a man, lives all that he professes to believe. Much of his power comes from a peace of mind which is expressed in an outward sincerity.

How then reconcile these personal virtues with his unflagging devotion to Nazi Germany? The proper nature of military loyalty is one of the most complex of questions. Does a soldier owe blind allegiance to his superiors, or must he be prepared for thought and action outside his professional sphere? One view is that there must be latitude for judgment, since undeviating steadfastness may become the handmaiden of evil. The other view is that, lacking absolute loyalty, a military system has no safeguard against anarchy.

For such a man as Kesselring, there could be no middle ground. That, too, is according to his nature. He could not turn like the men of July 20, twist like Rommel, retire to his tent like Rundstedt or blow hot and cold like Guderian. His task was the fighting of the battle. His view of duty was to stay the course. From that singleness of purpose came a strength which would have proved admirable in any worthy cause. But it is not infrequently true that the soldier who holds to an utterly simple ideal of obligation is fixed with an unshakable faith in the virtue of the object.

So it was with Kesselring. Possibly from the narrow American point of view, his strength was his weakness. But he could no more step out of character in what he did than in what he now writes of his life and work. One sentence toward the end of the book might better have been used as the opening line: "To the young I would say that the meaning of life lies in the endeavour to do right and that perfection is not to be found on this earth."

I can believe that he guided on this belief as on a polestar. The quality of his generalship will be well-studied through years to come; he left his mark on all who faced him. He had long since won the greater battle within himself which enabled him to come through the crueler trials of the post-war years with high heart, still undaunted.

S. L. A. MARSHALL
Chief Historian of European Theater

Detroit, Michigan
December, 1953

Foreword

I was finally released from prison on 23 October, 1952, and was fully pardoned shortly thereafter. The years I spent behind bars were a road I had to travel before I could begin to read the enigmas of life—or so it strikes me today now that these years have given me the time for reflection. There my thoughts were magnetically attracted to the past. I wanted to clarify my mind about the events of yesterday, so I might hope to understand today and be confident of tomorrow.

After my first year (in the American detention camp at Mondorf near Luxembourg and the remand prison at Nürnberg, where all we were permitted was a surreptitious glance at the American army paper *Stars and Stripes*) I was able from the middle of 1946 to study works of military science. In addition, newspapers, periodicals and books from many countries helped me to a deeper insight into contemporary events and trends. Through foreign publications I became familiar with American, British, French, Swiss, Italian and, to a lesser extent, Soviet ideas. The controlled German press had little to offer me, and I was therefore grateful for the varied abundance of foreign newspapers, through which, though cut off from the outside world, I yet had access to all the subjects that interested me, and which I supposed to be fairly accurately reported. Nevertheless, much of it made unsatisfactory reading. News stories and editorial comment are only useful in so far as their incentive is to serve the truth. Many "factual" reports, however, made one positively uncomfortable.

Whereas in other countries many of the leading actors in the drama have painted from personal memory as detailed a picture as possible of their side of it, the recollections of the chief German protagonists are missing. Consequently the historian lacks an essential element. Many people may be glad to hear why and how in this or that situation such a course was adopted in preference to another, and what motives influenced the decisions, large and small, of those who had to make them.

Accordingly, I decided that I would take up my pen and make my contribution. I shall try to speak only of matters in which I was involved and where I was able to form a more or less comprehensive picture of what was happening.

What I am going to write will, to the best of my capacity, be of people and circumstances as they appeared to me *at the time*. I am aware, of course, that however much I may aspire to objectivity I may in the last resort remain subjective, or at any rate give that impression. But the reader will have no cause to accuse me of trying to make out that I was always right. No one is unerring in his judgment and behaviour, and I shall freely admit the mistakes which I now recognize as such. A man with the experience of a lifetime behind him should not shirk the duty of self-examination and frank confession. This kind of writing requires, above all, personal candour, that is to say a willingness to set down one's motives and actions as conceived there and then. That so often hitherto this duty has been evaded would not justify my following a precedent I believe to be wrong.

If the reader wishes to understand my actions he must bear with me while I sketch my personal background. A brief summary may show that a military life is more than "playing at soldiers," and exacts a strenuous physical and psychological effort and a heavy responsibility.

A. K.

Contents

PART ONE

YEARS OF WAR AND PEACE: 1904-41

PART THREE

UNCONDITIONAL SURRENDER AND MY TRIAL

Contents

Illustrations

Kesselring with Crown Prince Umberto and General von Rintelen.

Following a conference with Marshal Graziani.

Mussolini visits Kesselring's headquarters.

Venice, February 1947—on the way to trial.

Camp Wolfsberg, June 1947.

Maps

Part One

YEARS OF WAR AND PEACE
1904-41

1

Service in the Royal Bavarian Army and the Reichswehr, 1904-33

Early years at Munich—With the Bavarian Foot Artillery—1917 Armistice negotiations on the Russian front—G.S.O. to II and III Bavarian Army Corps—1918 Demobilization work: formation of security troops and Freikorps—1 Oct. 1922. Transfer to the Reichswehr Ministry in Berlin.

I do not come from a family of soldiers. My ancestors once founded the "Chezelrinch" against the Avars, and later against the Hungarians, in what is today Lower Austria. Ritter Ouscalus Chezelrinch (1180) was the first to borrow the name. From these origins the Kesselrings made themselves respected as knights, patricians and priests in the German south and beyond the German frontiers in Alsace and Switzerland. My direct ancestors, however, have been settled since the sixteenth century in Lower Franconia as farmers, brewers and vine-growers. Some branches of the family adopted the teaching profession, to which my father, a town councillor on the education committee of Bayreuth, also belonged.

My youth was spent in our large family circle at Wunsiedel in the Fichtelgebirge, and in Bayreuth, where I matriculated from the Classical Grammar School in 1904. I had no difficulty in choosing a profession. I wanted to be a soldier, indeed I was set on it, and looking back I can say that I was always a soldier heart and soul. Not being an officer's son, I did not enter the army as a cadet, but as a volunteer *Fahnenjunker* or aspirant officer, being nominated by the C.O. of the 2nd Bavarian Foot

3

Artillery Regiment, with which I began my military career and
in which I served, except for periods at the Military Academy
(1905-6) and the Artillery School (1909-10) in Munich, until
1915.

Metz, the regiment's depot, being a garrison town and a fortress, was the best possible training ground for a young and
ambitious soldier. There was no new military weapon that was
not tested out there, and the training was hard. The spirit of
Haeseler and the closeness of the frontier meant that efficiency
had to come first. The racial links, moreover, between the Germans and the people of Alsace-Lorraine fostered the idea of
German unity. We used to pay visits to the battlefields of the
Franco-Prussian War, Colombey-Nouilly, Mars-la-Tour, Grav-
elotte and St. Privat, or across the frontier to Sedan. There was
no cheap militarism about our admiration for our fathers' sacrifices.

But Metz and its surroundings offered many other attractions
to the susceptible among us. Who could be insensitive to the
glory of a spring day with the hillsides of the Moselle ablaze
with blossom? Who can forget our wonderful rambles up the
wooded valleys, the Bronvauxtal and the Monvauxtal? Which
of us grudged a few francs to enjoy the beauties of Nancy or
Pont-à-Mousson? When we handed our visiting card to the
French customs officer at Pagny-sur-Moselle and crossed the
frontier with his blessing and cheery "Have a good time!" and
were greeted on our return at the same post with the friendly
question, "Well, did you have it?" we felt we were breathing
the European spirit.

All this was changed with startling suddenness in 1911. The
most innocent trip across the frontier was reported to Berlin
and Paris, heads were scratched in the Foreign Ministries, and
the upshot was usually unpleasant for the misunderstood offender. From this time on, the fortress alerts became more frequent, incidentally obliging my battery to haul its guns at the
double to man the Kronprinz fort at Ars-sur-Moselle. Since
the forts on the western front of Metz (Forts Lothringen, Kai-
serin, Kronprinz and Haeseler) were so near the frontier, speed

was doubtless necessary. We junior officers often argued that, in the event of a sudden outbreak of war, it was by no means a sure bet that we in Metz would occupy them before the French did.

At the date of my enlistment in 1904 the 2nd Bavarian Foot Artillery was a fortress artillery regiment. We were trained on a variety of guns, ranging from the 3.7-cm. revolver cannon to the 28-cm. mortar, but primarily on armoured batteries, as was consistent with our purpose on mobilization. We learnt to shoot accurately—even at long ranges—and to handle the latest gadgets used by reconnaissance, observation and liaison units. This included training in balloon observation, which fascinated me. I liked free ballooning best; it made up for the queasy hours in a tethered balloon in a gale or even those on cross-country flights. I soon learnt from personal experience that this business needed a good stomach.

The fortress artillery owed its organization as mobile "heavy artillery of the army in the field" to the Emperor Wilhelm II and to Inspector-General of Fortress Artillery von Dulitz. Here I was able for the first time to be instrumental in an important change. Although the initiative must be credited to my superiors, particularly to the ingenious O.C. Bavarian Fortress Artillery Brigade, General Ritter von Höhn, nevertheless without the army's enthusiastic co-operation in 1914 the new and decisive heavy artillery would never have been available. This does not mean that the war, if it had to come, did not come too soon. It interrupted the normal peacetime development of the new arm and both in point of organization and psychological preparation cut short the time needed to run it in.

Had the war not come when it did, heavy artillery would not have been regarded as a mere incubus by certain authorities. I remember the C.-in-C. of the Sixth Army, when this was moved from Lorraine to Belgium in 1914, declaring: "Now with the happy prospect of a war of movement we shan't want the heavy artillery any longer."

Since then I have often observed this instinctive rejection of any innovation that has not yet broken down prejudice. It is remarkable how strongly the *vis inertiae* is able to influence even the best intelligence.

The Bavarian Ministry of War required from aspirant officers full matriculation and, in comparison with other quotas, a long period of training with their regiment or in War School before they were commissioned. We followed the Prussian system only in our Military Academy and General Staff training, although in Bavaria also before World War I an Academy course remained a *sine qua non* for acceptance into the General Staff. This had its advantages and disadvantages, and during the war changes had to be introduced because of the shortage of officers. The longer training before an aspirant received his commission was, however, to his advantage, and during the time of the Reichswehr this instructional period was considerably—and rightly—extended.

The tragic events in Austria of July 1914 gave the latter part of my regiment's visit to the artillery range at Grafenwöhr an unusually warlike background. The proclamation of a "threatening danger of war," which preceded the order for general mobilization, found our batteries already in occupation of the western-front forts at Metz. In those days and during the first phase of mobilization the equipment and movement of the combat units stationed at Metz proceeded without a hitch—a proof of the excellence of the preparatory staff work.

I remained with my regiment in Lorraine until the end of 1914, when I was transferred, just before the new year, as Adjutant to the G.O.C. 1st Bavarian Foot Artillery in the Sixth Army area in which command my staff was incorporated. In 1916 I was again transferred as Adjutant to the G.O.C. 3rd Bavarian Artillery, to whose staff I was attached until the end of 1917.

When we were detached from this last I went to the General Staff and served on the eastern front as G.S.O. on the staff of the 1st Bavarian Landwehr Division, as representative at which I conducted the local armistice negotiations on the Duna. My opposite number was a Russian G.S.O., who was accompanied by a general of the medical corps as interpreter. Two things struck me: first, the abnormal interest of the negotiator in tactical questions of trench warfare; and secondly the behaviour of the soldiers' councils appointed to cover the negotiations. They struck me as callow, uneducated oafs who interfered with practical discussions and peacocked as if they were the officers' bosses. I thought then that such things could never happen in the German army. Barely a year later I learnt differently. What individual units did in Cologne in 1918 strongly resembled the behaviour of the Russian revolutionaries. But away with these dismal memories! We can only be grateful we were spared such scenes in 1945.

While I was with the Sixth Army Command in Lille in 1918, as G.S.O. to the II and III Bavarian Army Corps, I came into frequent personal contact with the C.-in-C., Crown Prince Rupprecht of Bavaria. We were invited to his table in turn, where the Crown Prince dominated the conversation. Whether the topic was politics, art, geography, history or statecraft, he had a mastery of it. Whether he had the same grasp of military matters it was difficult to judge, as any allusion to them was carefully avoided. During World War II it was often argued among circles "in the know" that we entered this war with "better brains" than in World War I. Though this view rather overshoots the mark, it may be said that every important post was occupied by a thoroughly efficient soldier who had had the experience of an excellent preliminary training as a G.S.O. in World War I. These men were younger and maintained a closer contact with the troops than the 1914 commanders, amongst whom were various members of princely houses who, with due recognition for their example, human qualities and general capacity, were not exactly "Fredericks." It is less easy to assess the officers of the General Staff. Numerically the imperial G.S. Corps had the advantage; its training was more uniform. But the G.S. officer of 1939 was closer to the man behind the gun— an advantage which cannot be too highly appreciated; in every respect he was subordinate to the operational commander, so that there was no possibility of a repetition of the duality of command that developed disturbingly in World War I. The commander alone was answerable to his own conscience, and—as the event showed—to Hitler and the Allied tribunals. That did not preclude the fullest co-operation between a commander and his Chief of Staff, and a high degree of independence for the Chief of the General Staff.

In 1918 I wanted to retire from the army, but my politically minded G.O.C. insisted on my staying on to carry through the demobilization of the III Bavarian Army Corps in the Nürnberg area. This demobilization was carried out under the direction of a political commissar, a young barrister who was a member of the Social Democrat party. It was a very strenuous time for me, the pressure of work being heavier than at any time in the field. In addition to the demobilization proper, there were new security troops and Freikorps to be formed and their distribution round Nürnberg and in Munich and central Germany to be organized. It was interesting work, as it gave me a unique insight into the revolutionary events of the period, but disheartening to have to witness the fanatical excesses of the mob after the storming of our G.H.Q. in the Deutschherrn Barracks in early 1919.

My cup of bitterness was full when I saw my devoted work rewarded by a warrant for my arrest for an alleged *putsch* against the socialist-influenced command of my III Bavarian Army Corps. Notwithstanding degrading episodes during my imprisonment after 1945, I do not hesitate to describe this as the most humiliating moment of my life.

As battery commander for three and a half years from 1919 to 1922 at Amberg, Erlangen and Nürnberg, I was brought into close contact with the serviceman. There were choppings and changings galore; an army of 300,000 men had to be reduced to 200,000 and then to 100,000, and a way thus to be found to cut down our large and extravagantly inclined wartime army to a modest peace force, the *Führertruppe*. But the work, being educational, was rewarding, and I was glad to be contributing my mite to the regeneration of Germany.

On 1 October 1922 I was seconded for service in the Reichswehr Ministry in Berlin, and there entrusted with a key ap-

pointment as G.S.O.1 to the Chief of Staff of the head of
Army Direction. My work in this post, which covered the years
1922-29, included every branch of training, organization and
technique in all departments of the Reichswehr. I was busily
occupied with questions of economy and administration, national and international law, besides having to deal with the
problems of the Interallied Military Control Commission. I
worked in close liaison with the *Truppenamt,* the forerunner
of the *Zentralstelle* of the General Staff. Because of my special
knowledge of the work of the Ministry and of regimental conditions I was given an additional assignment as Commissioner
for Army Retrenchment, a work of reorganization which was
to occupy much of my time as head of Seventh Regional Command in Munich in 1929.

After a further short term of duty in the Ministry at Berlin
I spent exactly two years in Dresden as colonel and divisional
commander with the 4th Artillery Regiment. This ended my
service with the army. On 1 October 1933 I was formally discharged, and was put in charge of the Administration Office
of the Luftwaffe with the rank of Commodore.

2

Flashes from the
Reichswehr Period

Work as G.S.O. to the Chief of General Staff, Berlin—Von Seeckt's
training—The resurrection of the German army—Reichswehr Retrenchment Commissioner.

I owe much to my time in Berlin. I was loth to go to the
Prussian capital, but I confess that after a few years I grew to
love it, and it became my favourite town. After this admission
there is no need to explain how deeply, as a "man behind bars,"
I have shared the sufferings of Berlin's tragic years. I loved
Berlin and its people with their cheerfulness, their spruceness,
forthrightness and zest for work. I used every now and then to
spend an hour in the early morning at a corner of the Potsdamer-
platz, that vantage-point so sensitive to the pulsations of the
awakened city, and watch the flow of people disgorge from the
buses and railway stations. It was another matter when in the
troubled days of 1923 I had to walk from Lankwitz to the
Bendlerstrasse, or when as an honest and therefore almost des-
titute captain—I lost my fortune after the war and army rates
of pay were extremely low—I went in mufti with my wife to
study the "situations vacant" advertisements outside the Kloster-
theater and had to footslog it for an hour and a half there and
back. Yet we endured all this gladly for the sake of the Sunday
excursions into the Mark. What had I, a South German, imagined the Mark to be like? I learnt to love its lakes, woods and
people too. The jam on the tightly packed morning and evening

trains was part of the fun—such carefree enjoyment blew away the cobwebs of service problems.

Professionally the Berlin years were a schooling for me. What could have replaced the debates, often held in my room, in the presence of Lieutenant-General von Seeckt, who knew so well how to listen and then sum up in a way that always hit the nail on the head? What a model General Staff officer and leader of men! Again, where else could I have gained such inside knowledge of political conditions but from the witty and brilliantly argued lectures of General von Schleicher? It was a pity he could not continue his influence quietly behind the scenes, but was thrust into the foreground in 1932 by the political crisis. Certainly nowhere else could I have studied in minutest detail the problems of every department of the army, learnt to understand their interdependence and shortcomings, and so helped to build up the Reichswehr. Naval technicians and aviation experts broadened my views, and so led me to support the idea of merging navy and army into a comprehensive Wehrmacht.

In 1924-25, in collaboration with Major Preu of the Army Organization Department, I wrote the first memorandum on the formation of a Wehrmacht General Staff, for which my previous contact with the *Truppenzentralstelle* was particularly helpful, my experience there having been destined to be a turning-point in my whole military development. In the work there one learnt to think and act in terms of the man in the firing line.

The work of the Reichswehr went forward industriously, animated by an *esprit de corps* that quickened the impulse to get results. We had become a non-political body outside all parties, deliberately trained by von Seeckt to be soldiers immune from the virus of Right and Left; a body whose presence and behaviour assured the bloodless solution of every internal crisis between the two world wars.

This non-political Wehrmacht thus imperceptibly became the political fulcrum of the popularly elected governments. On the question of the political or non-political soldier and commander I shall comment later. For the moment it is only necessary to add that exceptions such as occurred in the 'twenties during the

Ulm and Munich episodes were strongly condemned, and that
in the initial years of National Socialism we soldiers had no sympathy with it. The things I witnessed in Dresden in 1933 were
only tolerable to a decent citizen if he reminded himself that
far worse would have happened in a bloody revolution.

Until 1933 I avoided all personal contact with the party.
Their behaviour in the streets and on their parades had dis-
gusted me. I remember an officers' conference in Dresden in
this same year, at which the Reich Minister of War, General
von Blomberg, pleaded in a most insistent and unconvincing
speech for the loyalty of the Reichswehr to the National Socialist government. It was not until the end of October 1933, when
as an executive in the Luftfahrt Ministry I was able to appreciate the methodical qualities of the régime, that I gained more
favourable impressions. On this point also I shall have more to
say in due course.

The manpower limitations of the Reichswehr laid special
obligations on the High Command. As shield and buckler of the
state's authority it stood traditionally aloof from world events.
This gave it all the more time and opportunity to devote itself,
undisturbed and remote from publicity, to the second great task
of making the Reichswehr an experimental élite. As a regular
officer and when, after I was seconded to the Reichswehr Ministry in 1922, I had a hand in dealing with almost every question
affecting the Army Peace Commission, I had learnt from innumerable cases that the Interallied Military Control Commission was trying to fulfil the letter of its disarmament assignment
while ignoring the hard fact that time would inexorably present
the bill. The I.M.C.C. broke down because of the intrinsic un-
reality of its mission. Every German, and the Allies too for that
matter, knew that in practice the army of 100,000 men would
have no permanence as long as the rest of the world did not
disarm in accordance with the Treaty of Versailles. That we
soldiers were not content with a one-sided implementation of
the treaty should not be attributed to our legendary "militarism"
but to the vital needs of the nation and its geo-political situation.
I should add that the Social Democrat government then in

power, and later also the coalition government which included the Social Democrats, recognized the justice of a limited rearmament and supported the Reichswehr in its endeavours.

What was the Reichswehr itself up to? As an executive at the time I can answer that. The brains of the Reichswehr Ministry were concentrated on sifting war experience, incorporating its lessons in technical, organizational and educational programmes and framing new operational, administrative and technical directives. It goes without saying that "estimates" were a very important consideration. The main target was to keep abreast of technical improvements made by the Allies after the conclusion of peace and—when the time should be ripe—to resurrect the German army equipped with modern weapons. In training there were two main objects: first, to establish a prototype body of combined arms; and secondly, to train the private soldier for non-commissioned and commissioned rank. The political conditions prevailing dictated that our operations be restricted to "the defence of the Reich"—primarily, therefore, to the fortification of the eastern frontier and East Prussia and to securing them by a frontier defence force to be formed in an emergency. An effort was also made to close the obvious gaps in the Reichswehr by training ex-officers and N.C.O.'s and a limited quota of short-term volunteers. All in all, this glimpse of the work of the Reichswehr should suffice to show that life in the army was no *dolce far niente*.

Much of my time was occupied with the reorganization of the Ordnance Department. Here the fusion of the two branches, construction and supply, resolved the conflict of ideas that had previously subsisted between them. The General Staff's conclusions about the conduct of any future war formed the basis of clearly defined requirements in weapons, which were given by the Ordnance Inspectorate to the experimental stations for construction and to the Ordnance Supply Department for placing orders. These technical departments dealt directly with the industry. Trial pieces delivered by the factories were thoroughly tried out on the different experimental ranges of the Ordnance Department for serviceability. If they were passed, individual experimental units subjected the weapon to the severest tests in service conditions, any faults discovered being later eliminated by the supplying firms. It will be clear even to a layman that the interval between the placing of an order and the date of general issue to the troops ran into years, and in the case of heavy pieces, such as big guns, to six to seven years. A new type of gun, for example, was therefore sometimes already obsolete by the time it was issued to the army. For technical and financial reasons this was the right working method in peacetime. In wartime it had to be abandoned, though the departure from the established system had many repercussions and was often unsatisfactory to the forces in the field.

In my key post in the Ministry I found out that clerical warfare was growing to an extent that threatened to jeopardize the development of the Reichswehr. I felt that something should be done about it and asked for a general investigation. My request was granted, but I was by no means pleased to find myself appointed Reichswehr Commissioner for Retrenchment and Simplification. The objectives, however, that I set myself were:

> To release soldiers from office work so as to increase active strength.
> To cut down internal and external correspondence by wider delegation of authority.
> Gradually to build up an expanding cadre of executives who could act on their own initiative.

The results of my work were variously appraised. Although thousands of posts were done away with and the soldiers thus released for regimental duties, I was less concerned to present an imposing staff reduction than to infuse a new spirit into the command and administration. I could not help smiling when I heard again and again that some official had taken on another man and by so doing had snapped his fingers at me.

My friends in the army have often told me with a grin that I must have been a queer sort of Retrenchment Commissioner, because when it came to building up the Luftwaffe I just threw money out of the window. I could only reply that during my few years in the administration of the Luftwaffe I could not have spent so judiciously if I had not learnt the ABC of economy. When Reichsminister Schacht once told me that the Luftwaffe was being built too dearly I admitted he was right; one could, I told him, perhaps build more *cheaply*, but certainly not more *economically*, namely if construction and maintenance costs were properly collated.

3

Transfer to the Luftwaffe

1932 In Command of 4th Artillery Regiment, Dresden—1 Oct. 1933
Transfer to Air Ministry—The political expansion of Germany,
1935-37—The Röhm and Fritsch affairs—Intervention in Spain.

After my term in Dresden (1931-33) they wanted me back
in Berlin. I had felt very happy with my regiment; my family
and I had grown very fond of the garrison town, and I was not
at all keen to be recalled to the Reichswehr Ministry. But as
in the meantime I had been promoted to the rank of colonel I
expected a change, though not a transfer to the embryo Luftwaffe.

When, in September 1933, Colonel Stumpff sought me out
during a day-and-night exercise at manœuvres with the object
of interesting me in the appointment of Administrative Director
of the future Luftwaffe he got a very lukewarm response. I
wanted to stay with the army and recommended that the administrative work of the Luftfahrt, and later of the Luftwaffe,
should be taken over by the army. The matter was settled that
evening at a mess dinner, however, at which the foreign military
attachés and the Chief of Army Direction were our guests.
When I presented myself to Lieutenant-General Freiherr von
Hammerstein the following conversation ensued.

"Has Stumpff told you about your future employment?"

"Yes."

"Well, are you satisfied about it?"

When I said no and proceeded to summarize my reasons he
cut me short with: "You are a soldier and have to obey orders."

As it was no use kicking against the pricks of military discipline, I found myself on 1 October 1933 discharged from the army and taking over my civilian duties as a Head of Department in the Luftfahrt Commissariat, the forerunner of the Reichsluftfahrt Ministry.

While I was in this post I saw the restoration of German military equality on 16 March 1935 and the reoccupation of the demilitarized zone on 7 March 1936. The first of these we had longed for with all our hearts. It seemed to us a reparation for the injustice of the one-sided application of the Treaty of Versailles. The first news I heard of our entry into the neutral zone was on the morning of the day itself. From a purely military aspect, what I learnt could only be described as "impossible." The entry of a few battalions and single flights of reconnaissance and fighter aircraft was hardly more than a gesture. One could only presume that the politicians were assured of its success and hope that the Allies, who had left everything in suspense, would accept the step as a *fait accompli*.

As I have said, the officer corps of the Reichswehr was trained in deliberate insulation from ideologies. Since soldiering and politics seldom overlap at lower levels this was completely successful, individual exceptions only confirming the rule. And the Weimar democracy, by its sometimes unhappy way of doing things, made this segregation easier. We senior soldiers also steered clear of politics in the early days of National Socialism, which was all to the good. For us there was only one guiding star—the military oath, with no concessions to Left or Right. Critics will find it difficult to put a finger on any instance of backsliding either in the Kaiser's day or under the Weimar Republic, any disposition to quit the non-political corral being rigorously discountenanced.

This had been our training, old or young, before we transferred to the Luftwaffe, which soon came to be known as the National Socialist part of the Wehrmacht.

The personnel of the Luftwaffe, like all other members of the Wehrmacht, took the oath of allegiance to the Führer; they considered themselves unreservedly bound by it—what else was the meaning of an oath?—and kept it loyally. Hermann Goering, C.-in-C. of the Luftwaffe and later Reichsmarschall, was a former officer pilot, a National Socialist and a man of grandiose ideas. Though he exacted a great deal, he left the generals in the Air Ministry the greatest possible freedom of action and screened us from interference by the politicians. During my long military career I never felt so free from outside influence as when I was Administrative Chief of the Air Ministry, Chief of the General Staff of the Luftwaffe and a service commander during the formative years of the air force from 1933.

As members of the Luftwaffe, enjoying the protection of the prodigious personality of the C.-in-C., we were welcomed in every social sphere, including the National Socialist party.

Like all prominent Wehrmacht, state and party officials, we went as guests of the Führer to the Nürnberg Party Festival and the Goslar Harvest Festival in honour of the peasantry. We also appeared at the ceremonies in remembrance of the war dead, at the parades on Hitler's birthday, banquets in honour of distinguished foreign visitors and all big Wehrmacht occasions. I confess that much of what I saw made a strong impression on me and that I admired their brilliant and smooth-running organization.

It was possible to ignore the less pleasing things. I had no occasion for criticism since in the circles in which I moved there was no evidence of serious excesses. This might be disputed by citing Goering's extravagant luxury, which indeed we could not help noticing, but even if his eccentricities had not been popularly tolerated with an understanding smile we were not in a position to call him to account, for if we asked any questions we were told that the money came from voluntary commercial donations and from Hitler's privy purse. It was only years afterwards that I heard, for instance, that the costly and artistic birthday presents were the result of carefully laid schemes on the part of Goering's entourage. Anyway, I saw all this only as an outsider, for at the time I paid very little attention to the junketings in Berlin. Besides, my misgivings had ceased when Goering himself told me that his art collections would one day be given to the Reich as an art museum, as had been the Schack gallery in Munich. As a Franconian, I was not unfamiliar with the history of the art-loving kings of Bavaria, and this helped me to understand Goering in his role of Maecenas.

No attempt was made by any of the leading politicians to bring us into the National Socialist fold. To them we were useful soldiers, and that was enough; having taken the oath of allegiance, we were trusted implicitly. Goering knew that we could only cope with the work he laid on us if we were kept free of all political importunities. Anything which had to be done in that connection he did himself. Questions concerning us as members of the Luftwaffe, or the Luftwaffe as a whole, he usually dealt with after taking the matter up with Secretary of State Milch, who thrashed out our views at high executive level. This method prevented many a wrong decision and thus strengthened our confidence in Goering and in Hitler. It may seem surprising, but it was a fact that we generals of the Luftwaffe Ministry were not informed of political events (I exclude the negotiations which I had myself to conduct in 1945); and of course the service commanders and troops were still more in the dark. Rumours reached us as they did every other German. We can be blamed for discounting rumour in a time of political agitation only by those who have never lived in such a hotbed of wildly exaggerated scares. In retrospect, I can see that surprisingly little came to my ears; perhaps my refusal to listen to gossip was too well known or perhaps such tales were intentionally kept from me as a member of the "National Socialist" Luftwaffe in close touch with Goering.

Were I and many of my colleagues too naïve in accepting at its face value everything we were told officially? Yes, but we were soldiers strictly trained to observe a scrupulous veracity in official reports and therefore prone to believe those coming from our superiors. I had no occasion to alter my view, particularly since Goering treated his faults of commission with so natural a frankness that one supposed his faults of omission equally ingenuous.

A few instances may serve to explain this attitude.

The Röhm affair, 30 June 1934, in which the Luftwaffe was only marginally involved:

The dissensions between the army and the S.A. were as much a matter of common gossip as the inordinate ambition of the S.A. Chief Röhm, whom I knew from the General Staff. His friendship with Hitler had gradually deteriorated into an open hostility, and it did seem even to me that the fuse had been laid for a *putsch* against the army and the Führer. During the days of the *putsch* I was away flying in South Germany and had to rely for my information on newspaper and radio reports. Subsequent doubts I had as the result of rumours were removed by the very detailed statement by Hitler in the State Opera House to the assembled high-ups of the party, government and Wehrmacht. Because I had got to know Goering so well in the course of the years, I could not believe the rumour that he had taken advantage of the measures against the *putsch* to liquidate his enemy and rival. There were two sides to Goering's character; he could be just as considerate and sensitive as he could be brutal and remorseless. His brutality proceeded from fits of excitement and quickly ebbed with them, after which his geniality would break through with surprising suddenness, his good-heartedness often driving him to quite fantastic lengths to make reparation.

The Fritsch affair in 1938:

After a deluge of revelations it is difficult to summarize our point of view at the time. Even though years had elapsed since I had worked in close collaboration with von Fritsch, he had remained for me, as for every other ex-army Luftwaffe officer, the paragon of what a man and officer should be. For this reason I was particularly chary of believing the rumours of his moral lapses, tacitly hoping that they would soon be exposed as malicious slander and a way be found to clear his name. Later we Luftwaffe officers also were besmirched by rumours—often contradictory in themselves. I thought it impossible that Hitler or Goering could subject so universally respected an officer to a deliberate, intolerable humiliation. When Goering afterwards told me how he had succeeded in unmasking the informer and how glad he was to have done so—one could see the satisfaction in his eyes—I had not the slightest doubt that Goering's hands were clean. I presumed the same of Hitler when he had the Court of Honour's verdict read out before the assembled C.-in-C.'s of the army and the Luftwaffe by Artillery General Heitz, the president of the court martial, from which there emerged an extraordinary chain of coincidences, but also the complete exoneration of the C.-in-C. of the army. I should have liked, as would most of the rest of us, to have seen von Fritsch publicly cleared by his reinstatement in his former post. I could not imagine Hitler's reasons for not doing so, but concluded an explanation might be found in his failure to thaw the ice of a basic antagonism. This uncordial relationship made even an official collaboration difficult between von Fritsch, the typical Prussian officer weaned on the prejudices of the old imperial army tradition, and Hitler, who could not belie his Austrian breeding or forget the caste differences that separated them.

I was with Hitler before Warsaw in 1939 when the news of von Fritsch's death was brought to him. I was struck by his lassitude as, with a grimly solemn face and dragging feet, pausing every few steps, he climbed the long staircase to his observation post.

What can have been the thoughts which moved him at that moment?

Whether our indifference to political events was right or wrong, we had no need to, nor could we, bother our heads about them. Goering had reserved to himself the exclusive right to influence them and to represent us. This was beneficial for our work. Even if in retrospect I am obliged to admit our indifference to political questions was a mistake—and in my activity as Chief of the Luftwaffe Administration I must plead guilty to the charge—even so in practice another attitude would scarcely have made any difference. In 1936-37, when I was Chief of the General Staff and my duties did cover political questions, there were no particular complications as that year was quiet apart from the measures taken to support Franco in Spain.

When we received a report on a Sunday afternoon in July 1936, from a German member of the A.O. (Auslands-Organization der N.S.P.) living abroad, informing us of Franco's needs and Hitler's directives from Bayreuth, I was seriously disturbed. The Luftwaffe had just been able to organize its first commands and was in the early stages of formation training. The few established formations, such as the fighter units, were equipped with the first combat aircraft of our own production, the Arado, while the bomber squadrons with the Ju (Junkers) 52, though they could intensify their training, could not be expected to fight. The reconnaissance aircraft were somewhere between these two, and new types were being tested. In the 8.8-cm. flak we had a superior gun. On the personnel side the intervention was less of a headache. We had splendid human material whose keenness compelled admiration. But enthusiasm is no substitute for combat training in formation flying. Moreover, drafts to the Spanish theatre comprised our very best material, to the prejudice of the training work of the Home Command.

On the other hand, certain tactical and technical experiences were of immense value, especially, for example, the long-distance training of the ferry flights from Berlin to Spain via Rome. The excellence of the Me (Messerschmitt) 109 as it was gradually introduced gave our fighters a lasting sense of superiority, while the trials of the Ju 87 dive-bomber drew attention to the significance of this aircraft, which resulted in its becoming a decisive weapon until 1942. Finally, the experience gained from the use of the 8.8-cm. batteries against targets in the air and on the ground gave impetus both to their tactical employment and development as organized units.

We at home were accordingly faced with every kind of difficulty as the demand for personnel and technical equipment upset our training programme. Yet we did it—a feather in the cap of staff, troops, industry and the civil air transport, who shared the credit for this achievement. Field-Marshal Sperrle and his successors, von Richthofen and Volkmann, may claim that their airmen and the German army contingents made Franco's victory possible.

4

In the Air Ministry

Administrative work in the Air Ministry—New factories and buildings—Building up an administration—Relations with Goering and Milch.

I was again fortunate, as often before, in being brought into contact with people with whom it was a pleasure to work. I have already said something about Hermann Goering. I shall refer to him later at greater length, but here only a few remarks relevant to this period. From the very first day Hermann Goering had a clear conception of the end he had in view: to create an air force that would be decisive for Europe. In the subdivision of his programme, to our minds he set us almost impossible tasks. When the time came, at the end of so many months, to report to him on the progress made in the interim, he was generous in his praise, but immediately doubled his requirements for the next period; demands which, if apparently hardly possible to meet, were nevertheless once again fulfilled. We understood his challenge, especially his wish to create a "speculation command" if only to ensure our being armed in case the government's political action had repercussions.

The work was all the harder because of the dearth of airmen with operational experience from World War I in the Ministry and in the service. The heads of the most important departments of the Ministry were none of us airmen, but we were cleverly initiated into the mysteries of aviation by Secretary of State Milch. We soon realized that a man who is not an airman cannot build an air force, any more than a man who is not a horseman can form and command a cavalry division. So all of us—myself at the age of forty-eight—took flying lessons. We were now in a better position to have our say, though we did not have it all our way, either with the "old airmen," who had more experience than us elderly learners, or with the "young airmen," even if they were still raw tyros. But that was all right, as it gave us the inducement to work still harder at learning our job.

I have practised many kinds of sport in the course of my life and at different times have imagined there was no greater thrill than riding, motoring and ballooning. Today I have to admit that in a way life would have been dull if I had never held a joystick and so missed the heights and depths of a pilot's experience. With the exception of parachute jumping, I know at first hand every aspect of flying, with the combined arrogance and humility it gives you. Only in this way could we understand the airman's peculiar attitude to life, and so form an arm inspired with the true spirit and brotherhood of the air. We were bound together by a rare companionship which made the success of our stupendous undertaking in so short a time possible.

When in October 1933 I took over my new job, the Office of Administration was only making a start. With the benefit of my experience in Retrenchment, I set to work helped by men who were grand fellows as well as talented experts. The first task was to lay the foundations for our budget. In a few months we had completed our estimates in practical form for Ministry and service expenditure. The Luftwaffe has been accused of exorbitance in its demands and appropriations, but no one who followed the scrupulous examination of every single budget item is likely to make this charge. I was only a spendthrift with bare necessities. I constantly showed our plans, both psychological and material, to the competent authorities by means of circular flying trips, and so awakened their sympathies for air force requirements. These three-to-four-day flights helped one to forget the frustrations of office work and internal bickerings and drew us closer together without too much palaver. This method of working I made a guiding principle.

We discussed new steps to be taken in aircraft construction; we called up the majority of the younger generation of architects and artists and did our best to make the construction programme of the Luftwaffe, both aesthetically and socially, as progressive as possible. Large orders to the brick, cement and quarry industries resuscitated trade and reduced unemployment.

We made a radical break with the old tradition of uniformity in military buildings. I insisted that the architectural style should be suited to the surroundings, that plans must provide for the latest air-raid precaution requirements, that grandiose projects should have regard to economy, and that the state should have less hand in the erection of living quarters than private building firms. Of the achievements of the accommodation and building department of the Ministry there can be no serious criticism. Neither Hitler nor Goering had any influence on the style of the new buildings. Goering directly interfered only in the interior decoration and furnishing of the German Aero Club, housed in the old Prussian Diet. Later the Allies made the best of their opportunities for accommodation. General Clay no doubt knew very well why he requisitioned the Air District II H.Q. in Berlin-Dahlem for himself and his staff, and the Russians and the East Zone government why they took over the former Air Ministry as well as the Adlershof complex. And there are other examples.

Our plans for the re-equipment of industry were carried out with sound economy, at least while I was at the Ministry. The aircraft and motor industries were in the main made up of small firms who resisted expansion on the scale thought necessary by the Ministry because they did not believe the boom could last; and the guarantee given by the Government was regarded by many factory owners merely as a nuisance.

The Government put up all the money required for the building of shadow factories. My principle, on the whole endorsed by Secretary Milch, was to let the industry make money so that it could repay its debts to the Government out of its gradually accumulated reserves in order to attain the ultimate objective of free competition as quickly as possible. On the other hand, big cuts were made in personal salaries and overdrafts. That we, especially while the industry was in its growing pains, were not exactly popular, that we were also on occasions taxed with incompetence, was something we had to put up with; we were content that our personal integrity was not impugned. This battle with industry preceded a violent duel within the Ministry between the Technical Branch and my department. The former's standpoint was simple: to step up production in the factories working for the Luftwaffe to maximum regardless of dislocation, giving consideration only to air-raid protection; they were not interested in the financial aspect. In the tussle between our departments we, however, placed economic factors first, determining the capital investment available and its amortization. For all the helpfulness of the Ministries of Finance and Economics and the Reichsbank, the problem, which was not without its psychological aspect, would never have been solved if the big banks had not come forward to the rescue.

In the field of human interest our first task was to create a corps of officials, incorporating all grades from executives to legal clerks and including meteorologists and engineers. There were, if I remember rightly, more than sixty specialized careers. A few military and naval officials formed the nucleus; volunteers from other branches made up a strong contingent; the rest were ex-officers and people who felt themselves dissatisfied in private business, and employees with a good record. They were a heterogeneous collection which had first of all to be welded into some sort of unity.

Difficulties arose in the first months owing to the excessive demand for workers and their employment in remote places, and as a result of makeshift organization. They were, however, quickly overcome by mutual understanding, so that on my many visits of inspection, especially to remote building sites, I saw only contented faces and never heard any special complaints. But we also did our utmost to bring employers into the fellowship of the undertaking and to let no one outdo us in our care for the men's welfare. In this the Labour Trustees gave us their best assistance.

"A soldier must feel that he is a true soldier." That goes for an airman, too, and more so. Not only the airmen themselves, but also the women who were proud to go out arm in arm with them, will confirm that we succeeded in instilling this spirit into the men of the Luftwaffe. The sarcastic nickname "butterfly-tie soldiers" was tolerated with a superior smile. The achievements and spirit of sacrifice of Luftwaffe men in peace and war proved that a soldierly deportment was maintained even in their semi-civilian uniform.

The successes of the young German Luftwaffe in the first years of the war were a crowning reward for the efforts of its early years.

5

Chief of the General Staff
of the Luftwaffe

Death of Wever, Goering's Chief of Staff—June 1936 Kesselring Chief of General Staff of the Luftwaffe—Experience gained from Spain— 1937 Transfer to Dresden.

It was a black day when, on 3 June 1936, Goering sent for me and told me with understandable emotion that General Wever, his first Chief of Staff, had met with a fatal accident in Dresden when taking off in a He (Heinkel) 70. It was equally understandable that I, his comrade and colleague, should be staggered by the news. Wever, like myself, was originally an army man; he had behind him a brilliant staff career and would have earned the same distinction as a regimental officer. As it was, he was the very man for the post of C.G.S. In next to no time he succeeded in picking up the essentials of aeronautics and aerial warfare, in translating Goering's ideas into practicable shape and embodying them in axioms both operationally correct and instinctively acceptable to the airman.

Today we realize, more than ever, what Wever meant to the Luftwaffe. We were so short of senior officers at the time of his death that his loss was felt as a doubly tragic blow. It is incumbent on me particularly, his successor, to praise him, because I was in a position to appreciate in his work the sure touch of a master hand. For this reason I did not need to explore new ways, but could carry on from where he left off. This helped to establish quickly an atmosphere of trust between myself, the

General Staff departments and the numerous inspectorates. With the loyal support of exceptionally competent officers my work was made a pleasure.

As has been said, the intervention of the "Condor Legion" in Spain was an incubus imperilling the work of organization, though in the long run it proved valuable. As one squadron after another was recalled from its baptism by fire there was a welcome progress in formation training, and instrument flying from being regarded as a black art became a commonplace. Fighter, dive-bomber, bomber and distance reconnaissance squadrons were equipped with the prototypes of the Me 109, the Ju 87, the Do (Dornier) 17 and the He 111, although short-distance reconnaissance and sea-plane units had at first to be content with their obsolete, but still serviceable, aircraft. The flak artillery was equipped with the pioneer 8.8-cm., 2- and 3.7-cm. gun and air intelligence training attempted to reach naval wireless telegraphy standards.

In the instructional squadron, later expanded into an instructional division under the gifted General Foerster, a testing system was arranged to cover technical and tactical performance which acted as a filter for the service. For the parachutists a skeleton organization was set up on the aerodrome at Stendal which required no subsequent modification but had only to be expanded. I am still proud today of the share I had, along with Wever, in the gradual development of the parachute troops. They were able to carry out the first successful assault on Holland under my command, and were later to become un-excelled ground combat troops. They found a guiding, clear-sighted leader in Air Marshal Student.

In 1937 disagreements with my superior, Milch, over service and personal matters led me to ask to be relieved of my post. As I could not picture myself as useful in an operational command I wanted to be put on the retired list. Goering met my wishes by transferring me to Dresden, at the same time appointing me G.O.C. of Air District III. I was succeeded by my old friend Stumpff, who had built up the Officers' Corps of the Luftwaffe with a most tactful hand and had become a real father to the N.C.O.'s and men under his care. Milch remained as Secretary of State and Goering's deputy in the Ministry. I appreciated Milch as an expert, a splendid organizer and an unflagging worker, and I was glad when the cordial relationship that existed between us in the early years was gradually restored.

I gratefully recall the assurance when I left Berlin that I had been valued not only as a chief but also as a friend.

6

Chief of Air Fleet 1, Berlin

1937-38 Command of III Air Region, Dresden—Completion of Silesian airfields—Assessment of Czech "Maginot Line"—Spring 1938 Command of Air Fleet 1, Berlin—Occupation of Czechoslovakia—Social life in Dresden.

From the middle of 1937 until the end of September 1938 I was in command of the III Air Region in Dresden, comprising Silesia, Saxony and central Germany, and from 1 October 1938 Chief of Staff of Air Fleet 1 in Berlin. In Berlin I was responsible for the protection of the East German Zone, defined by the Elbe in the west and the Thuringian Forest and the Czechoslovak frontier in the south. East Prussia belonged in this zone, whereas the coastal and island stations and naval air formations were administered by the Naval Air Region VI, which came directly under the Air Ministry.

It will thus be seen that I was responsible for frontier districts which were exposed to political tension within a few months of my taking up my duties. Before leaving Berlin in June 1937 I reported to Hitler. I was invited to lunch by General von Brauchitsch, who had been appointed to command the Army Group in Leipzig. Neither during my interview with Hitler nor at lunch was any mention made of political or military measures against the Czechoslovak Republic or Poland.

My deepest wish to build up the young Luftwaffe and to make it an instrument equivalent to the army and the navy seemed to me unattainable. Even though many years of my military career had been spent on staffs and in ministerial offices my secret longing was for regimental service. Wading through

31

masses of paper and through the dust of files, I always tried to make a human contact where possible and so give my office work a value. And to some extent I believe I succeeded. Now I was to have a chance of using my theoretical knowledge in the practical field. It was with a feeling of elation that I climbed into my Ju 52, piloted by my old flying instructor and pilot Zellmann, and escorted by fighters in threes flew from Staaken near Berlin to Dresden.

The most important thing for me was to meet my subordinate officers and my men, to listen to their wishes and complaints, and to explain to them my views on our common task. This took time and limited my office work to a minimum. I could safely leave that to my industrious and talented Chief of Staff, Speidel. I gave particular attention to the training of commanding officers in air warfare and the use of the air arm in co-ordinated operations with the army. There were no large-scale manœuvres, war games, firing practices by the flak on the Baltic coast or bomb-dropping exercises in which I did not take part as learner or instructor. I was happy to let myself be taught without going so far as to emulate an old brigadier-general of mine who, during the criticism on the range, once gave a troop commander a lecture on the proper way to carry out his fire task. At the next day's criticism the latter countered the general's unflattering remarks by saying: "I only did what you told me yesterday." Whereat he received the unexpected rebuke: "Captain, do you want to stop me learning?"

Everyone must work together in the development of a new arm. One has to listen to the views of the men, ponder and recognize their merits, for in no other way can the result stand scrutiny and survive a rigorous test. In this way the Luftwaffe grew to maturity, and although still green at the time of its first campaign (Poland), it was able to play a decisive part.

The air force is an offensive arm, as air warfare is only conceivable in terms of offence. The inference was that the Luftwaffe—leaving aside mere protection against air raids—had to make all preparations for a hostile penetration in depth of Czechoslovakia and to advance our operational airfields to near the frontier. After the summer of 1937 I was faced with the task of reconnoitring a new air base between the Bavarian-Silesian and the Silesian-Czech frontiers for close-range operations and constructing airfields with the needful accommodation, technical installations, flak protection and supplies. The airfields in Silesia were duly reconnoitred and completed for operations against Czechoslovakia; in view of the narrow depth of Silesia they could, if the need arose, be used for operations against Poland. A battle practice lasting several days gave the reassurance that we should be able to fulfil whatever tasks might be set us.

But we all knew that we were still in the middle of our apprenticeship and that any interruption or even a hostile operation might set us back very seriously and jeopardize our further development. Goering and Hitler, too, were both aware of this. When, in May 1938, the order was given to prepare for an offensive against Czechoslovakia, I considered, as did Goering, that the more firmly the will of the German government was supported by a superior military strength, the more likelihood there would be of a political solution. Hitler, by a propaganda strange to us soldiers, had not failed to inform the enemy of the strength of the German Wehrmacht. In spite of the shortcomings of which I personally knew, I had the feeling, in common with the troops, that we should pull it off. Judging from the photographs in my possession, I could not share the widely held opinion that the Czech frontier fortifications were a second Maginot Line. I did not doubt for an instant that our army would capture the layout by assault, with my 8.8-cm. flak with their armour- and concrete-piercing shells paving the way. In order to dissipate the lingering misgivings of the army, airborne troops were to be landed behind the fortified line in the area of Jägerndorf to open the Sudeten front from the rear. The knowledge that they were being attacked from north, west and south must have a crippling effect on the Czech command and on the troops, and correspondingly boost our morale. In August I moved my operational headquarters to Senftenberg in the Lausitz so as to be closer to my units.

In the event the result of the Four-Power Conference at Munich on 29 October 1938 was a profound relief to me, sparing as it did both sides inevitable heavy sacrifices. The strength and depth of the frontier fortifications was nothing like what our intelligence reports had led us to expect; they could have been smashed by a violent bombardment of 8.8-cm. guns.

The strategic concentration of our air forces had shown that the Luftwaffe was on the right lines, but that the strengths and technical state of units were insufficient and that our frontier air bases required thorough overhauling. A practice operation carried out by the 7th Airborne Division under General Student demonstrated that airborne landings were tactically and technically possible and could open up new possibilities. But as I have said—we were only at the beginning.

In the spring of 1938 I assumed the command of the Air Fleet 1 in Berlin. Happy as I had been in Dresden, I was glad to get back to the capital. In Dresden I did not stand to be shot at and I could work more independently, but in Berlin I hoped to be able to preserve my independence even in my new and more important sphere. My own tasks were principally:

To weld the air and flak arms into a uniform, flexible and corps-conscious formation incorporating a modern signals service;

To disseminate operational principles and the principles of air-ground support for the instruction of flying units;

To realize our ideas of air-raid protection and to make the civilian population A.R.P. conscious;

Lastly, to build up the ground organization in areas close to the frontier.

My heart leaps when I think back to those months of constructive work. One could sense the gradual growth of the Luftwaffe towards perfection and readiness for use. I remember the first A.R.P. exercises at Leipzig and in central Germany and the valuable lessons they taught us for the civilian A.R.P. and the use of anti-aircraft artillery. Electrical location instruments were on the way—the spadework was completed and we had done a good job.

One more word about the life of the German soldier in the peace years of the Third Reich. As G.O.C. in Dresden, my social circle was on the whole restricted to members of the forces, above all the Luftwaffe. Private invitations alternated with little parties in the different regimental messes. Whether in the magnificent mess in the Air Academy or when entertained by the Luftwaffe Signals Service, older married people and youngsters mingled with gay informality. We only rarely met in the rooms of the Bellevue Hotel—that was too expensive—or in the better-class wine taverns. On Sundays or holidays we often made excursions into the lovely country around the city. The calls of duty and the amount of travelling we had to do made it inevitable that social intercourse with the civilian population and the party should be limited to a minimum. I cannot recollect that I ever encountered any improper opposition from party officials.

For a man who had lost his fortune in the inflation and was an enemy of all stock-exchange speculation and other manipulations, and had consequently failed to rehabilitate himself, entertainment was a budget item I could ill afford on my meagre pay. However, the extent to which I did mix with my colleagues and their families led to a real intimacy which was brought home to me in the years of my defamation in 1945.

Beyond that, apart from the regular invitations to the Führer, the Reichsmarschall and various Ministers of State, every political visit to the capital was a chore. Association with foreign attachés and air-force comrades at the Aero Club was a matter of course. Time had also to be made for military and scientific get-togethers and for visits to the theatre. All in all, an incubus on the busy soldier that could well have been dispensed with. It meant a practical undermining of one's health to get to bed after midnight every night, to be constantly on show and, into the bargain, to have to know everything, be responsible for everything, and be the embodiment of infallibility to one's subordinates.

At the beginning of 1939 we were suddenly snatched out of our winter's peaceful preparation for war and switched over to measures for a possible hostile operation against Czechoslovakia. We had no time to speculate on the justification or need for our intervention, so surprisingly did hints and rumours become war-like reality. Goering told me, as the commanding officer principally concerned, that the situation gave cause for anxiety because of acts of aggression committed by the Czechs, but that there was hope of clearing the air without bloodshed. This time, too, the strictest secrecy was to be kept about our strategic concentration so as not to make a political solution impossible.

As only one instance of the way the secret was kept, on the night before the invasion my wife and I were invited to a small party at Gatow Air Academy as guests of General Otto von Stülpnagel—who after the war committed suicide while on remand in a Paris prison. We left as usual between eleven o'clock and midnight. No one present had the least inkling of the hostilities that were to be opened on the morrow, and we were all astounded the next morning when the radio announced that Air Fleet 1 was on its way to Prague with its commander at its head. This report was not quite accurate, as after the talks with President Hacha during the night our invasion was no more than a peaceful entry.

During the following months I was often in Prague and other air-force towns in the part of Czechoslovakia allotted to Air Fleet 1. The taking over of the aerodromes went smoothly, though there was really no question of taking over, as the Czech air force disbanded of its own accord. The equipment found on them was incomplete and of inferior quality, and the few aircraft were unserviceable.

I was surprised and worried at the subsequent aggravation of the situation, and that the solution reached by the Four Powers at Munich had not been permanent and—incomprehensibly to me—had proved the source of even greater friction which might perhaps mean war. We accepted the acts of aggression attributed to the Czechs as facts, not as propaganda lies. We even thought it possible that the incidents were engineered in order to give the Western Powers a pretext for a renewed intervention in favour of the Czechs.

Least of all did we believe that Hacha could have been forced to sign the treaty. As soldiers we were glad that the annexation of Czechoslovakia had had no pernicious repercussions; the security of our frontiers had been unexpectedly strengthened, and the sympathetic co-operation of the Poles before, during and after this period led to the inference that Polish-German differences would somehow be settled amicably. We soldiers honestly regretted the immediate recrudescence of the old complaints of acts of aggression by the Poles.

Even if the Wehrmacht made preparations for any eventuality, the fact remains that responsible persons—above all Goering —strove to avert war. Individual measures were cited at the Nürnberg Trials sufficiently and convincingly. As one who lived through this period of tension only on the fringe, I must lay the blame on *one* man: von Ribbentrop, who gave Hitler irresponsible advice. I remember an incident in Goering's special train at Wildpark which illuminates the atmosphere then prevailing. I was with Goering waiting to hear the decision: "Peace or War." The instant Goering received the news of Hitler's decision, 1 September—X Day, he rang up von Ribbentrop in a state of the greatest excitement and bawled into the telephone, "Now you've got your —— war. It's all your doing!"—and furiously hung up.

7

The Polish Campaign, 1939

1 Sept. 1939, 4.45 A.M., the attack is launched with two Army Groups,
North and South—5 Sept. Crossing of the Vistula—16 Sept. Investment of Warsaw—17 Sept. Fall of Brest-Litovsk, intervention of Soviet Russia—27 Sept. Capitulation of Warsaw—1 Oct. Surrender of
the last remaining Polish forces, end of the fighting in Poland.

In the late afternoon of 25 August 1939, the day on which
Hitler had ordered the invasion of Poland, I was in the control-
room of Kolberg airfield for a meeting with group-captains and
wing-commanders when my operations chief reported that
Hitler had changed his mind again. The invasion was called off.

Our delight at this turn of events was plainly written on our
faces. I expressed the hope that the war which had seemed inevitable might be definitely averted. With relief I climbed into
the cockpit of my aircraft and flew back into the setting sun to
my battle headquarters at Henningsholm near Stettin.

My thoughts went back to the twenty-third, two days before,
when Hitler had summoned the C.-in-C.'s and the G.O.C.'s of
all three services with their Chiefs of Staff to his Bergheim. We
were not informed of the agenda. The meeting was preceded
by a conference with the Reichsmarschall in the S.S. barracks
in which he again went over our preparations for the air war
against Poland and listened to our views. Goering talked with
us for an hour without mentioning any irrevocable decision to
have recourse to arms. We knew, of course, that he was still
working to preserve peace by hook or by crook.

The subsequent conference with Hitler took place in the great
reception hall with its wonderful view of the mountains which

seemed so near one could reach out and touch them. He made us a lengthy, calm and controlled speech, the details of which I need not set down, as its text is public knowledge since Nürnberg. I was glad to hear no word of a final rupture, but from Hitler's exposition it seemed more than likely that this would happen. There were two things that worried me: first, the consequences of a war with Poland. Any other calculation than that England would regard a forcible solution of the German-Polish dispute as an irreparable affront was sheer optimism; hence Goering's indefatigable endeavours to save peace. My greater worry, however, concerned the attitude of Russia. Even though I believed that in spite of their relative unpreparedness the Luftwaffe and the Wehrmacht would prove their superiority over the Poles, the German armed forces were no match for Russia's military might. I was greatly troubled by this, but a weight was lifted from my heart when at the end of his speech Hitler informed us of Russia's neutrality and that a pact of mutual non-aggression had been concluded.

That evening I flew back to Berlin gravely thoughtful. The memory of the days before the outbreak of World War I returned to me, when I had been filled with the same uncertainty and tension, although then the grim shadow of war affected me as an individual only without far-reaching responsibility.

For us of the Luftwaffe war meant war in the air. But except for individual experiences in Spain we had no practical experience. We had evolved our own basic principles of air warfare and appropriate rules of strategy and tactics to the best of our knowledge, and these were in our bones. Yet there were no international prescriptions for air warfare. Hitler's attempt to get air warfare banned altogether met with the same refusal at international conferences as his proposal to restrict it to purely military objectives. We had, however, incorporated in our air-force regulations—as Chief of the General Staff I had a considerable hand in formulating them—those moral principles which our conscience told us must be respected. These included the limitation of attacks to strictly military targets—whose definition was only extended with the inception of total war—while those on open towns and civilians were forbidden.

We had envisaged the use of aircraft in close support of forces on the ground, airborne landings or landings by single parachutists not being foreseen. The essential discussions with the C.-in-C. of Army Group North, von Bock, were now concluded. As an old army officer I understood the needs and worries of the army too well not to reach complete agreement with him in brief talks. I was not subordinate to von Bock, but voluntarily felt myself to be under his orders in all questions of ground tactics. In all differences of opinion, such as inevitably occurred occasionally in all the campaigns—I worked in close co-operation with him both in that against the west and in Russia—our frank desire for the best in any given situation produced agreement with a few words over the telephone. Even in cases where air considerations had priority I sought ways and means to satisfy the army. Bock and I both knew we could rely on each other; our Chiefs—von Salmuth (Army Group) and Speidel (Air Command)—were exemplary aides. Co-operation with Goering as C.-in-C. Luftwaffe was good, while in Air Marshal Jeschonnek I knew we had a man of more than average perspicacity and generalship who knew his officers and men and was capable of defending his views coolly and persistently when dealing with Goering and Hitler.

Last-minute talks with all staffs and men under me—part of my peacetime organization had been transferred to a neighbouring Air Command—gave me the assurance that we had done all that possibly could be done to ensure the success of a swift and smashing blow. The mood was grim but confident. They knew they were about to pit themselves against a strong, ruthlessly fanatical and well-trained enemy, and one who by 1939 standards was also well equipped.

The fighters of the Polish air force numerically and qualitatively claimed our respect, although their bombers lagged considerably behind. With our Me 109's and Me 110's, about 500 German against 250 Polish fighters, we proposed striking vigorously at the enemy's ground organization (airfields and parks).

It was, besides, important to prevent the Polish bombers from making damaging attacks on our home bases. To attack the Polish armament factories was beyond the competence of the Luftwaffe, but some airfield installations, as at Warsaw, were objectives of bombing raids. We could afford to give these targets secondary place because, if the campaign ended as swiftly as we expected, Polish production would, anyway, have no further significance. On the other hand, it could be decisive if the Polish Command were disorganized at the very outset by fierce attacks on it and on its signals communications, including central W-T transmitting stations. Finally, those elements of the Polish army which could most rapidly move against our own must be attacked, if possible, in their billets.

The mission of operational air reconnaissance, flown by the reconnaissance formations of Air Fleet 1 and Army Headquarters, was to provide with all speed a picture of the enemy's movements in the back areas as far as and beyond the Vistula. A bomber formation was also given a special assignment to attack the Hel Peninsula in co-ordination with the navy, preparatory to a landing assault.

Our flak effectives—approximately 10,000 light and heavy A.A. guns in the whole of the Reich—were kept massed under the orders of the Air Administrative Area Command to protect the tactically important installations of the Luftwaffe such as airfields, the east-west railway system, and various central economic plants. Certain elements accompanied army units as regimental air-raid protection troops, large formations of more than one troop working together being then unknown. All in all, there was a striking discrepancy between our tasks and the formations available.[1]

This situation could only be balanced by an elastic strategy and by the initiative of individual formations and crews. The results of the first day guaranteed our hopes. Aerial photographs revealed that the Polish air force had been hard hit and general

[1] Numerically the army strength of the two sides was fairly evenly balanced —about fifty German divisions against about forty Polish divisions and some ten cavalry brigades. The German forces were better equipped and better trained, especially as the Poles had not yet completed mobilization.

mobilization disrupted. Observation of the targets already attacked was now carried out and nuisance raids made irregularly over the enemy's back areas. During the next few days it became increasingly evident that our immediate task was to support the army and to harass enemy strategic concentrations and troop movements.

It is a tribute both to the Polish High Command and to our own achievement that the Polish forces had enormous fighting spirit and in spite of the disorganization of control and communications were able to strike effectively at our points of main effort. Crises on the German side, as on the Tucheler Heath, in the Polish break-through battle on the Bzura and in the area covering Warsaw, were overcome by exemplary co-operation with the ground forces, and by throwing in every available close-support aircraft and bomber in a recklessly concentrated attack. The main brunt of the fighting was borne by the Stukas, fighters and pursuit fighters, numerous sorties a day being the regular thing.[1]

In my battle sector almost every Polish operational movement had to pass through Warsaw, and this dictated our strategy, namely to smash at the capital's traffic nodal points. In order to spare the city I had the bombing attacks on the bridges and railway yards within it carried out exclusively by Stukas and ground-strafers under cover of fighters and pursuit fighters, and a large number of 1,000-kg. bombs were dropped. Results on railway key-points were satisfactory, but the solidly built bridges withstood even the 1,000-kg. bombs, thus revealing the limitations of air attack—a lesson which was not learnt till the last years of the war.

In those weeks I was myself frequently over the Polish battle area, including Warsaw itself with its very respectable fighter and flak defence, and I can say with pride that our airmen successfully tried to restrict their attacks, as ordered, to militarily

[1] Fuller writes in *The Second World War* that the campaign was not decided by the numbers but by the speed of the Luftwaffe and the panzer forces which operated as an undivided whole.

important targets, though this did not prevent inhabited houses near the targets from being hit, suffering from the laws of dispersion. I often visited the Stuka squadrons on their return from bombing raids over Warsaw, spoke with the crews about their impressions and inspected the damage where aircraft had been hit by flak. It was almost a miracle that some of them got home, so riddled were they with holes—halves of wings were ripped off, bottom planes torn away, and fuselages disembowelled, with their control organs hanging by the thinnest threads. Our thanks were due to Dr. Koppenberg and his engineers who produced such aircraft as the Ju 87, which was still in use in Russia in 1945.

Towards the end of the campaign Warsaw was once again subjected to concentrated attack. In co-operation with the heavy artillery under General Zuckertort the Air Command made an effort to smash resistance and so end the war. This combined attack on the city gained its object within a few days, on 27 September. The assignment of the Air Command was chiefly to attack points out of artillery range or which could only be shelled with insufficient effect. Blaskowitz, the commander of the investment troops, could be justifiably proud. In a final conference with Hitler on 6 October 1939 he claimed the decision for the army artillery; I had to point out on behalf of the air force that Polish prisoners were terrified to the marrow of the Stukas and that the targets in Warsaw devastated from the air were proof positive of our share in the victory. A subsequent tour of the city made this plain.

An incident on the day of the city's surrender gave us a glimpse of Hitler's mentality. He had ordered a field-kitchen meal to be served on the airfield, and Blaskowitz, thinking that the occasion warranted a gala display, had extra benches and tables arranged in the hangars, the tables being laid with paper tablecloths and decorated with flowers. Hitler was furious. Snubbing von Brauchitsch's attempts to get him to change his mind, he left Warsaw without attending the meal and flew to Berlin with his aides. From that moment on, as later became evident, Blaskowitz was regarded with suspicion.

At the time we thought the intervention of Russia towards the end of the campaign quite superfluous, not to speak of the friction very soon caused by Russian fighters firing on aircraft of my Command. To swallow this merely out of consideration for the Russians was no simple matter, and we were all the more exasperated because the Russians showed little friendliness, even keeping back vitally necessary weather reports from us. This gave me my first insight into the strange bedfellowship of a coalition war.

The Poles had been defeated in a few weeks of fighting and their beaten country was put under military administration. The campaign had proved that as far as air strategy was concerned we were on the right road; our various crises and reverses, however, showed there was much leeway to be made up if we were to stand up against a more powerful enemy.

The army formations had to have constant strong air support, which meant even closer co-ordination and still closer support of aircraft, above all, of Stukas, fighters and pursuit fighters. But more bombers were also needed, with a consequent increased call on production as well as a higher standard of training.

Although in general all new aircraft types [He 126, Do 17, Me 110, Ju 87, He 111, Ju 88, Do 18, He 115, Ar (Argus) 196, the last three seaplanes] had stood the test of operations, even the fastest were too slow, had insufficient effective range and armament, and carried too little ammunition. Here were fresh urgent tasks for the technicians.

The flak arm had not had much opportunity, but where it had come into action to protect artillery it had fully proved itself and earned a special reputation in ground fighting. It was now as important to organize it in larger formations working together as it was to augment it.

The award of the Knight's Cross of the Iron Cross, with which I was invested by Hitler in person in the Reichs Chancellery along with the other C.-in-C.'s of the services, I regarded as a recognition of the performances of all the flying and ground personnel of Air Fleet 1. I think I may say without boasting and without depreciating the work of the army and the navy that without the Luftwaffe there would have been no *blitzkrieg* and our casualties would have been very much heavier. I also pledge my honour that the war, as I saw it, was conducted by us Germans with chivalry—as far as this is possible in war—and with humanity.

As the campaign claimed all my energies and attention, I did little more than note the occurrence of historical events that did not immediately concern me, such as the expected declaration of war by England and France—my resolve to devote all my efforts to the quick ending of the Polish campaign being thereby only strengthened. I took every opportunity of explaining to my men how we in the east could decisively help our comrades on the western front by rapidly smashing Polish resistance and releasing urgently needed forces for the west.

From my last headquarters at Königsberg I flew over my first headquarters in the Polish campaign at Henningsholm home to my family in Berlin, where the happy, intimate atmosphere helped me to forget the mental and bodily strain I had been through.

8

Between Campaigns—
The Winter of 1939-40

Extension of Command to North Poland—Reorganization of home
defence—Transfer to command of Air Fleet 2 in the west.

It may interest the reader to know that when A.O.C. Air
Fleet 1 I was not informed of the strategic concentration in
the west or of Hitler's plan of attack. I had to transfer the bulk
of my formations partly into my old Command district, partly
into those of the western Air Commands (Air Fleet 2 located
in Brunswick and Air Fleet 3 in Munich). The first thing was
to have them rested and re-equipped. At that time I knew nothing whatever of the vacillations of our planning and the tension
between Hitler and the C.-in-C. of the army; things I only learnt
after the war. This water-tight secrecy was due to a personal
ruling of Hitler's. There may be two opinions about this, but
the advantage, as I see it, is that commanders at all levels are
compelled to fix their minds on a single task, their own. In my
study of military history I have been particularly struck by the
extent of the influence on higher commanders of the views and
anxieties, advice and criticism of their neighbours. Here breadth
of vision has prejudiced depth. As far as I was concerned, I was
only too happy not to have to bother about other fronts whose
problems could only deflect me from my own. I had far too
great a respect for the men who were there in command to
assume they could be dependent on my advice.

Of course it is possible to exaggerate everything, and unhappily the course of World War II provides enough instances of such exaggerations which have had disastrous consequences. But in the winter of 1939-40 I was glad not to have to worry my head about the west. I was snowed under with urgent work in my own domain, the geographical limits of which were extended by the inclusion of the northern part of Poland, which meant that the air base organized during recent years in the eastern frontier provinces had to be advanced into Poland and reorganized and expanded where there were Polish installations. This work was entrusted to General Bieneck, a World War I veteran pilot, as Commander of Administrative Area Posen. On my many flights over Poland I was happy to see the ground organization everywhere shooting up so that by the end of 1939 the first pilot training schools, the bomber school at Thorn and the aircraft repair workshops at Warsaw were established. It was helpful that the training organization could be extended to Poland, thereby relieving the spatial limitations of Germany. As strong Luftwaffe formations poured into this zone an A.R.P. net was spread over all the area, which incidentally also helped the pacification of the country.

In my old Air Command district the organization of air protection now became a priority task, as with England and France our enemies air raids must be reckoned with sooner or later. First came the claims of Berlin, the central German industrial area with Magdeburg and Leipzig, Breslau with its adjacent coalfields, and the seaports, first and foremost Hamburg and Stettin. At this stage the East Prussian ports and the Czech industrial towns took second place.

As my custom was, I looked into everything personally on the spot, attended as many air-raid protection as aircraft-reporting exercises, as also flak artillery fire-control practices. The over-all picture of the state of defence of my district which I gained by paying surprise visits to various units during the festive season made me feel sure we had overcome our childhood ailments. Time must help and defence be further developed in accordance with the technique of air attack.

For the first time during the last quarter of 1939 Jeschonnek told me about his intended reorganization of home defence. He was anxious to incorporate all home anti-aircraft and A.R.P. services into a single organization, and we went into all the advantages and disadvantages of this in great detail. The new organization was not only good, but was the only possible solution which could provide the maximum of protection with the minimum of means. General Stumpff, later Chief of the Reich Air Command, and the flak expert, Weise, carried out our ideas. Goering assisted with directives. Even if he was a past-master at getting his subordinates to do his work, occasionally his very frequent hours of leisure were devoted to casual reflection which bore many fruitful suggestions for the Luftwaffe. Thus it was Goering's own idea to concentrate the flak troops in large formations, in flak divisions and flak corps, which paid ample dividends. The army flak formations remained under the orders of the Air Commands, however, and so under the C.-in-C. of the Luftwaffe, an intrinsically infelicitous arrangement which could endanger the unity of command unless the air force voluntarily played second fiddle.

On 12 January 1940, as Chief of the Berlin Air Command, I as usual conveyed to the Reichsmarschall our birthday greetings, and during the lunch which followed, at which all the "high-ups" of the Reich were present, I was glad of the chance to clarify a number of service questions. Whispers had been current the day before that there had been a flare-up between Goering and Hitler, though nobody knew the reason. When my appointment with Goering was put forward an hour I guessed this had something to do with this rotten business. I was right. Never before or afterwards did I see Goering so down in the dumps, and that is saying something with Goering's temperament. But he had reason enough for his depression. It turned out that a flying officer had made a forced landing in Belgium with a passenger carrying a draft of our plan of campaign. That this should have happened to an airman of all people was enough to unsettle stronger nerves than Goering's. The extent of the harm done, however, could not be gauged, as no clear report of the incident was available; we did not know parts of the plan the pilot had been unable to burn and had thus fallen into the hands of the Belgian General Staff and consequently into those of the French and the British.

When Air Marshal Wenninger, our sometime Air Attaché in London, who represented our air interests in the Benelux countries, arrived soon after me, he was unable to give an entirely satisfactory explanation either. We had none of us any doubts on that day that a court-martial sentence hung over the two unfortunates. But here, as altogether in the first campaigns, luck was on our side inasmuch as the importance of the capture—to put it briefly—was not recognized by the enemy and on our side the over-all plan was soon changed.

First I had to listen to a storm of abuse of the Luftwaffe commanders; Goering did not stop to think whether any competent officer of Air Fleet 2 could be held properly responsible. Its commander, Air Marshal Felmy, and Kammhuber, his Chief of Staff, were sent into the wilderness. All the rest of us were given a dressing down and extra assignments into the bargain. At me he snarled (there's no other word): "And you will take over Air Fleet 2—" pause—"because I have nobody else."

If he was not friendly he was at least frank!

At the lunch which followed this interview I was able to give Stumpff, who now succeeded me as A.O.C. Air Fleet 1, a rough idea of his new duties.

For me this was the end of the lull between the two campaigns. The very next morning, 13 January 1940, I was sitting in my old Ju 52 with my pilot Zellmann. With considerable icing-up we flew to Münster, where Air Fleet 2 had set up its battle headquarters in the magnificent Luftwaffe Signals barracks. My old Chief of Staff, Speidel, followed me there.

9

Air Fleet 2
in the Western Campaign

Strategic concentration in the west with three Army Groups, B, A, and C; main effort by A (break-through of von Kleist's Panzer Group in the Ardennes)—10 May 1940, 5.35 A.M., Launching of the offensive, air landings in Holland—11 May Capture of Fort Eben Emael—14 May Capitulation of Holland—17-24 May Break-through of German panzers to the Channel coast, battles for the pockets in Artois, Flanders and Dunkirk—28 May Capitulation of Belgium—4 June Evacuation of British Expeditionary Force completed from Dunkirk —5 June Offensive of Army Group B against the Seine and lower Marne—9 June Army Group A attack on the upper Aisne—10 June Italy enters the war—14 June Offensive of Army Group C on the upper Rhine front—14 June Occupation of Paris—16 June Pétain forms new French ministry—22 June Armistice signed between France and Germany.

Our Army Groups, effectively supported by the Luftwaffe, had surged unimpeded through Poland on a wide front and the Poles had quickly collapsed. How would it now be in the west, where we had to defeat the armies of two great powers entrenched in favourable positions? I faced the future with high hopes. Both the army and the Luftwaffe had given proof of their mettle in the Polish campaign, and, even more important, had learnt lessons which surely had given us too big a lead for the enemy to catch up. I was convinced that in the interval before the offensive began these lessons could be turned to practical account and that the gaps in our material equipment could be closed. For their part the Western Powers during the past four months had showed a hesitancy that might almost be interpreted as weakness.

When I took over my new command from Air Marshal Felmy, I found a remarkably advanced state of preparation. While the enemy had remained quiet we had flown a modest number of reconnaissance sorties and operations against shipping.

At that time Air Fleet 2 comprised the following formations:

Signals Command 2
Distance Reconnaissance Squadron 122
IV Group under Air Marshal Keller
VIII Group under Air Marshal von Richthofen
IX Group under Air Marshal Coeler (from 23 May 1940)
I Group under Air Marshal Grauert (from 15 May 1940)
Air-landing Group under Air Marshal Student
1st Fighter Wing under General Osterkamp
II Flak Corps under Generalleutnant Dessloch
Air Administrative Area VI (Münster) under Generalleutnant Schmidt
Air Administrative Area X (Hamburg) under Generalleutnant Wolff.

Air Fleet 2 was allotted to General von Bock's Army Group B for army support, the Group consisting of the Eighteenth Army under General von Küchler and the Sixth Army under General von Reichenau. It was also assigned to Naval Command North under Admiral Carls.

The following days were taken up with the hand-over and informational flights. I paid my first visit to Army Group headquarters as I found the contact with them too loose for my tastes. Von Bock was surprised to see me turn up instead of Felmy, but was genuinely glad to renew our old comradeship in arms. The offensive had actually been ordered for the middle of February, but though we considered it probable there would be changes in the plan they were not of sufficient moment for us to discuss them. I informed von Bock again about the organization and mission of Air Fleet 2, and told him we had no fear of letting him down. Two points I raised in greater detail: (1) that on the third day of the offensive the panzer forces of the Eighteenth Army would have to join up with Student's air-landing parties in or near Rotterdam; and (2) that contact must be made immediately with the freight-carrying glider parties on the Albert Canal by the army advanced detachments, as they were too weak to be able to hold the captured bridges alone.

Von Bock was not by any means sure that he could keep to the Rotterdam time-table, but when I made no bones about it that the fate of the air-landing group, and indeed of the Army Group's operation, hung on the punctual arrival of the mechanized army units, he assured me that he would do everything humanly possible. I made it easier for him to give me this promise by guaranteeing him the fullest air support. In order not to lose contact with the advanced elements of the Eighteenth Army, the units on their left flank would have to push forward. A gain of ground by the Sixth Army might also assist the main thrust of the Army Group on their left under von Rundstedt against the French.

VIII Air Group headquarters I found was on the best terms with the Sixth Army and the Hoepner Panzer Corps, an impression confirmed by a later visit to Sixth Army headquarters. Its Chief of Staff was General Paulus, whose name is familiar from the battle of Stalingrad. He made a specially good impression on me by his level-headedness and sober estimate of the coming trial of strength. As he was teamed with the temperamental von Reichenau not much could go awry.

IV Air Group was earmarked for long-range assignments where strong concentration was required; its mission was to support remote air-landing troops, to neutralize the ground organization on enemy airfields, and to observe and deal with troop movements in back areas.

IX Air Group was still in process of formation and was being trained for minelaying. It would probably be ready to go into action by the end of April or the beginning of May 1940.

Distance Reconnaissance Squadron 122 had already played itself in by reconnaissance sorties over the sea; it was a good outfit and did very useful work. Its losses were tolerable, regrettable as they were.

At the Air-landing Group headquarters (7th Air Division, 22nd Infantry Division, Air Transport formations, gliders, etc.) I found that a detailed operational and tactical scheme had been drawn up by Hitler. Air Marshal Student had made his preparations with care and imagination, ably assisted by his regimental officers, Captain Koch, Lieutenant Witzleben and others, in the laborious technical and tactical arrangements. I was myself not inexperienced in air-landing operations, but there was much new for me to learn before I dared put forward any suggestions. On questions of tactics I felt more able to interfere. I was pleased to see that Major-General Count von Sponeck, commanding the 22nd Infantry Division, was a sharp-sighted, vigorous and flexible personality with a good judgment of flying problems. Count von Sponeck was later court-martialled for making a retirement from the Crimea in disobedience to orders and was shot at the end of the war at Germersheim—so far as I know in a fit of panic by the summary order of Himmler or Hitler.

The mission of General Osterkamp, an old World War "Eagle," was to employ his fighters in close support of the army and to protect the Ju airborne landing aircraft while in the air and after landing. This again was virgin country, demanding flying skill, organizing ability and a quick eye for tactics.

II Flak Corps had to contend with difficulties ensuing from its too hurried formation. General Dessloch, an old cavalryman and airman, had acquired enough experience in land warfare to be able to accommodate the army. There was, however, some difficulty in fitting the flak troops into the columns on the march; no army commander wanted his formations split up, no one wanted to march behind the flak, but everyone wanted the flak to be there at the critical moment. This was a matter in which I had to intervene myself and to arrive at compromise solutions not always satisfactory, and in some cases bad.

After these initial flying visits to unit headquarters there followed from February till the beginning of May strenuous weeks of staff conferences, plan revisions and operation rehearsals, both

on the ground and in the air. At the end of these three months
I was well in the picture. The fairly costly change-over to the
He 111 (Bomber Wing 4) and to the Ju 88 (Bomber Wing 30)
was decided. Staffs and formations practised the drill for the
first operations and complete agreement was reached with the
army. On 8 May 1940 I was present at a final briefing of the
Air-landing Group, attended by all independent commanding
officers, at which last questions were answered. For my taste the
signals arrangements were rather too complicated, especially as
Student was reluctant to allow the 22nd Infantry Division much
rope. The conduct of the operation was further hampered because both Hitler and Goering had had a big finger in the pie—
the use of "hollow mines," for instance, which cracked the
armoured turrets of Fort Eben Emael, was Hitler's own idea—
and gave Student a certain privileged position which he seized
with both hands. In the very first hours of execution it became
evident that the Air Command, as the only stable pivot of the
air operation, would have to interfere to a very much greater
extent.

Student wanted, as I have said, to direct the battle himself
from the front. It would have been better if at the beginning
he had issued his orders from his battle headquarters in the rear
and only taken over control on the battlefield when the two
air-landing divisions could conveniently be directed from a
single forward headquarters. Of course the 7th Air Division
would have needed its own operations staff, but it would not
have been impossible to fix it. There were other points besides
which worried me. Despite their advantages, the Ju 52 had great
drawbacks as transport aircraft; they had no bullet-proof fuel
tank, and as their use for this purpose was an improvisation they
consequently had insufficient armament and range. The traffic
over the dropping zone necessitated on-the-minute timing for
several hours. Protection had to be provided over a stretch of
many hundred miles by our fighters, a problem almost insoluble
with the Me 109's short duration of flight; Osterkamp and his
first-rate pilots, however, managed to do it.

Meanwhile to synchronize the bombardment of the Dutch

airfields with the dropping of the parachutists was easier on paper than in fact. On the top of this, on the evening of 9 May a jittery order was received from the C.-in-C. Luftwaffe that two heavy-bomber squadrons were to operate off the Dutch coast in case of a surprise appearance of enemy ships. It arrived in my absence and my operations chief could not countermand it, despite his justified fear that it might interfere with the punctual timing of the parachute landings.

THE FIRST ACT IN THE WEST

The initial movements were carried out according to plan. I breathed a sigh of relief when the first favourable reports came in of the capture of the bridges across the Albert Canal, of Fort Eben Emael, of the punctual parachute descents on the bridge over the Maas at Mordijk and on the Rotterdam airfields and their joint capture.

Obscure reports of landings by Ju 52's on the coast south of The Hague, an oral report by the commodore of an air-transport wing of landings on the road from Rotterdam to The Hague with enemy attacks on the ground and from the air, and news of fresh fighting round the Rotterdam airfields with considerable aircraft casualties as landing operations continued poured in pell-mell and satisfied neither myself nor the C.-in-C. Luftwaffe. A reconnaissance flight by my operations chief at last set our minds at rest about the situation at Rotterdam. Information from the Air-landing Group was very slow to arrive, wireless messages coming in thick and fast only when there were calls for support, and telling us nothing about the situation of the 22nd Infantry Division.

Air reconnaissance presently established the fact that the seizure of The Hague airfield had been frustrated. On the morning of 13 May Student kept calling for bomber support against enemy strong points inside Rotterdam and the point of main effort at the bridges where the parachutists were held up. At 14:00 hours the sortie in question was flown, and its success finally led to the capitulation of Holland on 14 May 1940.

The indignation of the Dutch and the charges brought against the Reichsmarschall and myself after the war, repeated before the Nürnberg Tribunal, were on a par with our military achievement. Before the bombers took off, Goering and I spent hours of heated argument over the telephone as to how the attacks demanded were to be carried out, if at all. As a result I repeatedly warned the bomber wing-commander to pay particular attention to the flares and signals displayed in the battle area and to keep in constant wireless contact with the Air-landing Group. Our anxieties were increased because after Student's morning message our wireless communication was cut off so that the Air Command was no longer informed of what was happening in and around Rotterdam; there was the additional danger of dropping bombs on our own troops. Neither we nor the Army Group Command knew that meanwhile Student had started negotiations with the Dutch, that he had been seriously wounded and that General Schmidt, commanding the Panzer Corps, had taken over. The breakdown of communications at the most critical moment of the fighting was nothing unusual to me, an old soldier, gunner and airman. Hence my precautionary warning to the wing-commander which might even have prevented the 2nd Bomber Squadron dropping their bombs on the city.

The following is his report of this operation:

"Bomber Squadron 54, whose leader I was at that time, was given the assignment by Major-General Putzier to support the troops under General Student on the outskirts of Rotterdam by bombing the Dutch enemy out of certain parts of the city from where he was enfilading the bridges across the Maas and preventing the further advance of Student's troops. For this purpose the targets that were to be bombed were marked on a map.

"Shortly before the take-off a message came through from Air Command saying that Student had called upon Rotterdam to surrender and ordering us to attack an alternative target in case Rotterdam should have surrendered in the meantime (during the approach flight). The surrender was to be signalled by the firing of red flares from the island in the Maas outside the city. For the execution of the mission the wing was divided into two equally strong columns. In spite of the defence the attack was delivered at just over 2,000 feet, as thick smoke made visibility very bad and it had been impressed upon us at all costs to hit only those parts marked on the map. I led the right column, and as there were no red signals to be seen on the island in the Maas the attack was carried through.

"The bombs fell extremely accurately in the target area. The defence ceased firing almost entirely after the first bombs were dropped. Wing Commander Höhne, who led the left column, noticed red flares on the island, turned away and attacked the substitute target.

"When I made my report on landing by telephone to General Putzier he asked me if we had not seen red flares on the Maas island. I reported that the right column had seen none, but that the left column had observed a few, and asked him whether Rotterdam had fallen. I was told that communications with Air Marshal Student had again been interrupted, that apparently the city had not fallen, and that the wing had to fly the same sortie again immediately.

"The wing took off a second time, but was recalled by W/T while flying in as Rotterdam had meanwhile fallen. In conclusion I declare that this sortie was unequivocally a tactical operation, namely support of the ground troops by the Luftwaffe."

In view of its international importance I have thought fit to quote the material parts of this testimony, although it differs somewhat from my picture of what occurred. Regarding the international law aspect, I should like to add, in the light of my personal interrogation of the parachutists in Rotterdam, that to bomb the defenders of a city is not contrary to the Geneva Convention and tactically admissible as intended artillery support. The bombs fell on the target. The subsequent damage was chiefly due to fires which were fed by burning oil and grease. During the intervening lull in the fighting the fire could have been effectively got under control.

It may be of interest that the 7th Parachute Division was not fully trained in jumping at the beginning of the western campaign and consequently only part of the parachute troops could be used in the attack. The air-landing operation was carried out by 4,500 parachute jumpers, 4,000 of whom were dropped in Holland and 500 landed by gliders, near Fort Eben Emael; the remaining forces were landed by Ju's and seaplanes.

After the transfer—at noon on 13 May—of VIII Air Group to Air Fleet 3 (i.e. with von Rundstedt's Army Group) to support the advance of von Kleist's panzers across the Maas, the forces remaining to Air Fleet 2, chiefly IV Air Group and II Flak Corps, had to be reinforced to assist the Sixth Army and the left wing of the Eighteenth Army in their difficult crossings of the numerous canal sectors, to smash the various French tank attacks and to support our divisions engaged with the British Expeditionary Force at Löwen and Arras. These operations exhausted our men and material, and reduced our strength to 30-50 per cent. The transfer of formations to airfields near the front scarcely affected the number of daily sorties, as mounting casualties could not be made good at the same rate.

After the capitulation of the Belgian army I hoped—in the special interest of my flying formations—that the British Expeditionary Force would soon follow their example; in view of the brilliant co-operation between panzers and airmen, the superiority of German strategy and the strength of our mobile forces, this could, in my judgment, be only a matter of days.

I was all the more surprised when my Command—perhaps as a reward for our late achievements?—was given the task of annihilating the remains of the British Expeditionary Force almost without assistance from the army. The C.-in-C. Luftwaffe must have been sufficiently aware of the effect of almost three weeks of ceaseless operations on my airmen not to order an operation which could hardly be carried out successfully by fresh forces. I expressed this view very clearly to Goering and told him it could not be done even with the support of VIII Air Group. Air Marshal Jeschonnek told me he thought the same, but that Goering for some incomprehensible reason had pledged himself to the Führer to wipe out the English with his Luftwaffe. It is easier to excuse Hitler with so many operational tasks to occupy his mind for agreeing than Goering for making this unrealistic offer. I pointed out to Goering that the modern Spitfires had recently appeared, making our air operations difficult and costly —and in the end it was the Spitfires which enabled the British and French to evacuate across the water.

Nevertheless my misgivings led to no change in the assignment—was this refusal to admit a mistake pigheadedness or weakness? Our battered and gradually reinforced formations strained every nerve to attain their objective, with Air Marshal Keller himself leading his wing into action, and the number of sorties flown by the overtired formations higher than usual, with the natural result that the Spitfires steadily increased our losses. We were robbed of the chance of claiming even a moral victory by unfavourable weather which made flying even riskier. Anyone who saw the wreckage over the coastal waters and the material scattered on the beaches or heard first-hand reports of what was happening from returning fighter, strafer and bombing crews can have only the highest admiration both for the performance of our airmen and for the superlative exertions, ingenuity and gallantry of the English. We had no idea in 1940 that the number of British and French who escaped was anywhere near the figure of 300,000 given today. Even 100,000 we believed to be well above the mark. Hitler may have been influenced by other considerations in making his decision, such as difficulties of terrain and repairs to overworked panzers, but whatever his reasons the decision was a fatal error which enabled England to reorganize her armed forces.

The race to the Channel coast had ended in the improbably short time of just over three weeks—10 May to 4 June 1940, with the elimination of Holland and Belgium and the British Expeditionary Force. Against our losses of nearly 450 aircraft we could set the uniquely successful support of the army, more than 3,000 enemy aircraft destroyed on the ground or in the air, and, besides a considerable number of sunk or damaged warships, over 50 sunk and over 100 damaged merchant vessels and smaller craft.

THE SECOND ACT IN THE WEST

The curtain rose on Act II when, following brief talks by the generals on the operations of the past weeks, for which Hitler expressed his special thanks to all ranks, the Führer informed the C.-in-C.'s of the right wing assembled in the control-room of Cambrai aerodrome on 29 May—shortly before the fall of Lille— of his future intentions. He spoke with measured gravity, mentioning his fears of a possible strong flanking thrust by the main French forces which would necessitate the speedy regrouping of our mechanized columns. His summary of the situation was sober and included a warning against overoptimism and an extremely careful specification of dates and places. We separated easy in our minds, feeling that he had given very careful thought to the coming operations and was aware of difficulties which we, in the light of our experiences with the French and our own military performance, did not expect to a corresponding extent. It is noteworthy that no mention had been made of an invasion of England.

At the close of the Dunkirk operation a period of regrouping further south took place, during which continuous demands were made on the Air Command which resulted in a further weakening of our effectives. Our primary assignment was the tactical air support of Army Group B on the Somme and lower Seine and the protection of troop movements. Anyone who watched from the air and on the ground, as I did, von Kleist's and Guderian's panzers swing round from the northern manœuvre towards the Channel and drive south and southeast to the Somme and the Aisne could not repress a surge of pride at the flexibility and skill of the German Army Command and the state of training of the troops. Nevertheless that these movements could be carried out without a hitch in daylight is attributable only to our air superiority.

From an advanced battle headquarters north of the Somme I witnessed the astonishing success of the advance by the Fourth Army and the Hoth Panzer Group as far as the Seine, the less satisfying battles of XVI and XIV Panzer Corps at Amiens and

Péronne and their second regrouping in von Rundstedt's Army Group A. Meanwhile our fliers were making concentrated attacks on French troop movements on roads and railways, destroying bridges and largely contributing to the disintegration and subsequent surrender of the French armies in the field. It is a matter for rueful reflection that in these high- and low-level attacks civilians intermingled with the troops were hit, in spite of our airmen's efforts to attack only military units in formation.

We had to cope concurrently with other important assignments, partly in bad weather. After the occupation of the Channel coast we made extraordinarily successful sorties against British and French ships concentrating in the harbours and along the coast further south, thereby crippling the transport of British troops across the water. In the twenty days following 5 June 1940, two small warships and about 300,000 tons of merchant shipping were sunk, and four warships and twenty-five merchant vessels more or less seriously damaged. Similar results were obtained against rail communications and railway stations, for example at Rennes and in other parts of Brittany, where in one day thirty trains were smashed. On 3 June 1940 in a larger-scale surprise attack on the Paris air base more than a hundred French aircraft were shot down and three or four times that number destroyed on the ground. Here we demonstrated the refinement of our air tactics by low-level approach with deliberately misleading changes of direction and by high- and low-level and dive-bombing attacks.

The speed of operations, which led in an amazingly short time to the utter collapse of the French, can hardly be imagined. With the signing of the armistice on 22 June the campaign was practically ended. When I heard of the demobilization of certain army units my hope that Hitler would now end the war was not entirely unfounded, as I knew his action to be dictated as much by political foresight as by a secret predilection for the English which I nevertheless observed and which received increasing expression later. I recall an interview with him in 1943 when, on my appraising the military achievements of the English, Hitler threw back his shoulders, looked me squarely in the eye and commented: "Of course, they are a Germanic people too."

Overjoyed as we were at the capitulation, we yet did not forget to take stock. We were on the right road; the lessons of the Polish campaign had been put into practice with immense effect. Victory had proved the correctness of the plan of campaign. Its execution was worthy of the conception. The hand-in-glove co-ordination of Army Group B and Air Fleet 2 was classical; so was the tactical manœuvrability of our regrouping and concentration. Also the organization of the Luftwaffe in close and long-range formations and in flak corps had shown itself fundamentally right. The concentration of air power on a single target was the condition of victory even under more difficult conditions.

10

Before the Turning-point— Summer 1940

Preparations for the attack on England—Kesselring's personal reconnaissance of the Channel coast—Promotion to Field-Marshal.

"Lash your helm faster after victory," says an old proverb.
Hitler defied this golden rule. Even if he did believe in the possibility of diplomatic negotiations, to us soldiers it was incomprehensible that the first steps to demobilize parts of the army
were taken before the end of the war was palpably in sight.
Though it may be inferred that Hitler, at that time at all events,
was reluctant to cross swords with England and had no intention of extending the war to the east, yet he of all people must
have known that diplomatic negotiations are best promoted by
having a strong army ready for action behind you. That the
Luftwaffe was kept intact was not sufficient. It was bad enough
that not until the beginning of October 1941 was the aircraft,
flak and flak munitions programme keyed up to maximum production, although the experience of previous compaigns had
shown the inadequacy of air-force replacements and the over-
all importance of the Luftwaffe. It was also well known that
aircraft production cannot be rushed, and therefore that preparations for the increase of capacity and the development of new
types could not be started any too soon. Finally, we commanders at the front could not conceive how Hitler could hope to
reach an agreement with the English when day after day and
week after week went by without anything happening. The

only thing left for us to do was to rest our formations as far as the now intensified oversea aerial war allowed.

As I had to turn my attention in greater detail to this latter I learnt a great deal from the experiences of IX Air Group, whose assignments fell almost exclusively within this field. During talks with its excellent commander, Air Marshal Coeler, and visits to his formations I found that old naval men with knowledge of flying and great imagination were taking a hand in the game. Here a proper sailor's net was being knotted. The heavy formations of this group, in addition to observation of shipping traffic along the whole east coast of England, had to cover mine-laying on shipping routes and harbour entrances, and high-level and torpedo attacks on Allied ships. Our torpedo-carrying aircraft were always tied to the navy's apron-strings. This was understandable, as naval aviation is an appendage of the navy, though it was never placed under naval command; in any case our Air Command was hampered by the fact that we never developed any torpedoes suitable to our aircraft's characteristics. We did raise this question of providing torpedoes for fast, manœuvrable aircraft which could be dropped at great flying speed in 1940, but we ought to have exerted more pressure on the navy. One cannot withhold one's admiration from the torpedo fliers, however, for the recklessness with which they flew in with their old crates—I include the He 111—at low level through a hurricane of anti-aircraft fire and after releasing their torpedoes flew off with warships' broadsides on their tail.

We were better served with the mines, also developed by the navy. Sooner or later the answer is found for every weapon, and so, of course, it was with the mines we dropped from the air. The enemy's counter-measures were anticipated, however, by the continual provision of new types, so that as soon as they found the answer to one sort of mine we produced another which sent many ships to the bottom or blocked the channels until the game began all over again.[1] Our changeover from the magnetic to the acoustic mine was in line with this.

[1] The IX Air Group reported up to 31 July 950,000 tons of shipping sunk.

Regardless of further political developments the C.-in-C. Luftwaffe authorized the formation of Air Administrative Area Commands for Belgium and Holland. Simultaneously the air reconnaissance and lookout service was enlarged and a close-meshed network of signals communications organized. Once these advanced Area Commands were fully organized we felt more hopeful of being able to deal with the heavy raids which were certainly to be expected from Great Britain.

The real significance of this work did not become apparent until the middle of July, when we received the order to begin preparations for the air battle for England. I personally carried out the reconnaissance for the operations of the light formations on the Channel coast, where the standing grain made accurate observation difficult. The Area Commands with the Labour Service battalions attached to them had every airfield ready for occupation by the beginning of August and ammunition and fuel ready for the great offensive. While the flak and air-force Signals had more time to get settled the squadrons themselves only just had time to settle in on their airfields before the first operational sortie.

While we were so engaged and hastily completing our plans, armed reconnaissance aircraft were flying operational sorties against English shipping in the nearest ports and in the Channel, which was successfully covered by VIII and IX Air Groups and Group Captain Fink with his 2nd Bomber Wing, but also made considerable demands on Osterkamp's fighters and strafers. During this period we could not do more than disrupt the shipping traffic to and from England. It was more important that these bomber operations should be a practice for the task ahead and help formulate the principles of air-sea warfare.

From time to time British armament factories were raided, chiefly the Vickers Armstrong aircraft works at Reading, yet in contrast to British methods, notably at Hanover, Dortmund, etc., no raids were made on cities. The enemy's approach flights over occupied territory with Vickers Wellingtons led to such considerable losses that they were discontinued for a time, while British fighters were not yet out of the doldrums.

I was in the Reichstag in Berlin on 19 July 1940. The Reichstag speech, which contained, among other things, my promotion to Field-Marshal, made our minds easy. We regarded Hitler's peace offer as seriously meant, and reckoned with the possibility of England's accepting it. I had no idea at that time that many army officers did not consider the Luftwaffe Field-Marshals as their equals in rank. I am still today firmly convinced that none of us would have been made Field-Marshals after the western campaign if Hitler had not believed in the probability of peace.

I am both an army and an air-force officer, in the later course of the war holding both air and Army Group commands; I therefore believe I am in a position to appreciate the tasks of individual commanders in both services. If performance is to be judged by results, there can be no question that the Luftwaffe, both strategically and tactically, played a decisive part in army operations. Naval strategy is the pacemaker for air strategy. In both arms technical problems loom larger than in the army. There can be no doubt that an air operation demands profound knowledge and planning which, although on a different level, is not less complicated than that required by the army. Nor can it be doubted that air operations in the army battle zone or in sea warfare call for a high degree of knowledge and understanding of the rudiments of all three arms.

Results will demonstrate an officer's fitness to be a Field-Marshal, and no one will then ask about his origins, whether he came from the army or the Luftwaffe. But one piece of advice I give to all Air Field-Marshals: do not become a one-sided technician, but learn to think and lead in terms of all three services.

11

Operation *Sea-lion* and the Battle of Britain

Prospects for an invasion of England—Muddle-headedness of the programme—Part of the Luftwaffe—The opposing air strengths—The first phase, August to September 1940—Churchill and *Sea-lion*—The second phase, September 1940 to June 1941—Attacks on London—Industrial targets—Principles governing bombing missions—The Luftwaffe a stop-gap until the attack on Russia.

The preliminaries to Operation *Sea-lion*, which was to have had as its objective the invasion of England, reveal the planlessness of our conduct of the war. In neither the political nor the military field were closely knit preparations made for a war against England. Even in the autumn of 1939 when the offensive against the west was already determined there is positive proof that our preparations never envisaged an invasion of England. Granted that the O.K.W.[1] and Hitler were extremely wanting in foresight, and that Hitler into the bargain had not reckoned with a blitz victory over the Western Powers, even so the utter neglect of the invasion idea, obvious to every soldier, is incomprehensible. Anyone who knew the scrupulous care with which Hitler checked preparations before every other campaign and prognosticated the probable outcome must arrive at the conclusion from his hesitancy in the case of England that he wished to avoid an open conflict with her. In my view he seriously cherished the belief that England would grasp his hand with its

[1] *Oberkommando der Wehrmacht*, the General Staff of all three services. [Publisher's Note.]

67

offer of peace. All the same, the omission to make the necessary preparations was and remains a grave mistake. Besides, both Hitler and the German General Staff thought in terms of continental warfare and shied at a war across the sea—a view corroborated by Admiral Raeder. If the army was reluctant to tackle an operation against Great Britain, the navy was flatly opposed to it. We Luftwaffe generals, however, including the Reichsmarschall, were more positively minded. Seeing that we airmen have often been reproached with optimism, this more positive attitude—I purposely use the comparative—was in keeping with our record.

Nothing venture, nothing win! The trend of the war hitherto must be the first premise for a summary of the situation. Three victorious campaigns had demonstrated what the German Wehrmacht was capable of. England's expeditionary force had been wiped out in the field. To re-equip it must take months. The R.A.F. had been hit hard, their fighters having reached their nadir on 6 September, and many airfields, including those most favourably situated, having suffered with them. The British had no air-ground support bombers, while their medium bombers, for example the Wellingtons, had paid for their few sorties with very heavy losses. In general, their still available bomber forces could be held in check by flak alone and must sooner or later fall a prey to our German fighters, which had long yearned for just this kind of target. The British fighter forces could be dissipated, softened up and destroyed by appropriate tactics; in addition parachute troops could be used, in freight-carrying gliders, to shoot up, bomb or otherwise put out of action the radar stations and so deprive the home defence of its means to direct the battle. The British could not meet the demands for air supremacy in the classical sense for the simple reason that they had not sufficient air striking power to smash the invasion fleet, if this could be done at all, and what they had could be paralyzed.

The Luftwaffe by itself could not deal with the British Home Fleet; that was a task that postulated the employment of all available naval, air and military strength. Great importance had here to be attached to minelaying and to heavy coastal artillery. As the waters off the English coast were very heavily mined and mines could not be swept within the time available, those stretches of the Channel in which the Home Fleet could ma- nœuvre were greatly narrowed. Even at that time—and still less later in the light of my Mediterranean experience—I did not understand our navy's attitude towards coastal artillery. Of course one had to assume that the enemy coastal batteries would be neutralized, to which end cross-Channel gunfire and bomb- ing raids—to say nothing of smoke-screens—promised good re- sults. Yet to make an invasion dependent on the silencing of *all* the English coastal artillery in the assault corridor and neigh- bouring sectors was going too far.

This demand reminds me of a conversation with the Co- mando Supremo in 1942 when the Italian navy made the land- ing on Malta conditional to the destruction of the coastal bat- teries. I replied that this could not be done and went on to say that I had seen many assaults where the enemy guns had not been anywhere near neutralized, yet the success of the operation had not been endangered. Even if one or another ship were sunk—not necessarily involving the total loss of the crew—that was a tolerable loss to set against a success which might decide the campaign, indeed the war.

I also had a great belief in our Siebel ferries, in which I had travelled myself, and large numbers of which could easily be assembled. Even though in 1940 I lacked the experience of Tobruch, where two out of four British destroyers were put out of action by 8.8-cm. gunfire alone, or of Anzio-Nettuno, where thickly plated ships were similarly driven off by weak to medium coastal artillery, I was sure that our air defence could be greatly strengthened and minefields protected against enemy minesweepers by the use of numerous Siebels armed with three 8.8-cm. flak and light guns; they could also protect the crossing against attack by British light naval forces. I know the dislike of the navy for any craft whose design has not been based on purely naval considerations, but that does not argue that the ferries, first conceived in Siebel's ingenious brain, and our engineer assault boats would not have been as excellent a means of transporting troops across the English Channel as, for example, they were to prove in the Straits of Messina and between Sicily and Tunis.

The most arresting fact about *Sea-lion* is that the lessons of the German airborne landings in Holland were completely ignored and it was proposed to do without the support of parachutists. With proper planning enough parachutists and glider planes could have been made available to swamp the defence and radar bases on the coastal assault front, and to seize airfields on which the landing of one or two airborne divisions would then have been possible.

Extensive diversionary bombing of Essex, Kent and Sussex, as in the case of Holland and Belgium, would have confused the English command, defence and population, and alone have greatly facilitated the enterprise. In any event, *one* premise had to be fulfilled, namely that far from armament production being reduced it had to be stepped up to a greater pitch than ever before.

I expounded my views not only to Goering, but also to the G.O.C. Ninth Army, General Busch, and to the competent naval commanders. But the central purpose was lacking. During the weeks of preparation I became more than ever convinced that the operation would not be started. In contrast to our preparations for previous campaigns, there was not one conference within the Luftwaffe at which details were discussed with group commanders and other services, let alone with the High Command or Hitler himself. The conversations I had at my battle headquarters on the Channel coast with Goering and the military and naval commanders appointed for *Sea-lion* were also informal talks rather than binding discussions. I was even left in the dark about the relation of the current air raids on England and the invasion plan; no orders were issued to the Chiefs of Air Commands. No definitive instructions were given about what my air fleet had to expect in the way of tactical assignments or what provision had been made for co-operation of army and navy. I found this the more disheartening because, in the light of verbal instructions given me on 6 August 1940, I could presume that the air offensive which started two days later was intended to be the prelude to *Sea-lion*. But in the very first days of the offensive it was conducted on lines quite at variance with those instructions and never harmonized with the requirements of an invasion. Besides, every commander was bound to tell himself, in the light of our equipment at that time, that an air offensive lasting five weeks (8 August to 15 September 1940), even assuming the most favourable circumstances, must inevitably involve a wastage intolerable for the carrying out of an invasion—the more so because there was no apparent assurance that material and personnel replacements would be forthcoming or that formations could be maintained at full operational strength for several months.

In order to carry out an invasion it was necessary to stun the island defences by sharp hammer-blows and then suddenly to launch the attack with a scarcely depleted Luftwaffe. In this connection, however, it was forbidden to raid air bases in the London area, a mistake that made the battle for air supremacy problematical from the start. It is also questionable whether so much importance should have been attached at that particular moment to the neutralization of the English ports nearest to the Continent. However, if I had not been happy about the operational orders for the beginning of the Battle of Britain, various talks with the Reichsmarschall restored some of my faith in the prospects for *Sea-lion*. I could not imagine that precious air formations were being wasted attacking unsuitable targets just to mark time. It is only possible to understand the antecedents of *Sea-lion*, however, on the assumption that the High Command continually flirted with the idea of an invasion as a conscience-salve for its failure to make up its mind by reason of a number of political and military misgivings. I am forced to agree with the opinion of the British military historian Fuller when he writes that *Sea-lion* was often contemplated, but never planned.

The air battle for England also suffered from the muddle-headedness of the *Sea-lion* programme. It was clear to every discerning person, including Hitler, that England could not be brought to her knees by the Luftwaffe alone. It is therefore no good talking of the failure of the German air force to reach an impossible goal. It was likewise clear to us Luftwaffe commanders that, although we might gain a temporary ascendancy in the air, permanent air supremacy was impossible without the occupation of the island, for the simple reason that a considerable number of British air bases, aircraft and engine factories were out of range of our bombers. For the same reason only a few of their ports were open to our attack. The range limitations of our fighter aircraft increased the difficulty. We were thus not exactly pleased to hear talk of *Sea-lion* being washed out or postponed, rumours to which effect were already current at the beginning of September. Our disgust will be understood when it is realized that henceforth the whole burden of the battle for England would have to be carried, under aggravated conditions, by the Luftwaffe.

No doubt economic warfare against targets on or off the island was an essential part of the strategic war in the air which could have satisfactory results if target-setting was carefully planned, but to begin it as a substitute for a washed-out operation of a very much vaster scope without special preparation of all serviceable means was a bad makeshift with many drawbacks.

The 2nd and 3rd Air Commands were now given assignments which they could no longer fulfil effectively; they had neither enough aircraft nor aircraft of sufficient range. Just as in 1939 we had entered the war against Poland in a state of unreadiness, so now we were not equipped for an extensive economic war. To be sure, we made life more difficult for the English on their island, but we could not sever Great Britain's vital arteries.

English writers have exaggerated the strength of the German forces at the date originally fixed for *Sea-lion*, namely 15 September 1940. Churchill, for example, speaks of 1,700 aircraft. This figure is not correct, as may be checked by yearly production statistics. The 1939 production [1] of approximately 450 fighter aircraft can be written off as scrap in August 1940. Similarly of the total 1,700 fighters produced in 1940 about 600 must be written off as lost or crashed in the earlier operations in Holland, Belgium and France; and roughly 400 must be deducted because they could not have been delivered by August. At the very most our effective strength in fighters could have been 1,700 minus 1,000 = 700 aircraft. If we include from September onwards our Me 110's—two pursuit fighter wings to the number of 200—we reach a grand total of 900 fighters and fighter types against Churchill's 1,700.

The air war against England in 1940-41 may be divided into different phases, determined by political and military considerations.

The first phase, from 8 August to 6 September 1940, includes the air preparations for the invasion contemplated for the middle of September; in other words, the elimination of the English air defence simultaneously with the continuation of the campaign against merchant shipping to strangle supply lines and to cripple air-force armament production. The methods employed ranged from air penetration by strong formations of fighters to irregular fighter and low-flying attacks on air bases in Southeast England, reinforced by raids on airfields and plants by single bomber formations of varying strength escorted by fighters. The offensive against supply traffic in the sea areas off the east and south coasts of England was maintained by Stukas and Jabos, coupled with nuisance raids to disturb unloading operations in the receiving ports. Terror raids were forbidden.

After costly initial engagements the English fighters kept out of the way of the superior German forces, while part of the British ground organization was transferred to bases beyond the maximum range of our fighters. By the employment of small bomber units to bait the English fighters we managed to bring

---

[1] These data are taken from Baumbach's book *Zu Spät*. Ploetz in his *History of the Second World War* (Bielefeld, 1951) gives the total strength of the 2nd and 3rd Air Commands as 1,361 bomber and 1,308 fighter aircraft. Presumably this last figure includes the 400 undelivered fighters mentioned above.

them up again until even this chance of a battle became so rare
that no decision could be forced, as they were expressly ordered
to avoid any engagement. Our difficulty was not to bring down
enemy fighters—in Galland, Mölders, Oesau, Balthasar, etc., we
had real aces, while the huge figures of aircraft shot down are
further proof—but to get the enemy to fight.

The scores of aircraft brought down or hit had a different
significance for either side. English pilots who had to bale out
or make a forced landing over the island came down on their
native soil and, allowing for their injuries and the provision of
a new aircraft, could, sooner or later, be sent into action again.
A German fighter, on the other hand, landed in enemy country
and became a total casualty. If his engine were hit the German
pilot had a chance of alighting on the water, but this, too, often
meant a total loss despite the immediate action of our air-sea
rescue service and the help of our air-sea rescue buoys, as both
these security arrangements, albeit marked with the Red Cross,
were not recognized on the English side as protected by international law.[1] It should be mentioned that both in English waters
and in the Mediterranean we naturally sent in our air-sea rescue
service to save British airmen as well.

If our fighter successes were respectable despite the evasive
tactics of their English opposite numbers, they were also costly.
The sum of English losses, about 500 aircraft out of an initial
operational strength of about 700 Hurricanes and Spitfires, can
be laid against the loss of nearly 800 German fighter, bomber
and reconnaissance aircraft for the same period. The reasons
for the latter high figure have been given above. Aerial photo-

---

[1] Churchill thus expresses the English view: "German transport planes,
marked with the Red Cross, began to appear in some numbers over the Channel in July and August whenever there was an air fight. We did not recognize
this means of rescuing enemy pilots who had been shot down in action, in
order that they might come and bomb our civilian population again. We rescued them ourselves whenever it was possible, and made them prisoners of
war. But all German air ambulances were forced or shot down by our fighters
on definite orders approved by the War Cabinet."

There may be two opinions on the justice and admissibility of this order; but
anyone who has seen, as I have, the constant attacks made in defiance of international law on a German air ambulance and a crew in the water by Hurricane
flights can have only one.

graphs of hits claimed on aircraft industry plants at Liverpool, Birmingham, Coventry, Thameshaven, Hull, etc., and at such ports as Chatham, Newcastle and Sheerness showed satisfactory results. Stuka and Jabo operations against shipping, which I was often able to observe from my battle headquarters, were also extremely successful, being far in excess of previous months, though limited by the effective range of single-seater aircraft. Accounts of the success of minelaying operations from the air do not tally anywhere near, but the British have admitted it was. considerable, as was continually reported to me by IX Group.

Although we gained air superiority within a restricted area for a short time at the beginning of September, we failed to keep it consistently after we began to raid the London zone. But sure it is that outside the island itself we could move as freely as in peacetime, which points to the absolute inadequacy of the British bomber crews. They were also far from formidable as a defence against invasion; the Wellingtons were too little battleworthy and the German A.A. too strong and practised.

As a preliminary to *Sea-lion* the plan for the first phase of our air offensive against England was ill-conceived. When German and English writers say that the Luftwaffe lost the first round, that it failed to gain air supremacy and that in consequence the invasion had to be cancelled, that criticism is formally wrong. Let me recapitulate the essential factors. Air supremacy in an absolute sense, in other words mastery of the air, could only be won if the enemy air force accepted a trial of strength. This was not the case. The tactics of the R.A.F., right in themselves, can, however, hardly be considered a proof of strength or superiority; their airmen were good defence technicians up to a point.

The first air battles were by no means unsuccessful. At the beginning we could stand our losses in relation to the number of enemy aircraft shot down. Their defence was not yet fully organized and the initial fighting showed our tactical superiority. Not until the later air battles did we have to call it a draw.

The raids on armament factories, seaports, supply depots and camps, which were consistent with the idea of an invasion, had remarkable psychological results and achieved the practical effect of disrupting the enemy's economy.

In an invasion the German air combat forces would have done their job if the invasion planners had taken the necessary steps to gain only a qualified air superiority, if all dissipation of strength had been avoided and if the whole Luftwaffe had been available on zero day fully refurbished—conditions which could perfectly well have been fulfilled.

British strategy was confined to the mere defence of the island, with the application of all their technical knowledge and new technical devices. Their few unsuccessful night raids by single bombers in the French coastal zone do not alter this, but rather indicated that in the event of an invasion their bomber forces were not likely to be formidable. British raids on German air bases in occupied territory were mere pin-pricks, though terror raids on German cities were a more serious matter.

The beginning of the battle for the sky opened a new chapter in air strategy and deserves every air commander's most careful attention. As I was myself forbidden to fly against England I tried to fulfil my obligations as a commander by following the raiders as they went out from the Channel coast. Occasionally I interfered with operations and tried repeatedly to gauge any changes in atmosphere by talks with returning officers and crews. I was anxious to keep in touch with the feelings of the men and to issue my orders accordingly, but I dare say at times this habit of mine became a nuisance; I realized this when formations began to take off from airfields outside the radius of my supervision in areas to north and south. Still, I believe that by my watchfulness I reduced the number of losses, for if I saw an untidy formation I would send out a W/T order for it to return to base. Apparently both now and throughout the second phase the enemy was less dreaded than their pestilential Chief!

*   *   *

According to Churchill's *Their Finest Hour* England had to reckon with the invasion, which the Germans are stated as certainly intending to risk. However, the undertaking was pre-

vented by "the German failure to gain command of the air."
I agree with Churchill's view that the main opposition to the
idea emanated from the German navy's acute awareness of the
operational difficulties. ". . . the stipulated operational condition of undisputed air superiority over the Channel had not been
achieved." The way in which Raeder managed to bring home
to Hitler all the points against it in order to postpone the venture, if not to call it off altogether, is remarkable. In a word, the
Luftwaffe seemed to be to blame for everything. I myself, however, was able for days on end to observe the whole Channel
from my command post at Cape Gris Nez. I could see very little
sign of enemy air superiority, of their navy or indeed of any
consistent menace to the Channel—as was confirmed by my airmen. (It may be worth remarking here that British air attacks
against our small convoys—ferries and barges—between Sicily
and Tunis somewhat later hardly caused any losses because of
our powerful A.A. defence.)

If Hitler had really wanted to carry through the project he
would, like Churchill, whose character his own resembled in
this respect, have taken trouble with every detail (as with the
invasion of Norway) and imposed his will on all three services.
In that event so many vague orders would not have been issued
which made agreement between service chiefs difficult.

For the energy with which the British government raised the
defence potential of the island I have only admiration. My own
standpoint, however, reached as a result of my experience of
invasion methods elsewhere, is as follows. The value of fortifications and other obstacles is indisputable, but to overdo them
may be harmful if they cannot be constantly garrisoned, as they
may become useful points for advance enemy tanks, patrols and
parachute troops to hang on to. While recognizing the enthusiasm and devotion of the British people, I cannot believe in any
special combat value on the part of bodies like the Home Guard,
above all with inferior weapons; even if the regulars hold their
ground they are always cannon fodder, as the parallel in Germany in 1944-45 shows. The *Volksturm* had a great propaganda
effect, yet even though it was better armed than the Home

Guard it turned out a fiasco. In view of the sacrifice of life to be expected, the responsibility of sending such units into action is a heavy one. For our part we found that the best solution was to allot drafts of *former soldiers* to front-line regiments. Even taking the substantially higher morale of the Home Guard into account, one must not estimate its power of defence too highly.

During all this period the British could not put into the field in southern England more than fifteen to sixteen first-class divisions of the type required for a war of movement. Yet nothing can replace the lack of battle experience against a battle-tested enemy. The moving up of reserves will be delayed or even prevented by parachutists, air attacks, etc., and heavy reverses and losses will follow. I am thus convinced, contrary to Churchill's view, that at least until the middle of August a properly prepared offensive must have been successful—later its success would have depended more than ever on the Luftwaffe and airborne landings.

Our greatest danger lay, of course, in the Home Fleet, and this could only be averted by a concentration of all German naval and air forces, which would not have been helped by the German navy's hesitant attitude. Still, with serious planning and execution these difficulties could have been overcome. The means at our disposal—air and sea mines concentrated at harbour entrances, U-boats in superior numbers, destroyers, torpedo-boats and Siebel ferries as well as our coastal artillery and smoke-screens—could have paralyzed even these superior forces. One can very roughly say that in these operations the navy and coastal artillery would have had a 60 per cent share and the Luftwaffe 40 per cent.

Having observed British air activity for months on end, I can summarize my impressions of the situation holding good about September:

1. Air control of Holland, Belgium and northern France was unquestionably ours.
2. British day bombing attacks had been so costly that they had had to be called off.

German warplanes in flight to England.

| Kesselring | Bodenschatz | Goering | Speid |

Goering, Commander in Chief of the Luftwaffe, and officers watching a take-off for the first major attack on targets in the Greater London Area.

On the Channel coast:

Kesselring in conversation with Generals Jeschonnek and Loerzer of Air Fleet 2.

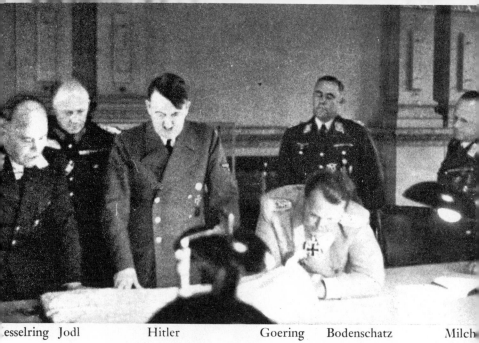

esselring Jodl   Hitler   Goering Bodenschatz   Milch

Kesselring's proposed strategy in Russia being
discussed in the Reich Chancellery.

General Yamashita and Kesselring in conversation at Brussels in 1940.

Leave-taking after a conference with General Hoepner, Commander of the 4th Panzer Army, during the double battle of Vyazma-Bryansk.

3. Their night bombing raids, at first directed against targets near the coast with weak forces and later against airfields, were having inconsiderable results.

4. Although the flak protection envisaged for *Sea-lion* was not yet available, raids on embarkation ports on the Channel coast were unimportant in their effect even according to our naval reports.

5. Night bombing raids against German towns had been becoming more frequent, though without causing any special damage, material or psychological.

In the event of an invasion the R.A.F., with its strength as it was at the time, could not possibly have undertaken the multifarious tasks allotted it: air reconnaissance, counter-attacks against landed forces including parachutists, neutralization of supplies, prevention of convoys from entering French ports, and provision of fighter escorts for destroyers. One does not need much imagination to see that the above jobs, involving attacks on German airfields, the Channel ports and the Channel itself with swarms of widely dispersed shipping, and on landed enemy forces as well as the protection of their own land and sea transport, would have been in striking disproportion to the R.A.F.'s strength. To this must be added the effects of our fighters, pursuit fighters and flak. As regards bombers, I cannot imagine that the British close-support forces, limited as they were in number and performance, could have done much damage, especially in view of the almost impenetrable protection that our Luftwaffe and navy could have built up with flak over the ports. With the heavy bombers, which until then had been used against targets in the heart of Germany, the case was different—but even here our strength in flak and night fighters would have kept their activity in the invasion zone within tolerable bounds.

To sum up, the attempt may have been difficult, even very difficult, but it would not have been hopeless. Every undertaking is a risk and needs, besides planning, relentless execution and a certain optimism. Churchill fulfilled these conditions in the highest degree from the defence aspect. But I feel I can say the same for the German commanders.

* * *

The second phase of the air battle for England, from 6 September 1940 to June 1941, saw the scrapping of the invasion idea. Our main assignments were now the disturbance of production and incoming supplies with the underlying purpose of slowing down British armament production and initiating a full-scale economic war. The "reprisal raids" were also started.

From the new nature of our missions those who could read the signs knew that sentence had been passed on Operation *Sea-lion*, and with it the opportunity missed to exploit a unique chance. The postponement of the invasion from mid-September to an indefinite later date, finally until the spring of 1941, could not alter this.

When Hitler ordered a reprisal raid on London this was only an apparent infringement of the new directive, as the targets selected fell under the heading "Economic War."

Our air strategy, the strength of raiding forces and targets were changed according to the weather situation, the enemy defences and the state of our training and equipment. It has been held against the Luftwaffe Command, not entirely without justification, that its efforts were too little concentrated, its results too dispersed. I myself, who am next door to a fanatic on the subject of "concentrated effort," have suffered extraordinarily from these charges. The changing of targets, which has been so much criticized, was forced upon us by circumstances in the autumn of 1940 and in the spring of 1941—apart from isolated cases when we had to obey an arbitrary, but unfortunately unmodifiable, order from above. Of course the obvious thing would have been to choose our targets according to their importance, raze them to the ground by incessant attack, and then watch for any signs of reconstruction so as to harass the workers and destroy their work. But if priority plans for the economic war were there, the means to carry them out were lacking. We needed four-engined bombers with great range of action, climbing power, speed, load capacity and armament; we had, moreover, no long-range fighters which could escort a bomber formation deep into enemy country; finally we were dependent on the weather, very changeable in the months in question, with the result that an effectively attacked target was saved from a follow-up attack in formation by lasting fog, rain and cloud. Surprise raids, perhaps once repeated, gave the best results without serious losses. But losses soon increased to an intolerable extent owing to the quick reaction of the British defence—fighters and A.A.—and quicker concentration of fighters over the target and on the approach route. With the alternative before us of letting the enemy's uncanny reading of our intentions bleed the Luftwaffe to death, we had no choice but to switch our targets, times and methods of attack.

The first grand attack on the military installations of London took place in the presence of Goering. Preceded by secondary raids and supplemented by night raids, it was completely successful. Goering was so impressed by the sight of the airborne squadrons in flight and by the effects of the raid which could be descried from his battle headquarters, that he let himself be carried away in a superfluous bombastic broadcast to the German people, an exhibition distasteful to me both as a man and as a soldier.

To accomplish our purpose, for all our zeal and ability, we needed luck. It was a mistake to count one's chickens before they were hatched. The very next day brought foul weather, which, as it did not break, severely hampered operational conditions and diminished results. The main targets in this and subsequent raids on London, which was bombed in varying strength by day and by night almost daily throughout September, were the war factories of this strategic, traffic and trade centre. Next, as alternative targets, port installations and various armament plants were raided with fluctuating success, the principal objectives being Southampton, Portsmouth, Liverpool, Birmingham, Derby, Chatham, etc.

The restriction of air raids to southern England was dictated by the limited effective range of the Me 109's, which could not fly without protection. An attempt to escort them with Me 110's (twin-engined pursuit fighters) and to use them independently in bombing operations was abortive; the Me 110's proved too slow and—surprisingly—too awkward in manœuvre, and in fact needed fighter protection themselves. At that period and even later fighter escorts had special difficulties. Cloud made it hard to fly in close formation or even keep together—we had not the instruments to help here—and the protection of the bomber squadrons was also endangered by the inability of some fighter formations to fly blind. Unluckily for us, the weather conditions were less of a handicap to the English fighter. The best solution in cloud was to group together individual pilots who could fly as well as fight in twos and threes.

Arrangements with the 3rd Air Command led to combined operations: simultaneous concentrated attacks and staggered raids on a variety of targets, and continuous all-day attacks on a common target. The defence was temporarily thrown into confusion by sorties made by bomb-carrying fighters and pursuit fighters.

The British terror raids on Germany were meanwhile becoming more frequent without achieving much material or psychological result. Our night fighters under Air Marshal Kammhuber harassed the enemy on the way over and gradually made themselves an indispensable component of our defence in depth.

Mussolini's offer to participate in the offensive against England by sending an Air Group was welcomed with some misgivings. The salient feature of German-Italian co-operation was the excellent camaraderie of the airmen. Without making any final judgment on the Italian air force, however, I am still convinced that the Italian aircraft were no match for the modern English fighters, not even for the Hurricanes. The Italian bombers could not be employed by day, and when later we went over to night bombing their blind-flying training was inadequate and they lacked proper instruments. I heaved a sigh of relief when the Italian formations landed back after a couple of small sorties against the port installations of Hull. Their losses were likely far to outweigh any possible damage they could do. Air Marshal

Fougier, who commanded them, was too shrewd a man not to realize this and used what time he could to get on with training.

The British defence was based on a powerful A.A. barrage, though this was not the decisive factor; its backbone was and remained the Home Defence fighter forces. Realizing this, I suggested to Goering, in addition to our raids with light-bomber formations, another method of attack with heavy bombers, from which I promised myself better results with less effort and smaller losses.

This marked the beginning of a new phase which got the most out of the skill and daring of individual bomber pilots. We did not give up heavy-bomber raids in formation, but from time to time instead of going for mass effect tried to hold up production by individual raids on vital parts of industrial targets, such as their power plants. These flights were, of course, planned in minute detail. I partly checked them myself. One or several alternatives were always provided so that whatever happened the bombs could be dropped on some important target. Although the crews were very enthusiastic about these raids, they were not very successful; such pin-pricks might certainly have a disturbing effect, but could hardly retard English output.

These different operational methods, however, enabled us to exploit the surprise factor and thus to carry out our mission less expensively; a succession of large-scale operations against military targets was accordingly staged in the form of non-stop raids on London, ports and armament centres like Liverpool, Manchester, Portsmouth and Coventry, and also on air bases. Convoys were dealt with by light-bomber formations and minelaying was intensified.

Yet notwithstanding all our efforts, whether in the form of mass concentrations or individual sorties, the total results remained unsatisfactory. What would it be like in the bad winter months when with the intensification of the economic war our assignments would be taking us further and further afield? If we were to deal a really damaging blow against the British war machine we should have to alter our tactics. And so, from November 1940, we switched to the night offensive.

The C.-in-C. Luftwaffe kept in his own hands the direction of operations of the 2nd and 3rd Air Commands against Great Britain in co-ordination with the 5th Air Command in Norway under Stumpff. The approach over broad stretches of sea and night raids had brought it home to us that this method of warfare strained the Luftwaffe to the limit. No one who has not experienced it can know what it means to reach home with the very last drop of petrol or to fly over hundreds of miles of sea on a single engine. Obviously the crews who carried out these operations in icing-up zones and under constant threat from British night fighters deserve the highest respect.

The general principles for these bombing missions were: (1) a choice of targets according to their importance to the British war economy; (2) attacks in large formations with follow-up nuisance raids to interfere with clearance work; (3) no targets to be attacked which had not been pin-pointed with the help of aerial photographs, the best available maps and the latest information about their location and military importance; (4) detailed briefing of all formations and lone raider crews, and a careful check with Group and Air Commands or the C.-in-C. Luftwaffe; (5) target reconnaissance and illumination by picked bomber crews in preliminary flights over the target, on the lines of the later famous English "Pathfinders." The enemy's countermeasures, growing in strength from week to week, complicated the difficulties of distance, navigation and weather.

Gradually, however, we adapted ourselves to every changing condition. All went well provided our wireless sets remained intact, but if they failed it was a nerve-racking experience for all ground personnel to bring in the returning bombers to a suitable airfield in bad weather and fog. For all their endeavours and the best use of every technical aid they were not always successful. In order to save at least the crews if not the aircraft, the aircraft would either be belly-landed on the coast or flown on to west or central Germany, for example as far as Neubrandenburg, while the crews would often parachute down. It is interesting that a plane properly trimmed by its pilot before he baled out over Brussels would outfly its remaining petrol to crash, for instance, at Perleberg or Stendal, about 350 miles further on.

We had a hard time of it during these weeks, whereas apart from U-boats and small craft, the army and navy could rest and prepare for the uncertain future. The Luftwaffe threw in everything it had in the hope of embarrassing the provisioning of Great Britain and delaying its rearmament. We hammered away at ports and production centres, and despite the multiplicity of targets a certain concentration was attained.

Our operational activity never let up throughout the whole phase for more than a day at a time, the weather being a determining influence. Our sortie graphs reached their highest point in the months of August and September but declined steadily until December 1940, to rise again from January to April 1941, with a further considerable falling off till June. According to operational reports and aerial photographs, the results achieved must have been respectable. All the same, as the Allies did later, we had overestimated the effects obtainable by bombing. There was no denying the damage inflicted by direct hits—photographs showed it—but the effect even of very heavy bombs was too restricted to be annihilating. Incendiaries, tens of thousands of which were dropped on vast target areas, were better, as the fires they started consumed what the heavy bombs had damaged but not destroyed.

Nevertheless the defence kept pace with the attack—even to tornadoes of this kind people can get accustomed. Every man of them put his hand to the work of shoring up and removing damage in a united effort which no one would previously have thought possible. Plastering with such a volume of high explosive that nothing was left alive was at that time as exceptional as the constant repetition of attacks on a single target. Yes, any hope of smashing Great Britain's war potential did seem wishful thinking.

As was later made clear, the tactical overwhelming of an inherently strong nation with a widely ramified war potential requires powerful and continually intensified day-and-night attack and terror raids continued over years. Exceptionally good results, as in 1940 against Coventry, were exceptional flukes. At Nürnberg before the International Military Tribunal I was questioned about this raid on Coventry, the destruction of which had aroused justifiable indignation in England. I explained that Coventry was marked on the target maps with an exact location of all its armament factories as the English "little Essen." The great success of the raid was attributable to the convenient distance which made it possible for our bombers to come over two or three times in the same night, to the exceptionally favourable weather conditions, and the illumination which helped navigation and the use of bomb-sights. The unpredictable consequences of even a precision bombing attack are much to be regretted but are inseparable from any attack in force. Fire and smoke clouds make it impossible to aim accurately. The dispersion inevitable in any bombing is thus considerably increased and punishes adjacent areas in no wise intended as objectives. Pacifist talk by a soldier is apt to be treated with suspicion; it is quite wrong, however, to question the sincerity of his feelings, for it is first and foremost the soldier with a sense of responsibility who with his knowledge of modern weapons can understand the full horror of total war.

I may remind the reader that the German government wished to have air warfare banned by international law and that the accusations brought against those in charge of this air war are therefore misdirected. I may repeat here that although in isolated cases purely terror raids were ordered by the C.-in-C. Luftwaffe, those orders were, however, modified by the Air Commands who appointed military targets. I can say unequivocally —and this has been confirmed by English war historians—that the first raids on open cities were flown by the R.A.F. It was furthermore only with reluctance that the German Command undertook reprisal raids, such as the September attack on London.

In the long run policy motives, which to begin with were kept secret even from me, even though I was destined to hold an important air command in the coming operations against Russia, led to the gradual throttling of the air attacks against

England. Thankful as I was that from then on operations across the Channel gave me more opportunity to study the problems of rest and refurbishment and the vagaries of the weather, the total burden on the Luftwaffe, however, was scarcely lifted. Only from May 1941 was there a noticeable easing of the strain.

On 24, 25, and 26 December 1940 and again on New Year's Eve I gave orders that no operational flights were to be made over England—but here my assumption that the enemy would do the same was unhappily wrong. I cannot entirely acquit myself of blame for often allowing myself to be overinfluenced by human feelings. I say this emphatically and without fear of contradiction, despite my condemnation to death for inhumanity.

A few days' leave at the turn of the year—the only ones I had during the whole war—did not bring me the rest I had hoped for because of heavy bombing raids on German towns in my administrative areas. I interrupted my leave and flew to Holland, where I had a serious discussion of policy with Kammhuber and Oberst Falck, the senior night-fighter commanders there, and gave them the alternative of either a basic reorganization or disbanding the night-fighter wing. I promised to do what I could to meet many individual wishes, but insisted that once this was done there must be tangible results.

And results there were. After this conference I remained in constant liaison with the night fighters, which—under Kammhuber as organizer, Falck with his operational experience and many another fine pilot, such as Lieutenant Prince Sayn-Wittgenstein and Hauptmann Streib, who was later our ace night fighter—rapidly won their spurs as a formidable defence arm. As "father of the night fighters" I was always invited to every important service or private occasion. Meanwhile technical improvements were the first step. Ground radar sets faultlessly registered the approach of enemy raiders; searchlights working hand in glove with radar, organized in a Searchlight Division, made possible successful "bright night fights," while radar sets mounted in the aircraft themselves gave us "dark night fight" successes. Further proof of the effectiveness of the new defence arm was that soon after the Group was formed the British night raiders preferred the overseas approach.

Although British raids on Germany in these months until 1941 inflicted wounds that caused a transient disorganization in the affected districts, their results were nowhere impressive. On the other hand, if enemy losses were considerable, they could easily be made good. The stepping-up of their night raids against our ground organization in the air administrative areas of Holland and Belgium might be seen as evidence of the effectiveness of our attacks on England. These attempts misfired as they had done before. If on fine days the British did not essay any day-light bombing operations, still we often ran into fighter patrols which sometimes scored fluke successes. Air Marshal Grauert, the gallant commander of I Group, was killed in just such an engagement. The less often the enemy flew into occupied territory, the more jittery our anti-aircraft gunners became. Between Christmas and New Year's 1940-41 I was paying a visit to Oster-kamp, and as I landed my little crate in a light fall of snow I was greeted by heavy fire from 2-cm. cannon. I raised justifiable hell. The excuse that an "English bomber" had been reported as approaching I was as little disposed to accept as the rather curious defence that the culprits were army flak. History re-peats itself: off Tunis in 1942 my Storch was also mistaken for an English bomber by Italian flak, which opened up on me; it was lucky for me that the gunners overestimated the allowance for speed.

Must this campaign in the air then, in its conception and results, be considered a failure?

The rapid ending of the ground fighting in the west brought the German Command up against a situation for which it was not prepared. Here for the second time the crass lack of a far-sighted plan was made particularly plain. It is a bad thing to drift on the current of events without having formulated either the next step or one's ultimate aims. No matter what the motives may have been which guided Hitler in his attitude towards England, I am convinced that in those months an attack against the island was never seriously contemplated. This was the situation in which the air battle with England was begun, a battle that committed us to nothing, but betrayed the aimlessness of wishful thinking, which could not help influencing the conduct of operations and its success, as indeed it did. Herein lies the key to the indisputable fact that in many cases results fell short of expectations. Considering, however, the state of its development at the time and the number of serviceable aircraft kept constantly in the air even in the most adverse weather conditions, it would be arguable to speak of the "failure" of the German Luftwaffe in the Battle of Britain.

As has already been explained, it is historically undemonstrable that the *Sea-lion* invasion had to be abandoned because the Luftwaffe was not up to its task and because of the impenetrable British defences. Had this been so, the uninterrupted series of bombing attacks on Great Britain could never have been kept up for the nine months after *Sea-lion's* cancellation. The fact was that because of the lack of a plan for *Sea-lion* the Luftwaffe was thrown in as a stop-gap to bridge the interval until the curtain rose on the next act—Russia. In justice to our achievement it must be said that if we never reached our goal we were certainly well on the way to it. That this is no disparagement will be clear to anyone who compares the ten months' battle for England with the Allies' three years' battle for Germany.

In a word, in the battle for England two worthy enemies were matched who surpassed each other in the performance of their highest duty.

12

The Russian Campaign till the End of November 1941

22 June 1941 Beginning of the invasion with three Army Groups, North, Middle and South—Advance of Army Group North through the Baltic states in the direction of Leningrad, of Army Group South in the direction of the Ukraine—Army Group Middle (two, then three infantry armies, two Panzer Groups): beginning of July encircling battle of Bialystok-Minsk—16 July Capture of Smolensk—Beginning of August, Encirclement of Russian forces at Orsha-Vitebsk—9-19 Aug. Battle of Gomel—9-19 Sept. Participation in the encircling battle of Kiev in co-ordination with Army Group South—2-12 Oct. Belated offensive against Moscow with three infantry and three panzer armies, double encircling battle of Vyazma-Bryansk—2 Nov. Guderian's advance checked at Tula—Advance of Panzer Group 4 halted at Moshaisk before Moscow—Crisis in the Russian capital.

Operation *Barbarossa*, the code name given to preparations for the campaign against Russia, wa. strictly top secret. Nothing leaked out. Staffs were as much in ignorance of what was in the wind as the troops. Nor for a month or two did I think it advisable for my own staff to be occupied with it. On 20 February 1941 a small planning staff was formed under Goering's personal guidance, housed in the Gatow Air Academy near Berlin. From time to time its director, Colonel Löbel, kept me informed of progress or asked me for a decision. At the beginning of 1941 I flew to Warsaw for a conference with von Kluge, the Commander-in-Chief there, and to give supplementary instructions about the ground organization in that area. I went back again in May to patrol the deployment base of my Air Command in the east and discovered that construction work, ostensibly held up by weather and difficulties of terrain, could not be completed before the beginning of June, but only in time for the revised Zero Day, 22 June. A check-up showed that the forces allotted me by Goering would not be strong enough to give Army Group Centre the support desired. In a heated conference with Goering in his command train north of Paris, with the backing of his Chief of Staff, my old friend Jeschonnek, I got my way; I was at least promised the minimum extra flying personnel and anti-aircraft guns on which I had insisted. I could understand Goering's state of excitement when he said that I was not the only one who wanted things; we had to go on fighting England as well. I stuck to my guns for three reasons: first, two campaigns had taught me the need of ground troops for air support; secondly, I was very sceptical about the continuation of the war in the air against England with seriously diminished forces; and thirdly, I believed that my insistence would give a fresh impulse to the augmentation of our air combat strength.

On 12 or 13 June 1941 I left the Channel coast to attend Hitler's final conference on *Barbarossa*. Officially I remained for some time in the west, the idea being to make the world believe that the bulk of the German air forces were still in operation against England under the orders of Field-Marshal Kesselring.

I have already mentioned when dealing with the *blitzkrieg* that when Hitler told me on the eve of the Polish campaign of the conclusion of a non-aggression pact between Russia and Germany it took a great load off my mind. That had been on 23 August 1939; we were now in the middle of 1941. Had the conditions so changed in those short two years that I could now quash the fears which had formerly oppressed me? By now the Continental Powers had broken the Allied front, and after the retreat from Dunkirk the British armies could no longer be used on a large scale, while the R.A.F. was not yet ready for major operations. Our northern flank was protected by Falkenhorst's army and Stumpff's air fleet in Norway, and our southern flank by Rommel's Afrika Korps and the Italians; the last blitz campaign had eliminated the Balkans as an enemy front. The intervention of the United States was questionable, or at any rate lay in the distant future.

Thus the two fronts were much less of an actual danger in 1941 than in 1939. Was it then so necessary to attack Russia? Hitler had again said in his final address to the generals on 14 June that the Russian campaign was unavoidable, that we had to attack now if we wanted to save ourselves from being attacked by the Russians at an awkward time. He reminded us once again of the points which made it seem unlikely that a friendship between Russia and Germany could be lasting, the undeniable ideological antagonism which was still not basically removed, the measures which Russia was taking on the Baltic coast and on her western frontier and which looked very much like mobilization, the increasingly aggressive behaviour of her soldiers towards the inhabitants of the frontier districts, troop movements in areas close to the frontier, the intensified building up of the Russian armament industry, etc.

In September 1939 in the 200-mile-deep frontier area there were 65 Russian divisions, in December 1939, 106, and in May 1940, 153 plus 36 motorized divisions—an estimated total of 189. The disposition of the Russian troops with a strong concentration in the centre—there were approximately fifty divisions in the Bialystok salient alone—might well be indicative of aggressive intentions. The Russian air arm ground organization, moreover, which was known to have been set up close to the frontier, had a positively offensive character.

Hitler's contention that the Russians would seize the first favourable moment to attack us seemed to me indisputably right. The Kremlin could easily manufacture reasons for a surprise attack. Time was on their side, however—and they were pastmasters in the art of biding it. I knew from the reports of Luftwaffe engineers who had quite recently travelled through Russia that an extravagant factory and armament programme had been begun which we would soon cease to be able to keep up with. Unfortunately Goering and Hitler thought them flights of imagination. I believe that today only an incorrigible optimist can suggest that Russia would have been content with her status after the end of the war with Poland.

If, then, a war was on the cards, what were the military prospects in 1941? On the debit side, the date proposed for the attack was pretty late, though this handicap could to some extent be offset by a limitation of the objective. On the credit side, in two major and two minor campaigns we had been able to accumulate experiences against which the Russians had no equivalent advantage. We were already veteran campaigners who knew our business from A to Z. Certainly, in the 'twenties we had developed tanks and aircraft side by side with the Russians, but since then we had a record of years of progress and proved experiment, whereas the Finnish war had exposed Russian weaknesses. To come to the Luftwaffe, I had every confidence in our fliers and knew that von Bock's Army Group, with which the 2nd Air Command would have to co-operate, need have no fear of being let down.

The battle would not be easy, there might be one crisis after another, the supply problem must cause unexpected difficulties. But was not the objective—to keep communism away from western Europe—so important that we must stake our utmost to achieve it? Hitler in *Mein Kampf* describes a war on two fronts as a dangerous mistake. It cannot be assumed—at least in my opinion—that he had forgotten his own views on the subject and let himself in for a war on two fronts without realizing the danger. Perhaps he believed, with the idea of "fighting from an inner line" at the back of his mind, that an opportune elimination of Russia would enable him immediately afterwards to turn round and smash the threat from the west with a concentration of strength. But one thing is sure—he was far from conceiving the idea of striking a hard, and perhaps decisive, blow at Russia from the countries bordering on the Mediterranean which would have enabled him simultaneously to wound England fatally at her most vulnerable spot. Obsessed with continental ideas, he disastrously underrated the Mediterranean's importance.

When I landed on 15 or 16 June 1941 on a really fine airfield north of Warsaw I found the organizational work at my head-quarters proceeding apace under the capable direction of my new Chief of Staff, General Seidemann; staffs and combat forces were on the spot or, as in the case of VIII Close Combat Group under von Richthofen, on the way from Crete. The aircraft on the airfields were very cramped for space; but if improved cam-ouflage, a good aircraft reporting service and powerful flak could not exclude every attack, they could in all probability reduce the effectiveness of Russian air raids to a minimum.

Easy as it may seem on paper, the responsibility of individual commanders was heavy. I had evidence of this when my very competent Senior Signals Officer, Dr. Seidel, committed suicide shortly before the opening of hostilities, apparently unable any longer to bear the burden of responsibility. He was succeeded by our former Air Attaché in Moscow, Colonel Aschenbrenner, an arrangement with which I was particularly pleased because of his knowledge of the Russians. It was owing to his mobility and sensitive control that the Air Command was always in the picture.

On my numerous flights in my twin-fuselaged, twin-engined FW (Focke-Wulf) 189 I familiarized myself with the breadth and depth of the assembly area and already had my first experi-ence of the torrential rains, so heavy that they might have com-pelled us to postpone the date of the offensive had it not already been made inevitable by the delayed arrival of troops from the Balkans. The Air Command had issued orders for strictest se-crecy; consequently on the airfields close to the frontier air-craft were only allowed to fly at low level. The tactical surprise of the Russian air units on their airfields is the more striking because after 20 June the Kremlin could no longer have been under any illusion about the sharpening of the situation.

My conference with Field-Marshal von Bock (Army Group Centre) did not waste much time; we understood each other. When I went back on the evening of 21 June to discuss any misgivings or ideas that might have occurred to him in the meanwhile I found him, in contrast to his mood on the eve of previous campaigns, rather dispirited, immersed in cogitation befitting a responsible commander before the beginning of a fateful enterprise. I realized once again the comfort in such a situation of a brief exchange of views between kindred minds. It was my intention in this campaign with its many imponderables to keep in much closer touch with Army Group headquarters and to maintain constant liaison through a Luftwaffe General Staff officer who had previously been in the army. He had to report to my command post every evening, explain the "army situation" for the day and discuss the measures proposed for the morrow, and similarly listen to the "Luftwaffe situation" so that he could explain that in detail to the Army Group Command.

As air commander I had rather a distant survey of the manœuvres of the army and received through the Air Groups (air service liaison) and the Flak Corps direct reports from the army front which sometimes differed very considerably from those from army headquarters. At every evening situation conference I assessed the army situation and instructed my intermediary, Uebe, to pass on my criticisms to the Army Group Command unless in urgent cases I had a telephone conversation with von Bock or my Chief of Staff rang his. Von Bock knew that I was not trying to teach him his business, but that my interference was only an understandable reaction of a partner, anxious to help a sister arm linked, for weal or woe, in a common purpose. Every morning, and often also again in the evening, I discussed in great detail with General Jeschonnek, Chief of Staff of the Luftwaffe, the events of the day and the next day's programme in order to enable Goering to further Luftwaffe interests at the Führer's situation conference and to bring them into accord with military intentions. In rare cases, for example at Smolensk and Moscow, I profited by this connection to urge my personal view of certain army measures to the fountainhead where the decision would be taken. All the same, the caption of this chapter is: exemplary co-operation between army and Luftwaffe. Relying on this harmony, I instructed my air force and flak generals to consider the wishes of the army as my orders, without prejudice to their subordination to me, unless serious air interests made compliance seem impracticable or detrimental. All my commanding officers and I prided ourselves on anticipating the wishes of the army and on carrying out any reasonable requests as quickly and as completely as we could.

The objective of the Russian campaign was clearly set forth in the order to smash the Russians in White Russia, that is to say between the frontier and the Dnieper. Hence our main weight had to be thrown against the Russian concentration area by von Bock's Army Group and the Russians wiped out by a lightning advance before they could break contact and retire to the vast steppes. Simultaneously the Russian bombers had to be pushed back to their rear bases east of the Dnieper from which they would no longer be able to raid the homeland of Germany. My orders from the C.-in-C. Luftwaffe were primarily to gain air superiority, and if possible air supremacy, and to support the army, especially the Panzer Groups, in their battle with the Russian army. Any further assignments would lead to a harmful dissipation and must at first be shelved. It was obvious to me that even this mission could not be fully accomplished immediately, but must be completed successively.

As regards the forces available to Air Fleet 2, I have already said that I had held out for minimum requirements, and my insistence had gradually had its reward. There were, in addition to an Air Command Distance Reconnaissance Squadron:

II Air Group (Loerzer), comprising one reconnaissance squadron, two bomber wings, one Stuka wing, one fighter wing of four squadrons, one destroyer wing, one signals battalion and one administrative area staff with a special war establishment. Close combat *Fliegerführer* II (Fiebig) was composed from these units.

VIII Air Group (Freiherr von Richthofen) comprising one reconnaissance squadron, one bomber wing, two Stuka wings, one ground-strafer squadron, one fighter wing, one destroyer wing, one signals battalion and one administrative area staff with special war establishment.

I Flak Corps (von Axthelm) and later
II Flak Corps (Dessloch). } each with three to four flak regiments.
Administrative Area Posen (Bieneck).

Zero hour was set for daybreak, against the wishes of the Luftwaffe for very convincing ground tactical reasons, that is to say at an hour when single-engined fighters and Stukas were unable to fly in formation. This was a great handicap to us, but we managed to overcome it.

We succeeded in gaining air supremacy in the first two days, helped by excellent air photography. Reports of enemy aircraft destroyed in the air or on the ground totalled 2,500; a figure which the Reichsmarschall at first refused to believe. But when he checked up after our advance he told us our claim was 200 or 300 more than the actual figure. From the second day onwards I watched the battle with the Russian heavy bombers coming from the depth of Russia. It seemed to me almost a crime to allow these floundering aircraft to be attacked in tactically impossible formations. One flight after another came in innocently at regular intervals, an easy prey for our fighters. It was sheer "infanticide." In this way the foundation for the build-up of a Russian bomber armada was smashed, and indeed all through this campaign Russian bombers never again put in an appearance.

After the first two days Stuka attacks on enemy front-line troops were reinforced by increasingly large elements of the other Air Command formations, the following assignments being carried out: neutralization of the enemy air force, a task that no longer required any specially detailed forces; support of panzers and infantry in mopping up local resistance or eliminating enemy outflanking threats, a task principally reserved for Stukas and ground-strafer squadrons; the smashing or holding of Russian forces trying to get up to the front or to pull out of the battle with Stukas, ground-strafers, fighters, light bombers, and practically everything we had; disruption of operational movements on the railways; and constant reconnaissance. Only a few days after the launching of the offensive I was flying solo in my FW 189 over the Russian zone, a proof of how completely the attacks of the first two days had paralyzed the Russian air force.

Fighting went on in the Brest-Litovsk area till 24 June, when its citadel was opened up by a 2,500-pound bomb. Meanwhile the Panzer Groups forged ahead and paved the way for the battles of Minsk and Bialystok (26 June till 3 July) which led to the capture of 300,000 prisoners, but not to the annihilation of the forces fighting there. Crises were inevitable as the mass of our panzer forces drove on towards the Dnieper and the "Stalin Line" while the Fourth and Ninth Armies were only gradually bringing up their non-mechanized divisions to the pocket. This operation with its crippling effect on the encircled Russians assisted the manœuvres of the German Panzer Groups in their attack across the Dnieper.

The 3rd Panzer Group, supported by von Richthofen's Air Group, captured Vitebsk on 9 July and so gained a favourable springboard for their successful operations north and northeast of Smolensk. Intermittent bad weather hampered their movements on the utterly inadequate network of primitive Russian roads, thus revealing the real face of the Russian theatre. The fact that even the fully tracked vehicles, including tanks, and most of all the supply services, had to rely on the arterial roads helped to warn the troops of difficulties ahead.

The battles for the Dnieper line (10-11 July) indicated the weakening of the Russian resistance, but also the presence of large, if poor quality, reserves.

The Luftwaffe played a decisive part in these successes. Our formations made concentrated attacks on the Russians as they moved forward or back on roads, footpaths and railways, and on their camps as they were spotted. Later again low-level attacks were made by Stukas, ground-strafers and fighters against the defence lines in various sectors of the river in the foreground. The difficulties encountered in moving forward the ground organization were even more noticeable with us than in the case of the army, for our ground staffs were insufficiently motorized and had no fully tracked vehicles. Moreover, over and above the few established airfields additional ones had to be reconnoitred and fitted up which were not directly protected by army troops.

On 23 June the Air Command kept its finger on the pulse of the battle by moving its command post to a railway train near Brest-Litovsk, and in the first days of July to a motor transport command column east of Minsk, in order to keep in close contact with units.

After the incredible gains of territory in the first weeks of the campaign the question of the continuation of the offensive soon came up for consideration. I supported the Army Groups, urging that the battle of annihilation which had now lasted for some weeks should be continued beyond the Dnieper in order to eliminate once and for all the Russian western army. But the High Command let itself drift on the current of events without instantly coming to a positive conclusion, although this vacillation was not yet perceptible at the front.

The fighting culminated in the encircling battle of Smolensk (from the middle of July till the beginning of August) which resulted in a great victory (over 300,000 prisoners again), but which yet brought no decision. Had we been able to close the gap east of Smolensk the result might have been decisive, but the urgent suggestions made by Goering and myself fell on deaf ears. In the course of a few days appreciable enemy forces were able, mainly by night, to trickle through a narrow gap of a few miles, through the middle of which ran a stream in a small valley whose ground cover hid their movements. If our ground-strafers had succeeded by day in restricting this seepage by unremitting attacks the Russians would not have been able to take such good advantage of the hours of darkness, over 100,000 of them at my guess thus escaping to become the nucleus of new Russian divisions. The failure to wipe out these forces later—I merely recall the costly battles in the Jelnia salient between 30 July and 5 September—could not be laid to the charge of the German troops or their commanders. Our divisions, including the Luft-

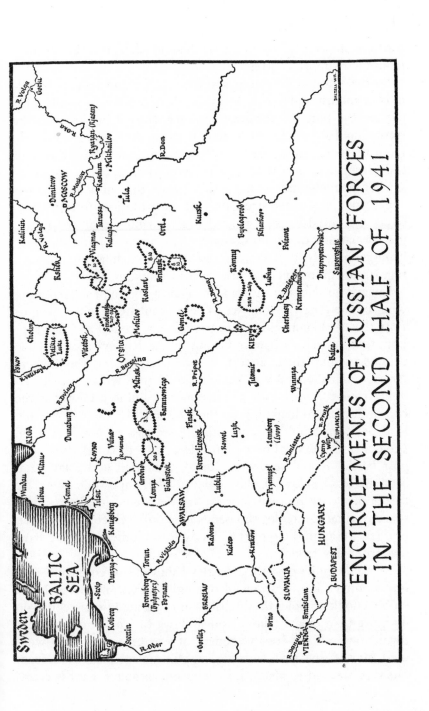

ENCIRCLEMENTS OF RUSSIAN FORCES
IN THE SECOND HALF OF 1941

waffe, were simply overtaxed, at the end of their tether and far from their supply centres.

So the word was: march and fight, fight and march, for almost a month and a half for a depth of nearly 500 miles, for part of the time in inclement weather; frontal battles with the retreating forces and with new Russian divisions brought up from the back areas, battles by the second and third waves of the German armies with Russian troops trapped in larger or smaller pockets and with guerilla bands that now made their appearance in greater strength, and with the low-flying, effectively armoured Russian ground-strafers which appeared in single formations of flight strength. Any normal hope of being brought out of the line for a rest, if only a short one, or of a regular re-equipment was just wishful thinking.

Enemy outflanking movements against the unprotected right wing of the Army Group set us new problems. From 1 August 1941 the Air Command had to provide air-ground and flak support for Guderian's Panzer Group in the Roslavl area (38,000 prisoners) and then, almost simultaneously, for the Second Army under General von Weichs, in a battle which was developing round Gomel (100,000 prisoners), and as a climax at the end of August to help mop up the Russian forces left in the low land between Smolensk and Lake Ilmen east of Velikiye Luki (30,000 prisoners). The commanders who directed these August battles—von Weichs at Gomel, Guderian at Roslavl, and Stumme at Velikiye Luki—achieved the impossible. Our air forces met with unusual success: we destroyed in a very short space of time 126 tanks, thousands of motor vehicles and fifteen bridges, to say nothing of the bloody losses inflicted on the Russian front-line troops.

At the beginning of these battles I moved my command post up to Smolensk, operations of our light formations being based on Shatalovka-Smolensk-Vitebsk. On the same line we could do no more than create take-off possibilities for the heavy-bomber formations. Heavy-freight gliders of the Giganten type were used for the first time to bring supplies up to Shatalovka from Orsha. Captured Russian M.T. vehicles, suitable for cross-country work, and native carts were brought into service. Our ground organization even appropriated captured Russian tanks, with which they beat off enemy tank raids on the airfields.

While in August 1941 we commanders on the central front were brooding over the *how* and *when* of the continuation of the offensive in the direction of Moscow, and our troops were kept uselessly kicking their heels, after much shilly-shallying the High Command, greatly to our annoyance, shifted the point of main effort to the south (21 August 1941).

Two opinions were possible about the necessity of turning against Budjenny's Army Group in the south at the beginning of September. The fact remained that large parts of von Bock's Army Group Centre and of my Air Fleet were left with our front facing south and had additionally to form a southern front in order to enable von Rundstedt's Army Group South successfully to envelop Budjenny's forces. After more than four weeks of fighting, however (from 28 August to 26 September), the fate of Budjenny's armies, and therewith that of Kiev, was sealed. Von Kleist's and Guderian's Panzer Groups joined hands on 13 September 125 miles east of Kiev. Over 650,000 prisoners, nearly 1,000 tanks and more than 3,500 M.T. vehicles were captured.

I would not be doing justice to the Luftwaffe if I omitted to mention the decisive performance of II Air Group. Without strong light combat formations, some of which had been given up to Air Fleet 4 in the south, it had to operate under conditions rendered more difficult because the Russians had learnt the lesson of previous engagements and almost completely throttled our communications by day. Bad weather hampered operations in closed formation. The skill of our crews was evident from the fact that railway lines in the battle zone were permanently cut. In one short section of the line twenty or thirty trains were held up which were subsequently smashed to pieces by destroyer attacks. Not until the last days of the battle did any formation targets appear on the roads; when they did they were relentlessly attacked with devastating results.

With the order of 21 August 1941 to attack in the direction of Kiev there was no more arguing about the Jelnia salient; it could be abandoned. After the preliminaries for the bomber sorties had been completed by the setting up of wireless beacons and the assembly of aircraft and bombs, the main target for all long-range bombers was the governmental, armament and communications centre of Moscow. Other targets, for instance the large aircraft works at Voronezh, the factories at Tula and Bryansk, the overcrowded marshalling yards at Bryansk, etc., which were only approached in bad weather in single fighter raids, were alternative, bad weather or tactical fleeting objectives.

The raids on Moscow caused me grave anxiety. Crews shot down had to be written off, the effectiveness of the Russian anti-aircraft guns and searchlights impressing even our airmen who had flown over England. Also as time went on Russian defence fighters appeared in increasing numbers, luckily only in the daytime. Results did not quite come up to my expectations, but in relation to the size of the target our forces were not any too strong, the dazzling effect of the searchlights was disturbing and the weight of bombs that could be carried was greatly reduced by the increased fuel load. But years later, when I was being interrogated in the Mondorf prison camp in 1945, the Russian woman who was acting as interpreter happened to mention "the terrible effect of our bombing"; I gladly revised the opinion I had at the time in the interest of my gallant formations and their crews. At all events, the continuous raids, besides the material havoc they wrought, prepared the subsequent breakdown of the city. A pity it could not be exploited.

August and the first half of September slipped by with variable weather, fighting on both wings of the Army Group and incessant sorties. I agreed with von Bock that the positions occupied by the Fourth and Ninth Armies were little suited for a winter campaign, especially as the enemy in front of us was being visibly reinforced. It was not a far step to the notion of trying our luck once again on this front. A successful encirclement might decimate the Russians and determine our tactics during the winter. Whether it would be possible after such a victory to push on in the direction of Moscow must depend on the strength and state of our forces, and, above all, on the weather, the great unknown factor.

Preparations for a fresh assault were pushed on from 15 September with coldly calculated ardour. My old friend from Metz days, General Hoepner, commanding the 4th Panzer Army—apparently impressed by the lack of success of Army Group North—had little confidence. Twice I explained to him the entirely different circumstances of Army Group Centre, made him see his really unique chance of a break-through and an outflanking operation and promised him reinforced air support. He gradually waxed more confident—and when I looked him up during the battle he was grinning all over.

As far as my own formations were concerned, the tactical frame was clear. The main tasks of the Flak Corps were on the ground. They were to be used as support and assault artillery with the point of main effort on the right wing. Our air-ground support fighters, following a practice which had already become axiomatic, were to blast a path for the army divisions. Our heavy bombers were to seal off the battlefield to the rear. In comparison to the most recent battles there were very few enemy aircraft to be observed, their air activity being at its liveliest on the southern wing.

The outside right wing was responsible for this battle, with 650,000 prisoners captured, being allowed to become another "ordinary" victory. The bad weather which the 2nd Panzer Army ran into in the southern area at the very beginning of September frustrated the hope of a wide turning movement on Moscow through Tula. Shocking flying weather hampered air support; it snowed and rained and the roads, already pitted with craters, were further churned up by the heaviest fully tracked vehicles, with the result that movements were slowed down until by 5 October they were almost brought to a standstill. Attempts to move single aircraft by means of flak tractors ended with the snapping of the tow-ropes or the tracks. When rations failed to come up the Luftwaffe had to supply parts of the 2nd

Panzer Army by jettison drops. The physical and mental strain
—the army units had no winter equipment—had become too
much.

This was the turning-point of the great sequence of battles in
the east. This and the aggravation of nervous tension were also
—as was later to become evident—too much for my old friend of
Reichswehr Ministry days, General Guderian, the tough and
resilient commander of the Panzer Army.

In the light of this development I hardly thought that the
strategic objective of the offensive was any longer attainable.
The filthy weather had completely reversed all the conditions
that had previously been in our favour. The state of the ground
was incredible, frost set in at the beginning of November, the
army had no winter clothing, and Siberian troops were now
making their appearance along with larger numbers of the extremely useful T 34 tank and ground-strafer aircraft.

Of itself it would have been no great feat—I was convinced
of this at the time—for Hoepner and Guderian to drive their
panzer forces straight through to Moscow and even beyond.
But Jupiter Pluvius disposed otherwise; the Russians were given
the chance to build up a thin front west of Moscow and to man
it with their last reserves composed of workers and cadets. They
fought heroically and stopped the assault of our almost immo-
bilized forces.

In that period of October the Siberian divisions had not
yet arrived at the front. It is still a puzzle to me, even today,
that our long-distance reconnaissance, although reporting lively
movement on the roads, never to my knowledge gave warning
of the strategic concentration of the Russian armies from the
Far East. But the increase of railway traffic which was reported
at the end of October ought alone to have warned the O.K.W.
to caution. The order to retire to a winter line ought to have
been given in the middle of November at the latest when the
army reported the arrival of Siberian units at the front.

Encouraged, however, by the encirclement battles of Kiev
and Bryansk-Vyazma the O.K.W. ordered the continuation of
the offensive against Moscow. The order was received with

little enthusiasm, particularly by the commanders primarily concerned, Field-Marshal von Kluge, who only gradually warmed to it as he became infected by the spirit of the front-line troops, and Hoepner, who, as I discovered from private talks, wet-blanketed the project. Kluge, more pushed than pushing, complained of Hoepner's hesitant leadership; Hoepner defended himself to me on the excuse of shortage of supplies. Things did not look any too bright when at the end of November I and my Air Fleet staff were pulled out of the Russian front and entrained in the direction of Berlin, to be followed a few days later by the staff of II Air Group.

As soon as I realized that we should have to spend the winter somewhere in Russia I indented for winter equipment, which by the good offices of my efficient transportation chief was delivered with the minimum delay. We also took advantage of the help of the Finns in constructing special heating apparatus to ensure that our flying formations were in readiness for sorties even in the greatest cold. On my departure I knew that my men were well equipped for the winter.

Was the Luftwaffe not strong enough to compensate for the symptoms of fatigue particularly apparent in the army and help to speed the further advance on Moscow? The achievements of Air Fleet 2 between 22 June and 30 November speak for themselves: 6,670 aircraft, 1,900 tanks, 1,950 guns, 26,000 motor vehicles and 2,800 trains. The incessant operations flown from 1 September 1939 till the middle of November 1941 had, however, severely taxed our resources, and the vagaries of the weather in the Russian autumn, rain, fog and cold, did the rest.

After the battle of the Bryansk-Vyazma pocket enemy movements in a formed body were only exceptionally observed; the concentration of the picked Siberian divisions were not spotted or at any rate were not appreciated as such. Pockets of resistance were isolated and small pillboxes widely dispersed, which made it extraordinarily difficult for fast-flying airmen to see and hit them, especially in filthy weather.

The T 34 tanks, which had now appeared in increasing numbers and could move even in the worst ground conditions, were a problem that imposed a terrific strain on our ground-strafer pilots, who had to fly recklessly over forests, trees and villages to deal with them. Army units were constantly calling for protection against the very low-flying Russian ground-strafer attacks, and sorties had to be flown to keep them quiet, though with little effect. Flak and pak would have been much more effective. As it was, in spite of all handicaps we continued to attack the tanks from the air, but we could not, and did not, do them any serious damage.

In order to exhaust all possibilities we moved up to airfields quite close to the army front on a line running approximately Orel-Yukhnov-Rzhev. Even so our success was not impressive. Even a powerful air force could not have helped the frozen and weakened German front decisively against an almost invisible enemy; it was still less to be expected of a weak and overtired air force.

*   *   *

The fighting on two fronts, in itself a mistake and certainly not generally wanted, need not, in the opinion of many people, necessarily have been fatal to the outcome of the war. We must therefore ask ourselves if the campaign in Russia with limited forces could have led to the capture of Moscow and the annihilation of Russian military power—that is to say the armies, military centres and armament works in European Russia—by the end of 1941. The starting-point of my argument must be the strategic plan adopted by Hitler. I know this central sector very well and I am certain that our worst enemies were the sporadic spells of bad weather and the bogginess of the roads, above all in 1941, but for which the capture of Moscow would have presented no problem. Nevertheless, if the inclement weather periods and their consequences are discounted as inevitable phenomena of the Russian theatre, the objective could still have been reached if Hitler had not wasted precious weeks in overlong deliberation and secondary operations. If on the conclusion of the encirclement battle of Smolensk at the beginning of September the offensive had been continued against Moscow after a reasonable breather, it is my opinion that Moscow would have fallen into our hands before the winter and before the arrival of the Siberian divisions. It would then in all probability have been possible to push forward a kind of umbrella bridgehead farther east which would have made it difficult for the Russians to turn our flanks and to bring up supplies to their fronts. The capture of Moscow would have been decisive in that the whole of Russia in Europe would have been cut off from its Asiatic potential and the seizure of the vital economic centres of Leningrad, the Donets basin and the Maikop oil fields in 1942 would have been no insoluble task.

But even with this operation Marshal Budjenny's Kiev group of armies would somehow have had to be dealt with. The fighting on that front would certainly have become violent and critical, but it would hardly have assumed a character decisive for the campaign. On the other hand, the capture of Moscow would have disorganized the Russian High Command, disrupted the apparatus of government and cut communications with the Far East. Keeping the strategic objective strictly in view, it would have been more correct to push on with the offensive against Moscow at the end of August or in September, after a suitable pause for refurbishment and for necessary regrouping. There would then have been ample time for an offensive operation with limited objectives against Budjenny.

A second question is whether Hitler's operational idea of going over to the defensive on the Dnieper with Army Group Centre so that the reinforced Army Groups on the wings could reach their important economic objectives mentioned above, was more correct than the idea of capturing Moscow.

When we reached the Dnieper two things had become certainties. First, the complete encirclement and annihilation of the Russian forces west of the Dnieper had failed; and secondly, it had become clear that fresh forces were still present or in process of creation in the area between Moscow and the Dnieper and that these could be provided with the needful reinforcements and supplies. It can be calculated that Army Group Centre was opposed by one and a half to two million men. Budjenny's forces facing von Rundstedt's Army Group certainly had the same strength, while those opposing Army Group North must have been somewhat less.

The mass transfer of Russian troops on the central front to points of main effort could not have been prevented for any length of time. The Germans could only reckon on a swift and sure success for the Army Groups on the wings if all not absolutely essential forces of Army Group Centre and all Luftwaffe units from the whole battle front—that is, from the west and north—had been fed to Army Groups South and North in addition to reserves, and also if these wing operations had been started at the very latest at the end of July or the beginning of August 1941. There is no reason to suppose that these operations could not have been finished before the winter, especially as there was no need to reckon with an early winter in the south as there was in the north. But today, as in 1941, I am doubtful whether the possession of Leningrad, the Donets basin and the oil fields would have been as valuable as the capture of Moscow as a governmental, armament and communications centre. Ergo: the primary strategic objective had to be Moscow even if it involved a deliberate limitation of the objectives set for the Army Groups on the two wings.

The third question is this: the successive encirclement battles of Bialystok-Minsk, Smolensk, Kiev, and Bryansk-Vyazma wasted time and put the brake on our Panzer Groups so that they were unable to fulfil their natural task of penetrating the enemy's lines and pushing on to their objectives regardless. Could this objective have been reached at all by clear-sighted planning and exact execution?

Even though in 1941 I lacked the experience of 1942-45, I believe that Panzer Groups 2 and 3 would have broken through the Russian lines of defence. But I do not believe that the second and third waves of infantry following in their wake could have defeated the million-strong Russian armies so quickly—if at all—that they could have caught up with and supplied the Panzer Groups in time, that is to say before they reached an inevitable state of exhaustion.

For this task the Panzer Groups were too weak. Our strategic mechanized forces had to be proportionate to the depth and breadth of the area to be conquered and to the strength of the enemy, and we had not anywhere near this strength. Our fully tracked vehicles, including tanks, were not adequately serviceable. There were technical limitations to constant movement. A mobile operation in 1,000 kilometres' depth through strongly occupied enemy territory requires vast supplies, especially if there is no chance of falling back on large and useful enemy stores. Our lines of communication and our airfields lay mostly in enemy threatened country, and were insufficiently protected. There was also little anticipation—for reasons I do not know—of the employment of strong airborne formations which for operations of this extent are indispensable.

All things considered, the Moscow offensive could only have succeeded if an interim halt had been called for the Panzer Groups in at least two sectors (Minsk and Smolensk) while they, together with the Infantry Corps, mopped up the enemy forces west of them; and only then if the further attack had been launched from a secure base.

In conclusion a few comments on the exclusion of additional sources of manpower and material. In August or at the beginning of September 1941 Field-Marshal von Reichenau, commanding the Sixth Army, suggested the creation of White Russian and Ukrainian divisions. This suggestion was rejected by Hitler at the time with the remark: "Let Reichenau—" of whom, by the way, he had a very high opinion—"mind his own military problems and leave the rest to me." Anyone who has ever seen what vast numbers of magnificent and willing Russians there were to draw on can only regret Hitler's attitude. From 1943 until the end of the war I had under me German-Russian formations, which, with no hope of realizing their cherished aim of freeing their country from the Bolsheviks, remained true to the bitter end; with their support on a larger scale in all probability our objectives could have been reached. Thus in the military field, and not only in the guerilla section, the price was exacted for the mistaken racial policy of Hitler and his associates. Immediate planned exploitation of Russia's human material and armament industries would have made the devastation of our production which we had to endure after 1942 very much more difficult and largely would have made up for our material shortages.

Part Two

THE WAR
IN THE MEDITERRANEAN
1941-45

13

The Mediterranean, 1941-42

10 June 1940 Entrance of Italy into the war—12 Sept. Italian offensive
(Graziani's Tenth Army) against Egypt, stopped on the frontier at Sidi
Barrani—8 Dec. British counter-offensive—17 Dec.-8 Feb. 1941 Italian
evacuation of Cirenaica with the harbours of Salum, Bardia, Tobruch
and Bengasi and the loss of 130,000 prisoners—February 1941 Formation of the German Afrika Korps under General Rommel—24 Feb.
Rommel's counter-offensive—March-April 1941 Reconquest of Cirenaica—11 April Investment of Tobruch—July 1941 First (unsuccessful) British counter-offensive at Salum—Autumn 1941 Successful attack on German-Italian supply lanes to North Africa by British
naval and air forces—18 Nov. Second (successful) British counter-
offensive in North Africa—28 Nov. Transfer of German 2nd Air
Command to the Mediterranean area—10 Dec. Relief of Tobruch—
December 1941 to January 1942 Rommel's retirement from Cirenaica
into the area of El Agheila.

I first became really interested in the Mediterranean theatre
when Jeschonnek rang me up one day in September 1941 and
asked me how I liked the idea of going to Italy or Africa. He
was sure we should very soon have to make a much greater
effort in that part of the world if we wished to prevent the collapse of the Italian position in North Africa. Weeks passed and
I heard nothing more. For my part, I was too actively occupied
with the problems of my command on the eastern front to give
the matter another thought, so that the first warning of my
transfer, which came to me from General Hoffmann von
Waldau of the Luftwaffe General Staff, took me by surprise.
However much I might welcome the prospect of a new assignment in sunnier climes I was sorry to leave von Bock's Army

Group and some of my own formations in a situation that was still obscure.

I flew to Berlin and reported to the O.K.W. and Luftwaffe G.H.Q. for my instructions. I was told that they had paved the way for my going into action in Italy through Hoffmann von Waldau, who had formerly been our Air Attaché in Rome, his successor in that appointment, General von Pohl, and our Military Attaché, General von Rintelen, in conversations with the Comando Supremo and the Superareo. I could therefore assume that my position had been clarified and that the most urgent preliminaries for the transfer of flying formations, especially into Sicily, were already under way. The title proposed for me, C.-in-C. South, seemed appropriate in view of the scope and nature of my task. I was given a final briefing by Hitler in the presence of Goering and Jeschonnek. The unfavourable situation of our supply line to North Africa, I was told, must be remedied by the neutralization of the British sea and air key-point, the island of Malta. When I objected that we ought to make a thorough job of it and occupy Malta, my interruption was brushed aside with the flat statement that there were no forces available for this. Not being in the picture, I did not press the point, though I had occasion to revert to it later.

I arrived in Rome in advance of my staff on 28 November 1941. It was not long before I found out the difficulties of a coalition command. Mussolini had made a change in the Super-areo command which met with my thorough approval by appointing as Secretary of State an old friend of mine who had commanded the Italian Air Corps in Flanders, Air Marshal Fougier; but Count Cavallero, the Italian Chief of Staff, could not swallow the pill of handing over to me all the Italian military, naval and air formations which he had earmarked for the new offensive. He protested that this arrangement was tantamount to giving up an independent command. His extreme concession was an offer to put his air force at my disposal.

Half-measures would get us nowhere; so, ignoring Hitler's instructions, I waived my claims to an over-all command, but insisted in return on an even closer and more confidential co-operation on the Italian side than had originally been contemplated. Cavallero gave me his word that no operational orders should be issued for the Italy-Africa war zone by the Comando Supremo without my oral or written agreement—a promise that was kept. Looking back, I see that this concession, affecting the national prestige and highly cultivated pride of the Italians, was the prime factor in the success of our collaboration. I have always preferred a voluntary collaboration based on mutual trust to a constrained submission which is bound to cause resentment. In all our dealings with the Supermarina, under the capable direction of High Admiral Riccardi and Admiral Sanzonetti, with the Superareo, with the High Command or with the executive officers of the military, naval and air force units in this command it was the same story of comradely helpfulness always shown to their German opposite number. On the highest level my co-operation with Count Cavallero was as good and loyal as it was to prove bad and treacherous after 1943 when General Ambrosio succeeded him. I personally was subordinate only to the King and to the Duce.

In Tripolitania I found a clear-cut organization on the Wehrmacht pattern. The forces of all three services were subordinate to the Governor-General, Marshal Bastico, as was Rommel. An ideal organization on paper, it was, however, foredoomed to failure in practice because Rommel and Bastico were continually at loggerheads, and Rommel was unwilling to budge an inch to avoid treading on the corns of the susceptible Italians. Rommel's great reputation, then at its zenith, was an obstacle to the introduction of any change, but at the same time it helped to smooth over certain delicate situations.

The salient feature of the military operations at the end of November 1941 was the inadequacy of our communications system across the Mediterranean. Every day showed more plainly the naval and air supremacy of the British in these waters. The battle of Africa had in fact taken a critical turn for Rommel. He was holding the pressure of the enemy east of Derna, but operations were greatly handicapped, above all by the poor fighting quality of the Italian divisions, and we could not exclude the possibility of our eventually having to evacuate Cirenaica.

Meanwhile Malta had assumed decisive importance as a strategic key-point, and my primary objective at the beginning was to safeguard our supply lines by smoking out that hornets' nest. Time was required to build up the ground organization in Sicily, to bring forward our air formations and the supplies needed to smash Malta's naval and air bases, as well as to secure the co-operation of the Italian air force in our offensive. For the moment it was impossible to do more than reinforce the air umbrella over the most indispensable convoys.

Rommel's army made its own demands. The excellent liaison established by C.-in-C. South with the Superareo, and likewise by the Air Officer Commanding-in-Chief Africa with the Italian North African Air Group could not relieve the German airmen of the main burden of the battle. The Panzer Army in the desert complained of the lack of support it received from our weak squadrons, commendable as their achievements were. But without the recklessly offensive spirit of our airmen, be it said, Rommel's army would not have been able to halt its retreat at the Gulf of Sirte (Agedabia on 24 December 1941, Marsa el Brega from 13 January 1942).

My secondary task, at Marshal Cavallero's request, was to iron out the recurrent basic differences between the Italian and German commanders in the field.

The German troops of all three services were of first-rate quality; only there were not enough of them. They were equipped with excellent material, in some respects better than the enemy's; but only in exceptional cases were they numerically strong enough for the tactical requirements. In addition the already meagre flow of replacements conditioned by demands elsewhere was being reduced to a trickle by extraordinary losses incurred during sea transport.

Every campaign presents new purely geographical problems. In North Africa our troops had first to get used to the peculiarities of climate, terrain and vegetation. They had to learn to adapt themselves to the combat tactics both of nature and of their new enemy. Once they became acclimatized officers and men were equal to any task.

In a general way, the feeling of comradeship existing between ourselves and the Italians could be described as good, even if from time to time exasperation at our allies' inefficiency, both in their staff work and in their conduct in the fields, troubled the friendly atmosphere.

Although the war was conducted from Rome, yet Italy felt nothing of it. The war—this was the impression I gained—was not being taken by the Italians with the seriousness demanded of them by their responsibility to the soldiers at the front. Where a general sense of urgency and exertion were called for they worked half-heartedly.

The root of the matter, in my opinion, was that the Italians were unwilling to make full use of their war potential. Mussolini often answered my complaints by saying that the Italian people had become wearied by long and exhausting colonial wars in the course of which too much precious blood had been shed. His explanation and mine may both have been right. But in 1944 the Italians seemed to me quite blatantly reluctant to tap their reserves of manpower.

In their dealings with me Cavallero and Ambrosio vociferously pleaded shortage of material as the excuse for their inability to equip their soldiers properly and for their failure to make full use of their available manpower. That also may have been true. But, in addition, they pursued a deliberate policy of hoarding quite beyond my comprehension. The discovery, after the defection of the Italians in 1943, of vast stores of unused war material is alone sufficient proof of this cheese-paring.

Their mobilization machinery was not adjusted to the requirements of an army of a million men or for a long emergency. As I was able to verify on more than one occasion, peacetime working conditions prevailed even during the most critical periods of the war. And although Cavallero accepted the principle of total war, and the initial steps were taken to weld the various organizations of civil life into a co-ordinated war machine, that machine very quickly broke down.

I never got the impression that the people knew from the start that the war was a life-and-death struggle. I rather think that the realization was first brought home to them, as the war dragged on, by air raids and territorial losses, particularly in North Africa. The contrast between the German and Italian cities affected me so strongly that I tried as far as possible to blot out these impressions, for example by rarely visiting the towns and villages, and then only when my duties made it imperative. I shall never forget the peaceful aspect of Rome at the time of the battles of Anzio and Nettuno. If Mussolini was unable to inspire a wartime spirit into the nation he ought to have abandoned the thought of entering the struggle. Yet it may be inferred from the bitter guerilla warfare of the Partisans against the German Wehrmacht that the Italian population were by no means utterly devoid of martial spirit.

As might be expected from a nation of southern temperament, the Italian armed forces were trained more for display than for action. Their barracks were ill adapted for combat training; their submarines' exhibition diving and the stunt flying of their airmen were no fit preparation for the real thing. Proper importance was not attached to combined operational training in smaller formations or indeed in the services as a whole, the latter a common failing in most countries. The lack of large training areas was a great handicap. Of even greater consequence, until well into the war, was the deficiency of good weapons and equipment. It was expecting too much of the individual soldier to ask him to stop a heavy tank attack with inadequate weapons, for example with 4-cm. anti-tank guns and dummy tanks, or to deliver an assault with tanks too thinly armoured and with insufficient firepower against a modernized enemy; or to expect ships without night-fighting devices or instruments for locating submarines to engage in battle with a modern enemy fleet, or fighters of inferior speed and insufficient ordnance to attack aircraft with maximum-powered engines.

To leave cities without even a semblance of protection apart from mediæval cannon and an almost non-existent A.R.P. (without radar, without a proper communications system and without convenient air-raid shelters) was to overestimate the individual's courage and the general discipline.

These few instances could be multiplied at will. It would thus be wrong indiscriminately to condemn the Italian soldier as poor material and unsuited for a long and stubborn war. Mussolini and his peacetime Secretaries of State must squarely shoulder the blame; if they knew of these grave deficiencies they ought to have kept out of the war. Another mistake was to rely on weapons of Italian manufacture, which were always going to be the last word but were never produced, instead of adopting proved German types and manufacturing them under licence, for example the newer types of German tank and the 9-cm. anti-aircraft gun.

Even if the lack of combat training facilities was particularly obvious in the Italian barracks, mere soldierly discipline fell far short of my ideal as a German officer. One had only to watch a simple changing of the guard to see that the Italian soldier had no enthusiasm for his profession. Perhaps as a differently constituted Northerner my standards of judgment were wrong, but I think events justified me.

I attributed this unsatisfactory state of affairs above all to the lack of contact between officers and men. An Italian officer led a segregated life; having no perception of the needs of his men, he was unable to meet them as occasion required, and so in critical situations he lost control. The Italian private, even in the field, received quite different rations from the officers. The amount multiplied in ratio to rank; and needless to say, along with the greater quantity the titbits went to the top. The officers ate separately and were very often unaware of how much or what their men got. This undermined the sense of comradeship which should prevail between men who live and die together. The field-kitchen, with its tendency to level out such distinctions, met with no favour in the Italian army. I frequently pointed this out, with its dangerous effect on morale, to Cavallero without eliciting any unqualified agreement. In fact I discovered for myself that while our German field-kitchens were literally besieged by the Italian soldiers, on the other hand when I was entertained in an Italian officers' mess tent the regulation fare there was very much better than the food served in my own staff mess. Marshal Graziani had to act with decision in 1944 to ensure the other ranks got their pay punctually and in full. That this actually required special intervention seemed to me the most typical thing of all.

The purpose of what I have said is not to play up the faults of the Italians, but simply to account for the often-observed failure of their troops. I do not imply that the relations between officers and men were not good in spite of everything. They were in the vast majority of cases. Yet this fact only proves the innate decency of the Italian common soldier and that it would have been possible to turn him into a tough and excellent fighter. I have seen far too many instances of heroism by Italian units and individual soldiers—of the Parachute Division "Folgore" at El Alamein, of the artillery at the battle for Tunis, of crews of tiny naval craft and torpedo-boats, of torpedo-bomber forma-tions—not to be able to say this with absolute conviction. But in war the issues are decided not by isolated acts of heroism but by the general training and spirit of an army.

On the other hand, the Italians adopted the strategic principles generally accepted by central European military powers. I have seen a great many commanding officers of all three services who unquestionably were first-rate strategists and tacticians. The system of work in the service ministries I found comparable to that of any other country. I came across no confirmation of the fairly prevalent view that the Italian subaltern had too little knowledge of service regulations. Rather I believe he had in-sufficient practice in applying them, that the lively intuition of the High Command was not in harmony with its executive arm, and that this was responsible for quite a number of reverses. The administrative work may have been thorough, but it was badly carried out. No doubt the southern character partly explained this. What struck me particularly was the inconceivable neglect of the coastal defences on the islands, and even on the mainland, and the stagnation, which leapt to the eye, in the development and production of modern aircraft after the departure of Balbo.

Needless to say, I lost no time in familiarizing myself with my new front. I inspected the German units and made contact with Rommel and the Italian commanders. My first visit was to Sicily. This was unfortunate, as von Pohl, who was flying to meet me there, had to come down in the Tyrrhenian Sea, causing me grave anxiety until he was rescued from his plight. The helpfulness of the Italian navy and air force, however, left a most promising impression.

North Africa came next. There I listened—for the first time— to Rommel's grievances, and learnt of German-Italian differences. I was also able to help A.O.C. Africa, the veteran General Fröhlich, in his difficult position, receiving his orders as he did from X Air Group, whose headquarters were in Athens—too long a way off. I also thought that Air Marshal Geissler, a most competent officer, had too little influence over Rommel, so that I presently placed A.O.C. Africa directly under the orders of C.-in-C. South. A visit to the Commandant of Crete, Air Marshal Andrae, gave me an opportunity to learn the problems there.

The result of these informative flights was to confirm my view that the menace to our communications from Malta must be removed, and to bring home to me the decisive importance of the Mediterranean to the war. Had I known then that Admiral Raeder, after the abandonment of *Sea-lion*, had also seen that the centre of gravity of the war against England lay in the Mediterranean, our joint endeavours might have succeeded in shifting our main effort to this theatre. Here Hitler's policy of secrecy reaped its own reward.

We were unable as yet to launch a decisive air attack on Malta, as our air base, Sicily, was not yet ready to take the forces destined for the operation, which in any case had not been assigned. Things had first to be improved by a series of intruder raids on the British island and by strengthening the protection given our convoys. Thanks to the keenness and skill of the German formations, results were astonishingly good. In January and February 1942 I was able to report to the Reichsmarschall in Rome with statistical proof that the tide had turned

—our shipping losses had been reduced from 70-80 per cent to 20-30 per cent. It was, however, clear to all of us that although we could pat ourselves on the back for a success which also made it easier for Rommel to take the offensive, the supply problem still remained the joker in the pack as far as North Africa was concerned.

Over and over again, sometimes with the support of the Comando Supremo, I urged Goering and Hitler to stabilize our position in the Mediterranean by taking Malta. I even persuaded Rommel to back me up. It was not until February 1942 that I succeeded in getting my plan approved. The occasion was an interview at the Führer's G.H.Q. Tempers ran high. Hitler ended the interview by grasping me by the arm and telling me in his Austrian dialect: "Keep your shirt on, Field-Marshal Kesselring. I'm going to do it!"—a typical sidelight on the tension at headquarters.

*   *   *

Tripolitania stood or fell with its supplies. The question why this problem was never solved is interesting enough to warrant discussion in detail of the conditions in the Mediterranean.

One would instinctively imagine that the Italians with their powerful fleet and Sicily and Pantelleria advantageously situated could control their *mare nostro* or at least close the narrows between Tunis and Sicily. I myself arrived in Italy with this purely theoretical belief. But I very soon found there is a world of difference between theory and fact. Our convoy traffic had various preliminary requirements to be fulfilled if it was to ply smoothly and successfully. It needed, first of all, a clear-headed directing organization. This did not exist at the beginning though Cavallero was by no means deaf to suggestion. From the end of 1941 conferences were held almost daily which were attended by all competent Secretaries of State and other heads of departments, and by myself or, if I was prevented, by General von Rintelen, with Cavallero in the chair. A permanent Supply Board was set up at the Supermarina, composed of specialists of every branch. The principle that depots and dumps of all supply material which might at any time be needed at the front should be kept crammed to capacity on both sides of the Mediterranean was recognized in theory; in fact at no time were the desired quantities available. The air raids on ports and depots, especially in Africa, during 1942 and 1943 made matters even worse.

The Italian supply service was in a somewhat better position than ours. They had the advantage of operating in their own *Imperium;* their sources of supply lay comparatively near and, all said and done, they had only one theatre to feed. In peace-time Tripolitania had had its own garrisons and consequently also a complement of stores. For lack of a through railway the colony had had an efficient heavy motor traffic system and a corresponding stock of vehicles driven by diesel oil, which, as the main problem was fuel, was an additional asset. A greater difficulty was that the civil population as well as the army had to be supplied from oversea—even with wood. Local production was on the upgrade, but still insufficient.

Unfortunately the different equipment of the German and Italian troops did not permit us to help each other out by recip-rocal exchange save in exceptional cases. Even differences of taste complicated an exchange of rations—the German soldier could only with difficulty be weaned from his solid, national diet and had to be literally forced to adopt a régime suitable for a hot climate.

For transport by sea we could muster the strong but hetero-geneous Italian merchant fleet, as well as a limited number of good German vessels which had been caught in the Mediter-ranean by the declaration of war. As there were no sea routes open, barring the traffic across the Adriatic and to Greece and the islands, the pool of ships ought to have been ample, but unfortunately it was not. The following main reasons, in my opinion, accounted for this—peacetime working methods in the Italian dockyards, inadequate distribution of raw materials and spare parts in the wharves, disinclination of Italian ship-owners to accept risks in their anxiety to keep their vessels afloat till the end of the war instead of bearing in mind that Italy's defeat might also cost them their fleet, failure to make the merchant fleet a part of the navy, its distribution in widely separated ports, and difficulties in the making up of convoys because of variations in the speed of single ships; and finally shortage of oil fuel and of coal.

All these deficiencies could only be remedied slowly, if never entirely. The conception of total mobilization was simply foreign to the Italian character.

Soon after the El Alamein position was reached it was clear that the ships still available were too few to sustain our extended supply line for any length of time. As the conditions for an occupation of Malta did not exist at this juncture, as the use of Tunis and Bizerte as supply bases was forbidden by the O.K.W. out of consideration for France, and as the newly opened sea route from Crete to Tobruch brought no appreciable relief, new steps had to be taken. These consisted in enlisting the help of U-boats, gunboats and destroyers for the transport of supplies of lesser bulk, the employment of air-transport formations, and lastly the use of seaworthy coastal sailing vessels for single trips.

In addition there was an extensive building programme for small craft and flat-bottomed boats. We had learnt from experience that vessels of small size and draught capable of 15-16 knots and midget ships of 6-10 knots, like naval barges and Siebel ferries, were safe from torpedoes. By giving them their own small-calibre armament and distributing strongly armed Siebel ferries among them few losses were incurred; in calm to moderate seas they could be used without risk and even at a pinch weather sea scale 5-6. In addition they made it easier to speed up the business of unloading, while, if necessary, they could avoid ports threatened by air attack and unload along the coast. It would have been very helpful to have fast ships able to do the greater part of the run under cover of darkness, but we had practically none, nor could they be built in so short a time.

C.-in-C. South placed a priority order for a total of at least 1,000 small vessels (naval barges and Luftwaffe Siebel ferries), including a new type of wooden ship of about 400 tons and special naval craft of up to 500-600 tons. But although the con-

THE MEDITERRANEAN AS A BASE FOR
OPERATIONS IN WORLD WAR II.

struction programme was put in hand, endless friction in the German and Italian armament machine prevented its maturing.

Early on the tanker problem had reached a critical stage. As tankers were fair game for enemy attacks, special protection for them was a *sine qua non*, and as camouflage was only occasionally successful, we soon started looking for new expedients. Petrol was already scarce and the loss of a 4,000-6,000 ton tanker meant an almost irreparable gap. U-boats, gunboats and destroyers were almost always used to transport oil fuel, but our small craft were also enlisted, as well as the Air Transport Wing with its daily carrying capacity of 200-500 tons.

The uneconomical wastage of aviation petrol by panzers and motor vehicles had also to be taken into account. Just as the tankers were at sea, so on land petrol dumps and motorized columns carrying fuel were favourite targets, and in this way a further percentage of our meagre fuel supplies was lost. Even if we suffered no decisive reverses before August 1942 the fighting was nevertheless fatally affected by our shortage of petrol, with the result that even essential operations could often not be carried through.

The Italian fleet was large enough to carry out all the work of protecting convoys, and indeed there were no German forces available for this. Only at the end of 1942 was a destroyer, constructed in a Greek shipyard, commissioned, which incidentally did very well. German U-boats, the ace of whose commanders was Captain-lieutenant Brandt, indirectly contributed by lying in wait for British convoys either in the east or the west of the Mediterranean as circumstances dictated, mostly off the chief ports, Gibraltar and Alexandria, but their rare successes could never be decisive.

For convoy work only lighter warships were normally used, and cruisers only by way of exception. The seaworthiness of the small craft was limited, as at sea scale 5 they mostly fell out. In view of this restricted capacity the following picture developed: in calm seas, in other words in fine weather, British sea and air forces would muster all their available strength and converge from Gibraltar, Malta, Egypt and Syria so that unescorted shipping with small defence power against submarines and aircraft was more or less helplessly exposed to enemy attacks. Unless the captain was skilful enough to outmanœuvre a torpedo, or unless our fighters were able to intercept the enemy in time or in sufficient strength, one or other of the ships in the convoy would be sent to the bottom or crippled. On the other hand, in stormy weather—which afforded considerable protection, and sometimes even immunity—the convoy could not sail because the protecting vessels could not weather the gale. As we were permitted to call on the help of cruisers for fast convoys in isolated cases only, while our antiquated gunboats and destroyers were kept constantly on the job and took a long time to overhaul, the total wastage in course of time reduced our quota of escort ships to below the minimum requirement. Yet the consequent holding of convoys in port meant delayed delivery of supplies which were only too badly needed.

By taking over and distributing ships lying in port in the south of France and refloating them, we did indeed achieve a temporary improvement at a sorely critical period (1942-43). The long-standing dispute, however, about the use of the three large fast destroyers and the submarines laid up in the ports of Tunis and Bizerte meant that the use of these was denied us—one of the disadvantages of a coalition command with an eye to prestige and post-war conditions rather than to the best use of all naval resources.

We did make an exhaustive attempt, nevertheless, to combat shortages by calling on German aid, which in fact was given in the form of fuel oil, raw materials and spare parts, by the equipment of Italian ships with locating instruments, and by the training of gun-crews and the despatch of German instructors—all measures which really came too late.

Another feature of the Mediterranean theatre was the efficiency and wide ramifications of the enemy system of espionage, the extent of which was unknown to me at the time and probably also to Admirals Riccardi and Sanzonetti. Though we could never prove it, we suspected that the times of our convoy sailings were betrayed.

In any case our counter-measures as a whole proved inadequate. We know now that the treachery of Admiral Maugeri was responsible for the sinking of many ships and the loss of many lives.

The Italian navy was regarded as a *pièce de résistance* and was therefore used sparingly—an attitude which caused special internal difficulties. Yet three times we managed to overcome these and get it to put to sea. A further trouble lay in its being stationed in different harbours; to assemble it cost time and wasted fuel. Finally, one or other battleship was either not ready to put to sea, or was not fuelled, or was in dock. Exercises in large formations could not be carried out mainly because of this same shortage of fuel. Gunnery practice was a rarity. On top of this there were extraordinary technical deficiencies which deservedly earned the Italian navy the nickname "Fine-weather Fleet." Its doubtful seaworthiness called for increased air protection, and that, with the limited strength of the Axis air forces in the Mediterranean, imposed ridiculous demands on the German Luftwaffe, whose hands were already full protecting convoys; the German airmen, who flew 75-90 per cent of all sorties, had consequently to be bled white. If the Italian fleet by any chance ever came within extreme range of the British fleets and a few shots were actually exchanged, it had to break off the engagement at the approach of dusk because of its inability to fire in the dark, and run for the nearest port—Taranto or Messina.

Italian shipbuilding policy was another cause for exasperation. A time when the uselessness of their battle-fleet, above all of their capital ships, was only too manifest, when shipyards were overcrowded and material in short supply, was chosen to round off the construction of the battleship *Roma*. Oblivious to the dangers of his armament policy, Mussolini, bursting with pride, had this "technical marvel" paraded before him in the Adriatic (it was sunk in 1943 when escaping from La Spezia to Malta by a German remote-control air-bomb), and I believe other capital ships were also completed or kept in service. Even a layman might have seen that with things as they were a lot could have been done to ease the supply problem by a realistic construction policy. I had long since ceased to believe that Mussolini's avowed intention to send the whole fleet into action at a decisive moment would ever materialize.

In conclusion I only hope I have done my best to paint the situation objectively. I have no desire to offer offensive criticism; I value too deeply the comradeship shown me by the Italians, and I had too many opportunities to watch their devoted work. My friendship with the Secretary of State of the Superareo, Fougier, and with many other Italian flying officers must vouch for the objectivity of my criticism of their air force.

Italian fighters could be used for purely protective purposes only; for operations their torpedo-bombers and bombers, and in odd cases their dive-bombers and fighter-bombers. I have already freely vented my opinion of their technical efficiency, or rather inefficiency.

My conclusion was that Italian fighters were employable in the less threatened zones, that is in the Tyrrhenian Sea and along the strip of coast off Bengasi and Tripoli, and to some extent also in the Adriatic and the Gulf of Pátrai. The danger zones over the Mediterranean, the areas south of Sicily and Crete, and the Aegean were flown by German fighter squadrons, including Ju 88's and Me 110's of the night-fighter formations, which were only partly suitable for the task. We shared the burden of operations over the African front. From the spring of 1942 our convoys were additionally escorted by one to three fighter-bombers carrying depth-charges, responsible for spotting and dealing with enemy submarines and warning duties. They were supported by torpedo-boats, also attacking with depth-charges and occasionally with gunfire. Tackling surfaced submarines with 2-cm. aircraft cannon had at least the effect of making the enemy dive.

The direction of operations was in the hands of Air Fleet 2 operations staff which issued its orders to II and X Groups and to A.O.C. Africa and called upon the Superareo for co-operation when necessary.

All German aircraft flew with extra tanks, all air-sea rescue aircraft were kept ready for take-off and rescue ships ready to put to sea or at their stations, while radar sets were installed at points of main effort. The strength of convoy escorts was determined by the degree of danger, the weather conditions, the time of day and the speed, size and importance of the convoy. At dusk the auxiliary fighters (Ju 88's and Me 110's) took over the work of protection alone, as the fighters had to be grounded before nightfall. The strength of the air-screen varied between two and sixteen aircraft. In difficult situations pilot aircraft (Ju 88's and Me 110's) would be used—it happened on several occasions that the formation had to be guided by one aircraft with direction-finding apparatus. If enemy aircraft were sighted approaching all available fighters would go out to intercept them before they could molest the convoy. Considerable risk, of course, went with these sorties because of the limited range of our fighters and the great distances to be flown over the sea, but that was part of the bargain. If British naval forces were reported on the route every available fighter-bomber, Stuka and torpedo formation would take off.

Since they had to break through an especially effective anti-aircraft barrage, these sorties put an incredible strain on flying formations. Being shot down generally meant a watery grave, although now and again bomber crews were successfully rescued, Allied ships reporting they had picked up airmen who had baled out over the sea. But at least the enemy squadron was kept from reaching the convoy.

This picture of the system of protecting convoys is enough to show how fearfully Axis air strength was overtaxed in wear and tear of aircraft and crews, not to speak of damage or total loss. From the tactical standpoint the use of airmen to protect convoys was unproductive, for the most part involving waste of precious flying hours. Still, this could not be helped, nor the unfortunate corollary of the increased difficulty of having the necessary quota of aircraft on the tarmac for purely combat purposes. As the over-all demands on formations grew continually heavier, so the crew's rest periods were steadily eaten into —and all as a result of what amounted to oversea routine flights.

In 1941-42 neither Germany nor Italy had organized any

special air-transport formations, every fighter squadron having only its own transport aircraft for local needs. These were used for operations for the first time in Norway and Crete, and then in the winter of 1941-42 on the Russian front, the air-landing operations against Holland in a sense paving the way. From this point on transport pilots were organized in wings under their own commanders, two or three of which I had at my disposal for emergencies on this arduous and thankless service, from Sicily, Italy, Greece, Crete and Tripolitania. In so far as these flights were not made by night they had to have fighter protection, or at least to be met at daybreak and defended while on the airfield at their destination. They put up a remarkable performance, which was even bettered once our six-engined Giants were in operation.

For a long time these flights were continued without loss, until the spring of 1943 when an air-transport wing of Ju 52's and a squadron of six-engined Giants were caught off Tunis by enemy fighters and almost completely destroyed. Our losses gave the American journalists occasion for critical comment, but these losses were not due to any shortcomings or recklessness on the part of Air Fleet 2.

In spite of the so-called Mobilization Supply Stores, in any case quite inadequate, Italy had not nearly enough coal or petroleum for her needs, and on both scores Germany had to help her out, although herself suffering from a scarcity of oil for her own war purposes. The result was a barter trade agreeable to neither party and which, anyway, in the end turned out unsatisfactory. Another consequence was that the meagre stores had to be distributed in widely separated depots and it was impossible to lay hands at any one given time on the oil needed for a convoy, with resultant delays. In case of definite shortage we had to fall back on the reserve stocks of the Italian High Seas Fleet, and once or twice even had partly to empty the battleships' tanks so as to be able to meet the escort ships' most urgent requirements. This again entailed delay, among other things. On the whole it must be acknowledged that Admiral Raeder generously answered the Italian navy's cry for help, while Air Fleet 2 similarly assisted the Superareo.

Coal was not equally important, for here we were able to help out in sufficient quantities for the needs of the freighters and transports.

It is difficult to say whether these conditions could have been at all improved, and avoid the charge of "knowing better" after the event. Certainly only by the Germans giving more and the Italians husbanding their resources more economically. But there is no doubt that owing to the difficulties listed above the necessary escort could not always be provided and favourable opportunities for running a convoy across the Mediterranean were missed.

On-the-spot control of loading and unloading was not within my province, but I learnt of shortages through the German landing officers who were partly under me, and I was able to confirm the justice of their complaints when I visited ports. My reports to the O.K.W. induced Hitler in 1943 to send Goering, and later Doenitz, to Italy to back up my importunity with the Comando Supremo and the Supermarina. Goering held long conferences and made tours of inspection, and the Commissioner for the Construction of Merchant Shipping was called in to remove the most blatant deficiencies. Things improved, but never as much as they should.

The loading and unloading organization worked far too leisurely. Delivery and loading of material was irritatingly un-co-ordinated. Air-raid warnings were unnecessarily prolonged. The unloaded stuff was left about on the quays for an unconscionable length of time and in this way was sometimes sacrificed to bombs.

It was long before a strong enough flak defence could be provided; and then it was almost always furnished by German flak artillery. This again weakened the airfield and panzer defences at the front.

I must admit that in Tunis, where C.-in-C. South had installed a controlling supply staff and a former senior Q.M. of the Luftwaffe supply service, all records were broken. Whereas in Bengasi or Tripoli it took two to five days to load a transport ship, the same thing could be done in half a day to two days at Tunis or Bizerte. In expectation of powerful air raids ships were towed away from the quays and anchored in harbour or out in the bay, many losses thus being avoided. In contrast the tactical error of letting a tanker sail from the well-defended harbour of Tobruch with its subsequent destruction reversed the conditions previously favourable for Rommel's offensive from El Alamein.

As the danger to big ships increased, the drawbacks of our unloading methods made me a propagandist for the construction of small and indeed very small craft. Only a few of these were lost en route and almost none in port with their cargoes still on board. This led to the issue of an order that valuable cargoes, such as tanks, must only be carried in ferries or flat-bottomed boats, and a maximum of six on larger vessels. The most effective defence against air attack was obtained by siting two troops of flak working together with six to twenty anti-aircraft guns.

Convoy traffic had always to be accommodated to whatever air and surface protection was available. Reconnaissance reports from agents, U-boats, aircraft and wireless monitoring services provided us with ample information, but it was a mistake to be so influenced by unverifiable reports in making a decision that all daring and initiative were paralyzed. Unhappily at times this did happen. Good reconnaissance ought to have been coupled with elastic leadership and the use of reliable ships.

The performance of the supply services from December 1941 to January 1942 will be appreciated if it is borne in mind that the German and Italian army and air combat forces were at that point decimated and had reached the Sirte position without any stores whatsoever and that their only supplies were those improvised from a ship stranded in the Gulf of El Agheila.

14

Malta or Egypt?
November 1941 to October 1942

21-30 Jan. 1942 Rommel's counter-attack in Cirenaica as far as El
Gazala—2 April-10 May German air offensive against Malta—26 May
New German-Italian offensive under Rommel—11 June Capture of
Bir Hacheim—21 June Capture of Tobruch—23 June Rommel crosses
the Egyptian frontier—1 July Rommel in El Alamein about sixty
miles southwest of Alexandria—Crippling of the German-Italian offensive—30-31 Aug. Rommel vainly attempts to renew the offensive
at El Alamein—23 Oct. British counter-offensive, beginning of the
battle of El Alamein—5 Nov. Rommel retreats.

At the time of my arrival in the Mediterranean area Rommel
had begun his retreat from Tobruch to the Gulf of Sirte. It was
followed, after his forces had been rested and losses repaired,
on 21 January 1942 by the counter-offensive which took him as
far as El Gazala. Both operations were characteristic of Rommel
at his best. The impression on me was the more enduring because
it was all new to me. In both cases I had to act as intermediary
between the Comando Supremo and Rommel. A certain willingness to meet the Italians halfway, even a formal correctness,
would have made the obvious antagonism less acute or less apparent. Rommel's retreat was in itself a blow to the Italian
Command in Africa and Rome and—rightly or wrongly—Count
Cavallero and Marshal Bastico felt Rommel's decision as a slight
to themselves and a danger to the Axis partnership.

We met in conference at Berta on 17 December 1941.
Feathers flew, and Rommel, having overridden the Italians' objections to his mobile strategy, promised in future to adjust the

movements of his motorized units to those of the other arms. I tried to pour oil on the troubled waters by pledging my word I would not surrender the key-point of Derna with its adjacent airfields until the Italian infantry had first been pulled back. The operation was in fact completed according to plan without dangerous losses. As usually happens in a retirement of this kind, the infantry divisions broke away remarkably quickly and Rommel was able to straighten his line without serious modification of his original plan. It goes without saying that our airmen and anti-aircraft gunners played a part in this manœuvre.

Rommel's decision to counter-attack on 21 January 1942 was the brain-child of his operations chief, Westphal, who conceived the idea one day when flying in his Storch over the more than meagrely held enemy front line. It was adopted in a flash and prepared and carried out with the utmost speed and secrecy. Rommel had got into the habit of keeping his operations a secret from the Italians until the very last possible moment because, not to put too fine a point upon it, he did not trust them. It is unquestionable that the first condition of a successful surprise is absolute secrecy, and every means to obtain it was certainly justified. But it was equally sure that such behaviour would add to the difficulties of the coalition command—Rommel was, after all, subordinate to Bastico and the Comando Supremo.

After Rommel had started his attack I informed Cavallero in Rome of the offensive. The possibility of another defeat threw him into a state of quite unusual excitement, and at my suggestion he flew with me to Africa on 22 January. He did not yet, however, go to see Rommel, but first visited the Italian unit H.Q. while I gave my attention to my Luftwaffe and the supply services.

In January 1942 we had a very clear picture of the strength, dispositions and fighting qualities of the British troops. I assured Cavallero that Rommel's offensive, even if it were halted, was no wild gamble. The British distribution of forces and the evident strain on their resources justified an operation that might lead to the capture of Bengasi, which, in its turn, would ensure our supply lines. After a deal of argument the conference with

the Italians resulted in an agreement on an attack with limited
objectives. The fact that in these discussions I played a concili-
atory part does not imply, as I have read since the war, that I
was against the operation. Cavallero corroborates this in his
diary. The Comando Supremo did not wish to take any further
risks, feeling that it could not sponsor fresh reverses.

Despite the agreement, I knew what to expect of Rommel.
In the full flush of victory he would not stop until the enemy's
resistance compelled a halt. I was right. The offensive, launched
with admirable vigour by our depleted forces and brilliantly
supported by the A.O.C. Africa, carried us by 30 January as
far as the so-called El Gazala Line. The glory for this success
belongs to Rommel, at that time an incomparable leader of
armoured formations and daring raids.

Weak as were the German-Italian air forces in Africa, they
were yet superior to the British. German fighters controlled the
battle areas, the British dread of the Stukas equalling our men's
affection for them. I was greatly impressed, however, by the
"magic illuminations" performed by British aircraft with flares
over the approaches to Bengasi. Their volume gave the impression that powerful bomber forces were being used, and all movement in the illuminated area was brought to a standstill.

I relate an insignificant incident simply because it was unique.
I myself flew Cavallero to the conference on 23 January in my
Storch, as this was the only aircraft on the tarmac and Cavallero
insisted on my accompanying him. The meeting lasted longer
than expected, so that we had to take off on the return flight
when the sun was already setting to land in the dark at El
Agheila. So a German Field-Marshal flew the senior *Maresciallo
d'Italia* over the desert in an aircraft unsuitable for night flying
and safely delivered his very suspicious passenger into the arms
of his numerous generals. The embracings and kissings that followed our landing are no flight of my creative imagination.

With the halting of Rommel's counter-attack at the El Gazala
Line (early February 1942) the German-Italian forces in Trip-
olitania were in much the same position as the British Eighth
Army had been in shortly before at Bengasi. The length of time

the enemy would be stunned by this successful blow would be determined by the question of replacements and supplies, particularly as the unfavourable season for campaigning was drawing to an end and the British supply lines were growing shorter. First priority was the reconditioning of the harbours of Bengasi and Derna, and within a few days of the former's capture the first ships were able to unload. It was a particularly fortunate circumstance that former German munition and other dumps were found intact; these supplemented our sea-borne supplies.

In spite of this unexpectedly favourable situation it was now urgently necessary to press on with the completion of our preparations for the air assault on Malta. Their protraction in view of the situation in Africa had been a nervous strain, but the success there had made the extra delay worth while.

At a conference held at II Air Group H.Q. in Sicily I convinced myself that everyone understood the detailed instructions issued for the attack. When I inspected the formations I found them confident and eager. The basic idea of II Air Group's orders was to surprise and neutralize the enemy's fighters, or at least to cripple them so much that they would not be any considerable danger to the ensuing bombing assault, while the three airfields were to be attacked at short intervals with heavy bombs, light anti-personnel bombs and machine-gun fire in order to destroy the aircraft on the ground and to render the runways at least temporarily unserviceable.

The objectives of further bomber raids were the airfields and harbour installations and shipping; the town itself was to be spared. Daylight attacks were to be concentrated and incessant, and given such powerful fighter protection that the British fighters would be kept away from our bombers and pursued until they were wiped out.

At night continual nuisance raids by single aircraft were to hinder clearing up the wreckage and repairs. An additional part of the programme was the sinking of the few supply ships making for the port by dive-bombing attacks, and the blocking of the harbour entrance by dropping mines.

This plan set all concerned a heavy task, but it was accomplished with comparatively small losses. Several factors made the battle against the island fortress difficult. There were natural shelters hewn out of the rock on the perimeter of the airfields and around the harbour where aircraft and stores could be safeguarded, and against which even the heaviest delayed-action bombs could not have a really devastating effect. Even an attempt to blow up the entrance with Jabo bombs was unsuccessful. Only searching and sweeping attacks with small-calibre bombs (contact fuses) offered reasonable prospects of success. The concentration of powerful British anti-aircraft defences on the shores, supported by naval A.A. guns protecting the harbour, put up a barrier of fire to be penetrated only by stout hearts and at the loss of many aircraft.

The vulnerable moments in the dive-bombing attacks were going into a dive and flattening out afterwards. These movements throttled the aircraft's flying speed and broke up the formation. Here we suffered losses which could only be minimized by sending in fighters to dive at the same time and by detailing special fighters to protect them at flattening-out level. The British fighters deserve recognition for their bravery and manœuvring skill, especially in the perfect handling of their aircraft when diving from a high altitude (30,000 to 40,000 feet) through the middle of closed German bomber formations. A tribute must also be paid to the organization of the unloading work. In an incredibly short time the ships and tankers entering the port were unloaded and the goods stored away in the underground, bomb-proof warehouses along the waterfront.

II Air Group Messina did a splendid job in the planning and the execution of the attack. Our distinguished and resourceful Chief of Staff, Air Marshal Deichmann, deserves special mention here.

Temporary interruptions of the air assault against Malta were caused by switching the attacking forces to convoys, the sinking of which was an indispensable preliminary to success against the island. In bitter battles these convoys, except for a few ships, were destroyed.

The main assault was begun 2 April 1942. On 10 May I could regard the task as accomplished. Thanks to its success, our ascendancy at sea and in the air in the supply lanes from Italy to Africa was assured. It would have been easy to capture the island after the bombing assault. That this did not happen was a grave mistake on the part of the German-Italian Command which came home to roost later. It is to the credit of the Luftwaffe that it restricted the battle to purely military targets, a fact which has been acknowledged by the British.

With the success of this attack the O.K.W. considered the tension so far relaxed that it transferred the greater part of our air forces to the eastern front. Of course sufficient forces were left in the Mediterranean to keep a watch on Malta, to curb the activity of the enemy's sea transport and to protect our own communications, without having to call on the forces of A.O.C. Africa. As time went on, however, these forces proved too weak to neutralize the island fortress or to deprive it of supplies.

Italy's missing her chance to occupy the island at the start of hostilities will go down in history as a fundamental blunder.

The O.K.W. very soon recognized the crucial importance of the island, but in spite of my reiterated arguments for its occupation, afterwards supported by the Comando Supremo and Rommel, they were satisfied with trying to neutralize it by air bombardment. This deliberate refusal to repair the first mistake was the second fundamental strategic error which placed the Mediterranean Command at a decisive disadvantage.

In contrast to C.-in-C. South, the Comando Supremo vacillated. At the all-important conference of Marshals at Sidi Barrani on 26 June 1942 after the capture of Tobruch it deviated from our fixed strategic directive and agreed to Rommel's proposal to continue operations towards the Nile. This decision sealed the fate of North Africa. To summarize my reasons for opposing it:

Rommel had previously lectured us on the situation. He declared that there was practically no opposition of any significance and that he could be in Cairo with his army in ten days. To this I replied:

"Even if I grant that Rommel has a deeper insight into the situation on the ground I am still unable to quiet my misgivings. I agree, of course, that the beaten enemy should be pursued to the limits of possibility if one can be sure of not meeting with any fresh opposition. But if the advance is continued, even with a minimum of fighting, the breakdown rate of armoured and motor vehicles must be very high. It has been alarmingly high up till now. Replacements to the requisite amount cannot be expected for a long time. Even if at the moment the British have no reserves worth mentioning in Egypt it is a certainty that the first reinforcements from the Near East are already on the way.

"I am competent, however, to speak for the Luftwaffe. My airmen will land near the Nile completely exhausted. Their aircraft will need overhauling, yet with totally inadequate supplies. They will be opposed by active formations which can be still further reinforced in the shortest time. As an airman I consider it madness to attack an intact air base. In view of the decisive importance of air co-operation, from this standpoint alone I must reject the proposal to continue our advance with the objective Cairo."

Rommel, asked by Cavallero to reconsider his opinion, stuck to his optimistic view, however, still guaranteeing to be in Cairo within ten days.

Bastico and Cavallero gave their consent. The Duce came over to Africa to be present when the army entered the Egyptian capital.

I regretted this decision, which a wireless message from Hitler told me was no further business of mine, also because the capture of Cairo would bring very little, if any, alleviation of our supply difficulties. Our supply lanes could only be regarded as secured by the capture of Alexandria, and then only if the Axis Powers had sufficient defence forces to frustrate attacks from Aden and Syria. At that time they were not available, nor could be brought up.[1]

[1] The fantastic idea of using Egypt as a base for an invasion of Russia from the Caucasus, if it was ever seriously considered by the O.K.W. (which I doubt), never got further than muddled speculations. The realization of any

In the spring of 1942 C.-in-C. South and the Africa Panzer Army were agreed that the next operational objectives must be Malta and Tobruch. Tobruch without Malta was not enough. The sea route from Athens to Crete and from Crete to Tobruch lay within effective range of the British air and naval bases in Egypt. It entailed the use of strong escorting forces which were beyond our means in view of the need to protect our convoys sailing from Italy. Furthermore the exigencies of the eastern front prevented the peculiar difficulties of routing supplies and replacements via Greece from ever being entirely overcome.

There was only one bone of contention between Rommel and myself: the order in which the two operations should be carried out. The protection of the sea lanes and receiving ports came within my province, and I therefore suggested to Hitler that the capture of Malta should have precedence, as a preliminary to a ground assault on Tobruch. Although Hitler agreed with this sequence, he later changed his mind. In Berchtesgaden at the end of April he endorsed Rommel's intention to launch the land operation from El Gazala first. I was enough of a ground tactician to be able to understand Rommel's urgency—also the preparations for the attack on Malta were not so far advanced that the operation could begin at once. I thought I could justify my giving way because the less time we allowed the British to gather strength the sooner we should reach our ultimate objective, the Italo-Egyptian frontier. After a victory in Africa the assault on Malta could not go awry—and in the meantime our preparations could be completed. Thus the clash of opinion between Rommel and myself did not come to a head until after the fall of Tobruch.

Hitler and the O.K.W. must share with the Comando Supremo the blame for that wrong decision. They were admittedly less able to appreciate the situation correctly once Rommel had got his propaganda machine working.

The German High Command, brought up to think in terms of continental warfare, did not find the overseas theatre con-

such plan would have necessitated the safeguarding of our supply lines, therefore the occupation of Malta.

genial. It failed altogether to understand the importance of the Mediterranean and the inherent difficulties of the war in Africa. It did not originate or follow any clear-cut plan, but allowed its hand to be forced by fits and starts. Hitler's personal fondness for Mussolini kept him from intervening in the conduct of the war in the Mediterranean even where intervention was essential, with disastrous results. The slogan was "Mussolini in Cairo."

At that period Rommel exercised an almost hypnotic influence over Hitler, who was all but incapable of appreciating the situation objectively. This curious fact no doubt accounted for the previously mentioned order I received when Hitler, impressed by the success at Tobruch, and probably at the instigation of Rommel's mouthpiece, Dr. Berndt, told me not to meddle with Rommel's operational plan and to back him up to the hilt.

Subsequently Hitler was certainly happy that the victory at Tobruch gave him an excuse to call off the distasteful Malta venture without loss of face. In this he found a loyal yes-man in Goering. Goering was afraid of a second costly "Crete" with "gigantic" casualties, although the two operations were in no way comparable. I told him repeatedly that after the air attacks of April and May Malta could be occupied with a minimum of forces and of losses, and that the effort required if we postponed the assault till later would be much greater and more wasteful. Meanwhile on the Italian side the Comando Supremo had to contend with the renewed hesitancy of the Supermarina.

With the decision to push forward as far as the Nile, Operation *Malta* was shelved. It was anyhow made impossible by the disastrous outcome of our attempt to advance into Egypt and by the transfer to Africa of the land and air forces destined for Malta.

All in all, a problem of great interest for the war historian and the psychologist. Our failure was decisive for the campaign.

The great success of the winter offensive of 1942 and the building up of the El Gazala front had compensated the retreat of December 1941. Rommel had recognized the weaknesses of the British, and faith in his leadership and his army soared again. He believed that time was on the side of the enemy, and that in the course of the next six months he must reckon with a considerable strengthening of the British and with a revival of their morale. He also knew that the élan of his own troops could not be maintained in a static war in the desert; besides, to pin down the enemy would require a costly expenditure of men and material which would pay no dividends. Delay would undesirably handicap the planned offensive, as I myself had agreed. Meanwhile his demand for the stepping up of supplies could be complied with owing to the success of our attacks on Malta. By the beginning of May Rommel's army, including its Italian components, was fully equipped and supplied, and there was even a certain surplus of reserves.

The operational plan was drawn up by Rommel and discussed with Air Marshal Hoffmann von Waldau, Air Officer Commanding-in-Chief Africa. It was his obligation to make the arrangements with the Italian A.O.C., who also had my fullest confidence. Naval co-operation came into question for a turning thrust from the sea in the enemy's rear and afterwards for supplies—matters which were settled with Admiral Weichold.

Surprise was the essence of the operation. Its aim was to deal an annihilating blow at the British front integrated with an outflanking attack from the desert which would be later supplemented by the landing of small but picked commandos from the sea.

The second phase was to be the investment and capture of Tobruch. Rommel intended to accompany the column on the decisive flank, but reserved to himself the direction of the whole operation. The front line was under the command of General Cruewell.

The plan was simple and clear. Although Marshal Bastico approved it, I did not much like the arrangements for the transmission of orders. Once before Rommel by remaining out on the flank had not been on the spot to direct the course of the battle. A stationary battle headquarters should have been set up.

The surprise came off, but the link with Rommel was severed. Reports of equal importance to our airmen and to General Cruewell went astray. The confusion of attacking and counterattacking tanks, often facing the wrong way round, complicated air reconnaissance and made every bomb a gamble. Since, despite this, our incessant air attacks did no damage to our own troops, those first and second days may be regarded as red-letter days for the Air Command.

Early on the 29 May General Cruewell was forced to land his Storch behind the enemy lines and was taken prisoner, leaving the front without a commander. On insistence from many quarters I agreed to take over the front-line command, as Major von Mellenthin, Cruewell's operations chief, could not accept the responsibility and no suitable army commander could be released. I then learnt the difficulties of a commander whose hands are tied by subordination to a headquarters that issues no orders and cannot be reached. Moreover, the stimulating effect of Rommel's presence on the decisive flank was offset by his immediate exposure to all the fluctuations of battle. One must have heard eye-witness accounts to realize what went on among Rommel's staff on the first day of the tank battle. But the second day decided it: a glorious one for our panzers and their commander.

I put through repeated R/T calls to Rommel to ask for a conversation whenever and wherever he chose. It took place on the south flank, and resulted in the co-ordination of flank and frontal action, which had meanwhile become urgent. It was a joy to watch Rommel's amazingly expert technique in directing a desert command. The situation was not exactly pretty. As I was preparing to land my Storch at Italian G.H.Q. where a conference had been fixed, I was suddenly fired at from the ground by machine-guns and 2-cm. guns in country which was supposedly in our hands. On the strength of my first-hand observation during this flight I was able to order before nightfall an operational sortie against an enemy force which had broken through and, driving west across Rommel's line of communications, might have wiped out the supply columns of the Africa Panzer Army. I flew straight to the individual formations, alerted them and sent out Stukas, Me 110's and Jabos, in fact every available aircraft on the tarmac. The attack was successful. The enemy suffered considerable losses and had to turn back. But when our aircraft landed in the swiftly fading twilight, I found that among other casualties I had lost two of my best, oldest and keenest desert crews. It was a weight upon my heart.

I had a later difference of opinion with Rommel over the strong point of Bir Hacheim, which was strongly held by Free French troops under General König and was a considerable threat. Rommel called for air support, and in the end strong dive-bomber attacks were made with petroleum bombs. The omission to synchronize air and ground attacks was responsible for the failure of these and subsequent infantry assaults. Our dispute over this cleared the air, however, and shortly afterwards I was able to congratulate Rommel on the capture of Bir Hacheim.

It was a sign of Rommel's vitality that immediately after the fall of the oasis Bir Hacheim and a short conversation with me he drove off with his armoured formations in the direction of Tobruch, the complete investment of which followed soon afterwards.

The achievements of our army and our air force up to this moment and beyond it must rank among the epic feats of military history, and this succession of battles was in fact the climax of Rommel's career. The Italian troops also fought well.

The attack on Tobruch had the impetus of previous successes; it was daringly planned by Rommel and Hoffmann von Waldau and dashingly carried out. I brought in from Greece and Crete every additional formation capable of diving. On the evening before the attack I paid a flying visit to each formation and made them a speech of record brevity:

"Gentlemen, if you do your duty tomorrow morning, tomorrow evening the broadcasting stations of the world will give out the news: *Tobruch has fallen.* Good hunting!"

The attack was launched with precision timing. The last bomb had hardly reached the ground before the assault, splendidly supported by dive-bombers and artillery, had carried the defence positions in such depth that the harbour was brought within range of our artillery. All the same, there was bitter fighting with not a few critical moments—but we won the day. Tobruch *was* captured, and the news broadcast to the world. Hoffmann von Waldau was decorated with the Knight's Cross of the Iron Cross and General Rommel promoted to Field-Marshal, to the indignation of the Italians. To have given him a higher decoration instead of promotion would have been more appropriate. A large number of prisoners were taken; huge stores of war material of every kind, including foodstuffs, supplemented our supplies, while the possession of the port expanded our communications system.

The victory was cheaply bought; it was a grave blow to the enemy's power of resistance, and the loss of Tobruch complicated the supply problem for the retreating enemy forces. The British Command was indeed confronted with a desperate situation, one which would have tempted a general less flushed with triumph than Rommel to press on in hot pursuit, as it did now seem possible to exterminate the whole British army. But this called for haste. On 22 June 1942 I visited the new Field-Marshal at his H.Q. in Tobruch and found him briefing his officers for an advance that very morning on Sidi Barrani—a plan that coincided with my view of things without prejudicing the attack on Malta.

Hoffmann von Waldau had concerted the tactical arrangements with Rommel, and von Pohl was moving up the ground organization into the Tobruch area, where there was a sufficiency of airfields; these had to be cleared of mines, made serviceable and protected by flak, which was, however, done in next to no time.

Meanwhile Admiral Weichold and the Italian Naval Command had issued immediate orders for the repair of the harbour installations of Tobruch. Whether ships could be brought alongside the quay or would have to be unloaded by means of lighters, I attached the greatest importance to putting Tobruch into use as a receiving port. Even if our petrol stores had been stepped up and the car park was crammed with captured lorries, the road from Bengasi or Tripoli to the front was too extended to ensure a constant stream of supplies for any length of time. Although after the capture of Sidi Barrani this tiny harbour was also put into operation, without the occupation of Malta the North African theatre was in no way secured.

The assault on the island must be the next step—as planned, and the preparations which had been going on since February completed. The allocation of forces in the plan had been so calculated that failure was out of the question. Two parachute divisions under General Student had been brought in, including the Italian 2nd Parachute Division "Folgore." [1] Troop-transport aircraft, heavy-freight-carrying aircraft and Giants for tank transport were available in ample quantities. In addition there were two to three Italian assault divisions, elements of the battle-fleet to shell the island fortifications and to escort the troop transports and assault craft, and air formations in rather greater strength than had been used for the original attack.

The draft plan of the operation broadly had the following shape:

1. Attack by airborne troops to seize the southern heights as a jumping-off base for an assault to capture the airfields south of the town and the harbour of La Valetta, shortly preceded by a bombing raid on the airfields themselves and anti-aircraft positions.
2. Main attack by naval forces and landing parties against the strong points south of La Valetta and, in conjunction with parachute troops, on the harbour itself, synchronized with bombing raids on coastal batteries.
3. Diversionary attack from the sea against the Bay of Marsa Scirocco.

In the meantime the first phase of the advance into Egypt was proceeding according to plan, its success proving Rommel right. But soon the resistance stiffened to such an extent that we had to envisage throwing in fresh troops or speeding up the refresh-

[1] This excellent division was quickly and successfully trained by our energetic parachute general, Ramcke. The exercises at which I was present showed the men were the right material.

ment of old formations. The fighting became tougher until the battles at El Alamein brought the offensive to a standstill and threw us back on the defensive. There were critical moments which could be got over only by the reckless intervention of armoured reconnaissance units and the Luftwaffe. Our army and air force were both winded; they stood in need of an immediate flow of reinforcements and material. In addition, Rommel was clamouring for new formations, which in fact were sent over from Greece and Italy, besides a second German infantry division and the German-Italian Parachute Division that had been earmarked for Malta. As these forces did not bring any vehicles with them the first thing was to make up for this by drawing on the complement of the German and Italian divisions, which thus still further restricted the mobility of all divisions. The result was that a large number of motor vehicles had to be found also for the flak and the air force—and this, on the top of the problem of feeding the new units, made ever-increasing demands on our supply organization. In order to cope with them we just had to have Malta; yet the withdrawal of the forces destined for the invasion made this impossible. Even I was eventually forced to decide against it, as the premises for success were just no longer there. The calling off of this undertaking was a mortal blow to the whole North African undertaking.

After a few days the enemy's counter-attack also petered out. The British army was evidently not yet strong enough to launch a decisive counter-offensive, the failure of single Italian divisions not being exploited.

The front was now stabilized in a sector where the strength of the flanking positions was very favourable, its breadth being suitable for our reinforced striking power. I now urged the resumption of the offensive as vigorously as I had intervened after Tobruch to break it off. The situation in the Mediterranean and North Africa had become as precarious as could be well imagined. In the east the British Eighth Army faced us built up to a new pitch of strength with a powerful air force and a secure and abundantly equipped supply base. In the west developments threatened of an unknown magnitude. In our rear our line of supply was seriously extended. With the revival of Malta's potency and the strengthening of the Egypt base the hour of disaster loomed perceptibly near.

Any hope of successfully surviving a war on two fronts hung on the possibility of settling accounts from an interior line with an enemy with whom we were already joined before the second one presented his bill. With all the immense disadvantages of a purely defensive operation which above all could not solve the supply problem there was no choice but to opt for an offensive solution, if there was the slightest prospect of success. In an offensive the Axis would have the initiative; it could decide the hour to strike. Everything depended on Rommel's striking as soon as possible, so as to hit the British forces while they were still building up their strength. In my view the extreme limit of time in hand was the end of August 1942.

The precarious plight of our communications system made it impossible to give a positive assurance that all supply requirements would be met. I promised to do all I could and to use my influence with the Comando Supremo to keep the stream flowing. I was now convinced that the situation in North Africa could be stabilized only if the Egyptian and Mediterranean ports were in our hands. A two-sided threat to our supply lines —from Malta and Alexandria—meant their permanent neutralization. Meanwhile Rommel flatly refused to give up the objective Cairo, so nearly within his grasp. Despite his intensive preoccupation with the planning of the offensive he saw to it that the fortification of the El Alamein Line would be strong enough to hold a large-scale British counter-attack, which he gave me repeated assurance it would. The sappers had a hard time, but Rommel could tell himself he had done all that man could do and he certainly explored imaginative new paths.

The British Eighth Army was probing the German front without any tangible success, yet with the disadvantage to us that they would shortly discover our defence scheme and artillery positions, and that in these skirmishes much material—not to mention lives—would be used up. On the other hand, the British were bound to conclude from the strength of our line that Rommel had abandoned the idea of continuing the offensive and was contemplating a defensive strategy to bring about a decision. The greater would be the surprise when he launched his attack.

By the middle of August the plan of the offensive had taken firmer shape. The decision was not taken until the very last minute—on 29 August, the attack to begin on 30-31, being delivered from a powerful right wing by panzer and motorized divisions. The Comando Supremo and C.-in-C. South had moved heaven and earth to assemble an adequate provision of petrol. At least C.-in-C. South cannot be saddled with the responsibility for the sinking of the tanker off Tobruch. After this loss, as head of Air Command, I was anxious to help out from my own reserves. Despite my assurance that I would put 500 cubic metres of high-grade aviation petrol at the disposal of the army the petrol problem remained acute; the more so as even this quantity was, for reasons incomprehensible to me, never delivered. I accept the responsibility for this—although I knew nothing of it till after the war—but I cannot grant that this omission was decisively important. The fact that all our motorized forces were engaged in more or less mobile defensive operations until 6 September, relying on the supplies which were still available at that time, is sufficient proof that there would have been petrol enough for the continuation of the offensive, especially as it may reasonably be assumed that, as in previous cases, stocks would have been replenished by captured stores. The defeat may be attributed to causes of a more psychological nature. I had at the time the conviction that this battle would have presented no problem to the "old" Rommel. Had he not been suffering in health from the long strain of uninterrupted campaigning in Africa, he would never have pulled out when he had already completely encircled the enemy—the British "Last Hope" position, as it was called, had already been outmanœuvred. I know today that his troops were unable to understand the order to retire.

Rommel was, as always, with the decisive wing. The attack

did not gain the ground expected in the first few hours because of strong enemy minefields; besides, the continuous and surprisingly powerful air activity caused losses and was specially harassing. This influenced him to call off the attack between 6:00 and 7:00 A.M. The order to resume it in the early afternoon was given, after reconsideration, already before I intervened. It is, of course, difficult to say whether the attack would have reached its objective if it had been pressed home. It is, however, sure that victory lay within Rommel's grasp and that the breaking off of the offensive gave the enemy an opening and correspondingly lessened the chances of the Panzer Army.

The strong minefields in these sectors indicated that Montgomery still expected Rommel to make another thrust from the desert. The British were justified in this assumption in view of the lavish mining of the German forward protective zone on our left wing and in the centre which made an attack there improbable. It was imperative, therefore, for our defence to shift the point of main effort to oppose the British left wing. The British minefields gave the Eighth Army the necessary time for counter-measures and pinned the German attacking forces down in a narrow corridor which offered good targets for the R.A.F. If notwithstanding—whether rightly or wrongly is not arguable here—we had pressed home the attack this bottleneck would have had to be carried in a single rush so as to enable us to make the final deployment in a less dangerous area and to evade the hammering from the air. This iron determination to persevere was lacking; that being so, and given our knowledge of the full risk of the gamble, the attack ought never to have been begun.

That in itself the operation held promise of success can best be seen from Montgomery's view of the prospects of a German advance in August 1942. When it failed I realized that the fate of the North African campaign was sealed. I no longer saw the glimmer of any major solution, only possibilities of holding the African position for a while in a reduced area. My preoccupation henceforward was to consolidate our position and for as long as possible to keep the Allies on this southern front from influencing the European theatre of war.

The fact had to be faced that our communications were no longer secure for any length of time. In the south, as elsewhere, time had gone over to our enemies' side.

The long-planned British-American landing which, in my judgment, would follow in North Africa, meant a pincers movement. Even though thousands of miles lay between the Allied armies the operation must result in a dissipation of the Axis forces and have an enormous moral effect on the isolated troops in Africa.

In any event, Montgomery had won a victory over Rommel the implications of which were greater than its immediate achievement, while on the German side weaknesses had been exposed that could only assist future British operations.

The R.A.F. was in the ascendancy, the war at sea could be from now on more effectively supported and Malta made virtually unassailable. With a more powerful air force behind it the Eighth Army was capable of tackling the most arduous tasks, especially with its increased confidence since its success on the defensive.

Was it right under these circumstances to wait for the British offensive in the El Alamein position? As post-war literature has laid the blame for that decision on my shoulders I declare unequivocally, first and foremost, that as Chief of an Air Command and C.-in-C. South I reserved to myself the right of consultation and interference, but that I was not Rommel's superior. Rommel was at that time subordinate to Marshal Bastico, and he in turn to the Comando Supremo; at the same time he felt himself responsible to the O.K.W., with which he maintained a close connection, with results that should not be underestimated. By this plain statement of the facts I do not seek to dispute my share of the responsibility as adviser, in so far as Rommel was at all accessible to advice. Hindenburg once said that he was occasionally held responsible for victories, but always for defeats. These words apply to me in this as in many other cases. I have a lively recollection of an episode after the end of the fighting in Tunis in May 1943. My two Chiefs of Staff urged me to refute the unjust and unjustifiable aspersions on my conduct of the campaign. I refused with the remark that someone must bear the blame in the eyes of the world and that, anyway, truth would prevail when the history of the war came to be written. Nothing can hurt a man who is acquitted by his own conscience. This is, besides, an attitude which stood me in good stead at my trial.

Having made my position clear, I think it must needs be added that neither the O.K.W. nor the Comando Supremo would have strongly opposed any serious intention of Rommel's to retire to a rear line. Rommel had hitherto always found means to get what he wanted. But he believed in the strength of the El Alamein Line. His troops were good and, according to previous African standards, numerically strong. Also, at the beginning, supplies were adequate. On this basis I could assume, without incurring the charge of being a gambler, that the line could be held against an offensive.

Looking back, I see it was a mistake to remain there. Whether the test of strength was made a few hundred miles farther east or west, or whether Montgomery's thrust was met by a delaying defence, was immaterial. All that mattered was that the Eighth Army should be stopped and our army sustained from a wider supply base, if possible, between Tripoli and Tobruch. It must, however, be remembered that the German and Italian army and air formations were in the main not motorized or at best insufficiently so; ill qualified to carry out a lengthy mobile operation, they even tied the hands of the commander. In addition the superiority of the British in the air might have played havoc with an army on the move. Whether Montgomery's strategy would be cautious or intrepid previous battles had afforded no means of judging; our impression hitherto indicated that he would carefully weigh all the risks. The greatest unknown factor was the time and the objective of the Allied invasion in the western Mediterranean. Events in any case did not justify the absolute confidence of Rommel and his deputy, Stumme, in the El Alamein position. Very possibly Rommel by a mobile strategy in a restricted area would have accomplished more than Stumme, who was unluckily killed the very morning of the day the first attack was launched. All things considered, however, it would have been better to have retired behind a rearguard to a more easily defended position, for which the Halfaya Pass would have been suitable; or else, under pretence of offering the main resistance from the El Alamein Line, to have accepted the decisive battle some twenty miles farther west in an area—the so-called Fuka position—which had all the advantages of the El Alamein zone and was better protected on the left wing by the terrain.

In either case we ought to have acted earlier, that is to say reconnoitred the position and lost no time in strengthening it. Yet neither Rommel nor Stumme ever mentioned any such plan to me. There was no need to make dispositions beyond the main decision because the course of invasion in the western Mediterranean must dictate all subsequent operations. Rommel and I often broadly discussed future developments in the late summer months when we flirted with the idea of evacuating North Africa and withdrawing the German troops to the Apennines or the Alps. Weighing the political-strategic pros and cons, I was, as I told Rommel, against it. I shall return to this later.

The decision, right or wrong, was taken. The Comando Supremo and the Italian Commanders-in-Chief of army, navy and air force, Bastico with his generals and admirals, Rommel and C.-in-C. South did everything humanly possible to prepare for the decisive battle. While Rommel went home on leave for reasons of health, Stumme, a veteran tank commander who had won his spurs in Russia, went over things with an unbiased eye and made effective improvements to the line. Being a man of a more even and genial temperament than Rommel, he did much to relax the tension among officers and men, besides managing to create tolerable relations with the Italian Command. But neither was he quite physically fit.

While all concerned were straining every nerve to increase the efficiency of the receiving ports, Tripoli, Bengasi, Tobruch, Sidi Barrani and Marsa Matruh, to provide them with better fighter and flak protection, organize new means of transport and accumulate a greater volume of supplies in the Italo-Greek area, the war on our own and the enemy's sea communications went on with redoubled fury.

In the event both sides had heavy losses but reached their goal. The Axis forces in Africa were kept fed, equipped and reinforced to the limit of their requirements, while on the other hand Malta's striking power was fully restored by the British. The way our convoys were being increasingly molested showed that freedom of movement in the Mediterranean could not be secured by merely defensive action; in fact we had to reckon that these harrying tactics, combined with the expected Anglo-American large-scale landing in this area, if successful, might cripple our supply lines altogether. On the top of this came very effective acts of sabotage against our air bases in Africa and Crete.

I could not reconcile myself to this slow ruination in idleness. It was clear to me by the middle of September that, as *ultima ratio*, an effort must be made to ease our supply situation if only temporarily by an air operation against Malta. I knew the difficulties well enough; the island was fully capable of defending herself and had a substantially strengthened fighter force on hand. The transfer of British fighter aircraft, taking off from aircraft carriers, was going on apace without our being able to do anything to stop it. Even though we were able to spot their approach by radar our fighters always arrived on the scene too late; we just could not overcome the difficulties of getting fast fighter aircraft into the area. It followed that as regards comparative strength the scales had tipped against us, German-Italian formations being so much in demand to shield our convoys. Finally, the British had learnt the lesson of the first air battle of Malta; they had widened their base and achieved the highest degree of protection from bomber attack.

The C.-in-C. Luftwaffe gave extensive support to the proposed operation, but still every requirement could not be fulfilled. The quality of the formations, however, made up for this to some extent. The fighter wing were old hands at taking on the British, and the bomber formations had years of operational experience. It was hardly possible, however, to place much reliance on the Italian bombers and fighters because their air-craft were obsolescent and the bomber crews had insufficient night operational training.

Once again Air Group 2 directed the attack, and yet the as-sault in the middle of October had not the success we hoped for; I broke it off on the third day because, especially in view of the expected landings, our losses were too high.

The surprise had not come off, and neither had our bomber attacks against their air bases. Instead, the battle had to be fought against enemy fighters in the air and their bomb-proof shelters on the ground. The British used a trick, now observed for the first time, of dropping strips of silver paper to interfere with our radar instruments, which hampered our fighter tactics and made the protection of our bombers less effective. They had indeed considerably refined their methods of defence.

The great assault on the El Alamein position came on 23 October 1942. With the death of the deputy Commander-in-Chief there was an atmosphere of bewilderment at army H.Q. until Rommel's return. Anyone who knows how decisive are the first orders in a defensive engagement will have no difficulty in understanding what the loss of General Stumme meant for the whole battle. It was a further misfortune that Rommel was not fully restored to health. Thirdly, the air superiority of the British was more than ever apparent. Incidentally, the so-called "Devils' Gardens"—mined areas laid out on a certain plan—did not live up to the promises made for them.

On 3 November 1942, when things at El Alamein were almost at their decisive point, I wanted to visit Rommel once again to talk the situation over with him. Owing to engine trouble over the Mediterranean halfway to El Daba I was compelled to alter my course and land on the nearest airfield in Crete in the late afternoon. When I landed in Africa in the early dawn of 4 November I was met by General Seidemann, the new A.O.C. Africa, who took me at once to Rommel.

Rommel drew me a picture of the way things had so deteriorated as to induce him to order a retreat. The right wing had already been pulled back from its dominating position. On receipt of his operational report Hitler had sent him a wireless message that he did not agree with this "cowardly evasion"; the line must be held.[1] In more than justified excitement Rommel had called off the retiring movement in order to fight and die in obedience to orders. I told him in the presence of his operations chief that there could be no question of any such folly, that Hitler's order must be ignored as it would result in the extinction of the German Africa Army and the final loss of Tripolitania. I also told him that I would accept joint responsibility for not carrying out the order and would immediately send Hitler a message to that effect. As things were, I said that Hitler must have acted on a false assumption seeing that our men were no longer in the line but on the open desert, so that for that if for no other reason his order could not be carried out.

I radioed the Führer a brief summing-up of the situation and the consequences that would follow the execution of his order, immediately adding a request that Rommel be given a free hand for his operations. Rommel also managed to get through a similar message.[2] That same afternoon—before I took off on my return flight—the sanction I had asked for was there. Precious hours had meanwhile been wasted. Why on this flight of all others did my engine have to fail me, a thing that almost never happened? What I managed to do on 4 November would have been of the greatest, perhaps of decisive, importance on the 3rd. There would then have been a hope that under the skilful leadership of Rommel and his second-in-command and with the inimitable discipline of his troops the army might have broken away with heavy losses to the enemy.

[1] Seidemann told me on the way to Rommel that faulty air reconnaissance had been the reason for the order to retreat; he had had to swallow the bitterest reproaches. He said that he had been up himself at daybreak and had confirmed with his own eyes the air reconnaissance reports of the previous day according to which there were no enemy forces either at the Siwa oasis or in the Qattara depression. Rommel had apparently been the dupe of a false Italian report. This corrects the statements made in the book *War Without Hatred*.

[2] I have read that Rommel also sent a personal ambassador—Dr. Berndt—to the Führer's G.H.Q.

I could now give more attention to my pressing tasks in the western Mediterranean and my endeavours to sustain a constant stream of supplies. It was the beginning of a very strenuous period, made intolerable by Rommel's attitude and exorbitant demands.

Thanks to the old African campaigners the threatening collapse of the Axis forces was averted. I watched the dénouement from afar. Single war pictures linger in my memory—the retirement of Ramcke's Parachute Division, who motorized themselves with captured vehicles taken from their pursuers; the pell-mell congestion of friend and foe along the Via Balbia, and other incidents. It was lucky for us that the enemy air forces had not yet been schooled to exterminate a retreating enemy albeit there were many opportunities, as, for example, at Halfaya Pass.

15

The Allied Invasion of North Africa and the Battle for Tunis

8 Nov. 1942 Landing of British and American troops in Morocco and Algeria—9 Nov. Landing of the first German units in Tunis—Consolidation of the Tunis bridgehead—December 1942 to January 1943 Surrender of the whole of Italian North Africa by Rommel—Advance of the British Eighth Army from east to west—February 1943 German counter-offensive from the Tunisian bridgehead against the British First Army and the Americans on the Algerian-Tunisian border—Failure of the offensive and defeat of an attempt to wrest the initiative from the British Eighth Army—March-April 1943 Contraction of the Tunisian fortress by a pincers movement of the Allied armies from west and south—12 May 1943 End of the fighting in Tunisia, capitulation of the last remaining German forces.

BEFORE THE INVASION

The Allied invasion of North Africa was preceded by an intensive war of nerves. For weeks contradictory rumours and reports flowed into my headquarters. The landing objective, the strength of the invasion force and its constituents were varied with consummate artistry. Naval movements off the West African coast indicated a possible landing there with a march straight across the continent. The overcrowding of troops and ships into Gibraltar, on the other hand, pointed to an objective in the Mediterranean, the sudden appearance of aircraft-carriers and large transports confirming the probability that the main landing would be attempted beyond striking distance from Gibraltar, Malta, Alexandria and Syria. Repeated sailings of ships from Gibraltar into the Mediterranean increased the uncertainty.

After critical assessment of all intelligence reports available I summed up the situation as follows:

The invasion would be strategically co-ordinated with the movements of the British Eighth Army in North Africa, therefore a landing on the African west coast was unlikely. It would be an enterprise without precedent, and the American troops lacked fighting experience.

The Allies must know that there were very considerable air forces in Italy and on the Italian islands which could not be neutralized by fighter aircraft operating from aircraft-carriers. Therefore landings very near the islands or the Italian coast were not feasible. For this reason also, a break-through in the narrows between Sicily and Tunis seemed more than improbable.

If the enemy landed on the north coast of Africa it would certainly be at such distance from the airfields in Sicily and Sardinia that bomber and torpedo-bomber sorties would have to be flown from the longest possible range. That would give the invasion fleet a certain measure of security. The enemy would not need to reckon with an attack by the Italian fleet either at such a distance from the latter's home naval bases. So Algeria with the adjacent territories came into first consideration as the likely invasion area. What amount of opposition the French would offer there was an open question. But even the barest token resistance might be to our advantage.

A landing in Sicily must be an alluring bait. It would cut the communications between Italy and Africa and would bring the war close to the peninsula itself. Although this operation might have a decisive effect on the campaign, it was unlikely because of the risk to the invasion fleet.

A landing in Sardinia and Corsica would be a great advantage as providing a stepping stone for a subsequent landing in Italy or in the south of France. Their occupation would bring Italy within range of the Allied air force. Under the circumstances this seemed to me strategically overambitious and I considered it improbable.

The south of France, too, seemed a tempting objective for
an invasion, but despite its size the invasion fleet was too weak
for so independent an operation.

On the basis of these calculations I proceeded to take appropriate counter-measures. The C.-in-C. of the Luftwaffe had
sanctioned the most urgent reinforcements for Air Fleet 2 which
I had asked for, among which were several squadrons which had
had operational training overseas. The air bases in Sicily and
Sardinia were overhauled, strengthened and provisioned. A similar check-up of the requirements of the torpedo-bombers was
made at Grosseto, the traditional torpedo-bomber base. Plans
were made for co-operation with the German air divisions in
the south of France. The necessary liaison was also established
with the Italian air force, though unfortunately the only help
the Italians could give us was a few torpedo-bombers. Air- and
ground-reconnaissance activity was stepped up. German U-boats
were disposed so that they could attack large convoys entering
the Mediterranean, and plans were discussed with the Supermarina in case the Allied fleet should after all make a surprise appearance off the Italian coast.

I had further asked the O.K.W. to order at least one division
to Sicily, where it could be held in readiness either to be moved
forward to Tunis or to oppose a possible landing in Sicily itself,
where coastal defence had been almost unbelievably neglected.

My request was not approved. In order, however, that I might
have at least some thing on the spot besides my local defence
battalion, a reinforced parachute battalion was kept in readiness
for action. A detailed inspection was made of the Italian defence
lay-outs on the island and in Italy. What I saw there opened my
eyes, and as a result I brought in German construction staffs.

On the day before the landing in North Africa I heard from
Goering. As the mouthpiece of the Führer—I had no idea that
he was staying at Berchtesgaden at that time—he told me that
my picture of the situation was all wrong. At the Führer's
G.H.Q. they were thoroughly convinced that the attack would
come in the south of France. It was my responsibility to see to

it that the whole Air Fleet could be sent into action to meet it.

My formations were indeed correctly disposed to deal with the primary task of striking while the ships were still at sea. The second step was to send to Corsica, and to central and northern Italy, ground crews, engineering staffs and stores, which had to be done with transport aircraft. But in general I did not believe in an operation against France.

Agents and U-boats kept on reporting that the invasion fleet had sailed from Gibraltar and passed through the straits, with details of its strength, composition and disposition—amongst other things that it carried long-distance reconnaissance aircraft. Successive reports confirmed that it was heading east—France and North Italy could therefore be ruled out.

Rommel was already in headlong retreat. Except for some isolated Italian posts and fort garrisons there were no combat troops in Tripolitania. Supply difficulties had been substantially aggravated, and unless the pace of the retreat could be slowed down considerable supplies must be written off as lost. Neither the Germans nor the Italians had made any preparations in Tunisia, and in view of the mutual hatred of the French and Italians it was certain that whatever measures were taken would be met with obstinate resistance. For C.-in-C. South the French colonies were taboo. It was forbidden to put in at any of the ports, supplies must not be routed via Tunis and Bizerte, and of course no German garrison could be moved to Tunis to guard against surprise attack. Even if all this was quite understandable as a major political issue, I was at a total loss to understand the refusal of my purely military demand for at least one division to be sent to Sicily. The limited strengthening of the German striking forces in the air could neither prevent a landing where their range of action ended nor halt or annihilate the troops once landed without the aid of parachute forces or army support.

I never clearly understood the ideas of Hitler and the Wehrmacht operations staff. Their fundamental mistake was completely to misjudge the importance of the Mediterranean theatre. They would not or could not see that from the end of 1941 the colonial war had taken on a different aspect, that Africa had become a theatre in which decisions vital to Europe were maturing.

The second mistake was their failure to guess correctly the objective of the Allied invasion. Perhaps Hitler also thought that there was no need to expect any immediate threat to the European theatre and that no major effort was therefore called for. I do not believe that he wanted to leave the initiative to the Italians; I am more inclined to think he trusted the French.

If the Allied invasion army were not opposed by fresh German forces it would mean the total loss of the German-Italian army in Africa. For there would be no hope of getting them out with nothing to stop the combined forces of the British Eighth Army and the invasion army with their strength in the air and their undisputed supremacy at sea. Further, it would mean the surrender of the whole of Tripolitania, the peaceful occupation of the French colonies and the capitulation without a fight of all effectives there; the Allies would capture an ideal springboard for a future landing in Sicily and Italy in the early months of 1943, and with it probably achieve the elimination of Italy as an Axis partner.

The obvious conclusion was that everything must be done to postpone a sequel to the invasion of a kind which might decide the war. As no preparations had been made by the O.K.W. and the Comando Supremo, measures had to be improvised to surmount the initial crisis, with a view to evolving an ultimate plan of action. My first preoccupation was how to delay the Allied landing and its expansion by the capture of the harbours and airfields between Algiers and Tunis, as well as to protect Tunis itself. Of equal importance was the building up of a bridgehead of our own covering Bizerte and the city of Tunis, in which the behaviour of the French troops and of the Bey might prove decisive. Further, all efforts had to be directed to the organization of an efficient supply base.

If there was a yawning gap between my plans and the event, was it for that reason necessarily so wrong to try to put into effect the ideas sketched above?

The British offensive in Egypt gave me, as I thought, a good insight into Montgomery's strategy. In a nutshell, he played for safety and was correspondingly methodical—which was not without its advantages for Rommel's retreat, assuming Rommel could break away quickly and far enough to make a gradually more systematic plan possible.

At the same time it had to be remembered that even a victorious army cannot keep up a pursuit of thousands of miles in one rush; the stronger the army the greater the difficulty of supply. Previous British pursuits had broken down for the same reason. A slow evasive action could deny them the use of the harbour installations of Tobruch, Bengasi and Tripoli, and the British lacked a strong air-transport supply organization. Similarly the tactical support which could be given by the R.A.F. close to the ground was limited. If Montgomery chose the alternative of pushing on, in a frontal or an outflanking movement, with a smaller force of mobile pursuit troops, these could be shaken off and valuable time gained for the main retirement.

The task was not easy, but worthy of a Rommel. In spite of all the difficulties, he would have pulled it off if it had not been for his own subconscious resistance. He wanted to get back to Tunis; if possible still further away, to Italy and the Alps—wishful thinking that clouded his strategical judgment.

Eisenhower's invasion troops certainly had the best possible equipment; they were eager to go into action, but they had no combat experience. As long as the British Eighth Army was fighting far away they lacked support on their wing. Even an unfledged German army, unacclimatized to Africa, could deal with this enemy in a difficult, mountainous and desert terrain, but it must be sent in quickly and in sufficient strength.

In our judgment of the invasion troops we Axis partners were of one mind. With regard to the strategy of the Africa Army, however, there was a divergence of opinion. Neither arguments nor orders had any influence on Rommel. What he wanted can be best expressed in his own words: he considered it his only task—at the beginning of December 1942—"to prevent the liquidation of his army." This led, as I have read in a study by officers of "the Rommel Panzer Army," to "the retreat of the beaten Panzer Army from El Alamein to Brega—except for rearguard actions—being regarded more or less as a 'route march' under slight enemy pressure on the ground and from the air while reinforcements flowed in from the back area."

I will not express an opinion here as to whether Rommel's independent behaviour ought to be regarded as a political stunt or as "fatal insubordination." One thing was certainly a mistake, which was to leave Rommel in his command at all. For so long as he was there it was impossible to remove the disharmony, with all its consequences for the conduct of operations. The basic strategic plan, as well as political and tactical considerations, made it impossible for the Italian and German Commands to fall in with his ideas.

Nor was the division of command calculated to make matters easier. I was solely responsible under the O.K.W. for the conduct of operations against the invasion army, while all other land and sea forces were subordinate to the Comando Supremo. I duly kept Count Cavallero and the Duce informed, and no decision was taken concerning the African theatre of war without my being consulted. But this was anything but an ideal arrangement—I had to make the best of a bad job.

NORTH AFRICA, NOVEMBER 1942 TO JANUARY 1943

The battle began with air attacks on the enemy invasion fleet. Although the flights delivering these attacks were brought forward as far west as absolutely possible, i.e. to Sardinia and Sicily, they had to make their sorties at maximum range of action. In the very first days the defence put up by carrier aircraft and powerful anti-aircraft guns was hastily supplemented by fighters operating from Algerian airfields. Results, despite the reckless determination of our pilots, were below expectations.

The landings themselves, according to the reports available to me, met with no marked resistance by the French. On 11 and 12 November the ports and airfields of Bougie and Bône were already in enemy hands.

It was not until the morning of 9 November that Hitler, roused by a broadcast speech by Admiral Darlan, personally spoke to me over the telephone and gave me a free hand in Tunisia—though he later qualified this by forbidding me to go over there myself. Enforcement of my first extremely moderate measures was deferred owing to the interference of the Wehrmacht operations staff, which just at that moment was made independent of Hitler. Everything had to be held up pending Pétain's consent to an intervention in Tunisia.

The occupation of the country was begun with an understrength parachute regiment and my H.Q. battalion protected by fighters and Stukas, the diplomatic negotiations having similarly been completed by Colonel Harlinghausen and General Loerzer on 9 November. It was hoped that negotiations with the French Resident-General, Admiral Estéva, would result in the French military and naval forces joining us or at least remaining neutral.

The talks started well, and to begin with relations between the French and German troops were excellent. Our parachutists went out on patrol against the enemy in French armoured cars. But all of a sudden the situation changed when an Italian fighter squadron, in breach of an express agreement and without my knowledge, landed near Tunis. At once friends became foes. Cavallero's immediate recall of the squadron to Sardinia when I intervened made not the slightest difference. More disagreeable still, Cavallero's action, taken for reasons of prestige, shed a false light on my intentions. I am sure that, but for this incident, Pétain's order, which later came in to the effect that the French colonial troops should march with us, would have been implemented to our advantage. As this did not happen I soon had to do something about the divisions under the command of General Barré. This gentleman's intentions and dealings were so inscrutable that I could not afford to waste any further time. After the energetic efforts of our consul, Moellhausen, had failed to bring the wily general down on our side of the fence, I had to end an intolerable situation by sending in the Stukas against the

French divisions. In war it is futile to bargain with unreliable auxiliaries.

Contrary to all expectations, we succeeded in building up a small bridgehead with a weak German division reinforced by flak. On 15 November General Nehring took over the command in Tunisia. He was splendidly supported by Dr. Rahn, later ambassador to Italy, and his colleague Moellhausen, and equally so by Admiral Meendsen-Bohlken in his dealings with the French Admiral Derrien. Nehring was faced with a task of immense difficulty, but one of extraordinary fascination for a young general. His appointment was regarded as an instance of my unbounded optimism. It never occurred to me to belittle the enemy, though I readily admit I put on a show of optimism. But optimism is one thing and underrating one's adversary another. As an example I quote an incident that has been the subject of much mistaken comment in the post-war press: the surprise attack by sixty enemy armoured cars on the Stuka airfield at Djedeida on 26 November 1942. Nehring rang me up in a state of understandable excitement and drew the blackest conclusions from the raid. Unable as I was to share his worst fears, I asked him to be calm and said I would arrive the following day.

At this point the bulk of the invasion army had come ashore and the negligible resistance of the French coastal defences collapsed. It must now take some time to assemble the raw Allied formations and to make an arrangement with the French, yet the Allies were certainly anxious to avoid repercussions and were not wasting a moment. The attitude of the Tunisian French, including the Arabs, had to be considered doubtful and at least potentially hostile, while the enemy's knowledge of the grave over-all German weakness would tempt him to scotch the danger from Tunis by surprise raids. There was one other unknown factor: the traffic problem. The enemy had ahead of him a march of 500 miles through strange, dangerous and mountainous country. Even if the railways were in running order they were inadequate for any large-scale movement of troops, not to mention their lying within striking distance of the German dive-bombers. Though there was little fear of an immediate major operation, we had for obvious reasons to expect raids and reconnaissance operations.

These and various other considerations forced me to realize that in the exceptional circumstances our small forces must be organized under an army H.Q. staff. My request for a Panzer Army H.Q. staff was met at the beginning of December 1942 when the 5th Panzer Army under General von Arnim arrived. Hitler assigned to von Arnim a junior general—Ziegler—who "without portfolio" was to prove a friend and counsellor to his harassed superior and a capable deputy whenever necessary. The efficacy of this arrangement depended on the mutual understanding of the two generals, and it stood the test.

Meanwhile Rommel was continuing his retreat and bombarding me with impossible demands for reinforcements, which I could not even begin to satisfy. The oversea supply lines had been curtailed, communications through Tunisia had not yet been organized and I had no justification for robbing my own air-transport formations. Malta, still in British hands, cast its shadow over everything. It was increasingly plain from the reports of my formations that even where a successful resistance might have been put up, they had given up fighting. Marshal Bastico's reports to the Comando Supremo did not mince words. Cavallero and I were quite clear that if this "marathon" back to Tunis were continued there would soon be nothing left of the Italian divisions, that the ports of Bengasi and Tripoli would fall into the hands of the British in a condition in which they could be put to immediate use, and the morale of the exhausted German troops would be seriously shaken. The Mareth Line (the southernmost position on the frontier of Tunisia) could not right the balance because there was still much work to be done on it.

Meanwhile the unstable relationship between Bastico and Rommel threatened to develop into an open feud. Cavallero tried to thrash this matter out at a conference at Arco Philene at the end of November 1942, at which the antagonism of both parties was mollified, but not removed. Cavallero explained the Italian point of view that Tripolitania must be defended within the limits of possibility and excessive demands must not be made on the stamina of the Italian infantry divisions—two conditions essential to the fortification of the defence line on the south Tunisian border. Here work was going on feverishly. From now on supplies for the Axis forces were to be sent up more plentifully through Tunisia.

By the end of November the Allied invasion army had gradually got going. On the 25th the first weak American column had advanced to Medjez-el-Bab. In the meantime the arrival of German and Italian army and air-force reinforcements had consolidated the position. By the transfer of a fighter squadron with a weak infantry escort to Gabès, the supply line to Rommel's army in Tripolitania was opened. The eight to ten British-American-French divisions were opposed by five Axis divisions, more than two of them Italians, the flak being combined into a single division under General Neuffer. Fighter, dive-bomber and reconnaissance formations sufficient for immediate needs were under the command of General Kosch, a former Austrian pilot.

The west front was over 250 miles long. Although it seemed out of the question to try to hold it with such limited forces, especially in artillery (at the beginning we had barely 100 guns), all the same I meant not only to hold it, but even to push it far enough forward by guerilla attacks to prevent us from being thrown back towards the sea by every successful enemy assault. The terrain helped, the only network of roads and railways being in the northern third of the west front. The middle third was more difficult to approach from the Allied area, and was also blocked from the coastal plain by easily defensible ridges across which there were few passes. The desert made it difficult to approach the southern third. I assumed that without experience of desert warfare the raw Allied troops would not immediately thrust towards these remoter areas. The southern front, facing south, was reserved for Rommel's army, and this I left out of my calculations, as for the time being it was not threatened. In the central sector the Italian divisions sufficed as a security garrison; though at the same time it was clear to me that if the enemy broke through, German units would have to be sent in. The upper third would be held by German troops. My plan was to deceive the enemy about our more than feeble strength by constant attacks at widely different places in the north and middle sector with forces of varying strength and to hamper the assembly of a strong enemy offensive.

In this way the 5th Panzer Army was to occupy a main defensive line, running roughly through Dj. Abrod-Bezha-Tibursuk along the Siliana in the direction of Sbeitla-Gafsa. As our ultimate objective I had in view the line Bône-Souk Ahras-Tebessa-Feriana-Gafsa-Kebili. This was the first position at a distance of about 150 miles from the coast which would enable me eventually to begin a counter-offensive. It was naturally strong, lent itself to hasty fortification and had useful communications which the enemy lacked in the whole of the southern part—even to the north they were not nearly as good as those in the Axis area. How simple this task would have been if only there had been *one* German division available at the beginning of the invasion or if the French had not turned skittish! With half the forces we could have done twice, if not four times as much at the outset.

After the first few weeks the headlong pursuit by the British in Tripolitania slowed down. Heavy rains in Egypt interfered with Montgomery's advance, and when Rommel reached the El Agheila pass at the end of November 1942 the Africa Army was out of immediate jeopardy. With the broken and waterless desert of Sirte and the well-fortified position at Buerat to fall back on prospects were very much brighter. That the troops thought so I was able to see for myself when I flew to the front before Christmas 1942 and again before the New Year. Nowhere any sign of depression, only disgust that they were not being given a chance to fight as they could have done, and an intense and justifiable longing for better supplies.

On 15 January an attack on the Buerat position was beaten off, while at Zemzem the Africa Army avoided contact with the enemy converging from the south. The same tactics were repeated over and over again until the capture of Tripoli. To give

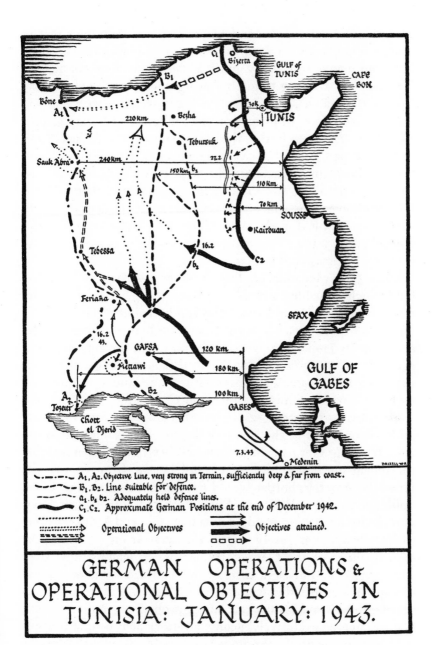

GERMAN OPERATIONS &
OPERATIONAL OBJECTIVES IN
TUNISIA: JANUARY: 1943.

one example: between 16 and 22 January, in seven days that is, the retreating army covered a distance of 220 miles (as the crow flies), an average of thirty miles a day. One does not need a General Staff training to guess that fighting went by the board. Clearly the Marshal's conference of 24 November 1942 had had no practical effect. In plain words, Cavallero and I were against a battle which might lead to the annihilation of the Africa Army or a large part of it. We were, however, both convinced that opportunities for counter-attacks with modest objectives must be exploited to the full. The fighting spirit was there. Given leadership even our lamentably small trickle of supplies would have been ample for this limited task. We were everywhere compelled to wage a "poor man's war"—yet it is amazing how Rommel had mastered it in 1941.

With the evacuation of Tripoli, where we had to leave behind much valuable material, the fight for the Italian colonies was virtually at an end—with the result that the Italians went into action with even less enthusiasm than before. Rommel's decision on 25 January, however, to send up to the southern Tunisian front the three divisions formed from a reorganization of the seven Italian divisions was a natural one, and was approved by the Comando Supremo and C.-in-C. South.

By contrast the strategy of the 5th Panzer Army H.Q. staff under von Arnim in the first months completely met the situation. If strong German formations had been available instead of the Italian units the objective of pushing the front forward as far as the Algerian border would have been reached. Successive stabbings by the 5th Panzer Army with the 10th Panzer Division led by its distinguished commander, General Müller, nevertheless slowly but surely edged the west front forward, the high qualities of the German soldier being demonstrated over and over again. The right wing of the Tunisian front, weakened though it was by the withdrawal of our assault troops, was manned by German units and left unprobed, the Allied attacks being delivered exclusively against positions held by the Italians.

While an assault on the Italians invariably resulted in loss of the position, sometimes in a break-through on a considerable front, the success of the German counter-attacks—as, for example, on 25 January 1943 when we took 4,000 prisoners—could not disguise the fact that the methodical execution of our offensive plan was seriously imperilled. There was no ignoring the significance of the Allied thrust from Faid towards Sfax at the end of the month, which indicated the beginning of an offensive that might well seal the fate of Tunisia if the Americans had the leadership and fighting qualities to cope with a tricky situation. As this was not so, this tactically effective manœuvre led only to an extension of the front and to a dissipation of enemy forces. The German Command must have been the veriest amateurs if they had failed to draw the consequences from this temporary advantage.

German airmen still controlled the air space above Tunisia, their low-flying attacks often having a devastating effect on the unfledged American troops, while the strategy of the Luftwaffe in the western Mediterranean was not unsuccessful either. But our forces were too weak in relation to the size of the operational area. The O.K.W. paid too little heed to the time factor when every day counted, and this decided me to fly to the Führer's G.H.Q.

In my talk with Goering I stressed the following main points: the need for fuel supplies, a more powerful armament for aircraft, more effective light (5-cm.) and heavy flak, an increased flow of decimetric and Freya radar sets and search radar for long-distance reconnaissance aircraft.

At the Führer's G.H.Q. I drew a picture of the situation as I then saw it, pointing out that the opportunity of winning the French over to our side had been bungled. The one chance of advancing the German front as far as Constantine could not be exploited for lack of troops.

"We have succeeded," I told them, "in the improbable task of building up a bridgehead and pushing forward a front which, though it will not be able to halt a major offensive, can be consolidated. To do so fresh reinforcements will be needed. The two or three Italian divisions are of small account. It is hopeless to think of pushing forward to the line we have to occupy with the available three and a half German divisions, including only one Panzer division, the 10th, and with a total of exactly 100 guns, on a front over 250 miles long. There is still time, but the sands are running out. As soon as the good weather sets in Eisenhower will try to seize the initiative and launch his offensive. As the attacker, he will have the choice of time and terrain, and by attrition on the secondary fronts will make himself strong enough to guarantee success, as we cannot match such a concentration of forces in time.

"The 5th Panzer Army is not yet in possession of the receiving points which guarantee the holding of Tunis in case of reverses. For this again reinforcements are essential.

"We are working like beavers on the work of fortifying the Mareth Line and its flanking positions, but it is no use expecting the work to be completed for six to eight weeks. If for no other reason, I consider a rapid retreat of Rommel's German-Italian army out of the question. At the same time I do think it of crucial importance that the British Eighth Army should not be allowed to link up with the invasion army, and that the Allied Air Commands on either side should be prevented from carrying out co-ordinated operations above the narrow fortress area of Tunisia. The work of unloading at the ports of Tunis and Bizerte which has hitherto gone smoothly would then break down.

"Our strategic objective must be to keep the two armies apart and to attack and defeat them, one after the other, from an interior line. I am against bringing back Rommel's army at once, because to do so would be contrary to the ground plan for the defence of Tunisia, but am in favour of pulling out parts of it, with the proviso that Rommel does not make the surrender of important combat elements a pretext for fighting even less than at present and for pulling back into Tunisia even quicker. I am bound to say in all frankness that since El Alamein he has not been fighting back with the uncompromising vigour I have been accustomed to expect."

I went on to explain that the African armoured forces must not retire behind the Tunisian frontier before the beginning or middle of February because of the pace of the work in fortifying the frontier positions. Further, a new system of command should be introduced: an Army Group Command, for which I suggested Rommel, and an Army High Command, which, for reasons of prestige, should be offered to the Italians. This must be ready to function by the beginning of February. In addition, I asked for two to three divisions, some batteries of artillery, some mortar units, and various flame-thrower and anti-tank battalions; and finally a strengthening of overseas communications by more active improvement on the expedient at present in view.

The strategic plan was approved and I was given wholesale promises that reinforcements would be forthcoming. An offer from Rommel of two motorized divisions from his army I interpreted as an excuse for accelerating his retreat, and consequently turned down—in the event we agreed he should give up *one* division with the express stipulation that no consequences should be drawn to the detriment of the conduct of operations. All Hitler's other assurances more or less evaporated in the course of time. It was apparently thought that the sop of Rommel's solitary division was enough to keep me quiet. I was fully alive to the difficulties of the High Command, and I believe that my attitude towards them was neither frivolous nor arrogant. But a man who has the command of a theatre of war must know where he stands, otherwise the ground is knocked from under him. In my personal talks with Hitler he only rarely went back on his word, but as soon as I was out of sight his interest in the Mediterranean theatre faded. It was too far away, as, incidentally, it was for many competent persons—for some it just did not exist.

TUNISIA, FEBRUARY TO MAY 1943

The salient feature of the fighting in front of the Mareth Line in February was that the defence was not conducted from a continuous line but from a succession of rearguard positions. In this action, artillery and Stukas were very effectively employed, but it was chiefly due to the rearguard division, the 15th Panzers, that the fighting in the area immediately protecting the fortress of Tunisia was maintained all through February. When the British Eighth Army reached the Mareth Line on 20 February the German-Italian troops were contained in a kind of roomy citadel, a fact which the arrival of reinforcements by sea and air did not alter.

The establishment of a direct link-up between the two Allied armies had not yet been achieved. Nor were there any perceptible signs of operational co-ordination in the air. On the other hand, activity against our shipping and air transport was intensified. The first raids by four-engined bombers from altitudes of 30,000 feet and over on our unloading ports introduced a new phase of the war in the air—how to repel them with fighter aircraft and flak was a perpetual conundrum.

Since the end of October 1942 the British Eighth Army had marched halfway across North Africa—over fifteen hundred miles—they had spent the bad winter months on the move and in the desert, and had had to surmount supply difficulties of every kind. Furthermore their forces were widely extended in depth owing to the lack of roads, which did not permit a parallel march for long. Accordingly in this sector of the front it was safe to assume that a lull would continue at least for several weeks.

On the western front the strategic concentration of the invasion army was far advanced. In this respect Eisenhower was ahead of Montgomery, but in fighting power the armies were to be assessed the other way round. This automatically suggested the idea of attacking the two Allied armies one after the other, beginning in the west, in a series of thrusts intended to delay their offensive at least for some weeks or even months. To achieve this end it was necessary to inflict such heavy losses in men and material that replacements would have to be brought in from oversea. A bold thrust into the enemy's offensive preparations held out the greatest promise of success, though the time was not yet ripe to seize the initiative from the Eighth Army. While on the southern front it was still possible to avoid contact with the enemy without risk, our objective on the western front, besides the destruction of enemy forces, was to advance the line in a sector where we could most safely discount the inevitable accidents of war and which would be easier to defend. Frontal clashes were unavoidable if only to pin down the enemy's front-line troops and to exploit every opportunity to improve our own local positions. Greater results might be expected from an outflanking movement—here the terrain in the middle sector (Sbeitla, Kasserine) was suitable as having the following advantages:

A sweep northwest would have a strategic significance. The near objective, Tebessa, was an important rail and road junction with huge depots of every sort. A break-through here would pave the way for a drive across the lines of communication, involving a perilous situation for the enemy's young and inexperienced troops.

Motorized units of Rommel's army could reach the jumping-off base in short marches; the country being sparsely populated, a high degree of secrecy was assured.

Similarly the distances to be covered by von Arnim's west-front units presented no difficulty. The American front being not yet consolidated, the move was an easy one and might prove decisive.

The onslaught must be followed through with persistent speed. Every day was valuable. Every man possible must be taken out of the line in order to strengthen the assault group. Any possible breakdown on the Tunisian western front would be compensated by the success of the drive behind the enemy's rear. We should then have gained the freedom of movement necessary to launch an offensive with all available forces against Montgomery's army. It was unlikely that the operation would be forestalled at the critical moment by a British assault on the Mareth Line, but should Montgomery be induced by reverses to Eisenhower's army to attempt a premature attack, the 90th Light Division would have to be rushed back. Any such counter-attack would have to reach the jumping-off position for Montgomery's assault on the Mareth, an operation that could not be launched out of the blue. The Mareth position was a line of natural defences fortified by blockhouses and strong points, but even a successful frontal attack could have no strategic effect, as an advance from the Mareth, even if it carried the Akarit defence line, would end up in the Chott Djerid salt marshes. Even allowing for the weakness of our most advanced defences—the Mareth Line—they were nevertheless strong enough to dislodge an initial foothold, as was demonstrated when the British actually stormed it. Its weakness was that it could be turned on the right flank; but even this hid no immediate danger, as the terrain itself was a delaying obstacle which would give the Germans ample time to regroup. A British turning movement could not be concealed and could be slowed down by counter-attacks from the air and on the ground. Finally, the rough and inhospitable desert zone separating the inner wings of the two Allied armies favoured the defence.

There were many objections to this intrinsically simple idea. The system of command was unsuited to the conditions of this theatre. The O.K.W. had indeed declared its agreement to the formation of an Army Group, but had expressly stipulated that the command should be left open for Rommel. Even though the operation against the Allied invasion army had been fixed on paper and by word of mouth, and even though no doubt existed as to the steps to be taken to prepare for the main effort, there was still no unified responsible command. Unfortunately, on the two most important days I was absent at the Führer's G.H.Q. so that I was unable to find the remedy in time. My Chief of Staff tried in vain to get the Comando Supremo to publish the order for the changes at the top which had been envisaged. So the 5th Panzer Division still adhered to their own operational plan, taking it for granted that the turning movement would have to conform. On the other hand Rommel also felt that he retained a freedom of movement, subject only to the demands of the situation—his habitual attitude.

The intention was that Rommel with his experience of desert warfare should strike a powerful blow at the British Eighth Army, to be delivered in conjunction with an attack on Eisenhower's forces. On 22 February 1943 I had a long talk with Rommel at his battle H.Q. near Kasserine and found him in a very dispirited mood. His heart was not in his task and he approached it with little confidence. I was particularly struck by his ill-concealed impatience to get back as quickly and with as much unimpaired strength as possible to the southern defence line, where Marshal Messe had been in command since the beginning of February. His apathy betrayed his reluctance or inability to grasp the significance of the operation which was then in progress towards Tebessa. My conversation with the C.-in-C. of the 5th Panzer Army, whom I had ordered to meet me on the airfield, was even less satisfactory. It was very one-sided and finally led to my calling off the attack on Tebessa after I had reconsidered the situation at my H.Q. at Frascati.

In view of the pigheadedness of both C.-in-C.'s—Rommel and von Arnim—I put into effect the new system of command at the same time, thereby believing I had created the most favourable preliminary conditions for Rommel's offensive against the Eighth Army. I deliberately refrained from interfering in the latter's plan of operations in order to leave him a feeling of independence. Of the two suggestions now elaborated, he decided on that which involved an extensive movement across the mountains, which was the basis of his own plan—General Ziegler envisaged an attack near the coast. Both draft schemes had their pros and cons. Each could, and indeed should, be successful if executed effectively and with the element of surprise.

The surprise at least did not come off. Rommel—quite rightly—discontinued his attack when he found that Montgomery's army was fully prepared to meet it. It is idle to argue the rights and wrongs of the matter, as the possibility of a betrayal, which was reported to me at the time, does seem to be authenticated by what I have read since the war. If this was the case, the Italian army commander, Messe, should be regarded as an accessory to the treachery of Admiral Maugeri in the naval sphere.

All our attacks from mid-February onwards (Tebessa and Médenine among others) failed to achieve the success we had anticipated. That there was a prospect of a strategic victory was proved by the extraordinary difficulties of the invasion army. But tactical successes could not retard the course of the campaign. The 1st German-Italian Panzer Army's thrust against Médenine was costly rather to the Axis partners than to the enemy and revealed the absolute weaknesses in our command and combat troops. It was now clear to me that the Axis armies had lost the initiative. The Army Group for which the new C.-in-C., von Arnim, was responsible would have to fall back, for good and all, on the defensive.

At the beginning of March 1943 Rommel left Tunis on a well-earned leave. I was glad to be able to recommend him for the Knight's Cross with Diamonds, but unfortunately my efforts to obtain the highest Italian decoration for this gallant soldier were unavailing.

The chances of a successful defence of the "fortress of Tunisia" were not altogether unfavourable, as long as the two Allied armies could be kept apart and their air forces prevented from co-ordinating. Our right wing was held by veteran German troops in well-constructed positions, and our left also ran through a zone strongly fortified in depth. The two interior wings of the Axis armies were in every respect weaker, the defence being partly in the hands of the Italians alone. Even if the units in that part of the line, such as the "Centauro" Division and the "Imperiali" Brigade, were by Italian standards first-class troops, nevertheless if left to themselves they were incapable of holding up an Allied offensive. If we had not had in reserve three German motorized divisions (the 10th, 21st and 15th Panzers) there would have been no alternative but to avoid any hard fighting and retire to the planned, but not yet constructed, Enfidaville Line. Rommel's pet idea would then have been realized. The advantages of this operation were obvious: the long flank running parallel with the coast would have shrivelled up, while the diminution of the fortress area would enable us to build up a better defence echeloned in depth and in some degree to compensate for the weaknesses in the line covering Tunis itself.

In terms of land warfare this was all true, but without entering into details, such as the insufficient depth of the area and the threat to both outside wings from the British navy, I would

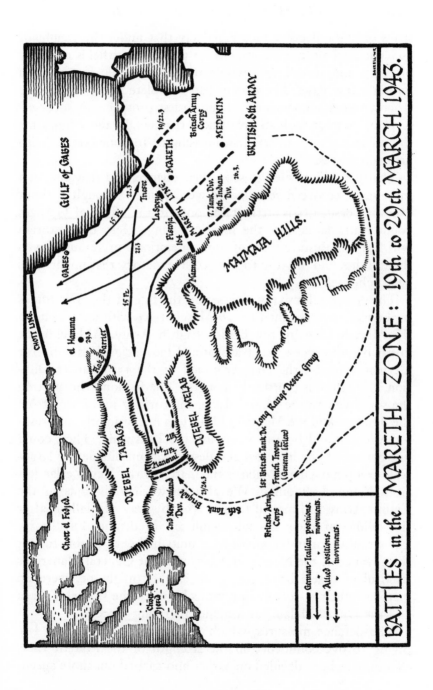

BATTLES in the MARETH ZONE : 19th to 29th MARCH 1943.

GULF OF GABES

CHOTT LINE

Chott el Fejaj

GABES

el Hamma
29.3

Falk Barrier

DJEBEL TABAGA

Chott el Djend

DJEBEL MELAB

2nd New Zealand Div.

5th Tank Brigad

Manenil
104 21Pz
21Pz
13/24.3

15 Pz
27.3

15 Pz
22.3

27.3

Tripoli

La Spezia

Pistoia
104

MARETH LINE

Mareth

Mareth

19/22.3

MAREATA HILLS.

7. Tank Div.
4th Indian Div. 26.3.

British Army Corps

MEDENIN

BRITISH 8th ARMY

1st British Tank Div. Long Range Desert Group

French Troops (General Leclerc)

British Army Corps

German-Italian positions.
⟶ movements.
Allied positions.
⟶ movements.

stress only the decisive factor, namely that under the weight of concentrated air and sea attacks on ports and airfields our supply lines and accordingly whole resistance would break down within a few days. The enemy had complete liberty of choice whether to attack—which had the rosiest prospects of success— or to be content with an investment that would allow him time to prepare, or even to start, an invasion of Italy or Greece with his main forces.

That the Allies failed to seize their chance, and that our own subsequent enforced retirements were carried through without excessive casualties is attributable only to the effect of German counter-attacks against the invasion army. Here the historian will see the justification of our operations in Tunisia even though they did not lead to the decisive victory that might have been achieved.

The Allied offensive which sealed the fate of the Axis forces in Tunisia was launched on 20 March 1943 with an assault on the Mareth Line by the British Eighth Army. Although the initial British success was transformed into a signal triumph for German arms by the counter-attack of the 15th Panzer Division, this last was too dearly bought. The flanking threat from the southwest to the Mareth Line, the turning movement from the desert round the Matmata Hills, was not promptly and resolutely countered by the army and the Luftwaffe. They could not get rid of the idea that the desert was unsuitable for large-scale troop movements such as the march of the New Zealanders from Foum Tatahouine. We also knew that divisions of the Eighth Army had moved farther west by way of Hallouf after the failure of their frontal assault on Médenine. Finally we knew that German reconnaissance units had been unable to halt the advance of the New Zealanders and that General Manerini's handful of desert battalions, good as they might be, were no match, in their ill-fortified positions between the Djebel Tabaga and the Djebel Melab, for a modern striking force.

The defence measures, which were not taken until too late owing to overconfidence in the strength of the Mareth Line, should have been decided on earlier and carried out more speedily. Also our air operations were unequal to the requirements of the hour. As the battle fluctuated in the area Maknassy-Gafsa-El Guettar very ugly crises developed which necessitated my personal intervention on the spot. At Maknassy, for instance, it was only thanks to the skill of Colonel Lang that the German-Italian army was extricated from a pocket. All in all, 21-27 March were crucial days for the interior wings, the seam of the two Axis armies. They exposed clearly the lack of energetic orders from a Corps H.Q. staff. I had asked for one often enough, but had never got it.

On 27 March the intensifying pressure of the Eighth Army against El Hamma, in front of which our hastily concentrated flak had erected a pretty tough barrier, and the increasingly worrying developments further north necessitated the abandonment of the Mareth Line and the withdrawal of the southern front to the Chott position. With the surprisingly swift collapse of this excellent dominating position on 7 April, in which the Italian divisions proved a broken reed, the end of the Tunisian campaign was in sight. Nevertheless, the retirement in good order of the German columns, hard pressed both frontally and on the right flank and hammered incessantly from the air for 120 miles, to the Enfidaville Line was evidence of their stamina and discipline.

Once this disengaging movement from the Chott position had begun our elbow room contracted sharply. The numerous operations staffs, supply services and so on were more of a hindrance than a help to further resistance. Inevitably they increased our casualties. My renewed request for a systematic comb-out of personnel—which amounted to a partial evacuation—was again refused by Hitler because he was afraid morale would suffer. So I had to be satisfied with getting out a few valuable military personalities. Flying formations and surface ships were almost entirely withdrawn to help in the preparations for the defence of Sicily. I, and my subordinates at H.Q., should certainly have made the order affecting the army more comprehensive.

The first battles for the Enfidaville Line began on 16 April 1943. Our counter-attacks on 21-22 April were so successful in holding up the enemy that Montgomery's army did not resume its assaults in this sector. After probing various sectors of the front the Allied Command shifted the decisive blow to that part of the line which had from the outset been the most critical because it covered the direct approach to Tunis. Eisenhower's divisions had been fighting since 7 April to capture the so-called Long Stop Hill, but not until the 27th did it eventually fall into the hands of the British First Army. Equal tribute must be paid to the assailants, above all to the British 78th Division. With the capture of these heights the gateway to the Tunisian plain had been smashed open; through it from 5 to 8 May four and a half divisions, shoulder to shoulder and supported by an unprecedented artillery bombardment and a rolling carpet of bombs, drove their irresistible assault. The flank of this powerful spearhead was covered by its own depth; the right wing was protected by French divisions and the left by four American divisions, which, with the experience gained in earlier if not exactly fortunate engagements, now advanced along the sea towards Bizerte.

With the capture of Tunis, following the break-through, on 9 May 1943 resistance was continued only by isolated units until, on 12 May, the last remnants laid down their arms. Up to this moment I remained in radio-telephonic communication with the German Command in Tunis from Rome. The last reports of General von Vaerst, who as army commander stood by the last gun to fire, of flak divisional commander Neuffer or of Air Marshal Koechy, who led the last Luftwaffe squadron to offer fight, were symbolic of the heroic spirit of the defenders of Tunis.

As long as the enemy armies were still fighting on separate fronts our air support, especially in the case of the 5th Panzer Army, was satisfactory. Our fighter pilots on the southern front were brilliantly successful in bringing down enemy aircraft. The Stukas and Jabos did equally good work until they could no longer stand up to the dive-bombers of the modern and superior enemy fighter arm and had to be withdrawn. The bomber formations of II Air Group, which were temporarily brought in from Italy to operate against the British Tenth Corps during its turning movement across the desert or to raid enemy airfields, were unable to redress the balance, especially as the crews, who had not been trained for desert warfare, had extraordinary difficulties with navigation and ground reconnaissance.

As the contraction of the battle area compelled the transfer of most of the flying formations from Tunis to Sicily, the number and effectiveness of our sorties decreased. In contrast, the Allies were able to operate concentrically with the heavy bombers of both their Air Commands to raid German shipping and the two receiving ports of Tunis and Bizerte, devoting all their light aircraft to almost unopposed support of their armies on the ground. This picture was constantly before my eyes when I badgered the O.K.W. for reinforcements and more supplies, and Rommel and von Arnim to make the most of their admittedly inadequate resources.

I end this chapter with a brief recapitulation:

To my mind Tunisia was the climax of a misconceived strategy. As I have already said, the main error, in my opinion, lay in a total misunderstanding of the importance of the African and Mediterranean theatre.

The second mistake was the insufficient protection of our sea transport and the gradual breakdown of our supply lines.

The third handicap seemed to me the difficulties of waging a coalition war. Too much giving way and too obvious intransigence were equally harmful. When Cavallero was succeeded as Chief of the General Staff by General Ambrosio, formerly C.-in-C. of the army, the situation became intolerable. The trustful relationship that had existed between Cavallero and myself deteriorated to the opposite extreme. I warned the Duce before the new appointment, and as my warnings remained unheeded I asked to be relieved myself. Unfortunately I yielded to the Duce's insistence and his assurance that we would "trust each other like brothers." Even then I already suspected—as is now sure—that the subsequent desertion of our ally was being discussed in the innermost circle of the government.

The fourth, and perhaps the most disastrous, error lay in our attitude towards France, whose African colonies Hitler incomprehensibly regarded, and insisted on our regarding, as taboo.

In this summary of the sources of error it is no good blinking the fact that we made strategical mistakes. These, if understandable, were partly the explanation of the relatively quick loss of Tunisia and the Allies' ability, as early as 1943, to create a new southern front in Europe with all its disadvantages to our general situation. These mistakes are all the more to be deplored since they were largely avoidable.

The *Allies* won a total victory. The final battles left the enemy with a sense of superiority which gave an extraordinary boost to his morale. The loss of Tunisia, following that of Tripolitania, was a particularly severe shock to the Italian Command and people. With the death knell of their colonial aspirations they woke up to the peril of their motherland, till then scarcely affected by the war.

Germany, as the leading Axis partner, had accepted the inevitable extension of the war to important parts of the Mediterranean with a certain lethargy and had missed the chance of exploiting her one opportunity to deal a mortal blow at England in a part of the world vital for her. The opportunity for spacious strategic planning and a comprehensive revision of political objectives had been squandered for good and all. At the end of this phase the Axis had lost the strategic initiative.

Great Britain, the classical Mediterranean power, had been able, with the aid of the Americans, to establish a jumping-off base for an assault on Europe from the south.

16

The Leap to Sicily

11-12 June 1943 Capitulation of the Italian islands Pantelleria and Lampedusa—10 July Allied landing in Sicily (with initial force of 160,000 men and 600 tanks)—12 July Loss of Siracusa and Augusta—22 July Surrender of Palermo—17 Aug. Evacuation of the last German bridgeheads near Messina, surrender of Sicily.

By the annihilation and capture of the Axis forces in North Africa the Allies had won freedom of movement in the Mediterranean. In spite of the uncomfortable narrows between Tunis and the Italian islands, Pantelleria, Sicily and Sardinia, the crossing could be regarded as sufficiently secured in view of the increasingly conspicuous inactivity of the Italian navy. The Axis air forces were a factor of diminishing importance.

The next move of the Allied forces was bound to reveal their ultimate objectives. The continuation of the war against Italy might have as its purpose her defeat and elimination, but also the conquest of a new base for offensives against the German eastern and western fronts and the central citadel of Germany itself.

Eventual landings in the south of France or in the Balkans, especially in conjunction with a reinforcement of Allied strength in the Mediterranean, might be assessed as a preliminary to operations with far-reaching strategic and political aims.

Since January 1943 I had been giving serious thought to these problems. I had formed a clear picture from information personally collected and from conferences with the Italian commanders on the islands, and had obtained from the O.K.W. and the Comando Supremo their approval for the first essential measures to meet the situation. There was good reason for urgency.

The optimism displayed by the island commanders was not proof against a sober examination of the facts. On the maps everything was in order, their plans cleverly thought out, in some respects too cleverly. But the only construction work done was mere eyewash. There were no prepared positions on the islands, which were inadequately defended and had unguarded tank obstacles more likely to hamper the defenders than to check the enemy—all so much gingerbread.

The coastal divisions I inspected were on a par with the fortifications. With such troops in these defences it was hopeless to offer resistance. There were differences: Corsica was the best, then came Sardinia; Sicily and the Calabrian coast left much to be desired. In April I turned the heat on, which, in view of General Ambrosio's hostile attitude, was only possible by tactful co-operation with subordinate departments. I made sure that the commanders of the islands were willingly carrying out my suggestions within the limits of their material and ability. The supplies that were gradually made available by the O.K.W. were inadequate despite their quantity, their distribution being determined by the expected strategic intentions of the enemy. I summed up the situation briefly as follows:

The occupation of the north coast of Africa could not be regarded as a final objective even if the annihilation of two armies justified the Allied expenditure of force in North Africa. The military defeat of the Axis forces there was a necessary preliminary to any further move and to the realization of the "Casablanca Plans," about which at that time we had no detailed information.

The conglomeration of British and American forces in the Tunisian area indicated first and foremost that the Allies intended to prosecute their operations in the western Mediterranean. Sicily lay within striking distance; the capture of the island would be an important step on the road to Italy. At the same time a diversionary assault on Calabria as complementary to the occupation of Sicily had to be reckoned with. As Pantelleria was incapable of putting up any show of resistance, its occupation had only a secondary importance. The enemy would gain more from an operation against Sardinia and Corsica if the Allied objective were the speedy capture of Rome. The effect on the Axis forces in Sicily and southern Italy of a successful assault on those islands was not to be underrated. On the other hand the Allies could not leave out of account the threat to their flank from Sicily, the extent of which it would be difficult to gauge. The possession of the islands, especially Corsica as an "aircraft-carrier," would facilitate an offensive directed against the south of France.

For an operation in the eastern Mediterranean the Allied forces in Tunis were far away. But the difficulties could be overcome. The Balkans could be reached across the Italian mainland; motorized units could be sent forward by road to Tripoli, Bengasi or Tobruch, and from there transported to the Aegean. The Allies knew that they need anticipate very little resistance on the sea. On the other hand, the combat air forces on the island of Crete, in the Peloponnesos, round Athens and the Gulf of Salonika, weak though they then were, could easily be reinforced and presented a potentially effective defence in depth to which the Allies could only with difficulty oppose an equal strength. But if the Allies were to land in the Balkans and launch an offensive against the rear of the German eastern front with the objective of joining up with the Russians, their success would not only affect the military situation; it would have political repercussions of at least equal importance.

Thus there were many alternatives for the continuance of operations. The experiences of the Allies' strategy hitherto made it easier for me to assess the probabilities.

The landing in Algiers would be considered a peacetime exercise; there had been no coastal defences to speak of. One could guess, with a probability nearing certainty, that the Allies would choose a task in the success of which they could be confident, taking into consideration their limited training, especially in amphibious operations, and their strength. They attached great importance to powerful air cover, and this could not be provided from aircraft-carriers alone. This meant the choice of an objective within easy striking distance of fighter aircraft operating from a fixed base.

These considerations ruled out the south of France, northern Italy and the Balkans (except an approach to them across the toe of Italy). Allied sea and air interests likewise pointed to Sicily, which could be successfully assaulted with the forces available and at the same time could admit a diversionary attack on South Calabria incidental to the main operation. It was not impossible that the enemy might bypass Sicily and launch his offensive in the direction of Sardinia and Corsica, enticed by the tempting bait of Rome as a long-range objective, but the imponderable difficulties made this unlikely.

The North African invasion had been virtually a peacetime exercise because it met with so little opposition. The German air attacks had to be delivered from great distances and were thus seriously handicapped. If in consequence almost no practical experience for the repulse of a sea-borne invasion had been gained, it was at least in theory possible to fix on its more obvious operational weaknesses.

While a mass movement of ships across the open sea offered promising targets to naval forces, including U-boats, and to bomber aircraft, the landing operation itself, with so many barges crowded in a narrow area, would be vulnerable to air attack and to coastal defences. The latter could be materially strengthened by mining the channels and the shore. While open coastal batteries, even if in concrete emplacements and under armour, could not stand up against a mass bombardment by naval guns, on the other hand concealed guns, well camouflaged in enfilading positions with heavies in the front line, could smash an assault and at least neutralize the Allied fighters.

In so far as it was still possible in the time and with the means available, all this had now to be considered in drawing up the plan and making preparations to defend the islands and the coasts.

In the very nick of time German construction staffs were brought over to instruct the Italians in the latest methods of static defence, followed by German construction troops and building material. From the draft-conducting battalions at that time in Italy new formations were improvised in Sicily, such as the 15th Panzer Grenadier Division (lorried infantry) and the "Hermann Goering" Panzer Division, as well as flying and flak formations, pending the arrival of the newly created full-strength divisions. At the same time an attempt was made to raise the fighting efficiency of the Italian units by feeding them with fresh supplies of arms and ammunition. Supplies were assembled in the places most likely to be unimpeded by enemy air attack, in such quantities that we could endure a temporary breakdown of communications.

At the time of the capitulation of Tunis the outlook in Sicily, as everywhere, was very black. I counted on the enemy's following up his victory, if not immediately, at least after the shortest possible breather. One extremely uncomfortable air raid on Marsala cost me the tragic loss of half my escort. Every day the enemy gave us was a day gained, however, and gradually a striking force was organized. Field-Marshal von Richthofen, the new C.-in-C. of Air Fleet 2, quickly made himself acquainted with the special problems of this theatre of war.

By the beginning of July—two months after the fall of Tunis —the islands had a defence which, though it ruled out a *coup de main*, was hardly powerful enough to withstand a large-scale planned invasion. Two German divisions were in Sicily, one reinforced German division in South Calabria and another in Sardinia, a weak German brigade in Corsica, and strong flak formations concentrated round Sicily, western Calabria and Sardinia. In Sicily these were comparatively strong and in Sardinia weaker fighter formations which could expect support from the heavy-bomber formations in Apulia, northern Italy, and in the vicinity of Rome. The main effort of the flak cover was centred at Messina.

The defence plan was thrashed out with General Guzzoni, C.-in-C. of the Italian Sixth Army, and the unit commanders on the islands at a conference in which the defence measures on the coastal fronts were fixed for all contingencies. In my final briefing of the German divisional commanders I drummed into their heads *one* point which Guzzoni and myself saw eye to eye.

"It makes no difference," I told them, "whether or not you get orders from the Italian army at Enna. You must go into immediate action against the enemy the moment you ascertain the objective of the invasion fleet."

I can still hear General Conrath of the "Hermann Goering" Panzer Division growl in reply: "If you mean to go for them, Field-Marshal, then I'm your man." I returned home feeling pretty confident.

While the army units were busy perfecting the drill, Air Fleet 2 was focusing its attention on the crowded North African ports. Von Richthofen, who was responsible to me, satisfied all my requests for reconnaissance and struggled to drive off the Allied raiders, who, from the middle of May till the middle of June, delivered each day more intensified attacks on our air bases and on the communications traffic plying across the Straits of Messina.

Unfortunately, at this very inopportune moment our leading fighter-pilot, General Osterkamp, was relieved by the German ace fighter-pilot, Inspector General Galland. There was nothing to be done about it. With Osterkamp's departure we lost the benefit of his invaluable local experience. The German air forces on the island, in so far as they were not withdrawn to Calabria and Apulia, were knocked out before the invasion even started— even on the Italian mainland they sustained considerable losses, and our fighters were too weak to redress the balance. Similarly our flak was unable to protect the airfields, harbours and railway installations—it was just not powerful enough. No flak is able by itself to cope with heavy and remorseless air attacks for very long; the dice must be loaded in favour of the attackers, especially when the fire-power of the ground defence is, anyway, inferior. The unique success of the flak defence of the straits themselves, where a very strong concentration, the employment of the longest-range artillery and a brilliant tactical direction combined most strikingly to frustrate the enemy air assaults, does not vitiate this.

The ferry service across the Straits of Messina was ably organized by Admiral Meendsen-Bohlken with naval barges, supplemented by engineer assault-boats and Siebel ferry-boats. On the other hand, our submarines were numerically inferior and handicapped by the narrowness of the area in which they could operate. I had lost all faith that the Italian navy would carry out any of the plans prepared for different eventualities. With Ambrosio in the saddle, our partnership was simply riding for a fall. There were often times when I reflected that it would be far easier to fight alone with inadequate forces than to have to accept so bewildering a responsibility for the Italian people's aversion to the war and our ally's lack of fighting qualities and dubious loyalty.

With the seizure of the islands of Lampedusa and Pantelleria (11-12 June 1943)—a particularly dismal chapter in the Italian record—our last doubts as to the objective of the invasion were removed. After one final check-up on all the preparations in Sicily I deliberately retired into the wings, since the defence of their native soil was pre-eminently the Italians' business.

Meanwhile the defence forces at our disposal were quite inadequate for even minimum demands, at least as far as could be deduced from the first amphibious landing.

The invasion fleet consisted of an assembly of large transport vessels and a covering escort. Of these the transport flotilla included merchant ships of all sizes, with landing barges on board, while the escort covered ships of every kind from battleships and aircraft-carriers to destroyers. Tankers also were among them.

The landings were made simultaneously at different points from landing craft carrying heavy weapons, including tanks, as seen from the shore appearing as a slow movement of widely and deeply distributed groups of countless small boats. Among the landing places, apparently chosen according to terrain and currents, the more practicable harbours were devoted to the unloading of heavy material and supplies. The transfer of fighter pilots to the airfields was remarkably swift.

If, despite my resolution, I interfered in the early morning hours of 10 July, the day of the invasion, by radioing an order to the "Hermann Goering" Panzer Division to go into immediate action, I did so only to repair an oversight. Once the enemy situation had been exactly ascertained all counter-attack divisions had to be in readiness to move and had to form up at midnight at the very latest in order to be able to counter-attack the enemy landing forces on the shore. Irretrievable hours were wasted, various other blunders delaying the completion of the movements; in spite of this the "Hermann Goering" Panzers very nearly scored a decisive success against the party which landed at Gela.

One disappointment followed another. The Italian coastal divisions were an utter failure, not one of their counter-attack divisions reaching the enemy in time or even at all—the "Napoli" Division in the southwest corner of the island had melted into thin air. The commandant of the fortress of Augusta meanwhile surrendered without even waiting to be attacked. Cowardice or treachery? Whether or not the court-martial promised me by Mussolini was ever held I never discovered. And all this against an overwhelmingly superior enemy of ten divisions, supported by strong airborne forces and several thousand aircraft with virtually no German air opposition.

On 11 July I realized the impossibility of remedying the confusion in the command by my telephoned directives, especially as I could scarcely get a connection with General von Senger at Italian Army H.Q. Thus on 12 July I flew to Sicily after first ordering the 1st Parachute Division to be flown over. Accompanied by von Senger, I visited all the front-line positions and the same evening watched the first masses of the parachute division land south of Catania—an operation continued in the days following as the British fighters' rigid time-table gave us repeated opportunities to risk the move.

My flight to Sicily yielded nothing but a headache. I had seen for myself the total breakdown of the Italian divisions and the tactical chaos resulting from their disregard for the agreed defence plan. The west of Sicily had no further tactical value and had to be abandoned. But even so the east of the island or an extended bridgehead round Etna could only be held for a short time. The two German divisions which were bearing the brunt of the battle alone were no longer sufficient—a third was urgently needed if the "Etna Line" were to be consolidated speedily. However, I no longer had to reckon with a landing in Calabria, a move I had been especially afraid of.

By the morning of 13 July I had already reached agreement with Hitler and Mussolini on almost every point, Hitler only making stipulations about the immediate transfer of the whole of the 29th Panzer Grenadiers—a finickiness which was to be paid for in the subsequent battles. It was not until 15 July that small elements of the division began to cross the straits.

During the night of the 15th-16th I flew to Milazzo, in North Sicily, by flying-boat, as it was now impossible for aircraft to make a landing, and gave General Hube, the commander of XIV Panzer Corps, detailed instructions on the spot. His mission was to dig in on a solid line even at the cost of initially giving ground. In defiance of the axioms of the Luftwaffe hierarchy I placed the heavy flak under Hube's command. Hube could hardly count on any air support in the daytime, so to compensate I was anxious to leave no stone unturned to accelerate the arrival of the 29th Panzer Grenadiers. I also told him that I was reckoning with the evacuation of Sicily, which it was his job to postpone as long as possible. The defence preparations on both sides of the Straits of Messina were proceeding apace and were now under his direction. I added that he need not worry about covering Calabria and Apulia, as they were unlikely at the moment to be the object of any large-scale operations.

The next day was again devoted to visiting the front and to a conference with Guzzoni, when I was able to clear up misunderstandings and get him to carry out necessary retirements—I left him with the feeling that our chances of holding the British Eighth Army were not entirely hopeless. The broadsides from the British fleet, which I then had an opportunity of seeing, made a powerful impression on me; after the battle of Salerno, on the grounds of a similar experience, I came to alter my views on coastal defence.

I was at the battle H.Q. of General Schmalz of the "Hermann Goering" Panzer Division when, to my immense relief, Colonel Heilmann, the commanding officer of the 1st Parachute Regiment, which I had privately written off, reported back. The parachutists had landed in front of the British lines without making contact with German troops on either flank. In the course of the fighting they were outflanked and encircled by Montgomery's advancing troops, but luck was with them and they were able to fight their way back. The idea of dropping airborne troops behind the British lines had been considered foolhardy when proposed, for the tactical principle that one's forces must be reasonably matched with those of the enemy holds good even for parachutists. Our landing *behind* our own front gave us an incredible fluke success when British parachutists were dropped there shortly afterwards and we were able to wipe them out; a success which, small in itself, considerably upset Montgomery's plan of attack.

On the whole I was satisfied. Hube was the right man in the right place, seconded by his excellent Chief of Staff, von Bonin. I was less pleased by the dilatoriness of the O.K.W., which retained parts of the 29th Panzer Grenadiers in Calabria and did not make the 26th Panzer Grenadier Division available, until too late, for the operations in Calabria.

Although, as in the earlier phases of the war in the Mediterranean, the official conduct of operations was in the hands of the Italians, in practice it was in those of the 14th Panzer Corps command and of C.-in-C. South. Our combined efforts to keep up appearances and preserve mutual respect had, in this phase, led to no personal discord between the partners. As for co-operation with Hube, it was absolutely ideal. The fact that I was for a long time *persona ingrata* because I took the decision to evacuate Sicily on my own initiative did not trouble me unduly in view of the successful military withdrawal from the island.

Hube got out his division in a delaying action with exceptional skill. The way he got them across the straits set the seal on his achievement as a commander.

It only remains to say that, for all its mishaps, the Axis Command was mighty lucky, helped above all as it was by the methodical procedure of the Allies. Furthermore, the Allied conception of operations offered many chances. The absence of any large-scale encirclement of the island or of a thrust up the coastline of Calabria gave us long weeks to organize the defence with really very weak resources. The slow advance of the main attack and the remarkable dissipation of their other forces over the island allowed the Axis Command to bring sufficient reinforcements into the defence areas as they were threatened. The enemy failure to exploit the last chance of hindering the German forces crossing the Straits of Messina, by continuous and strongly co-ordinated attacks from the sea and the air, was almost a greater boon to the German Command than their failure immediately to push their pursuit across the straits on 17 August. Unquestionably the troops on both sides had to face extraordinary exertions in the heat of a blistering midsummer sun in the rocky and almost treeless mountain regions, but the halt called by the Allies until 3 September, which was not absolutely dictated by the situation, was again a gift to the Axis.

The invasion of Sicily had been only slowly carried through, against a defence in depth, with the strongest possible support by naval guns and aircraft. This meant that the time had not yet come when we should have to reckon with operations far distant from sea and air bases. The Allies' strength lay rather in the vast amount of material they could squander.

The lessons learnt in Sicily led to the following conclusions: positions in depth were an indispensable complement to coastal fortifications, as, in view of the powerful effect of naval gunfire on visible coastal fortifications, a linear defence was useless. Despite the utter failure of the Italian coastal defence forces, concentrated fire against the enemy at his most vulnerable points, i.e. against unloading transport ships, approaching landing craft and men who had just disembarked, still appeared to be the best method of defence. In fighting from depth local reserves must be so strong and so close that they could *immediately* equalize their own repulses. The first main reserves must be brought forward so near to the coast that they could move up into their battle areas as far as possible in the hours of darkness.

17

Mussolini's Fall and
Italy's Defection

---

24 July 1943 Session of Fascist Council, motion of no confidence carried against Mussolini—25 July Arrest of Mussolini, Badoglio entrusted with the formation of a new government—12 Aug. Italy be-
gins secret negotiations for an armistice with the Allies—22 Aug.
Tenth Army headquarters staff set up in South Italy—3 Sept. Conclusion of a separate armistice between Italy and the Allies—3 Sept.
Landing of the British Eighth Army in South Calabria—8 Sept. Pub-
lication of the armistice by Eisenhower and the Italian government—
12 Sept. Rescue of Mussolini.

PRELIMINARIES

When on 31 January 1943 the *Maresciallo d'Italia,* Count
Cavallero, was dismissed it was natural I should ask Mussolini
to be relieved of my command. Cavallero and I were more than
comrades in arms and I believe he shared my sentiments. I stood
up for Cavallero and warned Mussolini against Ambrosio, whom
I had repeatedly heard unfavourably criticized by Italian officers
and who had not, in my opinion, the comprehensive ability to
hold a combined command. Mussolini begged me to reconsider
my request, gave me renewed assurances of his "brotherly confidence" and of his desire for a closer personal collaboration for
the future. Against my better judgment, I regret to say, I let
myself be persuaded.

Immediately I was aware of an atmospheric change in the
Comando Supremo. I refused Ambrosio's offer of the command
of all the Axis forces in Tunisia, guessing his motive to get rid

of me as a disagreeable and authoritative German commander and observer, and to remove my influence from Rome. The arrangement that no orders could be issued unless endorsed by me remained, which was the easier to carry out in practice as most of them were directly drawn up by my staff or my liaison staff. In spite of Ambrosio's sometimes intolerable high-handedness I remained loyal to him, only varying customary methods of procedure by ceasing to attend conferences in person and letting my Chief of Staff represent me. Interviews with Mussolini I restricted to occasional very urgent matters. If I had thought at the beginning that Ambrosio's conspicuous hostility to me was inspired by rivalry, many incidents soon made it clear that he was paving the way for a change of system and possibly much more. As Admiral Riccardi and General Fougier remained at their posts as heads of the navy and the air force, and as the new head of the army, General Rosi, was a gentleman and a friend, I honestly endeavoured to overcome my mistrust, relying on the absolute mutual confidence between Mussolini and myself. My original fears that by substituting Ambrosio for Cavallero Mussolini was digging his own grave were only temporarily dispelled by the cabinet changes of 8 February 1943. At that time neither I nor our Ambassador, von Mackensen, nor our Military Attaché, von Rintelen, believed in an immediate danger for the régime.[1] On 24 July even Mussolini still felt himself firmly in the saddle.

On that day I went alone to see Mussolini. As he had an important political conference he begged me to wait awhile. When I went in half an hour later his face was wreathed in smiles, and he greeted me cordially.

"Do you know Grandi?" he said. "He has just left me. We had a heart-to-heart talk, our views are identical. He is loyally devoted to me."

I understood his spontaneous delight; but when I learnt the very next day that this same Grandi had led the revolt against

[1] An eloquent example of Hitler's double-track methods of organization: it was not until after the war that I learnt that Himmler's agents were working in the intelligence service in Rome. Their information was not reported to me or to the Ambassador, but to Himmler and Hitler.

Mussolini in the Fascist Grand Council I had to ask myself which was the more astonishing: Mussolini's credulity or Grandi's wiliness. The day before, 24 July, von Mackensen had told me that he had positive information that there was no danger, and that Mussolini was still master of the situation.

The period between the change of cabinet and the fall of Mussolini was fully occupied with military and political Axis conferences at highest level, which, in view of the changing war situation, took a very varied form. The slightest incident was a flash of lightning, more suggestive than revealing.

Let me now briefly recapitulate the historical events. First and foremost, there was the battle for the reinforcement of the German troops in Italy, urged by Roatta, Commander-in-Chief of the army, but which Mussolini and Ambrosio wished to limit for incomprehensible reasons; the constant bickering about the disposition of the German and Italian formations; and Italy's startlingly exaggerated call for arms from 21 June. They wanted seventeen Panzer battalions, thirty-three batteries of artillery, eighteen anti-tank or assault-gun battalions and two thousand aircraft. This demand, which implied a complete change of course, I opposed at a conference organized by Bastianini, Under-Secretary of the Italian Ministry for Foreign Affairs. Although several Italians supported my view, Ambrosio flatly refused to revise his figures. Here was food for thought. The impossibility of fulfilling these demands also disturbed the O.K.W. and led to their refusal of the middle of July 1943.

Hitler's meeting with Mussolini at Feltre on 19 July did not solve the problem. Hitler did not assert his far-reaching claims to German leadership and Mussolini concealed his doubts on the advisability of continuing the war.

Keitel's and Ambrosio's military talks led to an agreement that German and Italian divisions should be moved to the toe of Italy, but neither of them wanted to take the first step.

At the front, meanwhile, relations between the German and Italian commanders were excellent. The Italian officers of all three services on my staff returned our friendliness, with the solitary exception of my Italian adjutant, who was something of a disappointment. He had been with me for years and I had always treated him with complete frankness. Though I took some trouble to get him another appointment, I sensed a change in his attitude towards me and the Axis alliance.

MY FIRST STEPS AFTER MUSSOLINI'S ARREST

The session of the Fascist Grand Council and the events following it showed our assumptions had been quite wrong. At it Mussolini had been deposed, and with him the Fascist régime. Just as Hitler in 1945 was cut to the quick by the revolt of his party friends, so the Duce was literally paralyzed by the desertion of his most trusted adherents. Even if his fall, or at any rate his arrest, could have been prevented if he had rallied round him the military units still loyal to him, including the Germans, his sublime self-confidence proved his own worst enemy.

When the news reached me on 25 July that Mussolini was under arrest—it was late in the evening—I at once asked for an audience with the King. After much shilly-shallying I was told that His Majesty was unable to receive me that night, but I was promised an audience for the day after. Before going to see the King I had an interview with Badoglio, who in answer to my questions merely informed me of what I already knew from the royal proclamation.

The gist of what he said was that the new government would fully respect its obligations under the treaty of alliance; that the Duce was being held in protective custody for his own safety. Badoglio then showed me a letter from Mussolini recognizing the change of régime, but he could not tell me where Mussolini was detained—only the King knew that. He begged me not to put any political difficulties in his way, which prompted me to point out that I was personally responsible to Mussolini and therefore had a justifiable interest in his whereabouts, quite apart from the fact that Hitler had an even deeper concern for his friend.

My impression of the interview was chilly, reticent and insincere.

I was later to see Colonel Count Montezemolo, who was acting as Badoglio's adjutant, turn up as head of the guerilla war against Germany.

My audience at the palace lasted almost an hour and was conducted with striking affability. His Majesty assured me that there would be no change as to the prosecution of the war; on the contrary, it would be intensified. He told me that he had had to dismiss Mussolini because the Grand Council had insisted and Mussolini had lost the goodwill of public opinion. He said he had made the decision with great reluctance. He did not know where Mussolini was, but assured me he felt personally responsible for his well-being and proper treatment. Only Badoglio knew where the Duce was! He said that he greatly admired the Führer and envied him his overriding authority, which was out of all proportion to his own.

My impression was that a mask of exaggerated friendliness concealed the reserve and insincerity of this interview, too.

HITLER'S FIRST REACTIONS

Mussolini's downfall and arrest poisoned the relations of the highest German and Italian state departments. Hitler saw in this sudden turn of events no ordinary government crisis but a complete reversal of Italy's policy with the object of ending the war as quickly as possible on favourable terms, even if it meant sacrificing her ally. His mistrust, which hitherto had been directed only against the royal family and its adherents, now vented itself in full fury against all Italian statesmen and military leaders. Past reverses in the field now appeared as deliberate sabotage, even treachery on the part of the High Command. The positions which the Italians had recently constructed or completed in the Alps were put down as preparations for turning the German front. Feeling himself betrayed, he was resolved to defend himself.

The first step, in Hitler's opinion, was to "mop up" the royal family and Badoglio—there would be no particular difficulty in clearing them out. Happily, he discarded this idea conceived in the first paroxysm of excitement.

An alternative plan, to forestall an eventual desertion at the first visible sign by securing the persons of the royal family and the leading politicians and commanders, was carefully worked out, but was not communicated to me.

Luckily there was no occasion to put this plan into operation either. It was subordinated to Hitler's wish to rescue Mussolini so that they could reshape a common policy together, a feeling of solidarity which prompted him to order its execution by any means available—in effect by S.S. Major Skorzeny working under General Student. Even though this harebrained scheme was kept secret from me, naturally I could not fail to get wind of it as all the threads ran together through my hands.

Among other measures contemplated it was only to be expected that Badoglio's proposal of a conference with Hitler would be rejected because the latter foresaw nothing would come of it. I had to agree with this view, but my concurrence did not prevent the differences between me and Hitler and his yes-men becoming even more acute. I was written down as an "Italophile" and consequently suitable for employment in Italy only for as long as my presence there could help maintain friendly relations with the royal house. For when the time should come to grasp the nettle and talk a different language the man had been chosen, namely Rommel, whose Army Group was already standing to in my rear with headquarters in Munich. My collaborators in Italy had likewise forfeited Hitler's trust—first and foremost our Ambassador, von Mackensen, with von Rintelen; next von Pohl, von Richthofen and Mackensen's successor, Rahn. We all accepted the King's word and the official assurances of the responsible statesman, Badoglio. We saw in the unaltered comradely behaviour of the soldiers at the front a guarantee that the King would keep his word even if the attitude of Ambrosio and the new Commanders-in-Chief gave rise to certain misgivings.

Roatta's struggles for military requirements, if dexterous, as far as I could see were above board. I liked working with him because he was the only person who now and then assumed responsibility for something. Even today I am not at all clear in my mind whether the general condemnation of Roatta as an enemy and a traitor was justified.

Admiral de Courten was ostensibly the most accommodating but turned out the biggest disappointment of the lot.

The new Secretary of State for Air, General Sandalli, had previously made quite remarkable admissions to von Richthofen. The few talks I had with him were most unsatisfactory.

Still—with the exception of Ambrosio—I had no reason for a positive general mistrust, a point on which von Rintelen agreed with me. But my continual efforts to dispel Hitler's indiscriminate revulsion only infuriated him. He once said of me in a long-suffering way, "That fellow Kesselring is too honest for those born traitors down there."

The turning-point came on 23 August at three in the morning when Hitler told me in Goering's presence that he had received infallible proof of Italy's treachery. He begged me to stop being the dupe of the Italians and to prepare myself for serious developments. This disclosure tied my hands. I could not disbelieve it, much though I regretted that the source of the information was not given me, and from this moment on all my endeavours were burdened by this political incubus.

Hitler's distrust of me personally, even if somewhat modified, still persisted. So I was as much surprised as the Italian government by the landing of Ramcke's 2nd Parachute Division on my airfield at Rome. I had long been begging for more troops and this addition was a godsend from every point of view, but I could have wished a less irregular procedure. The sudden appearance of the division in the Rome area, though it caused some resentment, obviously strengthened our hand, for from this moment the Italian government could not fail to realize that we had seen through their double-dealing.

When, shortly afterwards, German divisions and staffs began pouring into northern Italy the Italians' gloom deepened. Hitler's reason for this step was plain to every soldier—we had to anticipate the worst on the assumption that Badoglio designed to man the northern frontier fortifications against us and to block the railways to Germany, with the starvation of the German divisions defending Italy and their being handed over to the enemy as the sequel. Whoever controlled the Brenner and the roads and railways running eastwards into Austria and the Balkans and westwards into France had a stranglehold on Germany. The sinister behaviour of the Italians was thus responsible for Hitler's moving Army Group B into northern Italy, however much it might upset them. Even though on the whole the German troops and their officers were considerate of the Italians' feelings, there were blunders with repercussions affecting my prestige on the other side of the Alps. Von Rintelen had an unenviable task. At any rate it was now no longer possible for Badoglio to carry out his devilish ideas—for I cannot otherwise qualify such repayment for our loyalty and sacrifice of blood. In retrospect, I think this really was his intention, revealed more clearly by the increasingly peremptory demand that the German divisions in central and northern Italy should be moved to Calabria and Apulia. At this time the Italians were already negotiating with the Allies for a surrender.

The Italian government and the Comando Supremo, anyway, protested verbally and in writing against this "intolerable violation" of their sovereignty and on their side took military precautions.

Our measures included the reinforcement of the combat forces in the neighbourhood of Rome; these were gradually increased to more than five divisions, with the addition of Panzer units which, despite the exigencies of war, had hitherto been held timidly in reserve.

On 6 August Ribbentrop and Keitel met Ambrosio and Field-Marshal Guariglia at Tarvis, but these talks led to no tangible result. This came as no surprise as the antagonism had already become too pronounced. Both generals wanted concessions which would hardly have been argued under normal circumstances, Keitel wanting the Italians to send into action their divisions retained in central and northern Italy, and Ambrosio insisting that all the German divisions which had been moved into

Lombardy be placed under Italian command, which should also take over the guarding of the railways. Disagreement on these points prejudiced the discussion of other questions.

The second conference on 15 August, this time with General Jodl, was suggested by Roatta. From the outset a palpable tension brooded over the proceedings. Jodl—who was accompanied by Rommel, whom he introduced as the Commander-in-Chief of Army Group B, now in Italy—had been given clear-cut directives by Hitler. Jodl wanted C.-in-C. South, with all German forces in central and southern Italy, to be placed under the King, while all German and Italian forces in northern Italy should be under the command of Army Group B, which would continue to be subordinate to the O.K.W. Roatta repeated Ambrosio's proposal that all German divisions in the north of Italy should be put under Italian command, and also suggested the recall of the Italian Fourth Army from the south of France. The latter suggestion was agreed to, as the presence of these divisions in northern Italy was now offset by Army Group B, which controlled all key positions. On all other questions they failed to reach agreement. In fact after the fall of Mussolini C.-in-C. South became subordinate *only* to the King. In formulating his demands Jodl must have had some ulterior object in view. I was convinced at the time that he made demands which he knew it was impossible for the Italians to accept in order to force them to show their hand.

Despite this estrangement at top level, as C.-in-C. South I continued to carry on my business with the Italian departments with friendly impartiality. Even a conference with Ambrosio in the Comando Supremo on 21 August, to which the Commanders-in-Chief of all three services were invited, was outwardly correct. I was accompanied by my Chief, General Westphal, who had joined my staff at the beginning with an operation group and was later to become my sole Chief of General Staff. After a discussion of future plans Ambrosio asked for the transfer of one more German division to Sardinia. This I refused for purely military reasons. Even then I did not know that Ambrosio—as was proved—was aware that negotiations for sur-

render had already started. His request was so little determined
by the situation that I had to assume an ulterior motive.

Hitler's revelation of proved treachery on 23 August therefore was not so much of a bombshell. Ambrosio's object could
only have been to help the Allies by weakening the German
forces in central and southern Italy. I am very sure he would
have liked to get rid of the 2nd Parachute Division to smooth
the way for an Allied airborne landing in Rome so that he could
join hands with them and stab us fatally in the back from the
Campagnia.

MY EFFORTS TO CONSOLIDATE THE SITUATION

The gradual exacerbation of our relations had early prompted
me to consider what steps I should take if Italy surrendered. My
chief endeavour was to keep a firm leash on the Italian troops
and so on the Italian Command. This necessity outweighed the
risk of creating a new enemy if Italy dropped out—it was only
to be expected that as the war went on the Italians would try
to make things easier for themselves by ratting to the other side.

First and foremost, I attempted to reconcile our view of the
future conduct of the war with those of the Esercito, Supermarina and Superaereo by personal conversations or through my
staff. The Italian liaison officers unreservedly assisted me. But
the fact that, shortly before the surrender, the Italians agreed to
the movement of Italian troops to Calabria and Apulia made me
think. Was Jodl right after all in his judgment of Roatta? Was
not this merely a blind? Of course it is possible, though not
exactly probable, that Roatta, unaware of the current negotiations, only belatedly received Ambrosio's and Badoglio's sanction.

During these weeks I also made a personal contact with the
subordinate commanders in southern Italy and on Sardinia and
Corsica, whom I found both helpful and understanding, as well
as enjoying the confidence of their German brothers-in-arms.

During this period I had very little personal contact with the
active admirals. The Supermarina had been fully occupied with
operations in the Sicilian naval ports, yet had meanwhile under-

taken certain panic measures to put Taranto and Brindisi in a state of defence in case there were an Allied landing in Calabria. It had, besides, the leisure intensively to prepare for a major naval operation against the landing higher up the peninsula which had now become inevitable. Conferences about the action the fleet should take went on uninterruptedly between C.-in-C. South and the Supermarina. On the very day of the surrender I was to have had a discussion with Admiral de Courten—the navy was at long last to go into action against the invasion fleet off Naples—namely with the very man under whose flag the Italian navy put to sea from La Spezia to surrender to the enemy.

Von Richthofen and his staff dealt with the Italian air force. Though it had little more to offer, its ground organization was generously placed at our disposal, while Italian bomber crews and fighter pilots were retrained on German aircraft under German instructors and were practised in German tactics.

OPERATION AXIS

Unfortunately away from the front the picture was very different. Here there was justified suspicion that Italy intended to break her treaty of alliance and the O.K.W. had accordingly issued the order for measures to safeguard the German forces in Italy. These were referred to under the code word "Axis."

As the how, where and when of the Italians' laying down of their arms remained unknown factors, the basis for countermeasures was very modest. Since the most important thing was to be ready for every possibility, in the matter of tactics I issued no written orders, for example for steps to be taken in Rome, but only discussed my intentions with the competent officers.

My guiding principles were:

To evacuate the endangered fronts, including isolated island garrisons. All stores were as far as possible to be hidden and a bargain made with the Italian commanders to enable us to get away. Where difficulties were anticipated the measures in hand should be eased by the inconspicuous withdrawal of units and the removal of material.

On the islands and on the Calabrian front retirements were to be carried out without fighting, but where Italian units offered resistance the railways were to be cleared by every available means.

Liaison officers attached to Italian staffs were to keep a close watch over their activities.

Self-protection must be assisted by the evacuation of towns, and where this was not practicable German administrative centres must be assembled in defensible buildings.

The Air Command's rôle in *Axis* was to lay hands at once on all serviceable aircraft and anti-aircraft guns, the navy's to prevent the Italian fleet putting to sea with a view to using it later for German purposes.

The occupation of all important military signal stations was the final step in hampering if not entirely immobilizing the Italian Command.

The local defence units (army and flak) attached to my and Air Fleet 2's general headquarters at Frascati—the army units were in the Alban Hills—were strengthened and air-raid shelters enlarged.

This period before Italy's defection was for my commanders and me one of exceptional nervous strain. To me as a soldier this duplicity forced upon me by our allies and by Hitler was intolerable. I could not reconcile the apparently reasonable chance of our allies' playing us false with my implicit trust in my Italian associates, and my belief in the King's and Badoglio's word. This worry, on top of my far from pleasant exchanges with the Führer's headquarters, together with the burden of military work, the spread of the air war to the whole of Italy and the gloomy prospects ahead gradually frayed my nerves. Yet on the day of the surrender—which brought with it a bombing raid on my general headquarters, the Allied invasion in the Bay of Salerno and the flight of the royal family and the Government from Rome—I was glad to say I had done everything in my power both to prevent the Italians from taking this step and to safeguard the German cause from avoidable injury.

THE DAY OF THE SURRENDER—8 SEPTEMBER 1943

There was no indication on the morning of 8 September that the day would be fateful for the Mediterranean theatre. When the flak batteries opened up on the Allied bomber formation flying in over Frascati I was holding a conference to discuss defence measures. The first bombs fell close to my glass veranda just as I was leaving my office, while later raids made many hits not far from my air-raid shelter. The enemy attack caused less damage to the military staffs than to the town and its inhabitants. I immediately warned all troops to lend a hand. The raid was very illuminating because we found on a map in one of the bombers shot down the house in which I and von Richthofen had our headquarters exactly marked, indicating some excellent lackey work on the part of the Italians. It put my headquarters out of action for only a very short time, however, to the credit of the signals organization. Evidently the King and Badoglio had permitted this attack, although I could not and would not have raised any objection had I been asked to remove my headquarters to a less populated place. When I left my shelter a few minutes after the raid A.R.P. units and the fire brigade from Rome were already at the entrance to the town—certain evidence of foreknowledge of the attack.

I had to reckon with a landing on the night of 8-9 September and assume open co-operation between the Italians and the Allies.

But even after the morning's air raid there was no change in the behaviour of the Italian Command. I instructed my Chief of Staff and General Toussaint, Rintelen's successor, to attend a scheduled conference with Roatta at Monterotondo. I also spoke again with all commanders at the front, ordering them to stand by, and authorized the removal of naval headquarters from Rome to the Frascati area. In the late afternoon Jodl rang up to ask if the radio announcement of Italy's surrender was correct. As I had heard nothing about it I arranged for a later call. My enquiries were met with the astounding statement that the radio news had been a deliberate red herring and that the war would be continued. I thereupon categorically demanded an immediate official denial of this very dangerous falsehood, which was, however, never made, as in the meantime the Italian government was forced to make public admission of the truth. I got the first news of this again from Jodl, who informed me of a wireless message from Badoglio just received at the Führer's G.H.Q. I passed the information to Toussaint and Westphal, who made energetic enquiries and were told by Roatta that the whole thing was an inspired hoax.

The generals continuing their deliberations, it was late in the evening when Westphal reported back to me. He had already feared that he and Toussaint were being detained at Monterotondo. Between 8:00 and 9:00 P.M. Roatta rang up and solemnly assured me that the news had taken him by surprise and that he had not tried to hoodwink me, yet I am positive Badoglio and Ambrosio wanted to keep me in the dark so as to prevent me from taking immediate counter-measures. When the situation was clarified it was too late for me to act; the royal family and the Government had fled.

Although I was still able to speak to Jodl and my commanders at the front, the O.K.W. had to abandon us to our fate; C.-in-C. South was written off at the Führer's G.H.Q. After transmitting the code signal "Axis" I briefly told my commanders what I was specially concerned about for the next few days. As our air reconnaissance had reported late in the evening that the invasion fleet was still in the sea area off Naples, we might regard the gravest danger as exorcised, but its approach increased the responsibility of the Tenth Army in southern Italy, and incidentally my own, as I could expect no help from Army Group B. Meanwhile reports from Rome reaching me that night made things more critical than they really were—the diplomatic corps and all German nationals were being sent to Germany in the charge of our Ambassador.

THE LAST OF CAVALLERO

No sooner had the forces in and around Rome under General Carboni laid down their arms than I ordered the release of all the imprisoned Fascist leaders, including Count Cavallero. With one or two other Italians Cavallero was my guest. They all arrived in a state which passed my comprehension—I am wiser today now that I am an ex-prisoner myself. Cavallero fell on me and kissed me, a form of greeting new to me.

In consideration for their state of mind I merely pointed out that for their own safety it would be necessary to send them temporarily to Germany. They would travel by air in the course of the next few days. Cavallero was very distressed about his wife, who was seriously ill and in hospital. He begged me to allow him to visit her the next day—a request which I, of course, willingly granted. He spent several hours at his wife's bedside and overwhelmed me with his thanks. At supper on the second day I gave him to understand that I would take his wife under my personal protection and would see to it that their letters were forwarded while he was in Germany, where it was to be hoped he would not have to stay long. I also hinted that Hitler held him in specially high esteem and that Mussolini would certainly put him forward as Minister of War in his new cabinet.

During the meal Cavallero was exceptionally grave; I attributed this to the excitement of recent weeks and the parting from his wife. He said good night early and was escorted to his quarters by one of my officers. Early next morning I was startled by the news that he had been found sitting in the garden, dead, his gaze fixed on the Eternal City. I instantly ordered a medical and judicial examination, the verdict of which was conclusive: he had taken his life. A questioning of his Italian friends, among other things, brought to light that he had spent much of the night pacing up and down in his room and had gone out into the garden early.

As for the reasons, as far as I could discover Cavallero had been implicated in a plot against Mussolini, of which the latter might have known. The journey to Germany and Hitler's plan to form a new Italian government in exile must bring him again into contact with the Duce, which was more than he could face. In his desperate mood he saw no other way out. It was a pity that he did not lay bare his heart to me.

I have recounted this tragic episode because I heard it said in Venice before my trial, and also read allusions to the same effect in the newspapers, that Cavallero was shot by me or by my orders. I repeat here in about the same words what I said before the tribunal in Venice:

"I esteemed Count Cavallero and gave him my unqualified support because I had come to know him as a convinced friend of the Axis who perceived the greatest good in the furtherance of our common interests, to which—in the face of all opposition —he unreservedly devoted his life. With gifts far above the average, an able soldier of great distinction, he was a man who combined a high degree of energy with shrewd diplomatic skill and, in my opinion, was at that time the only man who could have reconciled the Italian war effort with the war economy. I say this deliberately in full cognizance of his inherent weaknesses and of the strong feeling against him among a part of the officer corps of the Italian army."

KING VICTOR EMMANUEL, MUSSOLINI AND HITLER

Mussolini was, of course, an absolute dictator, but he knew how to fulfil his duties to the royal house. Ultimately, however, it became startlingly clear how little inner harmony there must have been between these two during the long years they worked together. This is all the more striking because Mussolini's ambitions for an extension of power coincided with those of the King. Each may well have been false in his dealings with the other, thus paving the way for their common downfall.

Socialist journalism was Mussolini's school for politics, and he remained a politician to the end. He made himself master of diplomatic formulas and knew just where they could be useful, employing them first and foremost for the expansion of himself and his people. He was clever in applying for his own political aims the clamour for the strengthening and modernization of the army, navy and air force which he had himself instigated as minister for all three services. His military training was, however, insufficient for him to recognize the facts, the hollow kernel within the glittering display. Outwardly and ideologically the friend of Hitler, he yet envied him his military power and success, which was not the least reason why Mussolini let himself in for military adventures which brought his career to a tragic end.

At the time I came into closer contact with Mussolini he was past his prime, both in health and power. His absolute confidence in his followers was waning, he no longer had the physical energy to act with resolution and his decisions were increasingly prompted by his advisers, until after his reinstatement with sadly diminished powers on the shore of Lake Garda he surrendered more and more to the lethargy of philosophic speculation. He was now no longer a dictator, only a man who through the vagaries of life had glimpsed the mountaintops and for this reason alone should have been spared the brutal, revolting end which came to him.

The hour of Hitler's birth as leader of the German people was in World War I and in its troubled aftermath. From 1921 till 1945 he felt himself, above all, a soldier and still in the flower of his political vigour. That was why his political organizations were given uniforms, why he created a Wehrmacht both outwardly impressive and intrinsically effective. Supported by his excellent propaganda he really did become the idol of the masses. Small wonder that he gradually came to believe that he was unique and irreplaceable, that his destiny was to devote himself to Germany's greatness and her security for all time to come. This mission had to be completed in the years vouchsafed him, for he never believed he would have a long life. Yet the same man who in his early years allowed his paladins and liege men a really magnificent scope became literally transformed as the war dragged on. Because he believed his advisers were no longer serving him as he wished, and later that most of them had ceased to understand him, he felt himself deserted and betrayed. It is psychologically interesting that he whose superiority was unquestionable in many fields had inferiority complexes which resented any free expression of opinion and drove him to persecute any suspected or real opponent. By concentrating every responsibility on himself he undertook too much, and this overstrain led to his famous temperamental outbursts and snap decisions with their frequently horrible, inhuman consequences.

So fundamentally different for all their essential similarity, Mussolini and Hitler were the victims of their will to power and their own uncontrolled dictatorship. It would not have been enough, as Hitler intended, to place a senate above the Führer as a supervisory organ—*principiis obsta!* Such elementary forces need *from the first* a control which even the great ones of this world should create for their own and for their people's good. In whatever guise a dictatorship appears it is short-lived and crumbles of itself if it is answerable to no outer or inner laws.

18

The Battle of Salerno and the Struggle to Build Up a Defence Front South of Rome

9 Sept. 1943 Landing of the American Fifth Army under General Clark at Salerno—9-16 Sept. Battle of Salerno—From 9 Sept. Disarmament of the Italian formations in the German zone—10 Sept. Occupation of Rome—16 Sept. Discontinuation of the German counter-attack at Salerno—20 Sept. German units complete evacuation of Sardinia—27 Sept. The Allies capture the important air base at Foggia—30 Sept. German troops evacuate Naples—5 Oct. German troops complete evacuation of Corsica—October Battles for the Volturno Line, the Mignano Pass and on the Adriatic.

With the desertion of Italy Germany's purely military interests became paramount. In the first reaction they were all that mattered. The vacuum in the defence area was gradually filled by bringing up the 76th Panzer Corps and the Tenth Army, the latter created mainly by General von Vietinghoff's Army Group out of its own effectives.[1]

[1] I. Strength and distribution of German forces on 8 Sept. 1943

(A) C.-in-C. South (Field-Marshal Kesselring)

1. Tenth Army with: 14th Panzer Corps with 16th Panzer Division, partly in action, in reserve or taking over from the Italians, and the "Hermann Goering" Parachute Panzer Division resting and in action.
   76 Panzer Corps, engaged with the British Eighth Army in Calabria, with the 29th Panzer Grenadier Division (from Sicily and in need of rest), the 26th Panzer Division and the 1st Parachute Division in Apulia; one-third in reserve in the rear of the Salerno front.
2. The 11th Flak Corps in the Rome area with the 3rd Panzer Grenadier

The invasion of Sicily and its occupation had shown the objective of Allied operations in the Mediterranean—it was almost certain that the offensive would be continued against Italy herself. Her elimination from the Axis partnership presented the Allies with unsuspected opportunities: to intensify the air war on Germany, to strike against the southern base of the German-Russian front and against France. As C.-in-C. South I had to be ready for all these possibilities.

For a brief while when—incomprehensibly as it seemed—the Straits of Messina were not immediately forced, I was assailed by doubts. Did the enemy mean to use Sicily with its spacious harbours as a jumping-off base for some far-reaching operation in the Balkans? I did not take to this idea because for this the possession of sea and air bases in Apulia was indispensable. An invasion of central Italy north of Rome or from the Adriatic I ruled out after weighing the pros and cons; there were extraordinary difficulties inherent in either operation which the Allies had not sufficient strength in the Mediterranean at that time to overcome. A landing operation in Apulia must be accompanied by an offensive through Calabria to gain possession of the Abruzzi mountain passes. In any case an attack on southern Italy

---

Division (Lake Bolsena, Leghorn and south) and the 2nd Parachute Division south of Rome.
3. 90th Panzer Grenadier Division with Fortification Brigade on Sardinia.
4. S.S. "Reichsführer" Brigade on Corsica.
5. Air Fleet 2 with strong air and flak forces on the Italian peninsula, in Sardinia and Corsica.
6. Naval Command Italy with light surface forces in the Tyrrhenian Sea.

(B) Army Group B. (Field-Marshal Rommel)

1. 87th Army Corps with 76th Infantry Division, 94th Infantry Division, 305th Infantry Division and 24th Panzer Division.
2. 51st Mountain Corps with S.S. "Adolf Hitler" Panzer Division, 65th Infantry Division, 44th Infantry Division (Hoch- and Deutschmeister) and Doehla Mountain Brigade.
3. Witthöft Corps with 71st Infantry Division and smaller units.
II. The German land combat forces in southern Italy, including Rome, eight divisions strong, were opposed by the Allies' ten divisions and several brigades and groups, two airborne divisions, and five Italian divisions—in all seventeen divisions. There were eight and a half German divisions in northern Italy which took no part in the decisive battles. Two of them would have sufficed to repel the Allied landing at Salerno.

—whether as a main or secondary offensive—had to be reckoned with until the enemy's distribution, especially of their naval forces, should disclose a different intention.

Rome itself with its political and strategical importance loomed largest in all these considerations—if it could be reached only slowly over land it could be reached much more quickly by invasion from the Tyrrhenian Sea. The most obvious, indeed uniquely suitable, place to land, not counting an airborne landing in the vicinity of the city itself, was the Bay of Salerno.

On 3-4 September the Allies played their first card. Montgomery's army crossed the Straits of Messina and launched an attack over the mountains of Calabria. His advance, however, was slow. Apart from a landing at Pizzo at five in the morning on 8 September, the British, much to our relief, attempted no large-scale landings which might have seriously endangered the 29th Panzer Grenadiers and the 26th Panzers as they moved northwards towards Salerno and have impaired our defence organization there. A large part of the invasion fleet stood ready in the Tyrrhenian Sea from 8 September, the day on which strong Allied bomber formations had staged a midday raid on my headquarters at Frascati.

The principal question now was: where would the enemy land? The fact that the invasion fleet was making the crossing in the latitude of Naples did not necessarily mean that this was their objective. Equally on the cards were Rome and the Campagnia, where there were five good Italian divisions to support the landing troops and the terrain was eminently suitable for an airborne descent.

If the landing were made in the Naples area I saw no necessity to evacuate central Italy. Though the situation would then be serious it could still be controlled, especially if the O.K.W. acceded to my various requests that one or two of Rommel's Army Group divisions lying idle in the north should be sent to reinforce us in the south, and if they arrived in time. There might be some trouble with the Italian troops, but I could rely on General von Vietinghoff, who did in fact succeed in establishing amicable relations with the general commanding the

Seventh Italian Army in Calabria. I also believed that the German commanders on Sardinia and Corsica would reach agreement with the Italians there, or if the worst came to the worst would fight their way out.

All in all, the situation into which I had been manœuvred was anything but pretty. It still defeats me why Hitler chose to write off eight first-class German divisions (six in the south of Italy and two near Rome) and an overstrength flak arm instead of sending me one or two of the divisions already assembled in the north. I had explained to the O.K.W. often enough what the possession of the Apulian air bases meant in the battle for Germany, and how on no account must the plains there be gratuitously abandoned to the enemy. But as it was, even the obvious step of letting Rommel's North Italian divisions make contact with mine near or north of Rome was never taken. Rommel's idea that we should evacuate the whole of southern and central Italy and defend only the north had apparently taken such firm root in Hitler's mind that he turned a deaf ear to even the most self-evident tactical demands. But if Hitler had got his teeth into this idea the least that could have been done would have been to pull out the German divisions, Luftwaffe and naval units in South Italy in good time.

It was late in the afternoon when Jodl told me that the Italians had cut the painter. I had not much time to think. Nor was reflection necessary, for the despatch of the signal *Axis* had already set the wheels in motion. Only the situation in Rome still required running instructions. It was a blessing that I had no longer to pull my punches with the Italians and with the cutting of communications was now rid of Hitler's interference.

The report which came in that evening that the invasion fleet was still lying off Naples relieved me of a double anxiety: there was now no reason to expect a landing on the Campagnia coast and the chance of the 29th Panzer Grenadiers and the 26th Panzers being cut off in the toe of Calabria at the neck of the isthmus had become remote. The Allies were committed to the beaches of Salerno.

This news meant that we must hasten the northward movement of the two Calabrian divisions, at the same time delaying Montgomery's progress, in which the mountainous terrain would assist us. The situation in Rome must be clarified, and the forces there released be sent south to the Tenth Army, where assault divisions must be assembled in the rear of the Salerno sector. The "Hermann Goering" Division, resting in the Caserta area, would have to be sent back into the line as quickly as possible. General Heidrich, with the bulk of the 1st Parachute Division in Apulia, would have to act on his own initiative.

Air Fleet 2 now went into action against the invasion fleet, while the flak round Rome and the Luftwaffe ground organization was ordered to stand by for enemy air raids. The fact that the Allies had missed the chance of an airborne landing had eased the tension in Rome; left to themselves the Italian divisions, although outnumbering us by three to one, were no actual danger. It was to be expected that we should not be able to square accounts with our ex-allies without some clashes. In contrast, however, to the treacherous behaviour at the top, the old spirit of comradeship as a whole still prevailed, serious clashes occurring only at Rome and in Corsica.

The first reports from Rome sounded none too good, even if they were exaggerated. The 2nd Parachute Division was rushed to the southern periphery but was halted on the railway line to avoid fighting in the city, and attacks across the line, reported to me, were instantly called off. The parachutist assault on Italian army general headquarters at Monterotondo, if more difficult than I had anticipated, turned out a complete tactical success—the operations staff, with General Roatta in the van, had simply bolted. Meanwhile the 3rd Panzer Division, on its way south from Lake Bolsena to the northern outskirts of the city, met with very little opposition.

On 9 September an old Fascist serving with one of the Italian divisions told me they would offer no further resistance and were ready to talk. The Italian order to lay down arms followed soon afterwards. General Count Calvi di Bergolo and Colonel Count Montezemolo arrived under a flag of truce, and after a brief preliminary discussion I left the completion of details in Westphal's able hands. I demanded immediate demobilization and the surrender of all arms, but agreed that all soldiers might return to their homes. A wireless message from Rommel instructed me to send all Italian soldiers to Germany as prisoners of war, though I had received no word of his appointment as my superior. I decided to pay no attention to the message and telegraphed Hitler saying that, with my back to the wall, I must insist on being spared instructions which could not be carried out.

I had to be able to act as I thought possible and right, and indeed that was the last I heard of this. Rommel, too, would have been better advised if he had demobilized the Italians in the north, instead of letting them desert *en masse* to form the nucleus of the partisan guerilla bands. This Italian duumvirate of myself and Rommel, with Hitler's almost obsequious submissiveness to Rommel, was responsible for the rejection of my priority calls for reinforcements. Unfortunately the work of disarming the Italians and storing away arms, munitions and material in safety occupied more time and men than I liked in view of the tactical developments at Salerno.

The fighting on the beaches of Salerno, despite the Allies' overwhelming air superiority, their tremendous naval gunfire and our numerical weakness, went better than I had dared hope. By a stroke of luck on 11 September the first elements of the 29th Panzer Grenadiers, coming up from Calabria, though suffering from a shortage of petrol were able to counter-attack on the left wing. They were soon followed by the bulk of the division and the 26th Panzers. On the right wing a counter-attack was delivered by the 15th Panzer Grenadiers, those parts of the "Hermann Goering" Division which were ready to move following hard on their heels. The gap in the centre was filled, if thinly, by the 16th Panzers, previously in reserve, and a regiment of the 1st Parachute Division, which was still left in the area. The counter-attack launched with high hopes by the 16th Panzers on 11 September was hung up in country broken by trenches and became a sitting target for the Allied naval guns;

the left wing, on the other hand, under the command of the 76th Panzer Corps, successfully carried their own counter-attack on 13 or 14 September—it was actually reported to me in the late afternoon that there were hopes of their being able to throw the enemy back into the sea. Vietinghoff and I were rather more sceptical, and unfortunately we were right. How easily this critical time—"a dramatic week" even according to the English —might have led to a decisive German victory if Hitler had acceded to my very modest demands.

At the end of these crucial days the situation could be regarded as essentially unchanged. The left flank of the Salerno group was protected against Montgomery's very cautious advance by the rearguard of the 76th Panzer Corps and by natural and artificial obstacles. There was no formidable threat from Apulia, the British Eighth Army's dissipation of force, which we did not make the mistake of imitating, helping us considerably.

On 10 September I had already drawn on the map our successive defence positions in the event of a retirement from southern Italy; they were more or less kept to when we later withdrew. The impression I had of the first two days was that we must be prepared for a considerable sacrifice of ground, but that it might still be possible to go over to the defensive south of Rome, perhaps on a line running through Monte Mignano (the later Reinhard Line) or on the Garigliano-Cassino Line (later the Gustav Line). If there were to be any hope of halting the enemy these positions must be consolidated and fresh construction and fighting units brought up. It was up to von Vietinghoff and his Tenth Army to gain us the time we needed.

I did not depart from this basic idea. On 12 September I had my first conference with Vietinghoff, while talks with the O.K.W. on the provision of means for consolidation went smoothly enough. Meanwhile I kept my finger on the pulse of the situation by daily flights over and visits to the front, which were not always necessarily so enjoyable, while with my constant inspections of the progress made in fortifying our rear positions I must have been a thorough nuisance to the senior engineer officer, General Bessel.

With my exact knowledge of the position at the front and of the state of our defences I was thus able to draft a strategic plan for the coming months, which was on the whole adhered to without interference from Hitler. On 16 September in order to evade the effective shelling from warships I authorized a disengagement on the coastal front with the express proviso that the Volturno Line, to which the Tenth Army intended to fall back, must not be abandoned before 15 October. Naples was evacuated on 1 October after all stores had been removed. Vietinghoff and his brilliant operations chief, Wentzell, carried out the retirement in exemplary fashion and fought a delaying action on the Volturno till 16 October. It was not until two days later that the Allies began the crossing of the river. As I had hopes of three fresh and rested divisions (the 94th, 305th and 65th Infantry Divisions) being ready at the beginning of November I ordered the Reinhard Line to be in a state of defensive preparedness by the 1st.

On 4 November advanced Allied patrols were observed there. I had full confidence in this naturally very strong position and hoped by holding it for some length of time, perhaps till the New Year, to be able to make the rear Gustav Line so strong that the British and Americans would break their teeth on it.

In the meantime Heidrich and his depleted parachutists as they fell back were bringing the pursuit of the British 13th Corps to a temporary standstill, while in the Ofanto sector on 22-23 September he managed in an equally skilful evasive action to throw off the British 78th Division which had landed at Bari. On 27 September we lost the air base at Foggia after violent fighting. The 1st Parachute Division was driven back first beyond the Fortore and later behind the Biferno, although relieved at the end of the month by the 29th Panzer Grenadiers, who closed an awkward gap in front of the Canadian Division and covered the flank of the main body of the Tenth Army engaged on its left. I can only agree with an English writer's comment, describing the British advance through these mountains—"Why use a sledge hammer to crack a nut?"

So the O.K.W.'s refusal to release a single division from northern Italy for the defence of the Apulian air bases had resulted in their loss for us, which was a terrible blow. Nevertheless the situation was otherwise stabilized. By hotly contesting every inch of ground the Tenth Army had established a weak front from the Tyrrhenian to the Adriatic. On the latter side of the peninsula the outlook was less pretty; the 13th British Corps had made a surprise landing with strong forces at Termoli on 3 October and succeeded in building up a very considerable bridgehead. I happened to be at Tenth Army headquarters when the report came in, and immediately ordered the 16th Panzers to be rushed there with the mission of throwing the invaders back into the sea.

No time had been lost in issuing the order. I was therefore very surprised when, between 10:00 and 11:00 P.M. the same day, Westphal reported that the Tenth Army commander was still shilly-shallying while I was under the illusion that the division was racing to Termoli. As I did not share the commander's qualms I ordered my instructions to be carried out in double-quick time. The division arrived belatedly on 4 October and was thrown in piecemeal—Tenth Army headquarters bungled the whole thing and lost the chance of an assured success. The only way of offsetting our great inferiority was by foresight, intensive preparation, quick decisions and a high degree of mobility. The incident was a lesson both for myself and for the troops themselves, which, however, we showed later we had taken to heart at the time of the Anzio landings.

As I have said, I had high hopes of the Reinhard position. This last stood or fell with the holding of the Mignano Pass, which in its turn could not be taken as long as Hill 1170 was in our hands. But, as so often in war, our hopes were dashed. A local failure of the Panzer Grenadiers suddenly gave the enemy possession of the massif and a counter-attack by the only parachute battalion at my disposal failed to recapture it.

Two days before this enemy offensive at the end of November I was at 65th Infantry Division headquarters with Westphal. General von Ziehlberg took us over the ground and explained his dispositions on the map. There was no fault to be found with the right wing and the adjoining part of the centre. Terrain, fortifications and troops all promised well, and once the mountain battalions had occupied the Majella Block the right flank would also be covered. The left flank, however, showed increasing weakness as it approached the Adriatic, having little depth and unfavourable artillery observation posts; on top of this it was to be defended by a green unit. On the other hand, the tactical outposts were well located along a river, with excellent artillery observation from the main position. But for how long would they be able to hold it?

It is possible the battle might have gone differently if the commanders of the division and of the left-wing regiment had not both been seriously wounded at the outset, and the 1st Parachute Division had replaced the 65th Infantry Division on the Adriatic wing, a change I considered making, but without the time to effect it. The situation was also complicated by a number of coincidences: I was not on the spot on the critical day, being at 51st Mountain Corps headquarters in the Green Line (Apennines) where I could not be reached until the evening. Then unexpectedly the 44th Infantry Division (Hoch- and Deutschmeister) were late in relieving the 26th Panzers, which should have been asssembled in the rear of the 65th Infantry Division, thus reducing the strength of our reserves. Finally the 90th Panzer Grenadiers, who had been brought back from Sardinia via Corsica and assigned to the O.K.W. reserve, were not immediately available and, anyway, were not ready for action. As invariably happens in such cases, when they at last arrived in the battle zone they were sent into action precipitately and their counter-attacks were disappointingly unsuccessful. This unlucky start was put right in the next few days by their new commander, Colonel Baade.

After particularly stiff fighting from 6 to 13 December 1943 there followed a lull on this wing.

19

Cassino, Anzio-Nettuno and Rome, Autumn 1943 till Early Summer 1944

21 Nov. 1943 Kesselring appointed C.-in-C. Southwest—22 Jan. 1944 Allied landing at Anzio-Nettuno—February Fruitless German counter-attacks at Anzio-Nettuno—January, February, March Successful German defence in the battles for Cassino—12 May Allied large-scale offensive on the Cassino front, break-through on the Garigliano and at Cassino—22 May Allied offensive from the bridgehead at Anzio-Nettuno, break-through on the left wing of the Fourteenth Army—Retirement of the German Tenth and Fourteenth Armies—4 June Allied troops enter Rome, previously declared an open city by the German Command.

THE BRIDGEHEAD AND CASSINO

If the situation was militarily simplified it was politically obscured by the flight of the royal family and the Government from Rome. Dr. Rahn and our consul, Moellhausen, brought order out of chaos, however, by speedily succeeding in forming a strong administration. The conscription of labour battalions and the provision of food was subsequently carried out by the Italian bureaucracy under German control. It was a symptom of the general war-weariness that results were satisfactory only in exceptional cases and that the workers, although well cared for, yet remained unreliable. I gradually came to the conclusion that the conduct of the war in Italy would have been easier and more effective without the intermediary of an unpopular government—this being really the only question on which there was any basic difference of opinion between the German embassy and the military.

I followed with lively interest the evacuation of our troops from Sardinia and Corsica, satisfying myself on the spot of its completion. Thanks to the skill of General Lungerhausen and the complaisance of the Italian commanders on the island we were able to evacuate Sardinia without much fighting. General von Senger-Etterlin finally succeeded in getting the whole of our forces there, nearly 40,000 men, across to Elba, Leghorn and Piombino with their arms and equipment. The struggle for Bastia and the oversea transport from there to the mainland, moreover, caused me many anxious hours.

My constant plea for a unified command in Italy, irrespective of how it might affect myself, which I finally urged in person at the Führer's G.H.Q., had been at last acceded to on 21 November, when I was appointed "C.-in-C. Southwest—Army Group C." I tried to compensate for the belatedness of this decision by redoubled efforts to make good previous omissions. Our hands were no longer tied and the fortification-in-depth programme in the rear of the Gustav Line, with Monte Cassino as its central point, as well as the construction work ordered by Rommel, was now adapted to my needs.

After a short breathing space at the turn of the year the final battles for the position immediately in front of the Gustav Line began on 3 January 1944, and ended with the capture of San Vittore (6 January), of Monte Trocchio (15 January), and of Monte Santa Croce (also on 15 January) by French troops. Our new divisions only gradually got used to the peculiar conditions of the Italian front. Failures were very largely due to the shortage of high-altitude winter clothing and equipment and the divergence of opinion about the conduct of mountain warfare, which it took me some time to iron out.

The hard fighting of recent months had convinced me that the Allies' reckless expenditure of troops must conceal some ulterior objective. For a mere pinning-down offensive the strength of the effort was in too striking a contrast to the task. I did not believe that Alexander could be satisfied for much longer with the slow and costly way the Allied front was edging forward. Sooner or later he must surely end it by a landing, which, taking into account the enemy's systematic methods, could only be expected in the region of Rome. It was clear, furthermore, that such a landing would somehow be coupled with an offensive on the southern front. For both eventualities strong German motorized reserves were necessary. I had ordered the withdrawal of four motorized divisions from the line and hoped to have them at my disposal in plenty of time.

The Allied offensive on the Garigliano front was launched on 17-18 January with superior forces by the British 10th Army Corps; on 20 January the American 2nd Army Corps joined in by attacking across the Rapido. Our 94th Infantry Division was newly created and therefore not able to hold the offensive; the enemy broke through in force at Castelforte, and the Tenth Army, having to anticipate an extension of the offensive across the Liri Valley to the Cassino massif, was unable to seal off the gap with its weak reserves. As I saw for myself, the fate of the Tenth Army's right wing hung by a slender thread. In this situation—perhaps relying too much on a report of Admiral Canaris, Chief of Military Intelligence—I yielded to the urgent requests of the Tenth Army commander and sent him up the 11th Air Group under Schlemm with the 29th and 90th Panzer Grenadiers, ordering him to restore the situation on the 94th Infantry Division's front with all speed. The question is whether that was justified, especially as I had received an intelligence report also emanating from Canaris about the number of ships lying in Naples Harbour, according to which there was ample tonnage there for an invasion fleet.

I could plainly see the enemy's operational possibilities. One thing stood out: the assault begun on 20 January on the positions north of Monte Cassino by the American 2nd Corps and the French Expeditionary Corps was directly co-ordinated with the fighting on the Garigliano and contributed to its prospects of success. The alternative possibility of a landing was merely a hunch; there was no indication of the when or where. If I let down the Tenth Army commander his right wing might be driven in and no one could tell where it would be able to halt a retreat. At the time I foresaw a development such as actually occurred in the May offensive. If this uncontrolled retirement coincided with a landing the consequences could not be vouched for. How would Rome with its million population react? I did not believe that the American Fifth Army was attacking only to screen an invasion, but thought the Allies would wait until the progress of the offensive in the south would not only work in with a landing on their part, but also make possible local co-ordination in a kind of encirclement. At all events I believed I was not far wrong in assuming that Clark or Alexander would exploit the initial success on the Garigliano to turn our Tenth Army's right flank unless our counter-measures compelled them to call off the offensive. Against such a threat half-measures were useless—the counter-blow must of necessity be swift and effective. The need was to clear up the mess at the one point so as to have the strength available to meet any fresh challenge.

Meanwhile the invasion menace hung inscrutably over us—air reconnaissance had almost entirely ceased and the meagre reports that came in were inaccurate and misleading. On the three nights preceding the landing I had ordered an emergency alert throughout the whole of Italy. If I listened to the emphatic warnings of my staff against tiring the troops by a continuous stand-to and countermanded the order for the night of 21-22 January, I had only myself to blame.

The first hours of 22 January 1944—the day of the invasion at Anzio-Nettuno—were full of anxiety. That morning I already had the feeling that the worst danger had been staved off. Besides the hesitant advance of those troops which had been landed, this was mainly due to von Pohl, who on my direct instructions surrounded the beachhead with a ring of his batteries which it would be hard for tanks to penetrate. Meanwhile battalion after battalion was brought up and placed under the orders of General Schlemmer, whose mission was to push all units as they arrived as far south as possible so as to help the flak slow down or halt the enemy advance. Every yard was important to me. This order, as I found out on the spot in the afternoon, had been incomprehensibly and arbitrarily altered, which upset my plan for immediate counter-attacks. Yet as I traversed the front I had the confident feeling that the Allies had missed a uniquely favourable chance of capturing Rome and of opening the door on the Garigliano front. I was certain that time was our ally.

What followed in those days was a higgledy-piggledy jumble —units of numerous divisions fighting confusedly side by side. In addition to the 11th Parachute Corps I ordered the staffs of the 76th Panzer Corps from the Adriatic and of the 14th Army Corps in North Italy into the bridgehead area in order to create a solid operational frame. When on 23 January von Mackensen, the Fourteenth Army commander, reported to me at my head-quarters at Monte Soratte, I was able to tell him that I regarded our defence as consolidated and that we no longer had to reckon with any major reverses. I gave him two tasks: to strengthen the defence ring and to initiate measures to narrow and remove the bridgehead. The violent attacks on Cisterna on 25 January by the American 6th Corps and again on 31 January on Cisterna and Campoleone proved my judgment correct—small local en-emy advances were bought with heavy losses. Von Mackensen was thus able, without fear of any serious crisis, to assemble, instruct and send into action the reinforcements which now continued arriving till the end of the month.

Predominating as was my anxiety over the bridgehead, the situation of the 14th Panzer Corps northeast in the Cassino area demanded equal attention. Slowly but surely the excellent troops of the French Expeditionary Corps, side by side with the Amer-ican 2nd Corps, were gaining ground towards Colle Belvedere and Terello, which fell into their hands on 31 January. Here the peril could only be averted by picked German units under proved commanders—Heidrich and Baade—and the equally fine 211th Regiment of the 71st Division. And they did it; on 6 February the crisis was passed and the fighting died down on the 12th. Of this engagement Field-Marshal Alexander has writ-ten: "This battle was a German success."

Even the later attack, from 15-19 February, in which the 4th Indian Division and the New Zealand Division attempted to capture the monastery of Cassino and Cassino itself, could not alter this, despite the preliminary weight of heavy artillery brought to bear on the former and a bombing attack which was not only quite unnecessary but prejudicial to the subsequent conduct of the battle. Once and for all I wish to establish the fact that the monastery was not occupied as part of the line; it was closed against unauthorized entry by military police. Even though its art treasures and library had long been removed to the custody of the Vatican the heavy casualties distressed the civil population, and we could well appreciate the grief of the abbot.

At the bridgehead meanwhile the struggle was still in progress, the American 6th Corps aiming to break through to the Alban Hills, and von Mackensen to get a firm preliminary grip on Apulia before launching our main counter-attack. The Allied assaults were repulsed with heavy casualties on both sides, our counter-attack leading to the occupation of Apulia on 8-9 February and to the capture of Corroceto on 9-10. Allied counter-attacks misfired. Drawing the only possible conclusion from the miscarriage of their offensive, the U.S. 6th Corps now went over to the defensive, constructing positions in depth in the bridge-head. Even if the Fourteenth Army continued to keep our defensive measures in view, its chief problem was still to attack. Fresh units and supplies were brought up to the Army Group in remarkable volume. 2nd Air Command also did all it could, with an imposing concentration of flak and an operational strength reminiscent of past glories.

I myself was convinced, even taking their powerful naval guns and overwhelming air superiority into consideration, that with the means available we must succeed in throwing the Allies back into the sea. I constantly kept in mind the psychological effect of their situation on the staff and troops of the American 6th Corps. Penned in as they were on the low-lying, notoriously unhealthy coast, it must have been damned unpleasant; our heavy artillery and the Luftwaffe with its numerous flak batteries and bombers alone saw to it that even when "resting" their soldiers had no rest. The bridgehead garrison was numerically restricted; yet to bring in too many meant unnecessarily heavy casualties, while to leave too few might mean the loss of the bridgehead. The transportation of fresh waves presented difficulties and needed time. It seemed to me of paramount importance that we should attack as quickly as possible before the enemy had time to make good their losses in the late fighting and before the intermediate positions in the bridgehead were too greatly strengthened. On the other hand there was the need to acclimatize our unseasoned forces.

Both von Mackensen and I discarded the obvious idea of trying to unhinge the bridgehead by a flanking attack along the coast to the north of Anzio, as we should have had to assemble and attack under the flanking fire of all the naval guns without being able to make fully effective use of our own artillery; furthermore the co-operation of strong German panzer forces would be prejudiced by the densely wooded and mine-sown country. As the southern flank was automatically excluded because of its marshy, broken terrain, there remained only the sector between Apulia and Cisterna. I agreed to von Mackensen's plan to launch the main attack on either side of Apulia and to support it by two secondary attacks.

Hitler had von Mackensen report the plan to him and with the latter's agreement ordered the assault to be delivered by the Infantry Demonstration Regiment, recently arrived from Germany, and this on a very narrow front so as to guarantee a pulverizing effect on the part of our artillery bombardment. We had to pay for both these mistakes—I cannot acquit myself of a share in the blame. Even though the Infantry Demonstration Regiment was put to me as a crack one, I should not have accepted this just on mere hearsay but should have known a home defence unit with no fighting experience could not stand up to a major action. Another drawback was that the assault was fixed to begin at 6:30 P.M. on 16 February, a very late hour, as the regiment, being unfamiliar with the terrain, could only properly attack in daylight. It was in any case thrown back disgracefully.

I am firmly convinced that the 29th Panzer Grenadiers or the 26th Panzers would have carried the assault. The former of these showed its old fighting spirit in the attack on 18 February, which started from a difficult position without advantage of surprise and was pressed home as far as Route 82 to the last enemy bridgehead position, the Initial Line.

The failure of the second assault, ordered by Hitler himself, confirms this. Though I did not expect any very different result from a repetition of the attack at a different place, I could not countermand the order, as I was forced to acknowledge the political and military reasons which influenced the O.K.W. There was indeed a chance of partial success by reducing the bridgehead to the Initial Line. If that were achieved the Fourteenth Army would be able to husband its effectives and the Allies be made to wonder if the bridgehead could be held at all.

This time the assault was to be delivered from the opposite corner of the bridgehead, from Cisterna, with three weak divisions as the first wave. The lessons of the first attack were considered and measures of camouflage and diversion perfected, although I was not convinced this was necessary in so narrow an area. The first date fixed for the attack, 25 February, had to be postponed because of bad weather; even on the 28th there were periodic torrential downpours. When I visited the troops that day—as I always did before a major action—I had already made up my mind to another postponement, but the units detailed for the operation were so full of confidence that in deference to their wishes I let it stand. The bad weather conditions in fact favoured us rather than the enemy, giving us the chance of springing a local surprise if such were at all possible. The enemy would lose the benefit of tank support, while their naval guns and air force would be very greatly impeded. Improved weather on the 29th—the day of the attack—lessened these advantages, however, the drying ground helping the Allied tanks to get across country, and as our assault made no headway in the afternoon of 1 March I called it off.

In their renewed offensive against Cassino and Monte Cassino, which began on 15 March, the enemy made great efforts to soften our defences by dropping a weight of bombs in excess of anything hitherto experienced, by massed artillery fire and by the employment of the best British assault divisions, the 27th, the 4th Indian Division and the New Zealand Division. Yet at the end of it we were still on top. The 1st Parachute Division stood its ground, and on the night of 23-24 March, the British attack was discontinued.

Air Fleet 2 under the energetic lead of von Richthofen had not fully recovered from its serious losses in the battle for Sicily when the Salerno landing imposed a fresh heavy strain on our airmen. As, however, there was no need to carry out my original intention to keep our air forces for use against the Italian divisions near Rome in the event of an invasion south of the city, the Air Command could concentrate on the invasion fleet. A certain number of ships was sunk in this way, but the landing was not materially hindered. U-boats and E-boats, incidentally, had no success at all.

Both when in the air and on the roads during the subsequent fighting I could see for myself the inferiority of the Luftwaffe in strength and material, and could understand the army's criticism, undeserved as it was. We might score an occasional success, but no planned air operations were any longer possible with only about 300 aircraft to the enemy's 4,000-5,000. There is, however, no doubt that during the fighting round the bridgehead the air support given to the army was by no means despicable, while the flak support was extraordinarily helpful. Von Richthofen's recommendation that a Luftwaffe battle headquarters should be set up in the Alban Hills under von Pohl proved excellent. It had a direct view over the whole battlefield and far out to sea; aided by its liaison officers with the divisions, the command was able to follow the tide of the battle and promptly send in close-support formations, besides chasing away the very tiresome enemy artillery spotters.

BEFORE THE BATTLE FOR ROME

Unit commanders and troops had now been in action in part since July and one and all since September 1943, but well as they had done their achievement by March 1944 was by no means reassuring. With heavy casualties on both sides it was fairly safe to assume that before the decisive offensive was launched there would be a lull of some duration, during which the prescription for us was to assemble large reserves, if we were to withstand the coming shock. The Allies' idea of linking up the southern front with the landings was self-evident, if not yet realized. From now on fresh attempts in this direction were to be expected unless the Allies should seek to force a decision more cheaply by landings in the region of Civitavecchia or Leghorn. It was certain that their power to give battle had been lately enhanced, some divisions having grown into really large combat formations.

I believe this development was due to a cardinal error of our German propaganda, which could not do enough to taunt the enemy for their lack of initiative, thereby goading them into a gradual change of operational principles. The method of cautious and calculated advance according to plan with limited objectives gave place to an inspirational strategy which was perfected through the months remaining till the end of the war. At that time I took energetic measures to put a stop to this foolish propaganda, but it had already been effective to our detriment. In order to explain to Hitler and the O.K.W. how limited were the possibilities open to me I sent my Chief of Staff to discuss our problems with the Führer. These could be summed up in two main points: in the face of a perfect co-ordination of superior land, sea and air forces invasions cannot be held up, even in a well-constructed coastal position, without depth; secondly, our counter-attacks were as a rule beaten off by heavy artillery fire. In an area dominated by the enemy air force free operations only have a chance of success under special weather conditions or with a specially favourable ground layout.

Kesselring over the Russian plains in his FW 189.

Inspecting an anti-aircraft unit.

The siege of Malta.

A discussion at Berchtesgaden on the subject of Malta.

A meeting of Rommel and Kesselring in the desert.

Kesselring dons a parachute before the take-off.

In the course of the struggle for the Anzio-Nettuno bridgehead.

Kesselring with Crown Prince Umberto
and General von Rintelen.

Following a conference with Marshal Graziani.

Mussolini visits Kesselring's headquarters.

Venice, February 1947—on the way to trial.

Camp Wolfsberg, June 1947.

von Mackensen   Kesselring   Mälzer

The fighting so far had clearly ended in a draw, both political and strategic problems remaining unchanged. We were now faced with the economic necessity of making our theatre of war basically self-sufficient.

These considerations had been implemented by the fortification measures set in motion in September 1943. As a result the Gustav Line had been further consolidated in the probable battle sectors; it was so deepened by the construction of armoured and concrete switch lines and intermediate and advanced positions that even very strong enemy attacks could be intercepted in the back area. In the knowledge that single fortified lines cannot be permanently held against a modern assault and even positions in depth may well be lost, work was being constantly pushed on on the "C" Line south of Rome, running through Avezzano to the Adriatic coast, the ground of which had long been studied. This connected naturally with our positions investing the beachhead and their switch lines immediately south of Rome.

These fortification measures gave our strategy the greatest possible degree of freedom; it was nevertheless restricted by the air supremacy of the Allies and the undeniable weaknesses of the "C" Line. We had to accept the fact that mobile operations in country controlled by the enemy's air force—under a clear, blue sky, in rugged mountainous country or open plains, with few but easily detected roads and short, moonlit nights—could only have prospects of success with quite exceptional luck. The "C" Line was only in the first stages of construction and had the Tiber, the Aniene and Rome close behind it; its length also was a matter for anxiety. The lake front, however, between the positions of the Tenth and Fourteenth Armies was pretty securely protected by technical means and inundations. The adjacent coastal sectors to the north had been put in an adequate state of defence according to their degree of vulnerability. The most urgent matter was the construction of positions in the Apennines, where many more months would be needed before the defensive lay-out would pass muster.

Even though C.-in-C. Southwest was poorly served by air reconnaissance we had been able to form a more or less accurate picture of the enemy's effectives and from it to draw conclusions as to his probable intentions. With a probability bordering on certainty the Adriatic front could be ruled out of our calculations. On the other hand the Garigliano with its mountain spurs beyond Cassino and the Anzio beachhead had to be envisaged as battle-fronts, supplemented perhaps by feint or diversionary landings north of Rome in the region of Civitavecchia and by airborne landings in the valley of Frosinone. I calculated that the American Fifth and British Eighth Armies would open the offensive by launching a broad and deep attack against the right wing of our Tenth Army across the Majo, Petrella and Monte Cassino massif, with a connecting inward movement into the valley of the Liri. The rôle of the French Expeditionary Force, with its composition and direction of probable thrust, remained an important and dangerous unknown factor till the fourth day of the offensive.

How the battle was to be conducted was clearly laid down in my directive *Defence*, and I personally convinced myself that it was fully understood by all staffs and divisions. By and large those holding the front line had proved their worth. If the 94th Infantry Division on the right wing, whose behaviour in previous engagements had disappointed me, were overrun, an enemy break-through could be intercepted in depth. The valley of the Liri could be held if the pivots—Monte Majo on the right and Monte Cassino on the left—remained in our possession. With the 1st Parachute Division holding the Monte Cassino massif its defence was in the best possible hands. The whole left wing, as being uninteresting, was thinly occupied.

Our position surrounding the beachhead was almost ideally defensible. The Fourteenth Army had enough reserves, including flak, available to be able to repel a strong enemy assault without assistance. But should the co-operation of the inner flanks of the two armies break down the situation of the Army Group would be very gravely imperilled.

The Luftwaffe was under the direct orders of Goering. Even in his subordinate position von Pohl, in command of the flak, co-operated perfectly with us. The main flak concentrations were in the Liri Valley, at Valmontone and at Rome.

The signals network was also up to every requirement. Our naval command was instructed to intensify supply by sea and to improve our coastal defence with artillery and naval vessels. Compared with previous standards, the supply service—including rations and dumps in the back areas—was not too bad.

All in all, I could await coming events calmly, as we had done all we could in every field to meet the major offensive expected.

THE BIG SPRING BATTLE

The preliminary softening by artillery barrage and bombing, including a raid on Tenth Army battle headquarters, gave us a foretaste of what lay in store for us when the American Fifth and British Eighth Armies launched their offensive. As I saw for myself on the morning of 12 May, both the Tenth Army and 14th Corps headquarters had almost ceased to function; both had lost their commanders and their deputies were doing their best to carry on. In the first days of the assault, however, it became evident that my fears of an airborne landing or a fresh invasion had no substance; the movement and use of strategic reserves had therefore become less hazardous.

The first days of the battle also confirmed our guess at the points of the enemy's main effort. The fighting was fierce and costly; it was sad that the Army Group could not obtain a clear picture of the composition of the American Fifth, and especially of the French Expeditionary Corps. While the front south of the Liri to Monte Cairo retired to the well-constructed Senger switch line in very heavy, but evenly matched fighting, the movements of the 14th Panzer Corps got out of control. The 94th and 71st Infantry Divisions fought gallantly, but were too weak to hold the superior enemy. Quite apart from the fact that the Army Group was not in possession of data on which to make a far-reaching decision on 14 or 15 May, unexpected difficulties arose in bringing up the 26th Panzers and sending them into action. When on top of this the 94th Infantry Division, in disobedience to my express orders, assembled its reserves in the coastal sector instead of on the Petrella massif the gaps created in the front on the massif could not be closed. This meant the Alpine troops of the French Expeditionary Force had a clear path.

While the situation on the right flank of the 14th Panzer Corps went from bad to worse, the left wing and the 51st Mountain Corps gradually stiffened to hold their ground; the 1st Parachute Division did not dream of surrendering "its" Monte Cassino. In order to maintain contact with the 14th Panzer Corps I had personally to order these last, recalcitrant as they were, to retire, an example of the drawback of having strong personalities as subordinate commanders. This was also the reason why the 1st Parachute Division's reserves were not echeloned to the right behind the exposed flank of the 90th Panzer Grenadiers and why the 51st Mountain Corps was only belatedly retired.

So as to keep the line together the 14th Panzer Corps had to cling to the intermediate positions longer than seemed advisable in the tactical situation, with the consequence that the right flank of the Senger switch line could not be held. Failure to bring up reinforcements must seal the fate of the Tenth Army—for which a defensive victory by the Fourteenth Army at the beachhead could not possibly compensate. Any further advance of the American Fifth must also unhinge our Fourteenth Army. An emergency had thus arisen which induced me on 19 May to place the 29th Panzer Grenadiers at the disposal of the Tenth Army. When I gave the order I had every reason to assume they could reach a position of considerable natural strength by the morning of 20 May and would thus be able to close the gap.

That this did not happen was due to the Fourteenth Army commander's opposition to the transfer, the first news of which reached me on the evening of the 20th on my return to my battle headquarters. I could sympathize with his reluctance to part with his reserves, but in this phase of the battle I could not admit his arguments, especially as there was a danger that our positions

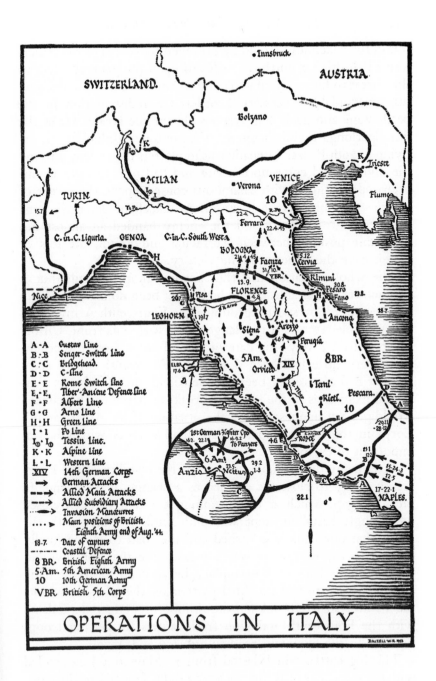

OPERATIONS IN ITALY

A - A   Gustav Line
B - B   Senger - Switch Line
C - C   Bridgehead.
D - D   C - line
E - E   Rome Switch line
E₁ - E₁   Tiber - Aniene Defence line
F - F   Albert Line
G - G   Arno Line
H - H   Green Line
I - I   Po Line
I₀ - I₀   Tessin Line.
K - K   Alpine Line
L - L   Western Line
XIV   14th German Corps.
→   German Attacks
⇢   Allied Main Attacks
⇢   Allied Subsidiary Attacks
····   Invasion Manœuvres
····   Main positions of British
     Eighth Army end of Aug. '44.
18·7.   Date of capture
     Coastal Defence
8 BR.   British Eighth Army
5·Am.   5th American Army
10   10th German Army
VBR   British 5th Corps

round the beachhead would be breached by forces of the American Fifth driving north. In order to open the general's eyes to this threat to his southern flank and to convince him my decision was unavoidably necessary I ordered a redistribution in the battle zone and made him responsible for the area as far as the line Sperlonga-Fondi-Frosinone-Valmontone. Unluckily on arriving at 29th Panzer Grenadier headquarters on 21 May I found the division had come up too late and had offered fight in unprepared positions—with calamitous consequences, the extent of which could not yet be foreseen. An excellent defensive zone had been thrown away and the enemy handed an almost impregnable position between Terracina and Fondi, the loss of which gave the Americans the victory.

The whole situation had thus become more difficult, but it was not yet irreparable. There had as yet been no offensive from the beachhead; by swift regrouping the Fourteenth Army could still assemble reserves at the danger spots within its front. Unfortunately by 23 May—the date of the offensive from the beachhead—very little had been done. The Fourteenth Army commander had apparently been unable to rid himself of a preconceived fixation as to the way the break-out from the beachhead would go. Yet unquestionably the situation of the American 6th Corps in the narrow pocket had disadvantages which it was important to exploit.

After many disagreeable interviews, the inability of the Fourteenth Army to close the gap led to a change of command. In fact, the gap, which at the beginning could have been closed by a single battalion, kept widening until 31 May, with the result that our flank was turned and the road to Rome finally opened to the enemy. It was a catastrophe that the divisions which fought with such exemplary bravery on the right flank and in the centre had no equal partner on the left. Meanwhile the Tenth Army fell back fighting stubbornly, effected a link-up with the Fourteenth and won fresh laurels by getting troops through to the mountain road to Subiaco and Tivoli.

This big battle, which lasted from 12 May to 4 June, ended with the surrender of Rome without a fight. Operations through-

out this period were immensely difficult; that with a few cata-
strophic exceptions the troops came through it as they did
speaks highly for their mettle.

In any case the Allies won a great victory, and the Fourteenth
Army took tremendous punishment.

That in the face of this disaster I nevertheless kept to my
unilateral engagement to spare Rome as an "open city" at least
shows that whether I relied on accurate knowledge or on intuition I did not regard the situation as hopeless.

20

Defence Stand in Italy, Summer 1944 till Spring 1945

---

6 June 1944 Allied invasion of Normandy—17 June Evacuation of Elba—June and July Retirement of Army Group C and stabilization of new defence fronts—26 June Evacuation of Pisa—12 Aug. Surrender of Florence—15 Aug. Second Allied invasion in the south of France—21 Sept. Loss of Rimini—30 Aug. Commencement of British offensive on the Adriatic front—September Stabilization of the German front in the Green Line (southeast of La Spezia-Apennines) — December British offensive in the Po plain—5 Dec. Surrender of Ravenna.

JUNE TILL MID-AUGUST 1944

The first of June marked the beginning of an appalling deterioration of the Fourteenth Army's plight. The fighting strength of the divisional combat groups retiring behind the Tiber and the Aniene had ebbed to a bare minimum.

The Tenth Army was in a better situation. By fierce and dogged resistance north of Petrella it had seriously delayed the enemy's advance and was still full of fight. But other difficulties presently arose: first, the roads along which retreat was possible were few and exposed to air attack; secondly, it was being pushed so far away from Rome and the Tiber that a rapid concentration in the area west of the river was hardly feasible.

I refused to budge from my determination to keep the battle out of Rome. This entailed the abandonment of a defence line along the Tiber to the sea and along the Aniene as far as Tivoli. These two intrinsically excellent positions were simply unhinged by the Allies as soon as they had entered Rome and chosen it as the starting-point for their next operations. Instead of defending the river line for several days our best hope was now to halt the enemy for a short while north and on either side of the city.

However difficult and strenuous the fighting might have been for the Allies in recent months, the capture of Rome was an undeniable victory. I tried to persuade myself that after weeks of bloody fighting the troops might succumb to the demoralizing influence of a capital city—only an exceptionally strong and ruthless discipline could force the pace uninterruptedly. But I did not really believe it, nor did I make my plans on this assumption. It was a relief that the enemy forces facing the Tenth Army east of the Tiber were being remarkably cautious. The ground was not so unfavourable for the delaying action I had in mind as it appeared at first glance on the map. In the first place, the roads immediately north of Rome and the intervening country, were very easy to block, which must considerably impede the enemy's motorized forces. On this everything else depended. Time had to be won by a delaying defence for the regrouping and replenishment of combat units at the front; time also to drain away non-combatant units to the rear and to bring up fresh reserves.

There was no need at this moment for much strategic deliberation. Enemy manœuvres which might be dangerous were easy to detect, and our own counter-measures followed inevitably from them. The American Fifth Army, though it had suffered smaller losses, had won the race and outstripped the British Eighth. In front of it now lay a country suitable for motorized forces and tanks; if it chose to press on, the broad high roads to the north lay open. In the British Eighth Army's sector, on the other hand, movement was still delayed by the terrain.

The enemy behaved very much as I had expected. If on 4 June he had immediately pushed forward on a wide front, sending his tank divisions on ahead along the roads, our Army Group west of the Tiber would have been placed in almost irreparable jeopardy, and I might have been induced precipitately to rush back the Tenth Army's motorized divisions across the Tiber to build up a new front south or north of Lake Trasimeno. But by the evening of 4 June and on the following day it no longer seemed necessary to start this fateful operation; I implemented my decision by keeping my headquarters at Monte Soratte north of Rome, although I detached the supply services. I believe that my remaining at the front inspired confidence—I was still in direct contact with units in the line at Viterbo on 6 and 7 June.

The Fourteenth Army's assignment was one of immense difficulty, but if every chance were taken it might be accomplished—despite a certain pessimism at its headquarters. Admittedly they had good reason for misgivings, as the American Fifth Army opposed their total strength of barely two divisions with three tank and nine infantry divisions. These numbers disheartened the army commander unduly; he paid too little consideration to the fact that the Americans had to deploy from a narrow pass through which only a fraction of their forces could advance simultaneously. Instead of worrying over calculations that were, anyhow, misleading, it would have been more important to delay the enemy's advance into the passes. This was possible immediately north of Rome, and there were other opportunities even farther north. It was, for instance, a grave tactical mistake to leave the pass at Civita Castellana undefended, the possession of which gave the enemy his first chance to make an initial deployment with mobile forces and fan out to the north and northwest.

Our general strategic idea from 7 June remained the same: to gather reserves arriving from the rear and from the side, both armies contesting every step of their retreat, to stop gaps and to effect a firm junction of the inner flanks. It did not matter whether more or less ground were surrendered; the main thing was to surmount our momentary weakness, to pull out our battered divisions and to rest and re-equip them.

The Allied High Command helped us to realize this operational plan. The even distribution of their forces over the whole front, already evident on 6 June, lessened the peril of a concentration at the seam of our two armies. The remarkable slowness of the enemy's advance and the subsequent hesitation of the

French Expeditionary Corps eased the situation. It was a reasonable assumption that the Allies, fully aware of the general state of affairs, would not pull their punches; according to our information Alexander had ample strength. Of course air reconnaissance could not dispel some uncertainties, but the picture of a "vacuum" was not correct. I was here, there and everywhere by day and by night and knew the picture. Actually roads and villages were jammed far behind the lines. Movements of supply columns and second-wave divisions towards the front and sideways movements of motorized divisions criss-crossed those of troops retiring from the battle-zone.

The Allies utterly failed to seize their chances. Their air force was not sent in to smash the helpless targets presented them on the battlefield, especially in the back areas, nor were Partisan uprisings supported by an airborne landing behind the battle-front. In fact no attempt was made at a tactical landing in our rear at all.

As soon as we were level with Lake Bolsena I ordered the defensive to be resumed at Lake Trasimeno. In doing so I realized, of course, that it would be a mistake to try to force a decision in this region, but it was vital to gain time to complete the defence lay-out of the Apennine front.

Even though I received repeated injunctions from the O.K.W. not to surrender so much territory I had to operate in the main as I thought necessary in the light of my own more accurate knowledge of the situation. Far from lending an ear to the frequent promptings of my supreme commander, I generally calculated the chances by investigation on the spot and gave my orders accordingly. In some cases I authorized a retirement after discussion with my Chief of Staff and operations chief at my battle headquarters and, perhaps, a further telephone conversation with the army commander concerned. I do not remember a single occasion when I was "on the mat" for acting "autocratically," apart from the evacuation of Sicily. When at the end of June and the beginning of July Hitler peremptorily demanded that the retreat be stopped and the defensive resumed, I flew to his G.H.Q. to reconcile my views with those of the

O.K.W. This time my operations chief, Staff Colonel Beelitz, accompanied me. After nearly an hour spent in explaining the development of the situation I ended by insisting I should be left a free hand in Italy. Hitler replied at equal length, trying to make me accept the principles of strategy valid in Russia. Beginning to lose patience, I made a short and heated reply the gist of which was this, if not my actual words:

"The point is not whether my armies are fighting or running away. I can assure you they will fight and die if I ask it of them. We are talking about something entirely different, a question much more vital: whether after Stalingrad and Tunis you can afford the loss of yet two more armies. I beg to doubt it—the more so as, if I change my plans to meet with your ideas, sooner or later the way into Germany will be opened to the Allies. On the other hand I guarantee—unless my hands are tied—to delay the Allied advance appreciably, to halt it at latest in the Apennines and thereby to create conditions for the prosecution of the war in 1945 which can be dovetailed into your general strategic scheme."

Hitler said no more—or rather he muttered a few words which, according to Beelitz, were not uncomplimentary. Anyhow, I had won my point.

After this interview I carried on as before on my own responsibility without asking the O.K.W. One instance among many others: Hitler sent a signal to the 1st Parachute Corps, when it was fighting north of Florence, sharply criticizing the behaviour of two divisions which were trying to retire. I was touring the front when I learnt that on receipt of this message Schlemm was about to throw in all his reserves. I interrupted my tour and drove straight to his headquarters, forbade him to sacrifice his last reserves and sanctioned his original action—which was much more correct in the situation. This was reported to the O.K.W., but they did not even raise a single query. They knew by now I was doing my best.

I followed the battle for the tank track west of Lake Trasimeno with acute tension, the divisions there holding out longer than I had any right to expect. The left wing of the Tenth

Army all along required no attention. The Fourteenth Army, however, even after von Mackensen had been relieved by General Lemelsen, needed special watching. It could no longer be said that the Tenth Army had better divisions or that it was generally helped by the terrain; and the enemy forces opposing the two armies were equally strong. But I could see that my directives were carried out by the Tenth Army less hesitantly and more energetically. With the failure of the Luftwaffe field divisions, however, Goering's vanity brought its own reward—he had not the heart to place Luftwaffe soldiers released from the ground organization at the disposal of the army as replacements. It was astonishing that Hitler put up with such amateurishness, for he knew better.

Thus by mobile tactics we succeeded in creating a gradually stiffening front. At the same time it was my objective to put up a longer resistance on narrow and better located fronts so that the wider and more unfavourable sectors could be vacated at speed without imperilling the purpose of the delaying action. My endeavours so to eke out the situation that the withdrawal to the Apennines should go smoothly made themselves felt in demands which did not always coincide with my generals' wishes.

Throughout the battle for Italy the army was excellently supported by the flak. On the other hand, during this phase air support had practically ceased, even our air reconnaissance being inadequate.

Meanwhile the important unknown factor was the latent flanking threat. After the beginning of the Normandy invasion (6 June 1944) the enemy had not the requisite landing tonnage in the Mediterranean to make a large-scale invasion deep into Italy probable for some time to come; on the other hand, tactical landings were always on the cards. Signs of preparations on Elba—the island had fallen on 17 June—suggested that this danger was once again impending. Otherwise what sense was there in capturing the place? But when this unique opportunity passed I could for the time being relegate this particular worry.

In an emergency rested divisions were ready for action on the adjacent coast.

There were no perceptible indications of a tactical landing in force on the Adriatic coast, where it was least to be expected. I also excluded airborne landings from my calculations, for it was certain that all the suitable means were required in Normandy. The O.K.W. had given specific orders for the defence of Leghorn and Ancona; but in this case also I was only bound by them in so far as I considered the necessity of holding these ports a part of my over-all plan, and they were both evacuated when the time came. Such *ad hoc* and rather panicky orders from the O.K.W. only defeated themselves.

The concentration of the deeply echeloned formations of the French Expeditionary Corps and the British Eighth Army on both sides of Lake Trasimeno and the stiff fighting there from the middle of June to the beginning of July were clear indications that the Allies were still driving towards Florence. I did not anticipate the enemy's objective would be a slow attrition of our Apennine position; I rather expected a rapid thrust across the Apennines beyond Florence or, if the mountains proved too difficult an obstacle, a switching of the main offensive in an attempt to outflank the Apennine position at its most vulnerable spot—the Adriatic coast.

During this phase I again inspected the progress of construction work in the Green Line in the Apennines. I found the positions better aligned and strengthened.

My general impression of the defensibility of the Apennine positions at this time led me to feel an immediate continuation of a methodical offensive to be improbable; the enemy's troops had been overtaxed and their losses considerable. To push on now would have little prospect of success.

I therefore gave orders with a view to prolonging the delaying action in the country immediately covering the Apennines, holding the Arno for a while and so by-passing Florence, which I wished to spare; I hoped also to economize my divisions by re-grouping and re-equipping them and bringing up new forces, my object being to man the Green Line with a garrison to guard against a surprise attack.

The fighting at Lake Trasimeno from the middle of June to the middle of July satisfied my tactical requirements. East of the Siena-Florence road, however, the best German motorized divisions were strung out like a string of pearls, though in sporadic encounters they did succeed in gradually halting the advance of the American 6th Corps. By pinning down these valuable German forces on this intrinsically uninteresting flank the American 4th Corps contributed largely to the success of the fierce Allied thrust between Siena and Florence.

THE 20TH JULY AND THE ITALIAN THEATRE

On the evening of 20 July Goering rang me at my headquarters. Up to that moment I knew nothing of the conspiracy. Goerdeler had made an attempt to approach me in 1942, but unsuccessfully, as I could not then be reached. There was no commotion among the troops either in the line or in the back areas. Except for a few officers to whom I had afterwards to lend my protection the news came as a complete surprise alike to army, navy, Luftwaffe and S.S. Of this I was heartily glad.

I have never come across any staff or unit in Italy where politics were discussed. The war was too hectic, the soldier too much aware of the obligations of his military oath, and the spell of Hitler's personality too ever-present and his criminal actions too little known for a conspiracy to prosper. But I think it historically important to speculate what would have happened in Italy had the conspiracy succeeded. If I may use an illuminating generalization, I had under my command large elements of the "republican" army, the "imperialist" navy and the "national socialist" Luftwaffe. These adjectives reveal the patent disunity of the services' attitude. In view of this in large part fanatical attachment to Hitler, an announcement of the latter's death and an appeal to the services' loyalty would have provoked the sharpest antagonisms, a mutiny against the renegades and traitors in the saddle and in all probability bloody clashes. Even if, in spite of the military oath, there was a leaven of anti-Hitlerism in the army in 1939, this was certainly no longer the case in 1944. As the youngest age class—ardently devoted to Hitler through the Hitler Youth Movement—was absorbed into the services the character of every formation had changed. With these boys in the majority in every unit, occasional expressions of dissatisfaction with the actions of the High Command were insignificant. Their attachment to Hitler was genuine; they swore by the Führer and were ready to lay down their lives for him. Even if individual generals and a few intellectuals, far-sighted or disgruntled as the case may be, were won over to the idea of Hitler's removal, his overthrow required more intensive psychological preparation, and responsible leaders were too uncertain of the Allies' sympathy. Casablanca was a reminder of this!

Since then our whole nation has lived through years of suffering, and excited argument has never ceased about the honour both of the conspirators and of those who refused to take part. Traitors or not, I have far too high a respect for the conspirators, whom with very few exceptions I knew or know personally, to doubt that they were inspired by the noblest motives.

AUTUMN 1944

Satisfied as the Army Group could be with the success of its delaying strategy even in the hard-contested sectors covering Florence and on the Adriatic—that is, until the middle of August—its endeavours to save divisions for the battle in the Apennines had been unfortunate, their release for this purpose being only feasible in a few cases.

I took the view that, after the two invasions in the north and south of France on which the fate of the whole war must depend, the withdrawal of my armies from a theatre now of secondary importance was inevitable. The recent deterioration on both main battle-fronts in the east and in the west and the tension on our own southern front meant that a good deal of self-confidence was needed by commanders to inspire the troops with the courage to stick it out. In this critical situation our plans were wrecked by accumulating orders to release divisions, and the troops received the impression that we were only muddling through.

At Army Group headquarters we attached great importance to co-ordinating our views with those of C.-in-C. West in case of an invasion from the Gulf of Genoa. I had asked the O.K.W. to determine a common strategy for the inner wings of the two theatres, but they dilly-dallied instead of issuing a directive. Graziani and myself were indeed informed of the state of the coastal fortifications and of the Nineteenth Army's forces in the south of France, but were left in the dark as to what they proposed to do if the Allies landed. As an "old hand" at invasions, I was very doubtful of the Nineteenth Army's chances if the blow fell there. The coastal-defence measures were inadequate and the troops had no experience of major fighting, not to speak of the enemy's air supremacy. It was clear that if the enemy made a successful landing the Nineteenth Army would be squeezed back onto the Alpine front and would have to be taken over by Army Group C. I did not anticipate a strong enemy offensive against the Alpine massif as being contrary to the strategic idea of an invasion of southern France, but that was all the more reason to expect that the enemy could secure his Italian flank, and possibly mount an offensive from it.

This view proved correct. But as, even when the invasion had begun, the O.K.W.—perhaps assessing the situation too favourably—still issued no directive and communications with the Nineteenth Army were cut, I moved heaven and earth to contact its wing and the 157th Mountain Division scattered in the mountains. The 48th Infantry Division on the coast was reached and from that moment was taken over by Graziani's Army Group, but reconnaissance thrusts were only able to reach single units of the 157th Mountain Division. The possession of the Alpine crest—more or less a frontier position—I considered decisive for subsequent operations in the northwest part of Italy. The capture of this dominating jumping-off position by the Allies would enable them to assemble strong forces and suddenly penetrate the upper Italian plain. This would mean a link-up with the Partisan bands in the area Turin-Milan and the unhinging of our positions on the Ligurian coast, which in turn—looking farther ahead—might well lead to our being manœuvred out of the Po plain. When this thrust came was immaterial. The Alpine crest position had to remain intact until the beginning of winter, when the climate would do the rest.

These considerations forced me to throw in the 90th Panzer Grenadiers to clean up the situation in the High Alps and to extricate the last remaining elements of the 157th Mountain Division. Even if I proposed to commit the Grenadiers only for a short time and to relieve them as soon as possible by an Alpine unit, nonetheless I had temporarily expended my reserves.

Theoretically ever since the beginning of August the Army Group had been prepared for a regrouping of the Allied forces on the Apennine front. After the middle of the month, however, there was no longer any doubt the British Eighth Army was getting ready for a decisive outflanking attack on the Adriatic. Even though we did not know how and when the offensive would be launched, everything had to be done to complete our preparations to repel it. I have also explained what efforts had been made to have reserves available, though because of the repeated interference of the O.K.W. they melted like snow in the spring sun.

The brunt of the attack caught the 71st Infantry Division as it was being relieved and moving back out of the line in the night of 25-26 August, when the British scored a surprise success. The 26th Panzers, moving in very late, got off to a very bad start which affected the whole front. In the night of 30-31 August the first Green Line—with no equivalent position behind it in the whole depth of the Adriatic sector—had to be surrendered.

In order to release fresh troops for the Adriatic front, regroupings had been going on for a long time from the western Alps along the Gulf of Genoa and across the whole breadth of the Apennines. The long distances, the enemy's air supremacy and a certain lethargy in the staff work, plus a justified regard for the enemy's combat activity, delayed the movement of the troops. But at the beginning of September the front in the western Alps and Liguria was secured and the reinforcement started of the specially threatened left flank of the Fourteenth Army north of Florence—a long way in front of the Green Line. The left wing of the Tenth Army on the Adriatic coast had also been strengthened by the timely arrival of experienced divisions. With these forces I hoped to be able to stem the advance. My hopes were realized; the battles of 17, 21 and 29 September brought a lull on the Rimini front.

The offensive launched at the beginning of September after several weeks of quiet against the inner flanks of the Tenth and Fourteenth Armies led to a retirement to the Green Line according to plan. The offensive was broadened and in the middle part of September assumed the proportion of a big battle—fortunately not before the slackening of the offensive at Rimini had become apparent. Whereas up till then I had thought it absolutely necessary for the 76th Panzer Corps to avoid contact with the enemy and had authorized evasive action, in the last ten days of the month I ordered persistent resistance in the hope of getting the enemy to call his offensive off, so as to help the Army Group obtain the freedom of action necessary to restore the situation at Bologna.

Nevertheless, with a quite remarkable precision the enemy managed to find the soft spots at the seam of the Tenth and Fourteenth Armies and to exploit German weaknesses. During those weeks the Army Group had repeatedly moved the inter-army border for geographical and tactical reasons. From the middle of October the situation south of Bologna gave matter for grave concern. If one or another sector in the Po plain between Bologna and the Adriatic were lost it might be of secondary importance, but if the front south of Bologna could not be held then all our positions in the Po plain east of Bologna were automatically gone—in which event they must be evacuated in good time so as at least to save the troops and material. Therefore all our strongest divisions must be fed to this part of the Apennines.

I spent 23 October, from five in the morning till seven in the evening, the time of my serious accident, visiting the headquarters of the Tenth Army and almost all the divisions at the front. I got the impression that the crisis was past and that side by side our good divisions could still defeat the enemy, as indeed took place between 25 and 26 October. My Chief of Staff often remarked that it was a miracle that the northern spurs of the Apennines could be held as they were. The fighting lasted eight weeks, four to six of them involving big battles in country difficult for the attack. The weather conditions were variable and ran through the whole gamut of a northern Italian autumn. The fighting was very costly, supplies insufficient and sometimes difficult to bring up, and our resistance for the most part stubborn. Where the attack came up against good divisions the enemy's efforts and losses were out of all proportion to the results. After October in comparison with previous weeks their gains were steadily less and their losses greater. Supported by technical weapons undreamt of by us and magnificent fighters as they were, nevertheless their belief in a quick victory ebbed, symptoms of fatigue became increasingly apparent and their blows feebler.

The battle of the Apennines can really be described as a famous page of German military history.

NORTHERN ITALY AFTER THE APENNINE BATTLES

My hopes of being able to repel the decisive offensive which was to be expected in the spring of 1945 in the whole depth of the Apennines had been shattered. But neither had the Allies reached their long-range objective.[1] Yet time was working for them far more than for us. What lessons were to be learnt and what conclusions drawn from the last six months of uninterrupted fighting?

The fierceness of the battles and the large commitment of men and material revealed the importance of the Italian theatre

---

[1] General Wilson on 2 July 1944 had ordered an advance across the Apennines to the Po, to be continued across the Po to the line Venice-Padua-Verona.

to the Allies, which had not declined with the invasion of the south of France. While the forces expended on it were replaced by foreign divisions (Brazilian, Italian), the close-support activity of the air force after a temporary slackening had been very quickly stepped up again to its former intensity, though their naval forces lay curiously doggo. Meanwhile guerilla warfare grew sharper with the expansion of the Partisan organization.

Allied strategy showed a remarkable improvement. True they had not been able to carry out their original far-flung plans, having conspicuously neglected to exploit the help of the navy and the air force to outflank or overhaul our troops in the peninsula. Tanks were still regularly employed on a narrow front. But—operations were in themselves more compact, each army's assignment was adjusted to its means and attacks were delivered at points of main effort in noteworthy breadth and depth.

The old Mediterranean divisions had further perfected their fighting efficiency and tactics. The support of the infantry by artillery and tanks was now supplemented by air reconnaissance, air artillery spotting and close support from the air with a degree of co-ordination by now classical. Technical expedients had reached a high stage of development and were used with great skill. On the other hand the initiative of smaller unit commanders showed no particular improvement, nor was this compensated for by the excellent signals network allowing wireless communication through multifarious types of instruments—which was more of a hindrance than a help. It was also to our advantage that the enemy continued to respect the customary right of units to be relieved after a certain period in the line, regardless of the local situation. Their troops were, indeed, badly in need of rest, as their replacements were of acclimatization and training. On the other hand, it was increasingly important for them to curtail the rest periods of the German troops, to harass their recuperation and to prevent them from accumulating any large stores of ammunition and fuel.

The situation created by the battles on the Adriatic and at Bologna made it reasonable to assume that the coming offensive would be a pincers operation against the main German forces.

In view of the importance of the bridges across the Po and the
water obstacles in front of it, the Allied air force would certainly do everything possible to smash our communications.
This might have a fatal effect on our supplies and the conduct
of operations in the spring of 1945.

It was difficult to co-ordinate our operations on the west and
east flank of the Apennine peninsula, for the circumstances were
fundamentally different. The whole west flank was not concen-
tric with the other flank where the main thrust was bound to
come; its rectangular shape concealed a number of difficulties.
A belated disengagement on the Genoa front could mean the
annihilation of the troops in action there. Moreover forces just
sufficient in the mountains were lost in the plains with their well-
constructed network of roads, and the Tessin Line was a long
way away—the danger from guerilla bands applying all over the
western part of northern Italy, retiring movements were doubly
threatened. At the same time, although the strategic value of the
whole west flank was very small, yet the armament industry
there was a hampering priority consideration which ruled out
any question of its immediate evacuation. There was indeed no
reason to assume that the western part of northern Italy was in
any danger either from the sea or the western Alps during the
winter months, though air raids on factories and lines of communication, particularly on bridges, were always to be expected. But the German-Italian forces in this area were weak,
and approximately four divisions could certainly not be left in
a forlorn outpost; on the contrary, they were needed, especially
the German ones among them, for the defence of the Tessin
Line and later of the Alpine Line. Without these divisions the
right wing of the Fourteenth Army would also be endangered.
If in order to cover this flank, however, it should become necessary to amputate the Fourteenth and Tenth Armies by withdrawing units from them, so serious a loss of blood would make
it impossible to hold their front. An operation had therefore to
be planned which took heed of all these various considerations
and could be set in motion at a moment's notice on the code

word—"Autumn fog." Only one difficulty then remained: the choice of the psychological moment.

The eastern part of the Italian front, at any rate east of the Isonzo, had no inner connection with the probable offensive area. The region east of Gorizia might gain importance if the retirement of the right wing of Army Group E (Loehr) were to denude Yugoslavia and open up the theatre of operations of Army Group C to Tito or Russian forces. In this event it would become necessary to protect this flank by creating a front towards the east; if Army Group E could not provide the forces for this there were none available. But even if Army Group C retired its left wing or was driven back in the direction of Villach, circumstances might arise to compel it to fight on both fronts, and this would overtax its strength. Army Group E led a life of its own in the Balkans engaged in scraps with Tito's guerillas, until the Russians loomed up as well. While from 1943 onwards C.-in-C. Southwest took care to protect Trieste, Istria and Fiume from sea-borne landings the possibilities of defending Yugoslavia and Italy against an offensive from the east and south were deliberately neglected. When the Russian threat to Yugoslavia became evident in the autumn of 1944 I instigated a reconnaissance of positions in the easily defensible country on either side of Ljubljana, and despite considerable guerilla activity their construction was begun.

Meanwhile a simplified chain of command in the southern area was an urgent necessity—I had no objection to the whole of the east Adriatic area being handed over to Army Group E provided that a common over-all command were created in the southern area whose first duty would be to see to the inter-army group seam. Otherwise, in spite of the disadvantages, the existing arrangement would have to stand.

These considerations were in accordance with the plans of Army Group C. The Tenth and Fourteenth Armies were to fall back fighting, if the necessity arose, to behind the Po and subsequently to the Alpine Line.

I believed these tactics would be agreeable to the O.K.W. and Hitler, for otherwise the construction of positions south and north of the Po, which had been going on with remarkable success all summer, was so much waste of time.

In the past half-year the German divisions had come through with flying colours. Tradition and campaigning experience made up for many deficiencies, and if commanders and junior officers needed training it was hoped this could be given them in the winter months. Our principal handicap, the lack of any operational or close support from the air, remained. It was not to be got over even by the allocation of strong flak, searchlights and other expedients. The danger to communications was bound to increase as the area shrank and bottlenecks (for example, the Brenner Pass) became more precarious. Whether it would be possible to stop the gaps in arms, ammunition and, above all, fuel supply remained an open question.

It would have been futile to minimize the coming struggle to oneself or to the troops. But it would also have been wrong to let oneself be actuated only by the difficulties because one feared the worst. The main question was: as we had failed to hold the Apennines, should a retirement behind the Po be made now or not until immediately before the Allied offensive, or should the decisive battle be accepted where we now stood more by accident than by choice?

I decided against an immediate disengagement in the late autumn of 1944, even under cover of strong rearguards. Our evasive movements could not long have been kept secret from the enemy's air reconnaissance and intelligence. In spite of difficulties of country and of weather, the Allies could have pushed forward after us and by the beginning of spring would have been able to launch a well-prepared attack on the Po Line. We should have made them a present of a large and physically difficult area which was still of the greatest importance to our strategy in every way—purely tactically, in its effect upon the air war and for economic reasons. This view also forbade me to set in motion Operation *Autumn Fog*.

Similarly I decided against accepting the issue on our existing line; to do so would have been to gamble the future of the Italian theatre on one hopeless card. Therefore, as the gaps in our defensive strength just could not be ignored, there remained a kind of "delaying strategy." I purposely say "a *kind* of" because circumstances would have to determine whether the battle assumed the character more of defence or retirement. If the Army Group decided on this procedure, then the problem was how to survive the winter as economically as possible. The "neuralgic" point of the whole front was the line south of Bologna. If the enemy attacked and penetrated our line or improved his own positions anywhere else it would only be of local importance. But, favourable as were the natural sectors east of Bologna, the conditions were reversed for an offensive from the south launched from the Apennines. A serious defeat here might prematurely have a bad effect on the whole front, particularly for the left flank of the Tenth Army. Conditions were made even harder by my decision to by-pass and so spare Bologna.

What was the attitude of the O.K.W. and Hitler?

When Hitler decided against Operation *Autumn Fog* in October I was not surprised. I had actually counted on this, and had merely put forward this first suggestion as a trial balloon to inform the O.K.W. drastically in advance about the development of the situation and the possible consequences. To start it at once would indeed have been against my deepest conviction— so difficult an operation had had to be carefully and calmly thought out and put on paper with an exact time schedule. Thus I did not accept the refusal in October as a flat rejection of my proposal, and I was confident of my ability to get it accepted if the situation became critical. In defiance of my critics I still maintain that the six months' continuous fighting from the Garigliano to the Apennines was more than merely contesting every yard of ground and that I always succeeded in persuading Hitler to agree to my suggestions and in extricating my troops from the most difficult situations without total loss. I was therefore optimistic enough to believe in the realization of this project at the decisive moment.

During the winter months I did not anticipate any excessive interference in the conduct of operations from the O.K.W., where Jodl's help stood me in good stead; he was sympathetic, in this case also, towards my handling of the situation and could prepare Hitler in homœopathic doses for the inevitable. That did not prevent my getting an occasional rap over the knuckles, however. Still, Hitler knew that in carrying out his directives I would go to the extremest lengths if I clearly saw the need for them. But he also knew that an order to stand firm could not tie my hands if I reached another decision after mature investigation mostly on the spot. I showed my independence on more than one occasion. Hitler had to fall in with my intentions when the task he set me gradually became incommensurate with the means at my disposal. Although the O.K.W. was anxious to do a great deal to help supply the Italian theatre, yet Army Group C, in view of the enormous German commitments on the main eastern and western fronts, was very sceptical about the realization of these intentions, and extensive measures of self-help were instituted, whose results were unpredictable.

During the autumn and winter the O.K.W. ordered the release of seven divisions. This was eloquent of the situation on the other fronts.

At this point I repeat that after the invasion I thought the weakening of the Italian front correct, that I had even offered to surrender divisions to a greater extent than was actually ordered. But I judged it wrong to adhere to the old strategic plans heedless of the depletion of our strength and the difficulties of supply. I told Hitler this for the last time on 10 March 1945.

THE WINTER PERIOD, 1944-45

On 23 October after a short night's rest I started out at 5:00 A.M. and drove from one division to another, beginning with the right flank. I was welcomed everywhere, and was able to give advice, encouragement and in some cases assistance by allocating reserves. I got the impression that the climacteric was passed and that we would be able to hold the northern slopes of the Apennines. Harassed throughout the day by British aircraft, I was driving along the main road from Bologna to Forli in the late afternoon on my way to visit the last two divisions when my car, passing a column, collided with a long-barrelled gun coming out of a side road. I came off the worst from the encounter, receiving a severe concussion and a nasty gash on the left temple.

Soon after my accident the story got about that the Field-Marshal was doing well, but that the gun had had to be scrapped. However that may be, I was taken by very roundabout ways to Ferrara, where I lay unconscious till the next morning. Meanwhile two specialists, Professors Bürkle de la Camp and Toennis, had been summoned to my bedside. After giving me an injection Captain Niesen, my staff M.O., who had accompanied me to hospital, sternly snapped: "And don't fiddle with your head. That's an order!"

This must have made a great impression on me as in fact I did keep my fingers off it.

On the second day I was visited by Frau von Oertzen, the head of the Red Cross. My face was a hideous mess and my sensitiveness at my disfigurement found expression when she came into the room.

"Do you know what real kindness is?" I asked her, and as she did not reply, "When someone can bear to look at me like this."

Hitler and the O.K.W. were seriously concerned at my becoming a casualty, and for several days Professor Bürkle de la Camp had to send in a daily bulletin to general headquarters. I was strapped into a Storch and flown from Ferrara to Riva in the safe hands of my engineer-major, Bäumler, and from Riva to Merano.

On 15 January 1945, after a fortnight's convalescent leave at home, I went to Bad Ischl for a medical overhaul at the Brain Hospital there and then returned to my staff headquarters at Recoaro. I had been away for nearly three months.

On my return I found that the Allies, as expected, had made constant attrition thrusts against our lines, and though success had been only local and not in any way decisive, they had blunted the mettle of our troops. Nonetheless the morale of officers and men was good, far better than I had imagined. Even in private no one mentioned throwing up the sponge; the men just knew they had to hang on. I was satisfied with the strength of units even though the state of training of some of them set me thinking.

More critical was the arms, ammunition and fuel situation, and worst of all our plight in the air.

The stage was set for the decisive battle. Whether our defence now took the form of a delaying action or of a retreat it was at least secured by prepared sectors and positions manned against surprise. This forbade the acceptance of a decisive battle south of the Po. Meanwhile the transfer of divisions to other fronts continued, and the indispensable flow of supplies was seldom fully maintained. Notwithstanding all this Hitler could not at first be prevailed upon to readjust his orders to the altered situation. But as the weeks went by without a veto on my plans I believed that at the crucial moment, as before, I could handle the situation as should be necessary.

Neither, unfortunately, on the question of a unified command could Hitler make up his mind. The question was continually examined by the O.K.W., an early settlement promised, but for reasons entirely beyond me nothing happened. I almost had the impression that Hitler was afraid to concentrate strong power in *one* hand in a distant theatre.

Then, on 9 March, I was summoned to Hitler, who appointed me Commander-in-Chief of the western theatre as from 10 March. Once afterwards—at the end of April—I was to meet up again with Army Group C when the Italian front was incorporated in my command along with other fronts.

BALANCE-SHEET OF THE ITALIAN CAMPAIGN

Any reassessment of the Italian campaign after the lapse of several years must decide whether our holding the deeply echeloned lines in Italy for two years can be defended from a military standpoint and whether the strategic principles followed achieved the best attainable results.

In the following reflections I shall ignore all political considerations. I have made it clear in another place that Italy's ill-timed entrance into the war was neither asked nor wanted and that, on the contrary, Germany had the very greatest interest in

Italy's neutrality. Any undue expansion of the theatre of war brought with it great disadvantages, consisting primarily in the excessive strain imposed on our war potential and in complications of supply and strategy. However, if our investigation be restricted to the military field we must find an answer to the question whether an early surrender of the whole or part of Italy would have been the better military solution.

To evacuate the whole of Italy and to defend the Reich from positions in the Alps would not have been to economize our effectives; it would have given the enemy untrammelled freedom of movement in the direction of France and the Balkans, have meant sacrificing an indispensable deep battle-zone and unleashing the air war on the whole of southern Germany and Austria.

Similarly to have evacuated southern and central Italy and held the Apennines and Alps only would not have resulted in any saving of men and materials, nor have appreciably lessened the danger of sea- and air-borne landings or the extension of the air war as above.

In both cases there would have been increased danger to supply lines.

For a retirement with certain prospects of success preparations ought to have been made long before, as early as 1942-43, when, however, it was not possible for political reasons.

The conclusion is that the battle for Italy was not only justified but even imperative and the problem one of simply doing whatever seemed best for one's own theatre irrespective of the general strategic plan. Of course if the objective was to bring the war to an early end, regardless of what chances remained of snatching a semi-political victory, then the Mediterranean war must be considered unnecessary, but this is a view I cannot share.

21

The Partisan War in Italy

The first organization of resistance—Outbreak of full-scale guerilla war after June 1944—Partisan successes—Establishment of a "Partisan wartime staff"—Aspects of international law—Excesses.

THE DEVELOPMENT OF GUERILLA WARFARE

The first signs that cells of resistance against the German armed forces were being created first became apparent under the Badoglio government (25 July to 8 September 1943). Colonel Count Montezemolo must be regarded as the moving spirit. As the count was Badoglio's aide it is safe to assume that this movement was called to life in complete agreement with the Italian government, at a time when it was Italy's declared intention to continue the fight at the side of Germany.

After the defection of Italy the network of spies and saboteurs spread, extensive assistance being given amongst other things to escaping Allied prisoners of war, who, joining with Italian soldiers who had taken to the mountains, themselves helped to build up the first guerilla groups. Among these latter, rascally elements were allowed to become a scourge to decent Italians. In the autumn and winter of 1943 isolated and not particularly dangerous bands, mostly composed of escaped prisoners of war, made their appearance in the rear of the Tenth Army, as a rule trying to fight their way across the front. Partisan bands began to be a nuisance in and on both sides of the Apennines for the first time in April 1944, being most active in the region of Florence, where, as their presence jeopardized our supplies, military counter-measures were required.

After the fall of Rome in June 1944, they became more aggressive, far more in fact than I had reckoned with, and this date may be called the birthday of the all-out guerilla war. Their accretion was particularly noticeable between the front and the Apennines, and at this period it may be estimated that their strength rose from a few thousands to a hundred thousand or so. This expansion was provoked by Badoglio's and Alexander's broadcast incitements and by the expected annihilation of the German armies in Italy. From then on the Partisan war was an actual menace to our military operations and it was vital to remove it.

After some desultory fighting costly to themselves, the Partisans drew in their horns during the winter of 1944-45, armistice agreements, the lull in the fighting at the front, amnesties and bad winter weather variously accounting for their quiescence. Their numbers then probably fell to some tens of thousands.

But the German Command had no illusions about this inactivity. Indeed when the thaw set in in the mountains they reappeared in stronger force than ever, their highest numbers, some 200,000-300,000, being reached in March-April 1945.

More efficient and even more brutal and ruthless in their methods were the localized bands in Istria, where they were influenced from the Balkans, and in northeast Lombardy, with a hard core round Gorizia and in the Alpine region to the north. Apart from a general harassing of our troops, the main purpose of these guerillas was to disorganize and hold up our supplies on the route through Villach into Italy and traffic to Yugoslavia from the west and north. In the mountains east of the line Fiume-Trieste-Gorizia the mass of the population were in sympathy with them.

The bands were generally localized, but with the changing aspect of the battle for Italy organized movements could be observed.

ORGANIZATION OF THE PARTISANS

The main feature of the Partisan organization in the early months was the absence of any kind of responsible leadership

according to Article 1 of the Hague Convention on Land Warfare, although later on, when the names of a few leaders became
known, things were not so bad in this respect.

In the course of months the following facts became increasingly evident to the German Command:

The highest responsible leaders of the Partisan movement
were located at Allied headquarters; we therefore assumed that
they composed a mixed control centre relying on both Italians
and Allies, the mainspring of their activities being the intelligence officer, although they were increasingly under the eye
of the operations branch. Sabotage and reconnaissance parties,
often composed of criminal elements, communicated with general headquarters through Allied liaison officers, in so far as they
did not act independently.

The organization of so-called brigades became observable as
early as April 1944; but this was more nominal than real. After
the autumn of 1944 it is possible to speak of a more disciplined
organization and leadership in Partisan-infested zones—for example, in the region of Alessandria. In those groups which had
a core of ex-soldiers the units were officered on military lines;
their scope and effectiveness was, however, small, their supplies
coming at the beginning from mostly involuntary contributions
by the local population, supplemented—in the matter of personnel—by parachute droppings or coastal landings from submarines.

Basically the Partisan organization presented the following
picture:

Group 1. "Reconnaissance troops" professionally trained,
making their appearance in very small groups. These were
bound to each other by oath and were gallant men who risked
their necks. Except that they violated international law no
objection could be taken to them. The sabotage troops also
belonged to this group; these increasingly violated the laws
of humanity, however, the criminal element being strongly
represented among them.

Group 2. Riffraff who robbed, murdered and pillaged wherever and whatever they could—a national scourge.

Group 3. The main Partisan organization. This, which as time passed took on an increasingly military character, regarded all Germans and Fascists as enemies and enlisted more or less support according to the attitude of the local inhabitants. In the areas in which they operated there were Partisan-occupied villages, even zones in which every man, woman and child was in some way connected with them, either as combatant, helper or sympathizer. Whether these people acted spontaneously or under gentle pressure made no difference. When a bullet killed a German soldier it was not possible for us to discriminate. At the same time there were whole zones that were only "Partisan-threatened" or even "free of Partisans."

Altogether the Partisan groups presented the picture of a motley collection of Allied, Italian and Balkan soldiers, German deserters and native civilians of both sexes of widely different callings and ages with very varying ideas of morality, with the result that patriotism was often merely a cloak for the release of baser instincts.

PARTISAN METHODS

The Partisan war was a complete violation of international law and contradicted every principle of clean soldierly fighting.

The chief blame must be laid on the shortage of leaders and the shortcomings of those available, which made any uniform organization and training impossible. Instead, the southern temperament could run riot, their "patriotic mission" combined with vicious instincts leaving few loopholes for compunction. In small groups or singly they ran amok without restraint, doing their nefarious work everywhere, in the mountains, in the Po Valley, in woods and on roads, under cover of darkness or of fog—but never openly. To the work of these bands must be ascribed most of the many acts of sabotage to military installations, dumps, railways, roads, bridges and telegraph lines and the equally frequent crimes against humanity. In the whole calendar of crimes—from ambushing, hanging, drowning, burning, freezing, crucifying and every kind of torture, not forgetting the poisoning of wells and the repeated abuse of the Red Cross—there is not one which was not an everyday occurrence.

All this was the easier because the Partisans almost always wore no emblems, hid their weapons or, again in violation of international law, went about dressed as Germans or Fascists, thus freeing themselves from the obligations a uniform carries with it.

In consequence there was considerable irritation on our side, for the German soldier in the infested areas could not help seeing in every civilian of either sex a fanatical assassin or expecting to be fired at from every house. The whole population had in any case helped in or connived at elaborating a warning system which placed every German soldier's life in danger.

Only in a very few exceptional cases did the bands accept fair fight; once they had stealthily done their mischief or if a sense of inferiority made them break off a fight, they melted away among the civilian population or as innocent country hikers.

When they did give fight they forgot all human decency, especially vis-à-vis the local inhabitants, so that fearful casualties often occurred among non-combatants, not to speak of the Fascist militia.

With German soldiers scattered over a deep zone exact statistics of our considerable losses cannot be obtained because every kind of disappearance was simply listed "missing." In the period June-August 1944 my intelligence officer reported to me some 5,000 killed and 25,000-30,000 wounded or kidnapped. These figures seem to me too high. According to my estimate, based on oral reports, a more probable minimum figure for those three months would be 5,000 killed and 7,000-8,000 killed or kidnapped, to which should be added a maximum total of the same number of wounded. In any case the proportion of casualties on the German side alone greatly exceeded the total Partisan losses.

THE FIGHT AGAINST THE PARTISANS

When the guerilla warfare started Italy had to be considered "occupied territory," in accordance with Article 42 of the Hague Convention, which both Axis and Allies had signed. Thus the Partisans were beyond the pale of international law from the very beginning, the pre-conditions for making Article 2 of the Hague Convention effective not being present.

The Partisan war was conducted by the enemy, however, with complete disregard for the definitions of Article 1, the text of which article justified the German Command in taking all counter-measures permissible by the terms of the Hague Convention or "custom of war."

My reading of history and first-hand acquaintance with guerilla warfare have led me to the conclusion that it is a degenerate form of war. The methods to which it resorts are so incalculable that, sooner or later, they must come into collision with the written and unwritten rules of international law, involving both sides in committing the most abominable crimes with almost mathematical predictability.

In full awareness of these conditions the German armed forces abstained from guerilla warfare—the sole exception, the proclamation of *Werwolf* in April 1945, is anything but a convincing counter-argument, being the act of S.S. and party leaders. In peacetime the German armed forces received no training or instruction in warfare of this kind, and thus were unprepared to fight the growing menace in Italy. It required vigorous intervention from me to make army commanders give it the same attention as the battle at the front.

Outside the forward zone the conduct of operations against the guerillas was, until May 1944, the special preserve of the S.S. Reichsführer, whose word was law in the officially declared "Partisan areas." I contended, however, that the battle with the enemy and the guerillas was an indivisible whole, and in the face of strong opposition from the S.S. the O.K.W. accepted my view, with the result that from the beginning of May 1944 I was given absolute authority in dealing with the guerillas in the

Italian theatre of war. In this the "Supreme S.S. and Police Leader" was personally subordinate to me and had to carry out my directives, although he could conduct operations against the Partisans in his zone on his own responsibility. This arrangement smacked of political jobbery and was militarily unsatisfactory. But it was workable, for a useful executive had been created in the "Partisan warfare staff" at the "Supreme S.S. and Police Leader's" headquarters.

In principle the command of an operation against the guerillas was given to the *senior* officer, irrespective of whether he belonged to the army, the S.S. or the police, the specified responsibility being in no wise affected.

For large-scale operations against the Partisans ordered by the Army Group, closed or mixed units under an independent command were kept in readiness. In this case absolute strength was not the determining factor but rather the suitability of a detachment for guerilla warfare.

Whereas at the outset we could be satisfied with infantry units the expansion and embitterment of the conflict required a continually increasing use of artillery, mortars, tanks, flame-throwers and other technical expedients. Well-trained and equipped men were locally organized into "raiding detachments" and drilled so as to be on hand at all times for immediate counter-measures over the whole back area in an efficient organization which was at the same time available both for defence against airborne landings and to serve as a substructure supported by such suitable geographical features as defiles, entrances to villages or fortified lay-outs, for the defence of the back area in case of an enemy break-through at the front.

Because it was active far in the rear and the troops in the line were not immediately affected, the High Command was inclined to treat the Partisan movement too lightly. Reports from the rear of attacks on platoons going back or stationed in the back areas arrived so late that what with the daily intensification of the fighting at the front there was little reaction to them. This apathy and lack of experience and, above all, our certainty of the coming extension of this irregular war induced me to order all possible measures to stop it or at least to limit its expansion. These were: police observation of resistance nuclei and later of the illegal organizations themselves; political appeasement, with the co-operation of the Vatican and the Italian princes of the Church, of political leaders, heads of administration and other influential persons; welfare measures for the population; pardons; release from military and labour service and from transportation to Germany; and radio propaganda. Attempts to bring about the cessation of hostilities, at least locally and temporarily—which were actually successful in certain cases—were also made.

It was clear to me by June 1944 that the Partisans might critically affect the retirement of my armies; I therefore tried to repair omissions by giving orders that the Partisan battle was to be fought in the same way as the battle at the front. Weapons which had hitherto been used exclusively at the front, such as tanks, artillery and flame-throwers, were to be employed everywhere where there was a chance that with their help the danger might be quickly removed. The best troops were only just good enough to be used in fighting of this kind.

I thus hoped by such energetic action and the use of disciplined troops to prevent the guerilla war degenerating into an arbitrary retaliation by poorly disciplined units—which I considered could only lead to chaos. This warfare had its own peculiar aspects to which tactical rules had to be adapted. Battle reconnaissance in the field had to be preceded by an early and continuous "enemy reconnaissance." The troops were not suitable for this work, which was reserved for the specially trained Security Service and the Secret Field Police. The strictest secrecy was essential to the surprise and success of any operation. The capture of a Partisan hide-out was of no practical use unless they defended it. It gradually became the rule to cordon off the Partisan area and either to close in from all sides of the pocket or to attack with assault troops from a stationary cordon line.

The crippling sense of uncertainty and liability to attack led to the development of a suitable defence against being ambushed. Instead of waiting to be shot at from a house we neutralized possible snipers by opening fire on the house or went on firing until the enemy was out of action. This was the only way to make sure of not receiving a bullet in the back. The protection of back-area communications for supply columns and the evacuation of the wounded had become especially important over long stretches of road if serious losses were to be avoided.

In view of the brutal, indeed very often inhuman, behaviour of the bands, for one critical period I had to order drastic use of weapons to curtail the extraordinary casualties we were incurring from a certain nonchalance and out-of-place mildness on the part of our soldiers. Unless one wanted to commit suicide the Partisan war involved a reversal of natural feelings, which in itself concealed grave dangers.

As a matter of principle I abstained from the use of bombers, which would naturally have been the most effective means, because in inhabited places I could not take the responsibility for injury to the civilian population. Events have taught me that this consideration is rewarded with very little thanks. In the future such scruples will have to go by the board—unless guerilla warfare is universally banned.

As it is, because of the peculiar nature of insurgent or guerilla warfare certain measures are permissible by international law which are alien to the soldier at the front. Unfortunately the articles of the Hague Convention for Land Warfare are insufficiently defined, the vague term "the custom of war" being partly used to cover this lack of precision. The questions that require clarification are: hostages and the killing of hostages; reprisals and their nature, extent and proportionality; collective measures and their pre-conditions; emergency decrees and judicial procedure.

It must be clear that the vagueness of international law and the loopholes left open by it lead in the heat of the moment to inevitable blunders and the death of victims on both sides. It is a sin against the spirit, in view of the different existing interpretations of international law—as, for example, between the continental and the Anglo-Saxon—to lay down a canon which a responsible commander cannot apply in practice on the strength of his own country's interpretation. Many of the above-mentioned acts, for instance reprisals, are "questions of opinion" which must be decided by the responsible commander after a thorough investigation of the particular case.

As, according to German regulations, only commanders above and including divisional commanders—who disposed of expert advisers—were authorized to order reprisals, there were ample guarantees against inconsiderate measures.

The fact, however, remains that the soldier who has just had a dastardly attempt made on his life and only sees red reacts quite differently from a hair-splitting prosecuting counsel or a judge from the safety of his bench.

THE SPREAD OF THE PARTISAN WAR. ITS EXCESSES

From the daily reports which came in to Army Intelligence from all parts of the battle-zone and were mapped and card-indexed, the constant spread of Partisan activity could be seen, the number of special incidents rising to five or six a day. While acts of sabotage on railways, depots and dumps were more or less localized and routine, the rest of Partisan activity was governed by the situation at the front, the areas and the frequency of surprise attacks changing constantly.

As the organization expanded the number of "Partisan-threatened" or "Partisan-occupied" areas multiplied, but they were a vital menace only where they were directly co-ordinated with military operations.

Since the war German soldiers have been accused of a large number of excesses; various incidents have also been made the subject of trials which have almost always ended with a death sentence on the accused. Surely with the passing of these sentences the last word cannot have been said!

Even if allowance is made for exaggerations and the extravagance natural to the Italian character and also for the pressure still exerted by persons belonging to former communist-dominated groups, it must be admitted that on the German side, too, abominable things were done. But the fact remains that only in a few exceptional instances has convincing proof been furnished of the guilt of German soldiers. The excesses or acts of barbarity that occurred in Italy must be equally shared among Partisan bands, neo-Fascist organizations and German deserter groups, whereas only the smallest fraction—if any—should be laid at the door of German military units. Perhaps also a good many incidents should be attributed to stragglers who overstepped the permissible limits of self-help.

It is matter for reflection that only a very few irregularities of this kind—there were perhaps three or five cases—were reported to me through official channels, and that the stories of crimes against civilians reported to me by Mussolini turned out, when investigated at my insistence by Germans, to be lies or exaggerations. This is partly explained by differences in procedure traceable to the variety of interpretations of the articles of the convention (for example, those covering the resort to, extent of and method of reprisals). Often the evidence is contradictory, so that German soldiers can be pronounced guilty on the assumption that the sworn testimony of witnesses on the German side is untrustworthy and that extracted by third-degree methods on the other side is axiomatically credible.

It may be objected to this argument that many such incriminating incidents were not reported, but were glossed over or even hushed up. As everything is possible in war, this may have happened in individual cases. But as I had built up a special reporting and observation network which would not have tolerated this practice for long I must take exception to any generalization. My service was supplemented by information passed to German units and staffs by the Italian authorities and the Church, and by my own frequent surprise visits to German and Italian units, headquarters and depots, not to mention the supervisory measures of my "special representative," General Hartmann. In addition there was the vigilant watch kept by the Field and Military .Police, the Secret Field Police and the Field Rifle Corps.

I believe that nowhere else were such precautions ever taken to maintain discipline and to protect the population. Within my command I myself intervened draconically at the first sign that immorality and corruption were undermining discipline or having a bad effect on our prestige, our friendly relations with our Axis partner, or above all on the welfare of the local people. By such means I was able in a very short time to put a drastic stop to the obvious demoralization of the Fourteenth Army.

If, in spite of this, during or after a war insurgents are officially recognized as patriots and heroes even by the governments of countries which have signed the Hague Convention, this means an utter contempt for treaties and the sabotage of every conception of right.

Part Three

UNCONDITIONAL SURRENDER
AND MY TRIAL

22

Commander-in-Chief West

23 Feb. 1945 American offensive on the Roer—Loss of the left bank of the Rhine—7 March The Americans capture the intact bridge across the Rhine at Remagen—10 March Kesselring C.-in-C. West—March American bridgehead created at Remagen—22 March The Americans cross the Rhine at Oppenheim—23 March British-American offensive on the lower Rhine, crossing of the Rhine at Wesel—28-29 March Fall of Mannheim, Wiesbaden and Frankfurt-am-Main—1-18 April Encirclement and capitulation of Army Group B in the Ruhr pocket—4 April Fall of Kassel—11 April Fall of Würzburg—16-20 April Battles for Nürnberg—18 April Fall of Magdeburg.

MY ASSIGNMENT

On 8 March 1945 I received an order to report to Hitler. When I asked the reason I was not told.

I arrived at general headquarters in Berlin towards noon on the following day. I was informed in the presence of Keitel and Jodl that I was to relieve von Rundstedt in the west. When I pointed out that I was needed in the Italian theatre and that, not being fully recuperated, I had not the necessary mobility for this decisive mission, they listened to my objections with understanding but thought it certain they would hold no water with Hitler.

The interview with Hitler that afternoon—at first in private—confirmed Keitel's and Jodl's prognostication. After a detailed exposition of the general situation he told me that the fall of Remagen had finally necessitated a change of command in the west. Without reproaching von Rundstedt he gave as his reason for taking this step that only a younger and more active commander who had experience in fighting the Western Powers and enjoyed the confidence of the man in the line could perhaps still restore the situation. He knew all about the difficulties of changing horses in midstream—I must, however, accept this sacrifice in spite of my impaired health. He had confidence that I would do everything humanly possible.

He then gave me a picture of the over-all situation, which I will only summarize:

The decision lay *in the east;* a collapse on the Russian front would mean collapse everywhere. However, as all our defensive strength was concentrated on that front, he was confident of the outcome there. He expected the enemy's main offensive to be launched in the direction of Berlin.

He told me that Schoerner's Central Army Group in Czechoslovakia and Silesia had recently fought magnificently. Reinforced and properly supplied, it would repel any offensive mounted against it. Busse and his Ninth Army stood firm on its left. As he expected the main assault to be delivered against it, it had been the best provided with replacements, material and fortifications.

His remarks about Schoerner's Army Group applied equally to Rendulic's Army Group South on its right; but although there was a possibility that Rendulic's left flank might be involved in the main decisive battle he was reckoning with only secondary attacks on the right flank.

The Ninth Army front was well equipped. Busse had ample infantry strength and Panzer and anti-tank units, to say nothing of army artillery and an overstrength flak distributed in great depth under the best artillery generals; good positions with excellent obstacles of every kind, above all a water defence line in front and in rear of the main battle-front, as well as Berlin with its circular defences and prepared positions for a successive retirement.

The Russians would never penetrate this front; he had personally convinced himself of its defensibility and had had

Heinrici's Army Group on the left of the Ninth Army must, however, be reinforced, though here he anticipated only secondary assaults.

The Southeast Army Group under Loehr had only a minor importance; its previous conduct encouraged him to believe it would continue to delay the enemy in co-ordination with Army Group Southwest and von Vietinghoff, who, he hoped, would uphold my tradition. Similarly he had no anxiety about Kurland or Norway.

In the west there had been months of bitter fighting, but the Americans, British and French had also suffered heavy losses. Once the Russian front had been reinforced the necessary replacements would be fed steadily to the points of main effort in the west. Even he could not make any fresh divisions available, but if a continuous flow of men and material was kept up there was still time to refit the exhausted units on the western front. The enemy could not ignore the natural obstacles behind which our armies were standing firm. The vulnerable spot was Remagen. It was urgent to restore the situation there; he was confident it could be done.

In this phase of the war the one and only question was to bridge the time until the Twelfth Army, our new fighters and other novel weapons could be employed in overwhelming numbers.

He largely blamed the Luftwaffe for previous defeats; but he had now personally taken over its technical direction and guaranteed success.

The Commander-in-Chief of the navy, Admiral Doenitz, would soon make his new U-boats felt and would substantially relieve the situation.

He was full of praise for the superhuman efforts and endurance of the people at home.

Arms production was co-ordinated in the hands of Saur of the Armament Ministry, in whom he had implicit confidence that he would satisfy the essential requirements of our armies in the field. There would, however, have to be some diversion of production to new units being formed, which would be the best the German Wehrmacht had seen during the war. He himself would be responsible for their getting first-rate leadership. So it was once again a battle for time!

Hitler's exposition, which lasted hours, was remarkably lucid and showed an astounding grasp of detail.

Afterwards Keitel and Jodl went into various points with me more minutely. Their answers to my questions brought the picture into sharper focus, but did not materially alter it.

My mission was clear: Hang on! It worried me the more because for the time being I had to command "anonymously," the idea being that my name should be still effective in Italy.

THE SITUATION AND PRELIMINARY MEASURES

In the night of 9-10 March 1945 I drove to C.-in-C. West's G.H.Q. at Ziegenberg, where the Chief of Staff, Westphal, my old Chief in Italy, gave me a detailed exposition of the situation as he saw it.

The main feature of the situation at the front was the enemy's extraordinary superiority in men and material on the ground and his absolute ascendancy in the air.

Our fifty-five weak divisions, without adequate replacements or supplies, were opposed by eighty-five American, British and French divisions in full strength. The daily strength of our infantry divisions had fallen to an average of 5,000 against an establishment of 12,000. On the other hand the daily strength of our few Panzer divisions was between 10,000 and 11,000. Altogether this meant at the very best one hundred combatants to every kilometre of front. There could be no talk of back areas, of pulling out even small reserves from the line or of garrisoning the numerous pillboxes of the West Wall. Rundstedt, appreciating the development of the situation on the Russian front, had put at its disposal ten Panzer divisions, six almost complete infantry divisions, ten artillery corps, eight smoke brigades and numerous other units. Compensation had indeed been

promised, but so far there was no sign of it. Westphal told me
that reports and his own personal observation led him to believe
that morale was still generally high. The troops were, of course,
war-weary and worried about their families at home, but they
went on doing their duty just the same. They were alive to the
importance of their task of keeping the rear of the Russian front
free. He believed he was right in saying that every soldier in
the west knew that he had a part to play in saving the soil of
our country and the Germans of the eastern provinces from the
Russians. This and the knowledge that the alternative was unconditional surrender were the linchpins that still held the front
together.

In the evening in a telephone conversation with the O.K.W.
I made no bones about my impressions. Seen at close quarters,
the situation appeared very much more serious than it had been
depicted to me. I told them my requirements must therefore
be fulfilled to the widest possible extent.

In the afternoon of 10 March I had an exhaustive consultation
about the situation in the air with General Schmidt, Air Officer
Commanding the Luftwaffe West. This Command, Schmidt
told me, was not subordinate to C.-in-C. West, although co-
operation was good. The interests of the military and air defence
of Germany were, however, sometimes conflicting; the Reich
Air Command, whose operations were directed by Stumpff's ingenious brain, could not, of course, always do justice to the
interests of the army. There were so many things to be done
and so few means to do them. Added difficulties were the Allied
air supremacy, the gaps and deficiencies in the Luftwaffe ground
organization, the technical and flying difficulties of the new
Strahler aircraft, the unpredictable changes of the spring
weather in the Rhine Valley, the shortage of petrol and spare
parts, the insufficient mobility of flak batteries and the inadequate training of their crews.

I recommended two points to Schmidt's special attention:
logical concentration, for the moment necessarily in the Remagen area, and the intensification of all efforts by the Luftwaffe

and the navy to destroy the bridge at Remagen and any auxiliary pontoons.

On the morning of 11 March I visited Army Group B, where, in the presence of its commander, Field-Marshal Model, I went into conference with General von Zangen, commanding the Fifteenth Army, and his subordinate commanders. They estimated that elements of two American infantry divisions and one armoured division with artillery were across the Rhine—where no equal strength could be mustered to oppose them. The weak points were, above all, the flanks of our line around the bridge-head. Supplies of ammunition were also running short. There was little prospect of liquidating the bridgehead unless supplies and replacements were speeded up and increased in volume.

The conditions behind the front were not very pleasing, so altogether I could not but regard the situation with apprehension.

In the late afternoon of the same day I went on to Army Group H on the lower Rhine, where I conferred with Blaskowitz at the battle headquarters of the Parachute Army. From this talk I gathered that the Army Group was fairly sure of itself if it were allowed at least another eight or ten days to re-equip, prepare positions, bring up supplies and rest. They liked their task of defending the Rhine.

Operations in Holland were directed by the Twenty-fifth Army under Blumentritt, whose forces were weak and insufficient for the purpose; his best troops were rightly in action on the left wing, where Schlemm's Parachute Army took over as far as the Ruhr and would have to bear the full brunt of the battle in the expected main sectors. The forces aligned between the Lippe and the Ruhr were weaker but capable of holding. (This unfortunately turned out to be an overoptimistic view.) Strong elements were held in reserve.

All I heard made on reflection a good impression, so that, remembering the unique performance of the Parachute Army west of Rheims, I felt I could look forward to the battles to be expected on the right wing of the front with confidence.

It was not until 13 March that I was able to visit the Rhine Palatinate for a local conference with Army Group G, with the Seventh Army on its right and the First Army on its left. Both armies considered the situation dangerous but not hopeless if mobile reserves were brought up. The Seventh Army was busy constructing the Moselle defence line; on its left flank it was engaged in violent back-and-forth fighting.

By the night of 13 March I had formed a superficial personal impression of the situation. Unfortunately pressure of time, the extreme length of the front and the difficulty I still had in getting about as a result of my injuries made it impossible for me to collect first-hand information by touring the units in the line. This was a pity, as I would have been able to form a more convincing picture of the situation and the state of the troops and perhaps would have come to another decision.

As I saw it the situation was this:

Strong enemy concentration of forces in the Remagen area in front of the First Army on either side of Saarbrücken.

Indications that the American Third Army was building up fairly strong concentrations in front of the right flank of our Seventh Army and was assembling in front of the Parachute Army.

Continuous heavy assaults against the right wing of our First Army south of Trier. Conspicuous neglect by the enemy of the Dutch front, of the Rhine sector below the Ruhr and of the upper Rhine front.

The grouping of the Allied forces made it difficult to guess their intentions. These might be:

(1) To exploit their lucky success at Remagen either so as to split the German western front in two and to link up with the Russians by the shortest route, or—which was less probable—to limit their forward drive towards the east and to attack the Ruhr from the south and the south-east.

(2) An encircling offensive against the only remaining bastion west of the Rhine—the Saar Palatinate—in order to
wipe out Army Group G and so by crossing the Rhine
to secure a jumping-off base for operations against South
Germany.

(3) A British offensive to force a Rhine crossing on the Parachute Army's front and so create a bridgehead which
would give them strategic possibilities in three directions.

In a word, the enemy was superior both in numbers and
material, and their air force controlled the battle area. After
very stubborn and costly fighting our forces had been pushed
back to the river lines and the still intact parts of the West
Wall, and only a fraction of them had been regrouped and re-
equipped. The necessary reserves were either not yet formed
or not in the tactically right positions.

The gravest danger lay in the fact that Remagen required
an increasing flow of reinforcements and by itself almost swal-
lowed up the replacements and supplies fed to C.-in-C. West,
magnetically attracting everything right and left. This made the
regrouping, resting and refurbishing of the other Army Groups
more difficult, if not impracticable. In fact, the counter-measures against the first enemy forces to cross the Rhine had not
been taken with the uncompromising fierceness which might
have ensured a swift and relatively easy restoration of the line,
and the fate of the whole Rhine front hung on our wiping out
or containing the bridgehead.

Our own Rhine Palatinate bridgehead was a gift for an enemy
outflanking offensive, which must be expected to begin very
soon. At the same time the Moselle, with favourable country
behind it, was a respectable obstacle, the West Wall and the
area on its immediate front in the First Army's sector could not
be overrun straightaway, and the West Palatinate, with its successive natural positions, presented extraordinary difficulties to
the attack and us with opportunities for a mobile defence.
Everything depended on bringing up the necessary reinforcements and reserves to the right place at the right time, though

the lack of any large mechanized reserves made this look doubtful.

The Luftwaffe disposed of considerable flak forces. Heavy losses had hitherto been partially made good by an improvised motorization of concrete emplacement batteries. A lot more could be done in this way. Indeed, more had to be done, as they were almost the only guns we had of long-range calibre and might help us considerably. Better supplied with ammunition than the army artillery, the flak could become the backbone of the front.

This meant a deliberate further weakening of our already weak air-raid defence. But our flak was in any case incapable of putting up an effective defence; also the main effort of enemy air attack had been shifted from towns and industrial centres to the battle-zones and troop-movement areas. After weighing the pros and cons I had to give preference to the front and lines of communication.

Our airmen were doing their best, but they could not score even a moral victory. They had lost heart; enemy attacks on their airfields and the unfavourable weather demoralized them. Perhaps something might still be done to revive the old elasticity of ground-air support and to regild the Luftwaffe's tarnished halo, or—was it too late?

The supply situation was bad; in some areas critical. Complicated by uncertainty as to the arrival of supply trains, it made wrong distributions inevitable. The railway network was badly battered, and if further stretches of line were put out of action could no longer be reckoned with.

Furthermore, symptoms of disintegration were perceptible behind the front which gave cause for uneasiness. The number of "missing" was a disquieting indication that a rot was setting in. The attitude of the civilian population in several districts, particularly in the Rhine Palatinate and the Saar, confirmed this tendency. Even among military staffs political talk could be heard which undermined the solidarity of resistance and nourished defeatism at lower levels.

Yet my orders were categorical: "Hang on!"

After our continual retreats for almost three and a quarter years even Hitler no longer expected a decision on the Rhine. Instead he ordered a shortening of the front in the hope the terrain would compensate for the weakness even he was aware of. The object was to gain time until events on the Russian front matured and until new divisions and new weapons became effective. In the case of the Saar Palatinate considerations of war economy were eloquent: after the loss of Silesia the Ruhr and the Saar had become absolutely decisive factors for the prosecution of the war. Another consideration was that as the enemy approached the Rhine, in addition to the chemical industry in the Saar, the important Rhineland armament factories—for example, Ludwigshafen—would have to close down.

A delaying action in the depth of Germany would, of course, have been one way of fighting the "battle for time," but this was equivalent to evacuating the industrial areas, which at this stage could not be considered.

Ergo:

Hold the Rhine and the Saar Palatinate bastion.

Remove or reduce the bridgehead at Remagen.

AGAIN AT THE FÜHRER'S GENERAL HEADQUARTERS

On 15 March 1945 I again discussed the situation with Hitler, the immediate reason being the unfavourable development in the Saar Palatinate.

In general Hitler agreed with my proposals.

He sanctioned the evacuation of the West Wall on the right flank of the First Army and the withdrawal of this flank to intermediate positions.

The difficulties of the situation at Remagen he realized, but wanted still more persistent efforts to narrow the bridgehead. Here he mentioned the importance of the Ruhr and the Saar, as well as the industrial area between the Rhine and the Main.

He told me that a full-strength division was being rushed from Denmark, but he could not promise more than this one without endangering his programme for building new divisions and consequently the continuation of the war. On the other hand, replacements and supplies, especially of tanks, would be forthcoming quickly and in volume. No reinforcements in the air could be expected for some time, though he had taken steps to speed up production of fighter aircraft.

As I drove back in the night of 15-16 March I had the impression that Hitler stubbornly believed we could defeat the Russians in the east, and that what was happening in the west neither surprised nor particularly worried him. He took it for granted that once the Russian front had been consolidated he would be able with the forces so released and his newly created divisions to clean up in the west. He was equally convinced that his orders to increase supplies would be carried out to the letter.

It was very different in fact.

The Danish division was not fully effective and was dispatched so late that I could not even consider using it at Remagen. By the time it had got halfway it had to be rushed to the Eleventh Army, which was in a tight place in the Kassel area. The arrival of replacements and supplies was continually reported, but they only came in driblets.

THE LOSS OF THE PALATINATE

On 19 March 1945 the situation in the Palatinate and also at Remagen had developed an intolerable tension. The right wing of the Seventh Army had been unhinged; the attack in the direction of Oppenheim, if accompanied by a simultaneous tank thrust beyond Kreuznach in the direction of Worms-Ludwigshafen, might place the whole of Army Group G in jeopardy. In addition the inner flanks of both armies in the middle of the Palatinate had been broken through, rolled up and partly outflanked. It was obvious the Palatinate could not be held. A "free operation" was no longer to be thought of.

I attached so much importance to the rapidly developing situation there that I was four times in the Palatinate between 16-17 and 21-22 March. A great deal depended on the behaviour of the Seventh Army; they must know that their tactics would decide the fate of the First Army, but that the latter's needs must regulate the pace of their own movements. They had a

difficult task. From a purely tactical point of view the First
Army was in an even tighter corner, everything hanging on the
holding of the left pivotal flank along the Rhine, which must
adapt the pace of its retirement to the centre. The Palatinate
Forest was a focal and pivotal point, as its possession was indispensable for later manœuvre.

While I was in conference at my headquarters with Minister
Speer and Herr Roechling, which was interrupted for a short
time by an air raid,[1] a report came in that American tanks had
reached Kaiserslautern. It was a good thing that the weak counter-measures on the right flank of the Seventh Army had slowed
up the impetus of the enemy advance. I personally convinced
myself of the consolidation of the Rhine bridgeheads at Speyer
and Germersheim, which were strongly reinforced with flak,
and thus night after night from 16 March I was able to watch
the rear elements of the armies stream continuously back across
the Rhine. Any enemy thrust from the north along the Rhine
in the direction of Speyer our air forces had orders to stop
regardless of losses, and I was relieved that the enemy's advance
did not make this necessary.

The last days of the final evacuation of the left bank of the
Rhine were left to the initiative of army corps and divisional
commanders. Thanks to their drive the innumerable difficulties
were overcome: traffic jams, air attacks on packed roads, lanes
and villages, and the breakdown of horse teams, motor vehicles
and signals communications. The chief credit belongs to the
First Army staff, which took over the command of all troops
in the Rhine Palatinate from 21 March, while Army Group G
and the Seventh Army had to build up the defence of the Rhine
on the east bank of the river. After the evacuation of Ludwigshafen on 21 March the only bridgeheads that could be held for
the passage of the last remaining corps were at Speyer, Germersheim and Maxau. On 23 March I was able to give the order to

---

[1] As in three earlier cases of attacks on my headquarters, the enemy must
have known the habits of the staff fairly accurately. The first assault on this
occasion was directed against the mess at dinnertime and my own sleeping
quarters and study.

evacuate these also, and this was completed on 24-25 March.

The enemy operation had been suited to the peculiar nature of the Saar Palatinate salient. He had chosen the earliest moment for his offensive, but had failed to exploit the opportunity for a pincers movement.

The enemy tank attacks were bold and, against the right wing of the Seventh Army, even foolhardy. Conspicuous was the swift succession of single operations—a sign that the step-by-step methods noticeable in Italy had been abandoned—the dexterous leadership and reckless employment of tanks in country definitely unsuitable for large-scale tank operations. In the light of my experiences in similar country in Italy I had not reckoned on the rapid success of the American armoured forces, assisted as they were by the partial failure of the exhausted German troops. I was, however, surprised that having once broken through they did not exploit their momentary opportunity to cut off Army Group G from the Rhine bridges with air support and so take the first step to its annihilation. That the Army Group, if sadly battered, got back across the Rhine in considerable strength and was able to build up a new defence line behind the river was due to this mistake.

The lion's share of the glory in the Palatinate falls to the Allied air force.

The reasons for the sudden collapse, which my talks with army and divisional commanders had not led me to expect, I shall try to explain as follows.

The troops had been in almost continuous action for months. The repeated emphatic order to stand fast had led to irreplaceable losses of the best men and material. In addition there were interfering instructions by Hitler, eloquent of his lack of acquaintance with the front, which wasted time before they were countermanded or modified. A battle cannot be directed from an office desk.

With all due regard for the magnificent performance of our soldiers, the heavy defensive fighting of the past months had been a greater physical and mental strain than I had allowed for in the light of my first enquiries. The advanced deterioration of the situation and the breadth of the front had made it impossible for me to visit the units in the line. If I had known the actual conditions on the left flank of the Seventh Army and on the right flank of the First Army I would probably have insisted more firmly on Hitler's altering my mission, though that could not have made any material difference to the outcome. Our issues of petrol and ammunition were in alarmingly small and irregular supply either for a running fight or a showdown. The American attack came so early that the grouping of reserves could not be completed.

The permission to evacuate part of the West Wall which I extracted from Hitler on the night of 15-16 March came too late. One day sooner and the rout in the Palatinate Forest would not have been so disastrous.

Our airmen were impotent and the bad weather in the Rhine Valley did not help. As against this the enemy air force was overwhelming, while signals communications in the Palatinate, already awkward, suffered considerably from bombing.

And yet, precisely because the situation was so desperate, our shrunken but loyal and spirited divisions put up a memorable fight.

THE OPPENHEIM CROSSING AND ITS CONSEQUENCES

I had deliberately put off till the last moment the evacuation of the left bank of the Rhine, including the bridgeheads, with the result that the bulk of the forces on the right bank could be at least meagrely refitted. Where the stiffest fighting had been, as on the left flank of Army Group G, the enemy did not attack across the Rhine for a couple of weeks. It was different on the right flank, where Patton's divisions forced a crossing almost immediately after defeating the German rear guards on the west bank.

The Seventh Army commander, in command on the right bank, was familiar with my views and had been warned of a probable attempt at a crossing. I was therefore the more dumbfounded when it was reported that the Americans had made an almost peaceful crossing at Oppenheim during the night of 22-23

March. Strategically this gave them the chance to thrust behind the First Army, still partly in action to the west of the river, and to secure the Frankfurt basin for further operations. As no preparation had been made for an immediate counter-attack an attempt had to be made with what strength we could muster to throw the enemy forces back over the Rhine while they were still weak. A picked division was sent into action with assault guns and adequate artillery, but stronger forces were needed and the counter-attack misfired through no fault of its gallant leader, Colonel Runge, who was killed in action—a very sad loss to me.

As Remagen had been the grave of Army Group B, it seemed that the bridgehead at Oppenheim would be that of Army Group G. Here, too, the bulge which soon widened into a gap consumed all the forces that could be moved from other parts of the front and all the replacements available in the rear. In Germany, it is true, we were on familiar ground, but very little had been done to fortify positions. Of course here as elsewhere support from the air was absolutely nil and flak support now very small.

The best general cannot make bricks without straw. The reasons why the German Luftwaffe was bled white and col-lapsed are not generally known. We lacked bombers of every kind. Production of fighters by this time had been almost brought to a halt by the penetration of the industrial areas and smashing of our railways. The technical performance of our jets was superior to that of the enemy's fighters and the training of fighter pilots was also adequate. But these highly evolved air-craft had their great disadvantages: dependence upon outsize, perfectly level runways, difficulties in taking off and landing, short duration of flight and high accident ratio. With the air space controlled by the enemy, take-off and landing required special protection which was not always available. Unfavourable weather conditions, particularly in the Rhine Valley in March-April 1945, hampered already risky flying.

At this time, at the suggestion of Army Group commanders, I considered retiring the whole Rhine front. But I finally decided against it as it would have been certain to degenerate into a rout. Our troops were dog-tired, almost incapable of movement, for the most part with no fight left in them; the still unorganized back-area formations were a hindrance; and the enemy was superior in every respect, especially in mobility and in the air. Unless his unchecked progress were throttled our retreating units must be overrun. Such an operation would have become an end in itself and not a means to an end, that of winning time. Every day gained on the Rhine meant a bolstering of the front, if only to sift out and reassemble stragglers in the maintenance areas.

The decisive blow was struck between Idstein and Aschaffenburg on 27-29 March. The Seventh Army under its new and energetic commander, von Obstfelder, now had the difficult task of delaying the progress of the American Third Army into central Germany and that of the American Seventh into the south. The incomprehensible behaviour of a Panzer division complicated the job of blocking the routes along which the Americans were pushing forward through Giessen to Hersfeld and through Gelnhausen to Fulda. But, worse still, our Army Group B, aligned on its right, had lost all influence over its own left flank, an awkward situation which was got under control by my sending into the area the 12th Army Corps deputy headquarters staff under General Osterkamp to deal with it. At the end of March the Seventh Army stood in loose order of battle covering Hersfeld to Fulda and the Spessart Mountains in the south.

The First Army had had to conform to the movements of the Seventh and stretch out farther to the right. On 30 March, however, it was driven back to the line Miltenberg-Eberbach-Heidelberg, thus endangering the consolidation of the vital Tauber Line.

The fanning out of the enemy forces from the bridgeheads at Oppenheim and at Mannheim from the south towards the east and then northeast violated the principle of concentration of effort, and its success was striking proof of the ebbing combat value of the German troops.

THE LAST CAMPAIGN
showing the Front on 11th March 1945

THE "RUHR FORTRESS"

I am weighing my words when I describe the task of Army Group B to establish contact with the forces of the Eleventh Army to the east as "an attempt to break out." That was exactly what it was because the psychological moment had passed, the mobile forces inside and outside the pocket were very weak, and the Twelfth Army, in process of formation in the Magdeburg area east of the Elbe, could not be sent into action for another three weeks. A further complication was that the left wing of Army Group H had been pushed back into the Ruhr, giving Montgomery's right flank freedom of operation against the left flank of the break-out forces. The attempt had, however, to be made, since the more favourable opportunities in March had not been taken advantage of or could not perhaps be exploited. But now was our last chance.

As it was, however, our efforts to assemble and my instructions given on the spot proved useless. When I got back to my battle headquarters at Reinhardsbrunn in the Thuringian Forest on the morning of 1 April my Chief reported to me that on an order from the Führer just received the attempt to break out of the Ruhr pocket was to be called off and Army Group B was to defend the Ruhr as "a fortress" in immediate subordination to the O.K.W.

I was more than flabbergasted by this decision of the O.K.W. It upset all our plans. The O.K.W. may have thought a break-out had no longer any prospect of success, and that an encircled Army Group might pin down enough enemy troops to prejudice a strong eastward drive. They may possibly also have believed that the Army Group could be rationed by the Ruhr and that greater supplies could thus be fed to the other units at the front.

In point of fact, however, there was only enough food in the Ruhr to feed the troops of both Army Group and population for at most two or three weeks. From a strategic point of view the Ruhr had no interest for Eisenhower; his objective lay far to the east. The only hope of pinning down strong investment forces lay in a stubborn and indeed aggressive defence, which, judging by what I had seen, was not on the face of it likely. Army Group B's 300,000 men could not remotely be replaced to close the gap between the Teutoburger and the Thuringian Forest.

The fighting on the perimeter of the Ruhr pocket developed as might have been expected and led to a capitulation on 17 April, the reason being the simple fact that officers and men had ceased to see any sense in continuing the war.

April 17 ended the tragedy of Army Group B. Model, its commander and a brave and dashing soldier, took his own life. Looking back today, who can blame him? He is in my thoughts now, and I shall always remember him.

THE ALLIED BREAK-THROUGH ON THE LOWER RHINE

While the impending catastrophe of Army Groups G and B was being played out, Army Group H was able to carry out its re-grouping and re-equipment comparatively unmolested. The enemy's air operations in a clearly limited area, bombing raids on headquarters, and the smoke-screening and assembly of bridging material indicated the enemy's intention to attack between Emmerich and Dinslaken, with point of main effort on either side of Rees.

The cloudless spring weather gave Montgomery the opportunity for a large-scale airborne landing and to make full use of his airmen for ground support, thus facing Army Group H with the greatest difficulties of movement.

The Canadians and Americans, supported by the airborne landing, sweeping forward as expected, I agreed with the group commander's idea of smashing both by every means at his disposal. But the result was that the Army Group had used up its main reserves before the situation at the front was nearly clarified. That was an error which had to be paid for later, and indeed was.

It was lamentable that the reserve divisions only scored one success in a dispersed attack in the direction of Dinslaken. If we had been more cautious in throwing them in on 23-24 March, and if Rees had been properly reinforced with artillery, the situation on the evening of 25 March would not have been so black. As it was, the location of these reserves, which I had omitted to correct, and the ill-judged use made of them not only lost the battle for the Rhine, but also shaped operations to come.

In consequence Army Group H accepted the inevitable with a certain fatalism which was obvious to me at every conference. The loss of the impulsive and brilliant Schlemm of the 1st Parachute Corps was very noticeable. With the switching of American forces to the right wing of the British the signal had been given for the break-through. As Army Group B had done, so now Army Group H moved its headquarters north, instead of coming in closer to the threatened flank as a visible acknowledgment that much, indeed everything, depended on its standing firm.

Instead on 28 March Army Group H, at a moment when only on its left flank was there still any front to speak of, thought fit to send in to me and to the O.K.W. an entirely supererogatory account of the situation. This reporting to the Supreme Command over my head had the great disadvantage that I could not express my opinion *before* I had passed it on to them and heard their decision, and also that it so exasperated Hitler that I could no longer hope to exert a decisive influence. Any general holding a high command should have known the right psychological approach to his superior, but this situation report was a perfect example of the way to rouse Adolf Hitler's wrath. While saying comparatively little about its own defeat and the reasons for it, it was concerned with Army Group B's predicament as an argument for its own retirement.

Strategically right or wrong, it was a psychological blunder to tell a superior that he was not capable of grasping the operational picture. Hitler took it as "insufferable arrogance" on the part of the General Staff. I feel justified in making this criticism because I was the Commander-in-Chief whom Hitler had deprived of liberty of decision in the Italian campaign. But in a quite different way. It was very plain to me what the Führer would decide in this case.

Being all along of the opinion that the Ruhr was not at that moment an American objective, and that the British Second and the American Ninth Armies would continue their operations in a northeasterly and easterly direction, that is that they would by-pass the Ruhr, I was most staggered by the elimination of the 47th Panzer Corps from the front. To feed reinforcements into the Ruhr now was a mistaken investment of capital. If simultaneously the front were to be torn open it would be more than a mistake.

The counter-attacks which I had ordered on the southern flank of the enemy spearhead were also abortive, so that during a personal visit between 28 and 30 March I once again put forward my assessment of the situation and my view of how to meet it. In so doing I wanted to anticipate a change of Army Group H command which I expected.

Angered by the pessimism of Army Group H's situation report, Hitler was once again prejudiced against Blaskowitz by his refusal to carry out a "Führer's order" given at the end of March (which I also thought impracticable) to attack the enemy forces converging on Münster from the north and south and to seal off the gap. He made this evident by sending Student to assist Blaskowitz.

On his side Montgomery had the most difficult assignment; his armies, which had suffered great losses in the preceding battles west of the Rhine, were confronted by a most formidable obstacle, defended by divisions with a recognized combat tradition, which, moreover, had had a respite of ten days and were backed by adequate reserves. The technical preparations for this manœuvre were exemplary, however, and the massing of forces was commensurate with the undertaking and the Allies' resources.

THE SITUATION ON THE UPPER RHINE IN MARCH

The upper Rhine was defended by the Nineteenth Army under General Brandenburger.

There was no longer any fear of an Allied thrust through Switzerland. The enemy's main offensive was unmistakably aimed in another direction. The efforts of the Nineteenth Army could not be increasingly diverted to its west front, which was naturally very strong; the Rhine was a barrier more on account of the swiftness of its currents than its breadth. The fortifications along the river were obsolete and inexpertly laid out. Hitler was aware of this, and so the transfer of the main battle-front to the Black Forest could be completed. The Black Forest massif, with positions on its edge and on the heights, protected the southern part of Württemberg against an offensive from the west. The Idstein block, opposite the Belfort depression, had been fortified in peacetime; even if the fortifications there were out of date and partly razed they still had a powerful deterrent effect, though elsewhere they were useless. The danger lay in a thrust from the northwest and north directed at Stuttgart, or even farther east through Heilbronn and Pforzheim and skirting the Black Forest. If the Saar Palatinate salient collapsed and the Rhine were crossed at Karlsruhe this danger might become acute, and thus to prevent or delay this happening was in the obvious interest of the Black Forest sector and the Nineteenth Army. The most seasoned divisions must and could, therefore, be transferred to Army Group G for the defence of the Saar Palatinate.

The tardy completion of the transfer did not correspond to the urgency of the situation, however. The two divisions moved arrived too late in Army Group G's area; they were sent into action precipitately and piecemeal and their success was less than it should have been. The difficulties of bringing up reinforcements lay principally in that of assembling relieving units. We had no closed formations and were forced to make shift with lavish improvisations. Time was too short to build up effective combat units. All the same, the Württemberg *Volkssturm* for example, did better than I expected. Very little could be done to make up for the lack of signals units, whereby operations were greatly handicapped. The Nineteenth Army had made the necessary preparations for defence within the possibilities open to it, and with due observance of the danger to its flank. It was given now a respite until the beginning of April.

I was appointed C.-in-C. West in one of the sharpest crises of the western campaign. After I had formed a picture of the general situation I felt like a concert pianist who is asked to play a Beethoven sonata before a large audience on an ancient, rickety and out-of-tune instrument. In many respects I found conditions which contradicted all my principles, but events were moving too swiftly for me to have time to influence them much.

My post was too important and my rank too high for me to shirk the responsibility imposed on me as C.-in-C. West. I am therefore answerable for everything done by my instructions. If I was unable to reconcile Hitler's ideas and orders with my conscience and my views, I could only interpret and modify them as seemed best. This frequently happened during this period, as it had before. The alternative was to have it out with Hitler. If after that I still remained unconvinced or failed to make him change his mind, I must ask to be relieved of my command. I knew the difficulties. I went to see Hitler four times in the first six weeks, frankly expounded my views on the situation and found him appreciative of my plain speaking. I was far too much a soldier not to know that I could not refuse to accept an opinion or to obey an order for which I was assured there were cogent reasons simply because I did not agree with it. I also saw the necessity for shelving many differences that arose during the last and extremest crisis of the war. I had myself always tried to make my subordinates understand my orders by explaining them in detail.

In the conditions I found in the west I felt utterly at sea. Different commanders have different methods, I told myself, and all equally reasonable in their different ways. My predecessor, von Rundstedt, rightly regarded himself as the heir to the tradition of the Supreme Command in World War I. The size of the theatre, the responsibility and the chain of command were the same. With his finger on the pulse of things, he issued his orders from his headquarters, almost never visiting the front and rarely using the telephone. Contact with his subordinates or superiors was more or less entirely in the hands of his Chief of Staff and staff officers. This system had undeniable advantages: the Commander-in-Chief was undisturbed and not exposed to the worrying impressions of the front. He was the remote High Priest who was referred to only with a certain awe. Even if my ways were different I could still understand von Rundstedt's, though I could not persuade myself to adopt them. The circumstances of the sixth year of the war were too different from the normal conditions of the first years. The laxity of discipline everywhere required personal contact with commanders and troops; direct influence could no longer be dispensed with, especially as agreement on so many points was lacking. This system was a nuisance for both parties, but the advantages outweighed the disadvantages. One had a glimpse behind the scenes and into men's hearts.

Convinced that the place of a commander is where a unit has had a reverse and a dangerous situation has arisen, I had chosen my battle headquarters close to the front and often moved them, but not until I was forced to by the enemy. I could not have wished for a better Chief of Staff than Westphal, with whom I had worked harmoniously in Italy. He knew my idiosyncrasies as I knew his.

There were three Army Groups in C.-in-C. West's command. I had myself commanded an Army Group for too long not to know the meaning of so high an authority. Their commanders had every right to insist on independence in their own sectors within the frame of their assignment. I also had the firm intention to respect it, though in practice abnormal occurrences often made me interfere. I did not like doing this, as, although I had been an old army man and army General Staff officer, I nevertheless came from the Luftwaffe and therefore had a certain compunction.

The Army Group commanders were World War I soldiers,

distinguished General Staff officers and leaders with exceptional experience.

Divisional commanders varied; on many of them recent months had left their mark. Under normal conditions some of them would have had to be changed, as they were not always up to the task of fighting under the difficult conditions prevailing in the spring of 1945. The cadre of generals when the German army was limited to 100,000 men had been too small, new formations had multiplied too fast and casualties been too heavy in the five years of the war for it to be possible to sort out the incompetent. One had to make the best of it, but at the same time it increased one's obligation to intervene.

In the course of the years it had become the practice in the German armed forces to retire high commanders. On principle I disapproved of it. In this way many quite outstanding military leaders were prematurely put on the shelf and were missed in the later years of the war, while really necessary retirements had partly to be deferred because there were no first-class generals to replace them. I only resorted to these last questionable means if I saw that the commander concerned had lost faith in the task assigned him and that his attitude was undermining morale.

A further difficulty was that Army Groups and even junior commands were in direct communication with the O.K.W. and Hitler. The sending of operational reports direct to the O.K.W. may have satisfied the curiosity and soothed the nerves of the High Command, but it thoroughly upset the routine of the superior staffs on the spot.

At the end of March I had to face the fact that the main part of my mission had not been accomplished. The Saar Palatinate had been lost with heavy sacrifices; the bridgeheads at Remagen and Oppenheim had been torn open and made the point of departure for extensive operations, as had even the lower Rhine, which had been crossed in an amazingly short time. In broad outline the enemy's objectives were clear: to separate North and South Germany with their main forces and to link up with the

Russians; the capture of the North Sea ports on the German right wing by the British; and the occupation of southern Germany by the American-French southern group.

How had these surprising results been brought about? There is no doubt that a good German unit in proper strength and with the essential equipment could still carry out its assignment. There is no doubt, also, that if each Army Group had had a few Panzer or Panzer Grenadier divisions and approximately equal air forces a "free operation" would have been feasible. The fact that Army Group H with Panzer divisions in reserve was nonetheless beaten does not of itself invalidate this contention, but it corroborates my view that a "free operation" could not have solved the problem. I therefore refused to listen to the constant clamour for freedom of action; this was a perfectionist memory of happier times now gone with petrol and other shortages and half-trained troops. I cannot deny, however, that the stubborn advocacy of this idea troubled me and in fact brought about something like a crisis of confidence between my commanders and myself. It was understandable that after five years of war my generals should have got different ideas into their heads, that politics and economics, as well as the military possibilities, should be debated. But all this could not be allowed to dominate the blunt issue that a real soldier will stifle all doubts in spite of damaging criticism and set so shining an example that his men cannot help following him unquestioningly. Even at that time I saw very many soldiers who radiated this strength.

My many years of experience against an overwhelmingly superior enemy had driven home the lesson, already learnt in World War I, that a purely local defence of the main battleline, as ordered by Hitler, whether in the interior or on the coast, never brought the expected results in the face of a combined ground, air and naval assault. Weak as we were on the ground and in the air, we had no elbow room. All we could do was to fight a "restricted war of movement" to hold an area previously decided on.

The differences between the Supreme Command of the Wehrmacht and the Army Command which had existed for years had meanwhile become increasingly evident. Their irreconcilable mistrust had a paralyzing and in many cases a disintegrating effect, with the consequence that the Army Command felt itself hamstrung and misunderstood. Hitler's attribution of failures to the perversity of army commanders and his frequent interventions in even the smallest tactical matters were scoffed at as armchair interference, his strategic orders and intuitions as amateur. This latent hostility was the grave of initiative, damaging to the unity of command and wasteful of energy.

The enormously costly battles of the last half-year and constant retreat and defeat had reduced officers and men to a dangerous state of exhaustion. Many officers were nervous wrecks, others affected in health, others simply incompetent, while there was a dangerous shortage of junior officers. In the ranks strengths were unsatisfactory, replacements arriving at the front insufficiently trained, with no combat experience, in driblets, and, anyway, too late. They were accordingly no asset in action. Only where an intelligent commander had a full complement of experienced subalterns and a fair nucleus of elder men did units hold together.

The unduly large number of stragglers behind the lines indicated that there were not many of these units left. The stragglers were a positive menace as a focus of infection and an impediment to traffic; they were at the same time a reservoir. Many of them were genuine stragglers who had been separated from their units in action or were on their way forward from hospitals and draft battalions and were unable to find their units. Others, the majority, were ducking out and trying to put the greatest possible distance between themselves and the firing line. Alarmed by my first impression of conditions behind the front, I took drastic measures. Successive interception lines were organized, and as there were still too many loopholes the net was drawn tighter by the institution of a "Field Raiding Detachment."

The Luftwaffe, which had for years been patently on the decline, could no longer be expected to do what was required of it. Coming from the Luftwaffe myself, I was the more distressed by its obvious inefficiency because I could no longer remedy it. The army's constant criticism that the air force did nothing was not justified, though certainly more energetic leadership might have produced better results. The Air Command's task was to concentrate *all* its striking power at the point of main effort of the moment, but it had lost its mobility. The organization of the air force into three air divisions might also perhaps have been changed to advantage by combining them into a single easily controlled formation and sending this compact force recklessly into action when asked for by a sector in distress.

In the quiet period of the war the party was active, in many places too much so; it had developed from a political organization into a definitely "supervisory" organization. Because the party apparatus was so big, many high-ups had been pushed up into positions for which they had no training and also lacked the qualifications of character. The itch to do something which is inherent in almost every German's nature manifested itself to an extraordinary degree in the meddlesomeness of party dignitaries. Bormann, head of the party chancellery, saw to that; it was his endeavour to prove to Hitler by frequent reports the justification and necessity for the existence of this "supervisory agency." It needed great force of character to stand up to this pressure from above. There were some who did, especially in the younger generation; but, all in all, by spying on the population and the armed forces and reporting to Hitler the party destroyed the willingness to co-operate and gradually caused intolerable friction and resentment on the part of officers and men.

As "Reichs Defence Commissioners" the Gauleiters also had military tasks, in this province working with the Military District commands. They had also the right to interfere in matters of administration and economy. The resultant quarrels and antagonism undid any good this arrangement achieved.

C.-in-C. West could maintain the necessary close liaison with the numerous Gauleiters only at the top level of the party. This made quick action impossible, and so a high party functionary with far-reaching powers was attached to my staff. This was a boon until the appointment of a fanatical party man threw a wrench into the works. I had no use for a spy on my staff. However, he was got rid of without remonstrance.

On the other hand, co-operation with a special representative of the Propaganda Ministry was in every way satisfactory; amongst other things he kept me currently informed of peace feelers or hopeful negotiations for an armistice.

MY RELATIONS WITH HITLER AND THE O.K.W.

During my long activity in Berlin both in the army and the Luftwaffe I had got to know everyone who mattered. That made my work easier. Through the Reichsmarschall, Hermann Goering, I have no hesitation in saying that we Luftwaffe Field-Marshals enjoyed a privileged position.

As during the building up of the Luftwaffe Goering dealt personally with all matters of outside importance we rarely came into direct contact with Hitler, and consequently our liaison was closer with the chiefs of the O.K.W. The first campaigns introduced no change. The Mediterranean and west theatres were so-called "O.K.W. theatres" which were no concern of the Army High Command (O.K.H.).

As C.-in-C. South and C.-in-C. West at the end of the war I had to work almost exclusively with Hitler and the O.K.W. By the end of 1944, after various ups and downs, I had won Hitler's unreserved confidence, which was certainly the reason for my transfer to the west. In Italy I had had to fight for a free hand, but in the end I got it; in the west I was necessarily restricted by the situation in the east. Between 20 March and 12 April I went to see Hitler four times, and he showed great understanding for my anxieties. In spite of our serious defeats he never uttered a word of reproach, certainly because he appreciated that the situation in the west had deteriorated too far to be effectively remedied.

Hitler received me at any hour of the night, listened to what I had to say without once interrupting me, showed great understanding for any questions I raised and nearly always made his decision on the lines I proposed. His mental elasticity was in striking contrast to his physical condition. In his decisions, he was less long-winded than formerly and treated me with quite astonishing kindness and consideration. Twice he lent me his car and personal chauffeur to drive me back to my headquarters and gave the driver meticulous instructions to be careful. The change to such evident solicitude from the correct politeness I had been accustomed to was a puzzling novelty, as my relations with Hitler had always been strictly official, and I could not help seeing the steadily widening rift between him and the Wehrmacht generals.

Hitler never asked me to do anything I could not agree to as an officer and I never asked him for a personal favour. I can only attribute the conspicuous proofs of his trust in me to the fact that he knew I had no axe to grind and that for years I had devoted every hour of the day to the performance of my duty.

In his morbid mistrust—finally of more or less everyone—Hitler ended by dealing with all state business himself. He was also unlucky in the choice of the men he kept close to him. Both of these were factors which had a bad effect on the services and the conduct of the war.

The last time I saw him, on 12 April 1945, he was still optimistic. How far he was play-acting it is hard to decide. Looking back, I am inclined to think that he was literally obsessed with the idea of some miraculous salvation, that he clung to it like a drowning man to a straw. In my view, he believed in a victory in the east, in his newly born Twelfth Army, in various new weapons, and perhaps even in the collapse of the enemy coalition.

All these hopes were illusory; after the beginning of the Russian offensive Hitler shut himself up and, more and more solitary, lived in an unreal world of his own.

The responsible executive of the O.K.W. theatres was General Jodl, with whom it was a pleasure to work. An astute and able strategist and tactician, he was the very man for such a post, especially as he was placid, level-headed and an indefatigable worker, though one could have wished he had had more operational experience. He had an extremely difficult position, as Hitler was by no means easy to influence and the unanimity of any suggestion jointly put to him was frustrated by the disharmony between the O.K.H. and the O.K.W. Those who presume to judge Jodl do not know what his diplomacy prevented and achieved—his critics should first show that under the circumstances they would have done better. As Chief of the Operations Staff of the Wehrmacht he overrode the O.K.W. even if in so doing he had to defend views and measures which he had fought relentlessly to change or modify. Jodl's colleagues, for instance von Buttlar, were trained, objective officers who cooperated intelligently in accordance with Jodl's ideas. Between Jodl and myself there were seldom any differences of opinion in our view of the situation or about the steps to be taken, and my staff and I could always rely on his backing.

With Field-Marshal Keitel I had less to do. His instructions relating to the creation of new units or replacements were based on Führer's orders, which, if arguable, could not be altered. For example, Hitler regarded the creation of fresh divisions as fundamental for the continuation of the war, which meant holding back personnel and material for this purpose. I and many other generals held the opposite view that new creations were in themselves uneconomical and that in the last phase of the war tactical victories were needed, not organization.

THE BATTLES IN CENTRAL GERMANY

The encirclement of Army Group B in the Ruhr pocket sealed the fate of central Germany.

The Allies' objectives were evident, and despite the diversion of an army to invest the Ruhr fortress they had the strength to reach them. For us the question of enemy concentration was no longer a riddle but had more or less ceased to matter, as we did not have the mobile forces or air combat strength to attack them with any hope of success. I call this period the "makeshift campaign" in which the goodwill of officers and men—morale in other words—was the governing factor.

That this area, roughly 150 miles in breadth, could not be defended by improvised units was clear. The widely separated forces fighting in this area accordingly had the task of delaying the enemy's advance until a stronger, organized striking force came to the rescue. This could only be the Twelfth Army created at the end of March. Only with its help could there be a certain assurance that the course of events on the Russian front would not be influenced from the west and the splitting of Germany into two halves be prevented.

The Twelfth Army thus was the all-important factor in the conduct of operations in the west—whichever way the situation developed it could be employed in the Harz Mountains for any task. Consequently the Harz and a certain area on the immediate front had to be kept open; at the best our strength was still depleted and it must not be used up prematurely fighting our way out of the mountains. The Harz also provided satisfactory opportunities for camouflage.

The weak German forces were thus withdrawn under compulsion to the Harz Mountains in the belief that a stand could be made there, even if thinly held. Besides, the order had been given to hold the Thuringian Forest as an important industrial area. Meanwhile the hope I had hardly dared conceive—that strong American forces would allow themselves to be drawn into the mountains by our weak troops—was realized. Under normal conditions it is certainly dangerous to conduct a decisive operation between two mountain ranges fifty or sixty miles apart or even if flanked only by one massif. As, however, the depletion of the German forces in the centre of the western front was known to the enemy, in this case there was no great risk attached, especially as with his mobile reconnaissance forces and all-powerful strength in the air he could smash any threat to his flanks. But in this way our Seventh and Eleventh Armies drew off strong American groups and stalled the enemy's progress, giving the Twelfth Army a chance to form up. The enemy may have been influenced by other considerations, such as inter-Allied political agreements, difficulties of supply, and a certain respect for German detachments scattered throughout the area.

The fact remains, however, that all opportunities were not exploited as they might have been and that therefore our armies on the Russian front were able to fight out the battle which decided the war without having to fear a threat to their rear from the Western Allies.

At the beginning of April my command post was located behind the points of main effort at the front and within reach of Berlin. In spite of this favourable position signals communications to the wings became increasingly difficult and the roads to the headquarters of Army Groups more roundabout and hazardous. By the elimination of Army Group B from the front and the tearing open of the German centre two separate threats had been marked off which no longer required a unified command. Readjustments were therefore made by a Führer's order of 6 April. A C.-in-C. was appointed for the northwest area with its southern boundary running through a line Hameln-Braunschweig-Magdeburg. The front south of this line remained under my command.

In these early days of April I was also notified of an arrangement which was to be put into force if it ceased to be possible to direct operations in the three theatres, northwest, south and east, from the centre. According to this arrangement, I, with a small O.K.W. staff under General Winter, was to take over the command of the whole southern area, including Italy, Yugoslavia and the southern part of the Russian front, as C.-in-C. South with plenipotentiary authority. In the north the same mission was to be allotted to Admiral Doenitz with the Wehrmacht operations staff. Hitler's destination was left an open question. The most interesting thing about this proposed reshuffle is that the command was given to two soldiers, while Goering, who was regarded as Hitler's successor, and the party were excluded.

On 8 April the Harz Mountains were declared a fortress by the O.K.W. and the Eleventh Army entrusted with their defence. When on 12 April the first enemy tanks appeared before Magdeburg and the battle for the Thuringian Forest was nearing its end the Harz Mountains still held out—the fighting there ended only on 20 April with the capture of the Eleventh Army.

Meanwhile in the middle of this part of the front from Magdeburg to Riesa the Twelfth Army hung on to the Elbe, fighting for the possession of this sector of the river. At the end of this period a new front had been established along the Elbe and the Mulde and the gap torn open on the Rhine in the middle of March was closed on the Elbe. But this front was also doomed as the enemy closed in on Germany simultaneously from east and west.

23

The End of the War

21 April 1945 Collapse of the German front in Italy—25 April Link-up of the American and Russian troops at Torgau on the Elbe—28 April Plenipotentiaries of Army Group C sign armistice at Caserta—28 April Mussolini shot—30 April Fall of Munich—30 April Hitler commits suicide in Berlin—Reichspresident: Admiral Doenitz—2 May Capitulation of Army Group C comes into force—4 May Surrender of Army Group G at Munich—5 May Capitulation of C.-in-C. Northwest—7 May Capitulation of C.-in-C. South (Kesselring)—7 May Instrument of German surrender signed at Rheims—9 May Ratification of surrender.

SOUTHERN GERMANY

Convinced that the last phase of the war would be decided in the central zone of Germany, I deliberately neglected the wings and gave special attention to developments in the centre. If the Russians and the Western Allies joined hands on the Elbe or in Berlin the situation on the flanks, however favourable it might be, would have ceased to matter. From then on there could be only one justification for continuing the war: the imperative necessity to gain time for the German divisions engaged in the east to fight their way back into the British and American zones.

As I have already explained, the situation in central Germany could only be influenced by the newly created Twelfth Army. For a long time I was not informed of the actual circumstances of this glorified phantom body. As the situation deteriorated I was always led to believe by Hitler in our talks and telephone conversations, and rather less extravagantly by the O.K.W. operations staff, that this army was a *deus ex machina*. But as soon as I realized that this miraculous force, only to judge by the whole state of its organization, could never be sent into action in time to restore even locally the central German situation, I thought it my duty to concentrate my attention on the touch-and-go situation in the south, and thus on 10 April I moved my headquarters into the Upper Palatinate.

In the south of Germany at the end of March the crossing of the Rhine by the Americans at Oppenheim and subsequent operations against the right wing of Army Group G had given the enemy a clear road to the northeast in the direction of Giessen and Hersfeld, to the east towards Würzburg, and to the southeast into the scantily protected plain in the direction of Nürnberg.

Farther south American forces had reached the Rhine Valley south and southeast of Mannheim and Heidelberg. The crossing of the Rhine by the 3rd Algerian Division and the 2nd Moroccan Division between Speyer and Germersheim at the end of March was followed by the switching of French troops northwards from the South Palatinate. These divisions advanced southeast, closely supporting the flank of the American army and mopping up the Rhine Valley in order to facilitate the passage of the river for the 9th Colonial Division and the French 5th Armoured Division.

The enemy's basic plan had already been fairly clear on 26 March. The picture now left no doubt that his strategic objective in the south was to open this area from the north. The advantages of this plan were the following:

The mass crossing of the Rhine could proceed in country already secured by Allied forces.

The difficult frontal assault against mountain fronts and river barriers, which would have been a costly business, would be avoided.

The left wing of the American Seventh Army operating in the south of Germany remained in contact—if only loosely—with the American Third Army advancing on its left.

The reading of these intentions could not, however, make up for the lack of strategic possibilities on our side. The only asset the German Command had in this area was the terrain. But even here the defence behind river lines (the Main) and mountains (the Odenwald) had been disappointing, part of the troops there having been taken while on the move and eliminated. Our endeavour must therefore be to man a position in good time and then do our best to prolong its defence until we could choose a favourable moment to withdraw to another. This meant putting up a fight behind selected natural lines and not only manœuvring. But at least the left wing of the First Army and the Nineteenth Army were lodged in defensible positions, the Nineteenth being concentrated in the right place on the northern edge of the Black Forest, to which all available forces had somehow to be brought up, even if it meant deliberately weakening the Black Forest western front. The depleted front positions were naturally very strong and could be more thinly defended. But there was no disguising the fact that an enemy flushed with victory could not be held for any length of time with forces inferior in numbers, training and equipment.

In order to give this plan of successive withdrawals a modest prospect of success, steps had been taken to fortify positions and to organize a defence supported by artillery and heavy weapons. But it was just in this field that deficiencies were worst.

Without going into day-to-day happenings I will summarize the tactical phases that seem to me important, with their critical peaks.

The break-through of the switch line between Miltenberg on the elbow of the Main and Eberbach in conjunction with the capture of the Main bridges at Aschaffenburg marked the commencement of two significant enemy operations. It opened the road to Würzburg (1-7 April) and from there to Bamberg (15 April)-Nürnberg and immediately beyond Mergentheim to Nürnberg (16-20 April).

The enemy did not change his tactical procedure; his armoured divisions probed in breadth and depth and, helped by remarkably rapid concentrations, opened the road for the infantry divisions to follow up. The swift forward onrush of his armoured forces in this phase was exceptional.

By switching divisions from the left wing of the First Army to the break-through wing, the commanders of Army Group G and the First Army showed remarkable flexibility. They arrived too late, however, even for the Tauber-Jagst Line, and with the troops available even the enemy's advance guards could not be halted.

This pressure also worried the O.K.W., who on 3 April ordered General Schulz, the new commander of Army Group G, to assemble a strong assault group under General Tolsdorff behind the right wing of the First Army to cut off the enemy group advancing on Würzburg by a northward thrust, and to establish contact with the 82nd Army Corps. This order was not practicable and was countermanded by me with the subsequent approval of the O.K.W. This instance, like the similar case of Army Group H (the offensive assignment given to Student), shows that maps and reports are never a substitute for personal observation.

The rapid advance on the Main had in our view given the Twelfth American Army Group the impetus to deflect southeastward the 11th and 14th Armoured Divisions fighting west and south of the Thuringian Forest, in order to cover and strengthen the American left flank, which was left as it were suspended in the air.

On the left wing of the First Army the divisions of the 13th and 80th Army Corps, yielding to enemy pressure, were forced to retire to the Jagst and Neckar-Enz Line, and then on 10 April to the Kocher; connection was now assured; after they reached these lines there was, in fact, a lull in the fighting, if only for a very short time. On 10 April the First Army stood on the line Prickenstadt-Uffenheim-Niederstetten-Ingelfingen-Kocher, with its right wing more or less on the western edge of the Steiger Forest. The switching of three divisions from the left wing of the First Army and the right wing of the Nineteenth into the threatened Nürnberg area weakened the strate-

gically important Neckar-Enz Line and the now equally important Kocher Line; their natural strength had, however, been so
well fortified that there was no need to anticipate any immediate
danger. It was only regrettable that the three divisions pulled
out were very late in arriving in their new combat area and
were not as effective as might have been expected from their
quality.

The necessity for these transfers was to be emphasized by
immediate developments on the army's right wing. The exhausted divisions of the 82nd Army Corps were unable to hold
up the pursuit of the American Seventh and Third Armies'
flank divisions; while the 36th Volks Grenadier Division and the
416th Infantry Division were cut up in the Bamberg area. Bamberg and Bayreuth were overrun on 15 April, and the country
to the south lay open to the enemy's advance.

To the west our movements were completed more tidily; the
front had not fallen apart. On 14-15 April we put up a fight
for the Aisch—magnetically Nürnberg drew the forces of the
American Seventh Army on.

This development must have led to a catastrophe if the 2nd
Mountain Division of the 13th S.S. Army Corps and the 17th
S.S. Panzer Grenadiers had not been available at the very last
minute. Simultaneously I was able to bring up two badly mauled
divisions—the 36th Volks Grenadier Division and the 416th Infantry Division—which had retreated through Bamberg, and a
few draft and emergency units so that they, too, hastily re-
equipped, were able on 16-17 April to build up a local defence
screen south of the *autobahn*. Unfortunately one regiment of
the 17th S.S. Division had to be withdrawn for the defence of
Nürnberg, which caused a temporary gap between the 82nd and
13th S.S. Corps which, as luck would have it, an American division slipped through. To close the exposed flank—Franconian
Switzerland and the northern Upper Palatinate as far as the
Naab—there were no forces available except a combat group at
the permanent military camp at Grafenwöhr. These Grafenwöhr forces (panzers and lorried infantry) were sent into action on the flank of the American 14th Armoured Division ad-

vancing from Bayreuth on Nürnberg. I was on the spot and watched the attack. Its meagre success was not entirely due to the weakness of the troops. Lack of experience at the front, insufficient combat training and dash were the chief causes. Thus, apart from the gap in the Upper Palatinate extending as far as the Naab, there was on 18 and 19 April a miserable line from north of Amberg through Schwabach, Ansbach and Hall in the direction of Lauffen.

With the establishment of this line the First Army once again proved its efficiency. Neither the command nor the troops could be blamed for the enemy's pushing forward a bridgehead across the Neckar on both sides of Heilbronn on 14 and 15 April.

The Neckar-Enz Line with its salient switch-line from Heilbronn to Pforzheim barred the gateway between the Odenwald and the Black Forest. A break-through on the Neckar front meant freedom of movement in country ideal for tanks north of the Suabian Alb, and an advance across the Enz threatened Stuttgart and the basin south of the town between the Black Forest and the Alb as well as the river itself.

It was evident already at the end of March that the southern boundary of the American Army Group was not venturing materially south of the line Ludwigshafen-Heilbronn. This meant that Baden and Württemberg were French operational areas.

On 13 April the French launched an offensive from the Karlsruhe area against our positions on the northern edge of the Black Forest, which by 18 April had led to deep penetrations in the direction of Wildbad and Herrenalb and to a partial encirclement of Pforzheim. Even behind a strong sector our troops were no longer able to make a stand. Consequently any "manœuvre" against so mobile an enemy must be foredoomed to failure. There was no disguising the fact that the Nineteenth Army was now incapable of fighting a delaying action. If even the best equipped corps—the 80th and 64th—showed little power of resistance behind strong natural defences, what could be expected of the local defence battalions and suchlike? In the open plains all tactics ended with a sprint for safety, but although defeat lent wings to flight the enemy moved still faster. Although the Nineteenth Army rallied in an effort at recovery, it could not halt the enemy sweeping east of Pforzheim.

The progress of the American and French divisions from Pforzheim, which by 20-21 April carried them to within distance of Stuttgart, was supplemented by an American thrust eastwards beyond the town. This severed the connection between the First and Fourteenth Armies. The 80th Army Corps was now in desperate straits, and when on 22 April the French Armoured Division pushed on in the direction of Villingen parts of the 64th Army Corps and the S.S. 18th Corps were equally in trouble. The battle for Württemberg was lost in the first days when it became plain that the Enz-Black Forest barrier could not be held.

On 24 April the Nineteenth Army with its decimated forces stood on the Danube and the Iller and was falling back on Kempten.

These days of defeat had sadly impaired the morale and fighting efficiency of officers and men in the south of Germany, besides deciding the shape of things to come.

On the right wing of our First Army the leading divisions of the American Third Army swept on into the denuded area east of Franconian Switzerland, threatened Weiden (24 April) and Neumarkt, and in the course of the next few days, in conjunction with the American 11th Armoured Division, invaded the Black Forest; between 26 April and 3 May they were in the region of Regen, Zwiesel and Cham. General Weisenberger's defence of the Naab was smashed or driven back.

The divisions of the 82nd Army Corps were likewise driven back, partly breached and finally rallied by the engineers of the Army Engineering School in the Regensburg bridgehead north of the Danube and by the S.S. "Nibelungen" Division on the other side of the river.

The S.S. 13th Corps had to follow; it was also breached in several places, though contact within the Army Corps was never lost. It was able to establish four bridgeheads between Ingolstadt and Donauwörth, to fight its way back behind the Danube, and to prepare a new defence line.

The decisive assault was launched against the 13th Army Corps on the left wing of the First Army on 19 April; it tore open the front at various places between Crailsheim and Backnang and opened the road to the Danube for the American divisions between Dillingen and Ulm. Nevertheless German combat groups were able to form a large bridgehead west of Dillingen from which they streamed back across the Danube on 24 April and were able to resume the defensive west of Dillingen as far as Ulm. The enemy's surprise success at Dillingen on 23 April and a converging movement by two to three American divisions on Ulm and beyond sealed the fate of these gallant combat groups.

All these events were overshadowed by the success of the Russians on 20 April in crossing the Oder on a wide front. The reaction to this situation was the creation on 24 April of an O.K.W. operations staff for South Germany under General Winter; it was subsequently accessible to me in my capacity as C.-in-C. South as a planning staff.

The enemy was acting in much the same way as in the preceding weeks. Even if in the last third of April the American armoured divisions had abandoned their temporary caution and had carried out deep raids into the Bohemian Forest, along the Danube and towards Lake Constance, the High Command's endeavours to bring the divisions of the second battle-line up to the same level and generally to maintain cohesion so as to avoid local reverses had some effect. Here, too, as in Africa and Italy, the French divisions had shown their skill in mountain fighting, which the German Command could no longer oppose with any equivalent strength.

The weakness of the German troops being patent, to say nothing of their inadequate training, equipment and mobility, a relentless pursuit and immediate penetration of the gap between the Seventh and First Armies might have given the Allies an earlier victory. The basic idea of the break-through by the 10th American Armoured Division was a tactical finesse which, equally energetically pushed home, might have had disastrous consequences for the First Army. Also the American 12th Armoured Division's dash for Dillingen showed genuine *élan*, which—to my surprise—seemed to flag after the passage of the Danube.

THE BATTLE FOR CITIES

On 2 April Hitler had given orders that all cities were to be defended. No doubt he believed implicitly that every German would make the last sacrifice to escape an uncertain fate and would thus share this point of view. If that was in itself an illusion, the order was in any case militarily doubtful and at least partly impracticable. The military problem was to blunt the edge of the enemy's striking force and so delay his advance. For that first-line troops were necessary—it could not be done with militia. The defence of a town demanded a high degree of tactical experience, training and combat discipline as well as a suitable terrain which could not be outflanked. This existed in only a few cases on the outskirts of the towns, and for that reason alone the order had to be sensibly interpreted. Accordingly—the whole western campaign is proof of this—on my orders we fought not in but for the towns, terrain and the nature and condition of the troops determining the battle-area. The defence of Ludwigshafen, Kassel, Eisenach, Schweinfurt, Nürnberg and Munich speaks for itself.

The battle for Würzburg was influenced by the Führer's order received immediately previously. Militarily unjustifiable, it was inspired by the Gauleiter.

The defence of Schweinfurt, which I watched most carefully, was conducted far from the town, being based on the circular positions which the existence of numerous flak batteries made possible. With the breaching of this outer ring both the defence and work in the town's ball-bearing factories had automatically to cease.

If my orders had been carried out the battle for Nürnberg would also have been fought before the town and on its outskirts. Because of the hallowed associations of the city of the

"Party Festivals" the Gauleiter disobeyed them, however, and continued the fight at the cost of his own life. Nürnberg did, in fact, pin down more enemy forces than we had reason to expect and than were necessary. I was myself in Nürnberg on 16 April, on my way to the headquarters of the First Army and Army Group G, during a bombing raid and saw for myself the damage done to the city. Fighting in the streets, tragic and unnecessary as it was, could hardly cause much more destruction.

The defence of Munich, the "capital of the movement," I twice forbade peremptorily, although it was urged on me by the Gauleiter.

Even where the tactical situation demanded the persistent defence of a town it can never be said it was carried to extremes in the sense of Hitler's order. I do not know of a single instance where this was the case.

THE DEMOLITION OF BRIDGES

Remagen, Hanau and Aschaffenburg were convincing examples of the disastrous consequences of failing to blow up bridges in good time. But neither these lessons nor Hitler's repeated draconic orders had any effect. Although the Danube front had been secured and special warnings had been given, the bridge at Dillingen fell into the hands of the American 12th Armoured Division on 23 April. It was the same story at other places. These instances of negligence revealed the inefficiency of a large proportion of the last drafts as we scraped the bottom of the barrel, as clearly as it did the general overtaxing of our resources. It went hand in hand with the inability to distinguish what was important from what was not, as shown in the sporadic demolition of *all* bridges. Military District VII and other administrative centres urgently demanded the preservation of various economically vital bridges although they could not be denied a certain military importance, and in these cases I forbade demolition while holding local commanders responsible for other security measures. There were, after all, plenty of other means, often more effective than dynamiting.

THE ALPINE FORTRESS

When about 20 April 1945 the order to defend the "Alpine Fortress" reached me at my headquarters at Motzenhofen, north of Munich, I tried to form a clear picture of what this involved. A great deal has been written about the Alpine Fortress, mostly nonsense.

The southern rim of the Bavarian Alps with its front extending towards Switzerland had been fortified during the time I was in Italy and was still partly under construction, garrisoned by S.S. security troops—lorry-borne infantry—under Gauleiter Hofer. In the north and facing northeast there were no fortifications, nor on 20 April had any been begun. Nor were there any troops permanently located there.

The battalions moved north in the last days of April by C.-in-C. Southwest under General Feuerstein had—so it was reported at the time, though apparently not correctly—military assignments inside Germany. The events of the last months of the war had brought many staffs and back-area formations from all four points of the compass into the Alpine Redoubt. As a result the area was overcrowded and food was in short supply, but under the circumstances prevailing in April 1945 an evacuation was out of the question.

The defence of this so-called Alpine Fortress would have required Alpine troops, of which, however, there were none left in the area—transport services and depots at home could provide mere cannon fodder. When at the beginning of May Rendulic with Army Group South wanted to retire into the Alps and fight on there till the bitter end, it took a long time to convince him the plan was impracticable.

The storing of food and equipment was to have been entrusted to S.S. General Pohl, but though he was supposed to be somewhere in southern Germany he was nowhere to be found; and as usual where the supply services or the air force was concerned, nothing was done.

From a purely military standpoint the Alpine Fortress would only have had value if it had been defended, not for its own sake, but as a means to an end; if it had been possible for strong general reserves of all arms not only to pin down large enemy forces by extensive sorties and air attacks, but also to smash them. This last was not possible, and everything else was merest make-believe.

THE SITUATION IN MID-APRIL 1945

Up to 20 April the main task of the whole of the western front had been to keep the rear of the eastern front free for the final battle with the Russians on which the O.K.W. pinned its hopes. Similarly after 20 April the *whole* front continued to fight with only one idea: to enable the eastern armies to retreat into the British and American zones.

I could not share the belief of the Supreme Command that the Western Allies, recognizing the danger of communism, would move forward and establish a front against the Soviet armies, although at the time when S.S. General Wolff made truce proposals, with which my name was associated, to the Americans in Switzerland he understood that Roosevelt had been convinced of the double-dealing of Soviet policy. The opinion was also voiced that the war with the Western Allies ought to be ended at once before the Russians had time to play their trump cards. Though there was much to be said against this view for military and political reasons, I personally was only influenced by the psychological argument—*how* must the surrender of all the German forces in the west affect those still fighting on the Russian front in the last, decisive battle? They would feel themselves deserted and betrayed to their pitiless fate, delivered *en masse* into the hands of the Russians. This it was our absolute duty to prevent. How this could be done was a moot question, but one thing must be attempted: to give them time to fight their way back into the zones occupied by the Americans and British, hard as it was to establish where these began. The event showed how right this idea was. Nothing can alter that, not even the fact that many Allied commanders put inter-Allied agreements before the claims of humanity and prevented

German soldiers from crossing the demarcation line or actually handed them over to the Russians after they had crossed it.

The pivots of the central western front—the Harz Mountains and the Thuringian Forest—which might have pinned down even stronger forces for a considerable time, had fallen in the middle period of April. The hectic march of events in central Germany made a planned counter-attack by the inchoate Twelfth Army from the Harz or the plateau north of it impossible. During this same period the west and east fronts were so close together that the one influenced the other, set the German Command almost insoluble problems and was the cause of serious friction. The area from which the battle-lines should have been fed had shrunk too small, especially the corridor along the Elbe from Magdeburg widening out to Dresden and the main concentration area from Greater Berlin to the Elbe, north of Tangermünde.

As the American Third Army swerved southeast, it was only a question of time before the first American forces north and south of the Danube entered the zone of Rendulic's Army Group South, with inevitable consequences for the latter. I planned a flanking thrust against Patton's army as it swept south, but the two German Panzer divisions (2nd and 11th) which should have delivered it were too slow in moving up across Bohemia. Subsequent orders to block the progress of the American Third Army on the southern fringe of the Bohemian Forest in conjunction with Army Group South were impractical.

From the end of March to the end of April the divisional combat groups that escaped eastward after the collapse on the Rhine and the Main covered over 250 miles. They marched, broke away, fought, were overrun, outflanked, battered and exhausted, only to regroup, fight and march again. An immense effort of endurance, for all its limitations, out of all proportion to what it did or could achieve.

The development of the situation in the north need not be discussed in detail, because from 6 April Army Group H was directly subordinated to the O.K.W. The improvement which Hitler had expected never materialized. Displeased with Blaskowitz's handling of the situation, he thought to remove an imagined lethargy by the appointment of Student. But on one occasion when the question was under discussion Jodl told him: "You may send up a dozen Students, *mein Führer*, but it won't alter the situation."

This, in so many words, was what all of us thought.

Busch, C.-in-C. Northwest, surrendered on 5 May, as on the following day did Blaskowitz in Holland.

THE END OF THE FIGHTING IN SOUTH GERMANY, AUSTRIA AND CZECHOSLOVAKIA

The Russians had broken through and were closing in on Berlin towards the end of April. While the decisive battle of the war was awaited there, the British and American forces in southern Germany were astonishingly passive. One had the impression that they had packed up.

Our resistance in southern Germany was, anyhow, petering out. The Nineteenth Army was beaten, its remnants standing on the Danube and the Iller. The Danube was crossed by the enemy at two places and he was rolling up the left flank of the First Army with a thrust from Ulm. The 80th Army Corps on this flank was threatened with encirclement and destruction.

Weak American forces stood on the former Austrian frontier. Attempts to advance along the northern bank of the Danube through the Bohemian Forest into Czechoslovakia had apparently no more purpose than to protect their flanks.

C.-in-C. Southwest (Army Group C, Italy) had suffered such serious losses in the fighting south of the Po that retirement was difficult and a stand in the well-constructed Southern Alps Line jeopardized.

C.-in-C. Southeast (Balkans) was engaged in heavy fighting under a clearly impending threat to its right wing, the retreat of Army Group C in Italy increasing the danger from that side.

There was a lull in the fighting in Austria (Army Group South under Rendulic), behind which front there stood considerable reserves.

Army Group Centre (Schoerner) in Czechoslovakia was heavily engaged on the right wing.

The only large German formation behind the front and still intact was the newly created Twelfth Army, but it had been committed in some strength against the west, and threatened on two sides as it was, was too weak to avert its doom.

Nevertheless, our armies in the east, including C.-in-C. Southeast and the Twelfth Army, had preserved a considerable inherent strength which made immediate concern for them superfluous, whereas those in Italy and Bavaria and the Seventh Army were on the verge of collapse.

Under these circumstances was there any excuse for continuing the war?

As all available divisions were now squeezed together into a narrow space the German forces still in the field were more than ever condemned to a common fate. Whether they stood their ground to help their neighbour or dragged him with themselves into the abyss, there was no way out. For example, the disintegration of our front in South Germany must critically endanger other groups in the Alps, the southeast, southwest and south. If the armies in Italy were eliminated it meant the end of those in Bavaria and an increased and immediate danger for the Balkans.

In the psychology of battle, where all are involved in the same fate, fluctuations of morale spread like wildfire, while even more serious are the effects of independent action taken without consideration for the whole. The primitive duty of comradeship made it impossible for a decent soldier to throw up the fight knowing that his comrades were holding out in their last battle. It was unthinkable to surrender or abandon a position if it meant life or death to his fellows that he stand firm.

Such were the reflections which whirled with tragic intensity through my mind. It was no longer a question of fighting to obtain a generous peace. The absolute duty not to let our German brothers-in-arms fall into the hands of the Russians was all that mattered now. For this reason, and this alone, we just had to fight it out to the bitter end.

During the last years of the war the question of how far its continuance could be justified had increasingly preoccupied me. Clearly a commander's chances of influencing the morale of his subordinates and troops depended on his adopting an unequivocal attitude to this question. After Stalingrad and the capitulation of Tunis, "victory" had become an impossibility. Speculation as to whether the successful invasion of Normandy had finally sealed our fate was beside the point now that the collapse behind the western front had extinguished the last hope of a stalemate and our straits were desperate.

This was the reason why since the autumn of 1944 I had supported S.S. General Wolff's plan to contact the Americans in Switzerland. I had convinced myself, as a soldier, that at this moment of the war negotiations with the enemy on a political level were imperative, and such was the purpose of this approach. From the political aspect, the Allies had never disguised their intention to destroy Germany, above all National Socialism and "militarism," which meant the greater part of the nation and all its leading caste, the propaganda which reached us being so framed that we were left with no hope at all of national survival. Confronted with this determination of the Allies to destroy us—proclaimed in the formula "unconditional surrender"—we had only one reply: to sell our skins as dearly as possible, that is, to fight on as long and as stubbornly as we could in the hope of wearing the enemy down and so perhaps making him more willing to negotiate. Once before, in 1918, we had thrown up the sponge and as a consequence been compelled to accept the ruthless dictate of Versailles. Certainly none of us wanted a repetition of that.

Round 20 April this whole question began to trouble me really urgently. The defensive battles in both east and west had disappointed our hopes. Berlin was in danger. Yet once again I made my decision for holding out.

The orders which reached me from Hitler's headquarters were so emphatic that a soldier could not act "independently." In the last two months of the war Hitler's orders had become so many adjurations to halt the Allies' advance or to gain time by a delaying action until the confidently expected victory in the east was won on our native soil and the creation of a new army—"the very best"—restored an equilibrium; and until various new weapons, above all the "People's Fighter," could be made effective.[1]

However, as the Americans ascertained after an exact study of the damage to our production, only greatly increased air-raid protection could have had much effect on the outcome, though it could probably not have prevented it. In this way political intervention might conceivably have led to a tolerable peace.

The German soldier in the line, who knew no fear as long as he had a weapon in his hand, trembled, in the most literal meaning of the word, at the thought of being taken prisoner by the Russians. To leave our comrades in the east in the lurch at this fateful moment was impossible for any commander, but especially for me who had the responsibility for the Russian front from Dresden southwards. We simply had to fight to give our eastern armies time to retreat into the British and American zones.

The urgent advice I gave the three eastern Army Groups under my command to enter into local negotiations with the Russians was rejected by all of them as quite hopeless. For the same reason at the beginning of May the armies of Army Group South at a conference at Graz demanded that we go on fighting. I forbade this by a definite order to break contact with the enemy and to fall back by forced marches into the American zone.

* * *

The Alpine massif (as distinct from the fictitious Alpine Fortress) in this last phase was the rallying point for Army Groups Southwest, Southeast, G and parts of South. It could not be held for very long, but long enough for the eastern Army Groups to evade the Russians. The pace of the latter's retreat was dictated by those units which were most advanced and most dependent on the movements of the rest.

[1] The People's Fighter—Volksjäger—was the Heinkel 162, a turbo-jet fast fighter which Hitler believed could be mass-produced cheaply and with which he hoped to flood the skies.—*Translator's Note.*

The retirement of the main forces of Army Group E in the Balkans through a narrow bottleneck required time, and might become impossible if there were unfortunate developments on the right flank and a gap be torn open by the recoil of Army Group C in Italy. Reinforcements had thus to be fed to its right wing and the measures of the two Army Groups co-ordinated. Still more decisive for the Balkans was the behaviour of Army Group South in Austria; a premature retirement, particularly of the right wing of this Army Group, would blockade Army Group E, which would then be at the mercy of Tito.

A penetration of Army Group Centre's front in Czechoslovakia together with a possible outflanking threat from the north might complicate the retirement. Therefore here, too, the first necessity was to stiffen the pressure-points with all the reserves that could be made available. From the behaviour of the American Third Army towards our Seventh Army it could be deduced that Czechoslovakia was not an American zone of interest, which meant that no critically dangerous operations against Army Group Centre need be anticipated.

In South Bavaria the enemy had succeeded in doing in the shortest space of time what I had considered highly improbable —the strongest sectors had been overrun with hardly an effort. Now the question was—would the entrances to the Alps in the sector from Reutte to Bregenz be held? The exceptionally favourable country made the task seem feasible. Again, would all the French forces or only those colonial divisions trained and experienced in mountain fighting follow the remnants of the Nineteenth Army into the Alps, or would they call a halt on the northern fringe of the mountains? Had our propaganda about the "Alpine Fortress" been effective? The possibility of striking at the rear of Army Group C in Italy might tempt the enemy to carry the offensive into the Alps.

As it turned out, the French pushed on into the Alps and made an outflanking thrust to the north. On 27 April they had already reached the northern fringe of the mountains and by 30 April had fought their way into the Alps on a wide front. After the capture of the Zirl and Fern Passes I agreed to the capitulation of the Nineteenth Army. Certain incidents of this period in the Alpine region were by no means pretty. Gauleiter Hofer's behaviour was hard to understand, and he interfered so alarmingly in the conduct of operations that I actually had to transmit an order that the Innsbruck Gauleiter's instructions on military matters were not to be followed. In other ways, too, he did not put his cards on the table. The uncomfortable result was that half-measures were ordered and carried out with insufficient forces, that orders were either executed in the stupidest way or not at all, and losses incurred through double-dealing or plain treachery. Which might have been avoided.

Even in these last days the First Army continued steadfast in exemplary fashion. Certainly there were breakdowns, for example at Dillingen and Wasserburg-Mühldorf. But special credit is due to the army command and subordinate commanders for their ingenuity in finding new expedients and to the troops for their skill in evading the constant threat of encirclement. Among many instances I mention only General Ritter von Hengl, who with a mere handful of men withstood attacks from the north, from the south and finally from the west and proved by this gallant stand that well-disciplined German troops could preserve their morale even in an utterly hopeless situation. Farther east the Americans had reached Ischl and Hallein, and on 7 May they accepted the surrender of the German troops there.

In Austria, where the Seventh Army was co-operating with Rendulic's Army Group South, more could have been achieved. But these events are still in too close a perspective for us to pronounce judgment. At the beginning of May I was at Zeltweg and Graz conferring with the eastern commanders, accompanied by Winter, my Chief of Staff as C.-in-C. South, who was a special help to me in these worrying days. The general impression I received of the situation in the three Army Groups, Southeast (Loehr), South (Rendulic) and Centre (Schoerner), was unexpectedly good. None of them were in immediate danger, operations against Army Group South having been generally brought to a standstill. But if that front gave no cause for anxiety, the situation as a whole was understandably depressing. On the other hand reserves were more numerous, stronger and better composed than I could have expected. Equipment was good, supplies no problem and, compared to the west, unusually abundant. On the second day I gave the order for an accelerated retreat into the western zone; though its execution was complicated by the surrender of the staff of Army Group South the previous night. (The capture of Loehr by Tito's Partisans and his subsequent condemnation to death were sad blows.) The bulk of Army Group South and a large part of Army Group Southeast were thus able to retire to within reach of the American zonal frontier and later to cross it after my urgent representation to the Americans.

The forces of Army Group Centre were not so fortunate, the high-handed action of individuals in the Seventh Army making it almost impossible to carry out the orders given it by Schoerner. It was unfortunate that this Army Group went on fighting beyond the time limit when total surrender became effective.

I AM GIVEN PLENIPOTENTIARY POWERS

In effect my new activity began with the arrival of the O.K.W. Staff South on 24 April, although I did not receive the official order until the beginning of May. The development of the situation required some such solution, the personality concerned being immaterial. I had been informed of the draft plan as early as the middle of April; so when, in spite of my representations, it was not put into effect by the end of the month, in my own absence at the time I sent Dr. Hayler of the Ministry of Economics to Admiral Doenitz with the request that my position be immediately regularized. This was accordingly done.

With the transfer of my headquarters to Bavaria my functions as commander, hitherto of a purely military nature, were greatly enlarged by political assignments. That these multiplied when the south was cut off from the north is explained by the fact that every government department was represented in the south by a minister or secretary of state, who (as did the Reichsleiters and Gauleiters, including those from the Czech Protectorate) tried to establish liaison with the supreme military commander, whose voice alone counted for anything.

It was essential to co-ordinate the command of the armed forces with the Gauleiters and to organize public security during the time between the surrender and peace.

Even among the Gauleiters there were some who wanted to end the war at once and others who wanted to fight till the last man. Those of Augsburg and Salzburg are examples of the first category, of Munich and Nürnberg of the second. At a conference held on 3 May at the headquarters of the O.K.W. Staff South at Königsee the Gauleiters there represented refused to accept the situation and demanded that we should go on fighting or at least that the National Socialists should be left in control, as otherwise order could not be maintained. If I refused to give the order they proposed to fly an ambassador at once to Admiral Doenitz to make it clear that this demand was unconditional. It required a long tirade to awaken some glimmer of understanding for the facts. They must realize, I told them, that the world had not waged war against us for over five years with the purpose of crushing National Socialism in order to leave the party at the helm when they had won it. It was clear to me that the party had trained its men exclusively for the domestic arena and had entirely neglected to teach them the rudiments of external politics.

* * *

Readjustment to the period following the surrender called for a completely fresh start and the obliteration of any idea of a guerilla war.

This end was achieved. The few who took refuge in the mountains and escaped capture do not count, nor do they belong to the so-called "Volunteers."

An administration composed of men who were neither politicians nor suspect as National Socialists was now needed for the transition period until the occupying powers took over. This idea was generally appreciated and, in spite of the shortness of the time, was partly put into effect; it covered the organization of local voluntary defence squads against pillage during the period of "anarchy" and their replacement later by a local police force sanctioned by the occupying powers.

Thirdly, steps had to be taken to feed the population and the armed forces until such time as the occupying powers took over the responsibility. The rationing of the troops was only a problem where the sudden influx from the Russian front into impoverished or inaccessible districts held up supplies.

Surplus stocks in military stores were handed over to the civilian population in order to avoid looting.

Secretary of State Dr. Hayler had most efficiently organized the continuance of a rationing system, and drawn up measures to encourage wholesale and retail trade. The last only required the sanction of the occupation authorities, which it was expected would be given after a conference with General Eisenhower. This conference, however, which was also to have embraced a number of other points, never took place.

I proposed to General Devers that technical troops of all kinds should not be disbanded, but should be strengthened by technicians drawn from all formations and used, under a scheme to be discussed with and supervised by the American authorities, for the immediate repair of bridges or in a few important cases to build new ones, to make the most necessary repairs to the railways with their rolling stock, and finally to get the telephone system working normally. We had also prepared to make speedily available labour parties and horse teams for distressed agricultural areas.

The American Army Group declared its general agreement with these proposals; C.-in-C. West thereupon prepared the necessary instructions so that all that was needed to commence this most urgent work was the approval of American general headquarters. This was, however, refused!

To cite but one example: there were at the end of May 15,000 signals servicemen waiting on the alert to repair the public telegraph and telephone network. I am convinced that by the end of 1945 the communications system and economic life would have been in a state in which reconstruction would have been possible and the Americans saved much subsequent expense, if the influence of Morgenthau had not permeated the American military mind.

PROBLEMS OF LEADERSHIP AT THE END OF THE WAR

My ideas about the ideal chain of command and the construction of a command organization for all three services in individual theatres of war are too extensive to be dealt with in detail, but I should like to mention one or two points which may be of general interest.

The system adopted by Hitler of setting up organizations working on parallel lines—that is, independent of each other but active in the same field—can only be understood from the standpoint of a dictator filled with mistrust of everybody. It was fatal to the conduct of a war, the main disadvantages being mutual distrust between the army and the S.S., between the Administration and the party, etc., different rules of precedence, and independent spheres of jurisdiction, etc.

In a war which demands a unified authority and economic structure, excrescences such as the party offices were bound in some way at some time or another to be injurious. If anyone wanted to undermine the structure of the armed forces of a nation he could not do better than apply the organization, or rather the disorganization, beloved of Hitler.

A centralized control of newly created formations was obviously essential, for only through it could the drafting and training of manpower be accommodated to what war material was available. Careful advance planning of new formations was also right. But it was wrong to neglect priorities (for example, air force over army equipment) and in the last resort to take into account only the requirements of the moment; it was wrong to hold back personnel and material for new formations until a change in the situation made their employment of doubtful value —whereas their immediate use might have saved the collapse of a front. Such new armies as Hitler pinned his faith to had no justification unless they were strong enough and well enough equipped and trained to influence the campaign decisively. In

1945 this was no longer the case. I maintain that the battles on the Rhine—considered purely as ground operations—would have had a different result if all our available combat strength in men and material had been sent to the front at the turn of the year or at latest in January-February 1945. All the forces at the disposal of C.-in-C. West after this date were barely effective without a solid leaven of veteran units. But to harp on this was preaching to deaf ears.

CAPITULATION

At the end of March General Röttiger, who had been my Chief of Staff when I was C.-in-C. Southwest, repeatedly rang me up to beg me to visit him urgently to discuss the situation. I had no time to bother with Army Groups which were not under my command. But when he did come under my command in April I went to Innsbruck on 27-28 to meet him—a saving of time, as it lay halfway between us. The conference took place in the Gauleiter's house in the presence of von Vietinghoff and our Ambassador in Italy, Dr. Rahn. S.S. General Wolff, who was also to have attended, was held up somewhere by the Partisans.

The Gauleiter made a long introductory speech in which he expatiated on the political situation, a recent conversation of his with Hitler and the hopeless military situation in the southern theatre. He wound up by expressing the opinion that we must examine the question of a surrender before it was too late, though we should, of course, only decide in favour of it if there was no opportunity of going on fighting. He then left the room for a moment and Rahn and Vietinghoff remarked that the Gauleiter had sung a quite different tune only a few days ago. This made me prick up my ears.

Vietinghoff next reported on the military situation, which had deteriorated alarmingly and must lead to a débâcle. He considered it necessary to debate the question of surrender and to make a definite decision. There was still time. Dr. Rahn was silent.

As I did not then know that the overtures to the Americans, to which I had some time previously consented, had already taken the form of negotiations for surrender, I made my decision from a military standpoint. I have never ceased to regret that Wolff, with whom I was associated for better or for worse, was not present; he would certainly have put me wise.[1] I argued that our action must be dictated by the general situation. As soldiers we had to obey orders. These forbade capitulation unless we could conscientiously say that there was no other way out. We must also consider the indirect consequences; the premature surrender of Army Group C would create an untenable position for Army Groups Southeast and G north of the Alps. We must also not overlook the psychological effect of such a step on the officers and men fighting around and in Berlin. Our own interests must take second place. Besides, I told them, I assumed or rather hoped that the actual situation at the front would develop more favourably than we now feared, as it had so often done in the past.

My decision to go on fighting met with no opposition, and I had the impression that I had stiffened Vietinghoff's back. But had I known in detail the steps which were then being taken to arrange a general surrender I would probably have decided and acted differently. I should have been morally bound to keep any contract made. If I am not to be wise after the event, I cannot say today how I would have acted then. But probably I would not have chosen the way which later seemed right to C.-in-C. Southwest.

The developments following the Innsbruck conference with its half-confessions were anything but pretty, and in fact embarrassed both sides intolerably. When I returned from a visit to the front late on the night of 1-2 May my Chief reported to me that General Schulz considered any further resistance by his utterly defeated armies useless and asked for immediate authorization for an armistice.

---

[1] I had informed none of my own officers, not even my Chief of Staff, of the negotiations with the Americans, not wishing to compromise them.

I gave it. And the following day von Vietinghoff broadcast the news to his troops. At the same time I reported this to the O.K.W. in a message in which I placed myself at their disposal for this arbitrary and punishable action; briefly outlining the consequences of C.-in-C. Southwest's capitulation, I requested sanction for the surrender of Army Groups E and G, and it was granted for the latter.

On 3 May I appointed General Foertsch, commanding the First Army, to conduct the negotiations. He possessed the diplomatic and political qualifications for this difficult task and was given detailed instructions the same day at my headquarters at Alm. On 4 May the requested negotiations took place at Salzburg; Foertsch returned extremely depressed. Even our very slender hopes were disappointed; the negotiations amounted to no more than receiving orders. It was Casablanca in operation! The same thing happened to C.-in-C. Southwest—whose representative had informed me at our interview on the night of 1-2 May of the special concessions likely to be made to his Chief! The copy of the surrender negotiations I asked for contained no mention of these.

During these same days I made my first approach to Eisenhower regarding the surrender of my troops in the field against the Americans. Eisenhower replied that he would enter into no negotiations that did not involve all German forces everywhere. I thereupon asked the O.K.W. to take the further steps required, which was immediately done.

The unconditional surrender became effective for Army Group G on 6 May. I had already announced the expected surrender on 2 or 3 May in order to avoid any further fighting and useless bloodshed. I thanked the troops and appealed to them to maintain by their behaviour the reputation of the German armed forces. I explained on this occasion and in various addresses to units that our unexceptionable military behaviour was the only thing which could preserve the respect of the Allied soldiers, and that it would be of inestimable value to subsequent negotiations at a higher level.

I had gained the impression, also confirmed by the American commanders, that our men after nearly six years of war and in a hopeless situation were still conducting themselves properly.

On 6 May my headquarters staff was the only group in the Alps which had not yet surrendered. I decided to transfer a reduced staff to Himmler's special train, which was standing masterless in a siding at Saalfelden, and again entered into communication with the Americans. My Chief of Staff meanwhile remained at my old headquarters to work out the details of the surrender according to my meticulous instructions. I had advised S.S. General Hausser as my special representative to see to it that the surrender of the S.S. troops proceeded in exact observance of my directives; that—in a nutshell—no follies, such as escape into the mountains, should be committed at the last moment. He, the most popular and ablest of the S.S. generals, succeeded in carrying them out, which did not prevent battle-tested and well-disciplined S.S. troops from being meted exceptional, and not always very humane, treatment.

I now had time on my hands and was able to contemplate my future. Should I do that which would absolve me from inevitable further burdens? As my demise would only place them on someone else's shoulders, I decided not to.

I had not long to wait before an American major arrived with a few soldiers, who were received by my escort; he informed me that in the course of the next few days General Taylor, commanding the 101st Airborne Division, would come and see me. This very junior but unarmed and courteous American officer—incidentally after the war he was American Commandant in Berlin and more recently Commander-in-Chief in Korea—invited me to move my quarters to the Berchtesgadener Hof, after details of the disarmament and surrender of my staff had been arranged. I was allowed to keep my weapons, medals and Marshal's baton and was driven to Berchtesgaden accompanied by the general.

On the way there I was able to address various units on the lines I have indicated.

At Berchtesgaden the best rooms in the hotel were given my companion and myself; I was allowed to move freely, but requested to do so only in the company of a certain agreeable Lieutenant Brown, who was born in Munich. That I was able to visit the Russian-front Army Groups at Zeltweg and Graz without an American escort is a small indication of the exemplary behaviour of the American general, but also a symptom of the tension between the Allies. General Devers, the American Army Group commander, who paid me a visit on one of these days, was noticeably aloof, although preserving traditional military courtesy. His attitude made me more clearly aware of my new situation.

In the course of the next few days, beginning in the train, I was interviewed constantly by Allied newspaper reporters; the interviews were conducted without incident and one might almost say with mutual understanding. I there made the acquaintance of Kurt Riess, who afterwards specially pleaded for me. Again and again I asked to be allowed to speak with General Eisenhower in order to urge upon him useful measures for the troops and the population. Instead, on 15 May 1945 I was taken to the camp at Mondorf, near Luxembourg, via Augsburg, where I had to leave my medals and Field-Marshal's baton. I may add here that neither of my two Chiefs (Winter and Westphal) nor any of my other officers or men imagined a bad end to my removal. They all knew me intimately, were familiar with almost every hour of my war activity and never dreamed of a trial or a death sentence. Nor did they think that instead of being taken to Eisenhower I would be sent to a special camp. Why was it thought right not to lay the cards on the table?

At various times and in various aspects the question of surrender has occupied every German commander, though this is primarily a political concern of the Government.

Secondarily, surrender can be a military matter carried out with the approval or on the orders of the Government. The surrender of Army Group G is a perfect example of the first case, the general capitulation of the German armed forces of the second.

A capitulation may become necessary if an army is beaten, if resistance has become senseless and futile, and if its elimination as a fighting force causes no immediate damage to military and political interests. But it must also be borne in mind that flirtation with the idea of surrender softens morale and impairs the will to fight. Examples of surrender which, despite disadvantages to the general situation, were the only possible way to end the fighting are that of the Tunis armies and of Army Group B in the Ruhr, though with obvious differences.

Finally there is the surrender for which military commanders can accept responsibility if the continuation of the fight either pins down no enemy forces and is hopeless by reason of inherent weakness or if it is no longer possible to influence the outcome of the war. In either case the effect on neighbours or the whole must first be very carefully examined.

Surrenders planned in advance and suddenly carried out regardless of neighbourly obligations betray a large measure of irresponsibility; though their pretext is usually political, the commander concerned has no more than a very limited comprehension of the general situation. Examples of this kind are also furnished by World War II. In this technical age such far-reaching decisions, taken without consultation with a superior authority, should become increasingly exceptional.

The whole question brings us back to the old problem of the "political soldier"—for whom, I repeat, the German armed forces had no place, the product of General von Seeckt's training being the soldier whose "constitutional loyalty" was divorced from party agitation.

The International Military Tribunal at Nürnberg nevertheless sentenced these soldiers to death, and demanded instead an attitude capable of exerting a decisive influence on major foreign political questions, of removing criminal elements in critical domestic situations or of overthrowing governments with criminal tendencies.

Between these two interpretations of a soldier's code there is an unbridgeable gulf.

In mid-1947 I dealt at length with this question of the "political soldier" without reference to the special case of the Third Reich, in an essay from which I now quote:

"I require of every senior officer in a high position of authority the political discernment which will help him to obtain a deep and proper insight into events of political life within and without his own country. This perception should enable such an officer to play his part as responsible adviser to the head of the state with full knowledge of his responsibility, to foresee military requirements, and at the same time to accommodate them to political circumstances. This delicate but indispensable collaboration may, of course, lead to serious conflicts of conscience and to external disputes in which the military leader must take into consideration the effects of his attitude on foreign policy.

"I do not, however, in any way recognize a 'political soldier' who implements his personal political views by personal political action and thereby misconstrues the true meaning of the word 'soldier.' Such soldiers arrogate to themselves prerogatives which no head of state or government can tolerate unless they are willing to surrender them. Even today, in 1947, examples bearing out this view are to be found in many countries."

In the above I wanted to emphasize that an officer, above all a high-ranking officer, stands above parties, but also that every soldier owes obedience to the legal government and the legal form of state. He must be bound by the military oath, which enjoins obedience as a categorical imperative and says neither more nor less than that the soldier must obey his superiors and the legal government. To relax these obligations is to encourage *coups d'état* which very seldom purpose what is best for the state or for the people. In this way the armed forces which should preserve and protect the state become its destroyers. A few instances to the contrary prove nothing, but suggest that in rare cases release from the oath may be an ethical duty for a soldier with very high responsibilities. This man must know that he is treading the narrow path between "Hosanna" and "Crucify him!"

One more point: there is an inner contradiction between politics and soldiering. Only exceptional persons can combine the two. There is some truth in the remark that a soldier who gives his attention to politics ceases to be a good soldier. I know from my own experience of war that political discussions in critical military situations can influence military performance. A division of power seems to me the sound solution. The fact, however, remains that troops are as good or as bad as their commander. The age of enlightenment we live in demands an officer who can grasp the interrelations of politics and explain them to his men. Only thus can the "civilian in uniform" evolve from a "party political civilian" into a "state-thinking soldier." The difficulty of this task cannot be overestimated, because we Germans, embroiled in wars for the best part of two centuries, have neglected political education and in the parties and politicians of the extreme Left and Right have to deal with people whose attitude towards the state is one of more or less fanatical negation.

Therefore the paramount law remains the education of the "civilian in uniform" as a loyal and patriotic soldier, and his firm allegiance to the state and the constitution through his oath.

My Post-war Experiences

FIRST YEARS OF IMPRISONMENT

Negotiations now proceeded to make the instrument of "unconditional surrender" effective–yet far be it from me to revive the period following the surrender with all its painful incidents. I hold the view that we must remove our differences to draw closer together in our old, crumpling Europe, to learn to understand one another, to find the road to a united Europe that will supersede the petty state divisions which are a thing of the past. I always believed in Briand's idea, but any remaining doubts of the necessity of a new order in Europe were removed when I became an airman. When, starting from Berlin in the slow aircraft of 1934, one had to consult the map after an hour's flight to avoid crossing the Czechoslovak frontier, it brought things home to one. As I explained to an officer of the American Historical Division in early 1948: "If I have opted for the west and in my diminished sphere of activity am fighting for the realization of a European federation, and incidentally also for the American Historical Division, this means a lot for a man who feels that he has been unjustly condemned to death by a British tribunal."

Hard as it may be for the individual, we must learn to forget. But much that has happened and much that is controversial must still be discussed, not in a spirit of recrimination but in order to learn from our mistakes for the sake of the future.

My life was now a bitter progress through every type of Allied camp and prison. In the "Ash Cage"—what a significant name!—at Mondorf in 1945 I met the former great ones of the German state, the armed forces and the party. Count Schwerin-Krosigk, the Reich Minister of Finance, and I may claim to have soothed those troubled spirits and brought them closer to one another. The officers and non-commissioned officers who guarded us were sympathetic fellows, in marked contrast to the camp commandant, Colonel Andrus. Perhaps that is the reason why he was made the commandant of the International Military Tribunal prison at Nürnberg. We all without exception found that this American officer discouraged the idea of a comity of nations. The younger American officers thought that I did not belong in this camp and tried with a kindness which I more than appreciated to effect my transfer to another camp with less of a charnel-house atmosphere. That their efforts were unsuccessful does not alter my opinion of these officers, who were above the hate psychosis.

At Oberursel I was well treated and had only a few days' experience of the mischief-breeding conditions of a hutment interrogation camp. But what I saw there was not pretty. I came to the conclusion and found it later otherwise confirmed that the intelligence service may so transform a man that in one's dealings with him it is impossible to suppress a dislike which can ripen into fear. The job leaves its mark on the man. Much might have been avoided if so many emigrant Germans had not been roped in. It is asking too much to expect objectivity and humanity of men who have been driven from their country after tragic experiences.

Nürnberg—to know it as a prisoner on remand is never to forget it. Five months' solitary confinement, with no grounds given—from 23 December 1945! At exercise or at church one felt oneself a leper. In the intervals there were long hours of cross-examination as witness for Goering—as the lawyers said to me: "At last a classical witness for a change!" Two incidents from my appearance as a witness stick in my memory. In a lengthy explanation I was justifying the legality of the air attacks in the first days of the Polish campaign—relying on the Hague Convention of Land Warfare our Air Ministry had drawn up appropriate regulations for air warfare. The prosecutor, Sir David Maxwell Fyfe, concluded his cross-examination on this point with the remark: "So you allowed so and so many Polish towns to be attacked in violation of international law?"

Raising my voice in the dead silence of the courtroom: "I have given my evidence as a German officer with over forty years' service," I replied, "as a German Field-Marshal and on oath! If my statements are so little respected I shall make no further depositions."

The startled silence in the courtroom was broken by the prosecutor's: "I had no intention of being offensive."

Later, defending counsel, Dr. Laternser, wanted to know something about the Partisans in Italy. The Russian prosecutor, Rudenko, instantly sprang to his feet. "The witness," he declared, "seems to me the least fitted to speak on this subject." (There was so much I could have said about it!) That from a Rudenko about whose career I was tolerably well informed! I regretted that the tribunal had not the same personal knowledge. Anyway, after lengthy deliberations out of court that was the end of the subject.

Dachau followed Nürnberg. My comrades who travelled with me were warned not to converse with me; I was similarly warned, with the effect that on arrival at the Dachau "blockhouse" I just *had* to talk to all my cell inmates, squeezed together as I was in a tiny cell with Field-Marshals von Brauchitsch and Milch, Secretary of State Bohle, Ambassador von Bargen and a subordinate troop commander. Our warder was a gypsy who developed an extraordinary interest in my watch. In the blockhouse I relearnt the art of standing still when my thoughts ranged all the more actively.

When physical weakness caused our removal to a hut and we were allowed to move freely within the compound, the interest of the S.S. prisoners in our fate was refreshing.

After that it was Nürnberg again, and then Langwasser, where, after a brief reunion with many comrades there, I was picked out to share a strongly barred prison hut with Skorzeny. My stay there had the undeniable advantage of comfortable quarters, the best American food and kind prison guards. However, I was soon removed to another hut, where I was watched even during my most intimate occupations by three persons, two with tommy-guns and one with a flashlight. My life went from one extreme to the other. Two days later I was taken away with Field-Marshals List and von Weichs and a junior officer in a magnificent car to the American Historical Division's camp at Allendorf. Our escort was an officer and a gentleman, his kindness making us feel that we were among people of our own kind. The officers of the Historical Division, under their excellent Colonel Potter, went to great trouble to alleviate the customary hardships of camp life. At Allendorf I began to persuade a number of generals and General Staff officers to participate in the compilation of a history of the war. As my main argument I pointed out that this was our only chance of paying a tribute to our soldiers and at the same time influencing Allied historians in the interests of truth—the recording of our experiences being a secondary purpose. Our chief difficulties lay in the lack of documentary material. All the same, our work, in my opinion, has been useful evidence for any final account of the period. I cannot name all the officers of the Historical Division who deserve my thanks for their understanding of our situation and that of our families—there were too many. Almost without exception they were, and are still, the ambassadors of goodwill and "fraternization."

In the autumn of 1946 I spent a month in the well-known "Kensington Cage" in London, where Colonel Scotland held the sceptre. There are various opinions about the Cage, but personally I was treated with remarkable consideration. My almost daily interviews with Colonel Scotland brought us closer together and helped me to realize his fairmindedness. (In fact he took it on him to move strongly for my release.) When one evening some jack-in-office was insolent to me I reported it to the colonel, with the result that afterwards the normal regulations were not exceeded even by this particular N.C.O.

I should like, incidentally, to quote in brief a conversation I had with an interrogating officer of Jewish origin about this time, the subject of which was the growth of anti-Semitism in the world then finding surreptitious expression in many quarters among the Allies.

"You have failed to understand the signs of the times," I told him. "It is not impossible that you are missing a unique opportunity of laying a foundation for the Jewish people which would have given it an unassailable position in the world. You had every right to demand the punishment of those who committed crimes against the Jews and repaiation for the harm they did. Every German and the whole world would have understood that, and world-wide help would have flowed in to you. But to be guided by the idea of revenge is fatal because this mentality only leads to fresh injustice."

Evidently impressed by this argument, he replied: "Yes, but you are asking a great deal of us Jews."

"I know," I agreed. "But is not the attainment of ultimate peace worth this stake?"

The advantage of Allendorf was that we were generously allowed visitors, so we were able to spend the Christmas of 1946 and see the New Year in with our families—a comfort which meant a great deal to our wives, whose endurance in the following years is certainly attributable to these visits.

On 17 January 1947 I was transported via Salzburg to Rimini for the opening of my trial. Colonel Potter with another colonel escorted me to Frankfurt, and there handed me over to two very pleasant English officers. As a symptom of the confusion of the times, in Salzburg these last and myself were guests over one day of a private American resident, only to spend the same night in bunks in what had formerly been stables. Again at Rimini we were met by a fair-sized delegation of officers. It cheered my heart to see in these brief intervals that comradeship does not draw the line at frontiers or between victors and vanquished.

I am always happy to find that soldiers are often better and more sensitive politicians than those who feel they have a vocation for that profession. It is ironical to record that soldiers, so frequently repudiated, defamed and ridiculed by the whole world, in times of real need are called to leading positions and overwhelmed with honours. One has only to glance at the single example of America to see this (Marshall, Eisenhower, MacArthur). Should this not induce people to judge soldiers with less hostility and prejudice?

MY TRIAL

On leaving at six in the morning for Venice-Mestre I was given a touching send-off by the inmates of the camp, who had all supported me—I promised to stand up for their honour and Germany's. As the arrival of my counsel was delayed by incidents for which the Germans were in no way responsible, the prosecutor wanted to open the proceedings without my being represented or only given the assistance of a judge who had been called as a witness for the prosecution. Again it was an English officer who intervened and told the prosecutor: "This trial must not be allowed to become a farce from the very start."

My trial had been preceded by those of von Mackensen and Mälzer in Rome in November 1946. Both, like myself, were accused of the shooting of 335 Italians in the Ardeatine catacombs near Rome on 24 March 1944, and both were sentenced to death on 30 November 1946. I gave evidence on behalf of my subordinates—but in each case in vain.

My trial at Venice-Mestre lasted more than three months, from February to May 1947. It was a terrific strain—more so even than the six days I was on the witness stand in Rome. From what a British officer at the end of a long talk said to me after the trial on the day the death sentence was passed: "Field-Marshal, you have no idea how much you have won the respect of all British officers during your trial, and especially today," it may be taken that I held my own. I replied: "Major, if I had behaved one iota differently, I would never have deserved to become a German Field-Marshal."

With the exception of the Judge Advocate, the military tribunal was differently composed from that at Rome. The Judge, the only legal official, whose duty it was to advise the military judges, who had no judicial training, performed the same function at all the other major trials—which ended, almost without exception, with death sentences. If the Judge wound up his final speech by saying that I "stood in the twilight" I can safely say that there was no twilight about his glaring prejudice. A Swiss newspaper wrote at the time that he was "the second, and the better, prosecutor."

The court was not constituted in accordance with international usage. In addition to a general (Hackwell-Smith) it comprised four British colonels. During the second half of the trial the president seemed to enjoy his rôle of temperamental inquisitor without the inconsiderate treatment to which I was subjected being in any way questioned. Colonel Scotland, who has dealt with *The Kesselring Case* in a pamphlet, gave his opinion of the tribunal to the effect that all right-thinking people in Great Britain and in Germany should reach their own verdict on the victims of these two trials, which could be described as the worst instructed ever convened by order of His Majesty. . . .

Now to the case itself. The bill of indictment presented to me comprised two heads: Count 1 accused me of being a party to the murder of the 335 Italians, already mentioned; Count 2 charged me with inciting by two orders the troops under my command to murder civilians by way of reprisals and in violation of the laws and customs of land warfare—the result of these orders being the killing of a total of 1,087 Italians. To the bill of indictment, as short as it was ominous, sworn statements by witnesses—so-called "sergeant-affidavits"—were attached as evidence—nothing else.

In his summing up the Judge Advocate advised the judges that if they accepted that the responsibility for all reprisals had been transferred from the armed forces to the S.D. (the Security Service of the S.S.), they must acquit me. This, it seems to me, is the key factor of Count 1. I have to deduce from the sentence—"Guilty—death by shooting"—that the court did not consider this proved. Yet my Chief of Staff and my operations and intelligence officers—as was afterwards corroborated by the clerk who kept the official German day-to-day account of the war—testified on oath that by a definite order Hitler had transferred the authority for carrying out reprisals to the S.D., which even the S.D. commander admitted in the course of the trial.

Why then was the verdict one of "guilty" in the face of this evidence? It can only be assumed that the sworn testimony of my officers was considered untrustworthy, which was incomprehensible to all of us. Finally I told myself that it could simply be explained by a different interpretation of the meaning of the oath. During the two trials I became increasingly convinced that in the Allied procedure the oath was regarded not as a means of promoting the truth but as an instrument of pressure to extract more than the truth justified from the unfortunate victims.

As I had the right to assume that the court must consider the foundation of the case as at least doubtful—there could be no question of proof—on the internationally recognized principle, also practised in British courts, that the accused must be given the benefit of the doubt, I hardly expected a verdict of guilty.

From the proceedings—no reason has ever been given to substantiate the verdict—it may further be inferred, in the light of the instruction given to the military court by the Judge, that the legality of the reprisals was accepted. In addition, the court must have considered it proved that von Mackensen and I had not permitted any reprisals on *our own responsibility*, of which we had been relieved by Hitler's order, but had, on the contrary, tried to achieve a deterrent effect by the execution of those who were so liable according to international law. Such a deliberate attempt to disobey Hitler's orders should at least have been regarded by the court as an honest effort to exercise humanity.

Hitler's ukase fixed the reprisal ratio at one to ten and appointed the S.D. to carry them out. By this order the armed forces were eliminated and deprived of all say in the matter.

The court does not seem to have been agreed over the question of this ratio—our efforts to reduce which it ignored—but in any case to have considered it as exceeding what was legally permissible. If this is so, it is all the more surprising that Allied commanders are known and proved to have ordered reprisals in the same or even a higher ratio without there having existed in their cases a critical military situation or the pre-conditions for an "emergency" as was the case at Rome. I refrain from giving an opinion here on whether the reprisal ratios fixed by Allied commanders were justified, as the whole question of reprisals, which I dealt with in detail in Chapter 21, is admittedly open to argument. It is, anyway, difficult years after the event to pronounce judgment about the rights and wrongs of a case without knowledge of the atmosphere prevailing at the time. It would not have been a bad thing if my judges, just because they sat as victors, could have taken this into consideration. The fact that an Italian tribunal—that is, a court set up by the nation most affected by the shootings—had returned a verdict of acquittal on the same count in the case of Kappler, a member of the S.D., may have distressed the conscience of the British judges. I still think they were trying to make up for what they thought an error of justice.

In a general review of the question it must not be forgotten that the reasons for the reprisals were the extermination of a company of police, elderly, respectable Tyroleans, in the course of their ordinary police duties of protecting the Italian population, and the slaughter of a number of local people going quietly about their business by Italian Communists pursuing their disruptive ends under the cloak of patriotism. This was not the first case. Because of previous assassinations Romans had been warned of the consequences of further acts of terrorism by public notices and by the Church—which should have been taken into account.

I was told by an English friend that I was thought to have accepted responsibilities that were not rightly mine, though this cannot apply to the case of the shooting in the catacombs because I proved to the court that the armed forces had no control over the S.D. This question is, however, not worth arguing.

As I have already said, both von Mackensen and I did all we could to prevent reprisals—a point which was not appreciated by the British tribunals. The Fifth American Military Tribunal at Nürnberg, on the other hand, clearly formulated its more understanding view as follows:

"To escape the legal and moral stigma attaching to such acts it would be sufficient to prove that any such criminal order was circumvented whenever opportunity offered."

Von Mackensen, Mälzer and I were sentenced to death through the failure of our attempts to circumvent one of Hitler's orders, for which we were in no way to blame, as we had in the matter of reprisals been deprived of authority.

Under these circumstances the court's inability to establish the indictment, unfavourably commented on in every quarter, emphasizes the travesty of justice.

As to Count 2: I have described as objectively as possible in Chapter 21, the growth, combat methods, etc., of the Italian guerilla bands and the nature of the German counter-measures the latter of which make plain my fundamental attitude on all questions of guerilla warfare. I quote as a rider a sentence from a letter I wrote at the end of 1945 to de Gasperi, the Italian Prime Minister, asking him, in view of the renewed and utterly unjustifiable persecution to which I was being subjected, to use his high office to publish the true facts—

". . . I sympathize with the grief of Italian fathers and mothers at the death of their sons. I bow my head in silent respect for their sorrow and for all those who died for their country, in so far as they were not the instruments of an alien communism. But do not these men and women also believe in the anguish of German mothers and fathers when they received the news of their dear ones ambushed and shot in the back or hideously done to death in captivity? Do they not understand that it was my duty to protect my soldiers from such a fate? . . ."

The foundation of Count 2 of the indictment was in connection with orders issued by me on 17 June, 1 July, 15 August and 24 September 1944. I confine myself to those points which were held as incriminating in the prosecutor's final speech.

"The fight against the bands is to be prosecuted with every available means and with the greatest severity. I will support any commander who in his choice and severity of means goes beyond our customary measure of restraint." (Order of 17 June.)[1]

In the first English translation the word "means" was rendered "methods"; so read, the sentence may appear to support the charge. It struck me that at the subsequent trial of S.S. General Simon at Padua the prosecutor, who had been junior counsel for the prosecution at my trial, again used the word "methods." Was it right to have retained this mistranslation?

"Here also the old principle obtains that a blunder in the choice of means to accomplish the purpose is better than omission and neglect. The bands are to be attacked and destroyed."

This excerpt is clearly a directive; it was addressed to all commanders down to divisional commanders, who had to issue orders at times necessary for individual cases within the framework of this secret document. Its purpose, as of others which followed it, was to prevent the fighting degenerating on both sides into inevitable chaos and to oblige commanders to devote their personal attention to the neglected guerilla war; in other words, to give it the same importance as the fighting at the front and to permit the employment of all available means in waging it.

It was believed that the words "I will support any commander, etc." could be construed as an intention to back up *any* reprisals. That this is not so is, however, evident from the plain

---

[1] *"Der kampf gegen die Banden muss daher mit allen zur Verfügung stehenden Mitteln und mit grösster Schärfe durchgeführt werden. Ich werde jeden Führer decken, der in der Wahl und Schärfe des Mittels über das bei uns übliche zurückhaltende Mass hinausgeht."*

fact that the order has nothing whatever to do with *reprisals* as such.

My second order of 1 July 1944, in contrast to that of 17 June, is purely a combat order; it contains, however, under paragraphs (*b*) and (*c*) principles for such reprisals as might have to be envisaged:

(*a*) "In my appeal to the Italians I have declared out-and-out war on the guerillas. This declaration must be no empty threat. I make it the duty of all soldiers and military police to use the severest means in case of need. Every act of violence on the part of the bands is to be immediately punished.

(*b*) "Where bands make their appearance in considerable numbers a percentage of the male population resident in the district, to be decided on at the time, is to be arrested, and if acts of violence occur they are to be shot.

(*c*) "Where soldiers, etc., are shot from villages the village is to be burnt. Culprits and ringleaders are to be publicly hanged."

This order was my reply to a significant appeal broadcast by Field-Marshals Badoglio and Alexander for the murder of Germans and the intensification of the guerilla war. I do not believe that the accusation relative to paragraph (*b*) would ever have been made if the British authorities who framed the indictment had known article 358d of the American *Rules of Land Warfare*.

"Hostages, arrested and held for the declared purpose that they shall serve as security against illegal action on the part of enemy combat forces or of the population, may be punished or put to death if illegal actions are nevertheless committed."

Moreover, the American conception of right goes so far as to permit the summary execution—that is, without previous legal proceedings—of Partisans and guerillas. I did not, however, need to make use of this right, as in no proved case were members of bands put to death *after* hostilities without a previous sentence

by court-martial. If the tribunal sought to infer the contrary
from my order of 24 September—"I further order that in future
courts-martial must be convened immediately on the spot. . . ."
—this is incomprehensible, because it was pointed out in court,
and supported by proof, that the decisive words in this sentence
are "immediately on the spot." They do not mean that courts-
martial were first to be set up—on the contrary, they were already there; the words were intended, rather, to remind soldiers
that effective *legal* means existed for the punishment of viola-
tions of international law if only they were properly applied. If
the tribunal was of the opinion that my directives were an incitement to "terrorism of the Italian civilian population" it must
be objected that "the civilian population" or "women and chil-
dren" are nowhere mentioned, and therefore cannot have been
meant. All German Commanders-in-Chief, army and divisional
commanders whose place of residence was known at the time of
my trial made verbal statements in court or sent sworn written
statements that they never understood the directive in the sense
given it by the prosecution. Only one Commander-in-Chief in
the London "Kensington Cage," under the strain of an understandable cage-psychosis, made critical remarks about my orders; these were not made under oath and he retracted them as
a *voluntary* witness before the court *under oath*. As the tribunal
apparently did not accept this correction as valid I may perhaps
be excused for explaining this incident more fully.

My order said: "I will support any commander who in his
choice and severity of means goes beyond our customary measure of restraint."

The witness remembered this as: "I will support any commander who in his choice and severity of means goes *far beyond
the authorized means*."

Objection can rightly be made to the second wording, but—
it was wrong. Even if one wished to attach significance to other
written and oral statements made by witnesses not under oath,
the remarks of the witness—"this order involves a great danger
for the troops," and "the Field-Marshal's orders give the troops
too much liberty"—cannot be construed as an incitement to

terrorism of the civilian population. Besides, the court must have known from the evidence of the Chief of Staff of the competent army commander that the morale of the troops was in fact not endangered.

It seems unimaginable that after clarification of the deposition as a whole the court could adhere to the written statement made by the witness in London. Yet so it was!

The final words of my order of 1 July read: "Looting in any form is forbidden and will be most severely punished. All measures must be harsh but just. The good name of the German soldier requires this."

These words, which present the meaning of my orders in the true light, are sufficient refutation of the court's verdict.

My orders of 21 August and 24 September might have convinced even prejudiced judges that no kind of terrorism was envisaged.

The following is an extract from that of 21 August 1944:

"In the course of major operations against the bandits incidents have occurred in recent weeks that seriously harm the good name and discipline of the German armed forces, and no longer have any relation to retaliatory measures.

"As the combating of the bands must be prosecuted by the severest means, innocent elements will occasionally be affected.

"If, however, a major operation instead of pacifying the district only leads to greater unrest among the population, as well as creating very difficult provisioning problems which in the end must be shouldered by the German armed forces, this will be an indication that the operation was wrongly conducted and can only be regarded as pillage.

"The Duce himself, in a letter to Dr. Rahn, our Ambassador to the Italian government, has bitterly complained of the manner in which various operations against the bands have been carried out and of retaliatory measures which in the last resort have fallen on the population instead of on the bandits.

"The consequences of these whole undertakings have very seriously undermined confidence in the German armed forces, thereby creating fresh enemies for us and assisting enemy propaganda."

Extract from my directive of 24 September 1944:

"The Duce has once again conveyed to me written statements about acts committed by members of units stationed in Italy against the population, which contravene my directive of 21 August 1944; the manner of their commission is outrageous and such as to drive decent and spirited elements of the population into the enemy's camp or to the Partisans. I am no longer willing to condone such behaviour, being fully aware that such cowardly outrages result in hardship for the innocent.

"The Duce's complaints are being forwarded to the High Command authorities, and the competent general is being asked to have the worst cases investigated, to report the result of the investigation to me and to pass the matter to the responsible commander for a final decision. These officers will also report the result to me."

In reference to these orders, however, it is a fundamental point that official investigations made at the time did *not* prove the guilt of German soldiers. Moreover, I gave evidence, supported by proof, before the tribunal that I investigated every report of an offence committed by my troops, and, if it was substantiated, had the offender committed for trial. If the order of 21 August were to be read as an admission of incitement to terrorism implicit in those of 17 June and 1 July, that would suggest that I gave criminal orders only, by another order given shortly afterwards, to make my subordinates responsible for crimes in the meantime committed by them in the line of duty. This hardly fits in with my reputation for overeagerness to accept responsibility, nor, if this had been so, would I have remained for one minute longer the "popular" Commander-in-Chief, to whom those who served under me remain loyal even today. The fact is that the accusation was not proved on any count. Even in the case where I admitted the possibility of my troops having violated international law an Italian court-martial returned a verdict of acquittal.

A few words about the sergeant-affidavits. Such affidavits were not taken down before a person authorized to administer an oath, but were made years after the event on the basis of statements by sometimes over a hundred people who were still subject to pressure on the part of the Partisans and Communists. Most of the cases tried by the Italians in the meanwhile proved that the statements of witnesses were either untrue or wildly exaggerated, and thus that no value could be attached to them as evidence. It transpired that the misdeeds in question had to be partly booked to neo-Fascist formations, for example the Brigata Nera, or to Italian criminal elements wearing German uniforms. The English investigating judge confirms this in a petition submitted on my behalf in which, in view of his special knowledge of the methods employed during the war by the Germans in Italy, he strongly urges that von Mackensen, Mälzer and myself should not only be released from prison but pardoned.

Here, too, it must be said in conclusion that all the German and Italian witnesses who appeared for me must have been considered "untrustworthy," whereas the Italian witnesses' fairy-tales and the British sergeant-affidavits have been accepted as "trustworthy." For us in the dock, brought up in the German concept of justice, it was again incomprehensible that no benefit of the doubt should have been given and the sentence "Death by shooting" consequently have been passed.

My four counsel—Dr. Laternser, Dr. Frohwein, Dr. Schütze and Professor Dr. Schwinge—before the event refused to believe in a verdict of guilty. Later, when the Judge Advocate announced "guilty" on *two* counts, they confidently assured me there could be no question of anything but a very lenient sentence. In spite of my contrary belief, they stuck to their opinion. It accordingly came about that when I heard the death penalty announced on both scores it was I who had to comfort my counsel. This is the sober truth, which I now record because it seems to me to throw a piercing light on the proceedings. It is idle to waste words criticizing the faults of the tribunal procedure adopted by the victorious powers for all war crimes trials which are well known.

On the evening of the day on which sentence was pronounced I confided the thoughts which moved me to the following letter:

"6 May 1947. The fatal day is over. I foresaw this outcome, not because I did not believe I had acted legally, but because I doubted the world's sense of justice. My counsel and many others considered the verdict impossible. In their opinion alone I should find justification, even if my conscience did not already afford it me. This had to be the verdict, because

(1) my trial was preceded by the trial in Rome, for the confirmation of which the Judge Advocate fought desperately;

(2) the Partisan war, which is still glorified today, could not be allowed to go down to history as a criminal operation, and

(3) the German officer and with him the military profession in general had to be dealt a mortal blow."

Today the Western Powers blindly overlook the fact that they thereby outraged their own future. I am reminded of a conversation at Nürnberg when a well-informed acquaintance said to me:

"You will be liquidated one way or another. You are too big, too popular. You are a danger."

This remark revealed to me my mission: to testify that we behaved with decency. My personal behaviour was dictated by my name, my rank and respect for the German people. I have tried not to fall short of what these required of me, and, with God's help, I shall worthily endure the worst that may befall me. I can say of myself that in my life I have sought the best; if I have not always succeeded, let those judge me who have never made a mistake. The condemnation of Pharisees cannot touch a man who has or has had some self-respect. My life has been rich because it was filled with work and cares and responsibility. It was not my doing that it had to end in suffering. But if in this situation I can and may still be something to my comrades, if men of standing are still glad to have a talk with me, this is a great grace. If I am acknowledged even by my former enemies and all men shake their heads and are appalled at the sentence passed upon me, that means a great deal. If Italians declare that instead of being put on trial I should have been awarded four golden medals, that is symptomatic of an effort to rise above the bad emotions of today.

In 1950 and 1951 the Bavarian denazification court, dealing with the same subject matter as the Venice trial, reached the decision "not implicated." Although I—and moreover the British—saw in these proceedings an infringement of the principle *ne bis in idem* I was grateful for this clearly stated criticism of the tribunal's verdict.

I have said earlier in this chapter that the tribunal ought at least to have noted the legal position as doubtful. According to the practice of international justice it ought, therefore, to have entered into my activities as a whole—in my counsel's opinion this consideration alone could have acquitted me. I must here state categorically that the Judge Advocate, who otherwise industriously noted down almost every word, yet laid aside his fountain pen with an air of boredom when the witnesses were being examined on such evidence as is given in the following section, showing a patent lack of interest.

Painful as it is for me to thrust myself and my deserts into the foreground, I feel I must bring up one thing which has already become history. However many prominent persons may dispute the fatherhood of the measures which I shall now discuss, the fact remains that I alone had to bear the unusual responsibility for the decisions taken. I think it right to go into the matter in some detail here because I believe that the German people and the other peoples of the western world ought to be told that, in spite of the war's bloody doings, German soldiers were guided by humane, cultural and economic considerations to an extent which conflicts on this scale have very seldom admitted.

MEASURES FOR THE PROTECTION OF ITALY'S POPULATION AND CULTURE

As C.-in-C. South I prevented the planned evacuation of the million population of Rome. In contrast to the 1914-18 war, in which cities close to the front were generally voluntarily or compulsorily evacuated, Rome, fourteen miles from the front, had increased its population by almost half. The evacuation of the city, even if it had been limited to certain categories, would, in view of Allied air strategy, the lack of transport and difficulties of feeding, have certainly led to casualties running into hundreds of thousands.

On Himmler's orders the Jewish community in Rome was to have been deported to an unknown destination. I myself made it impossible to execute this. That I should still today be pilloried as a common murderer and criminal by the Jewish community in Rome shows little discernment.

I also succeeded in preventing the evacuation of other overcrowded towns and villages by measures explained below.

The Italian administration, hampered by shortage of transport and other difficulties, was not in a position to feed the population of central Italy. Even the help given by the German supply services proved inadequate. Credit is due to us for getting the feeding of the population organized on proper lines, for helping out with food from German depots and the provision of military freight space (railway wagons and lorries). At the risk of depriving the soldiers at the front a minimum subsistence was thus ensured for the Italians. I also sanctioned the neutralization of the port of Civitavecchia and its being made available to the Red Cross. In addition the Vatican assisted from its own limited resources. Although every lorry travelling on the roads between northern Italy and Rome was clearly marked with the Red Cross, all these measures were rendered difficult and costly by Allied air attacks.

Anyone who was in Rome during the war knows how often German technical troops had to be used to repair the bombing of the water mains, and every Italian ought to know that the water supply and other public utilities were left intact even when the German troops retired, because we refrained from blowing up bridges and other installations at the risk of substantial military disadvantages.

Finally it should be noted that losses from air raids in the nearly always overcrowded villages and towns were kept within bounds by German initiative and the provision of men, weapons and material.

From September 1943 measures for the protection of the Church and Italian culture in general were carried out, almost unaided, by the Germans, partly at the instance of various princes of the Church and the Italian Ministry of Education. This work finally became so voluminous that a special "Art Preservation Branch" had to be set up at my Southwest headquarters under Dr. Hagemann. Instructions for the preservation of art treasures were so far-reaching that most proposals had to be submitted to operations branch regarding their practicability.

The work of removal was undertaken in successive stages, depending on the ground and air situation in Italy; but even so requirements could hardly be satisfied, and gradually all manner of expedients had to be resorted to. In the following account I confine myself to what was done by C.-in-C. South.

The simplest measure was to forbid trespassing on premises of cultural value in towns and in the country by notice-boards bearing my signature. I signed hundreds of these and can say that not a single case of infraction was brought to my notice. Works of art, archives and libraries were removed to safety from many of these castles, churches, etc., where freight space was available. For instance, the world-famous art treasures of the monastery of Monte Cassino were removed to Orvieto by the "Hermann Goering" Panzer Division and subsequently handed over to the Vatican on my orders for storage in Rome, not to speak of many other art treasures directly rescued by German troops and delivered to the Vatican. The second task was the removal of the Florentine works of art to different secluded villas in the region of Florence, from where, as they became threatened, as in the case of the monasteries of Camaldoli and Sant' Ereno, they were conveyed to the South Tyrol. The Villa Medici at Poggio a Caiano, near Florence, with its precious Florentine works was excluded from the defence zone by my direct order. In addition art treasures provisionally deposited at Marzabotta were eventually stored at Ferrara. In the end lack of freight space made it inevitable that art treasures should be left in their towns, but in that case they were walled in in bomb-proof shelters. This was invariably done where the town could not be declared a "hospital" or "open" city. Even Verona, which as a central traffic nodal point was a special magnet for Allied air raids, fell into this category.

Secondly, cities and towns of cultural interest and ecclesiastical tradition were eliminated from the battle-zone as hospital cities. The Allies were informed of this, usually through the Vatican. The declaration of a "hospital" city involved the evacuation of all military offices, except those connected with the medical service, as was done, for example, at Agnani, Tivoli, Siena—later declared "open"—Assisi, to which the most important works of art in Umbria were brought for safety, and lastly at Merano—an instance of reciprocal respect for the Red Cross.

There were certain military and diplomatic difficulties in making the declaration of an open city thoroughly effective. We tried to do this for a great number of places, but our efforts were not in every case successful. Sometimes as a solution we fell back on the "neutralization" or "demilitarization" of a town. In either case this meant the evacuation of all military offices and troops, making the town out of bounds for all military personnel and cordoning it off by military police, diverting traffic and blocking roads. That these measures did not always meet with the enthusiastic approval of the troops and also gave rise to serious military misgivings is self-evident. Rome is a good example; already declared an open city by Cavallero and Badoglio, it was confirmed as such by myself as C.-in-C. Southwest and kept rigorously free of troops.

The orders prohibiting the defence of medieval towns like Orvieto, Perugia, Urbino or Siena entailed further demilitarizations. Florence, with its unique art treasures, was declared an open city as early as February 1944. I could not accede to the Cardinal Archbishop's request to renounce the defence of the city, as I could not obtain a similar concession from the enemy, so the road through it was blocked by various demolitions, which unfortunately involved the destruction of the wonderful bridges across the Arno.

Pisa was spared damage to its familiar cultural monuments by timely evacuation.

San Marino—as Siena—was, tactically considered, the central point of an important line of defence. The fact that in spite of this I declared it an open town may be seen as a criterion of my complaisance.

On the Via Emilia in northern Italy the cities of Parma, with its magnificent Farnese theatre in the Palazzo della Pilotta, Reggio, Modena and Bologna were all "neutralized" in July 1944. At that time Bologna was the key point of our defence. Petitions from the local mayor and the Archbishop of Bologna that their city be declared "open" were sympathetically considered and led to various security measures. Actually the historical heart of the city was not contested, the chief credit for which is due to General von Senger-Etterlin, commanding the 14th Panzer Corps. Ravenna was early demilitarized and later evacuated without a fight. Venice was chosen as a collecting point for all art treasures in eastern Italy, and in the face of strong opposition by the navy the problem of its preservation was satisfactorily solved.

Vicenza was in practise neutralized by the diversion of all military traffic and the evacuation of the town.

Padua was also completely demilitarized at the request of the Bishop of Padua, thus enabling the precious Giotto Chapel, among other things, to be preserved.

Similar protection was given the monastery of the Certosa di Pavia, south of Milan, by my direct order.

These few instances of the activity of C.-in-C. Southwest may suffice to indicate that the German armed forces did all that was humanly possible to protect Italy's ancient culture. Those who do not know Italy may perhaps be unable to form a correct picture of the extent of our endeavours. They may, however, appreciate them better by comparing the Italian cities listed above, which suffered little or no damage, with German cities like Würzburg, Nürnberg, Freiburg, Dresden and many others. This should give thoughtful minds in other countries matter for reflection.

During the war I received numerous letters of thanks from the Church and civil authorities. Out of these I should like to quote only one excerpt from a letter from the Archbishop of Chieti:

"For eight months we, the people of Chieti, were only seven kilometres from the line of operations held by the Germans. During all this time I received no offensive treatment from the German commanders, especially not from Field-Marshal Kesselring or the generals under him. On the contrary, they, and particularly Field-Marshal Kesselring, supported and helped me in every conceivable way as far as the military situation permitted when the question arose of saving the town of Chieti and anything that could possibly be saved. . . .

"Summing up, I must declare upon my conscience, and I say this without fear of contradiction, that the attitude and behaviour of Field-Marshal Kesselring deserve all public praise. And this is also the opinion of my clergy and—as far as I know—of all right-thinking people in Chieti. We have to thank Field-Marshal Kesselring that in the midst of general destruction our town was spared. I owe a special debt of gratitude to Generals Günther, Baade, Feurstein and Mälzer for their good deeds to this town under the guidance of Field-Marshal Kesselring. Their names and the name of the Field-Marshal will always be blessed here.

"Dear Dr. Laternser [my counsel at my trial], in writing these words I have followed my conscience as archbishop and am very happy to have been able to make some contribution, however small, towards establishing the innocence of Field-Marshal Kesselring. I end this testimony with a prayer to the Almighty that it may enlighten the judges so that they may give judgment in conformity with justice."

AFTER MY TRIAL

I travelled from Mestre to Wolfsberg in Carinthia by the same train as my officer witnesses, but separated from them. My comrades were very depressed. The British commandant at Wolfsberg, however, was a man of understanding; he treated me, as he did von Mackensen and Mälzer, as an honourable soldier. I am grateful to him and to the officers and N.C.O.'s of the camp, thanks to whose kindness my stay in the "bunker" there was endurable. There was one exception, a certain American captain, who had been an Austrian refugee, who had a heart of stone full of hatred and revenge, whose hands improperly used the innocent. I heard a year later that nemesis had overtaken him and brought him where his cynicism had sent the poor wretches he persecuted. I shall always remember, however, our German chaplain, Gruber, who excelled as a shepherd of souls and in good works.

Wolfsberg was an Austrian camp. We did not feel that we were strangers and intruders, but rather the centre of a closed circle of internees who knew how to enrich life by artistic creation, lectures and work. Soon after my arrival a former S.S. major approached me and told me that everything was prepared for my escape. I thanked him, but said firmly that I would never give my enemies (I could not regard the tribunal in any other light) a pretext for believing that they had treated me justly; I would rather miss a chance of freedom which would be an admission of my guilt.

On 4 July the death sentences passed on my comrades and myself were commuted to life imprisonment. Then and afterwards I often said that this reprieve was an aggravation of punishment. When an English colonel once asked me why, I could only answer that there were limits; for me, a German Field-Marshal conscious of innocence, "death by shooting" would have been an end worthy of a soldier, whereas to have to live with criminals in jail was a humiliation and dishonour.

The transfer of von Mackensen, Mälzer and myself from Wolfsberg to Werl in October 1947 was a sign of the comradeship that bound us three together. We had the impression that our officer escort were trying by their special solicitude to dissociate themselves from the verdict and the execution of the sentence, which even they found hard to understand. When the great gates of Werl prison closed behind us it was like a physical pain of amputation from the world. That there was no difference between us and the professional criminal was made very clear when we were marched to the office of the deputy governor, whose duty it was to inform us that we could be allowed only the same privileges as the worst felons.

Years passed in the vicissitudes of prison life. The dreariness of the time until 1950 was to a certain extent compensated for by the better treatment of the years that followed. I was rather abashed to discover that we could only get our requests forwarded to the German, and more especially the Bavarian authorities with the support of the British and American control, which last, however, went to the limit of their competence to satisfy our economic wants—for example, the pay due to us as prisoners of war and remuneration as convicts. Besides Lieutenant-Colonel Vickers, the last governor of the Allied prison, whose kindness was only limited by restrictive orders, I should like to mention General Bishop, whose intervention gave the first impetus to later improvements. In the legal field I cite only *one* name: Sir Alfred Brown, senior legal adviser to the British High Commissioner, who helped us nobly and evidently suffered inwardly as a responsible jurist under the conditions of justice he had to represent. I was less favourably impressed by a distinguished general, who, after a cursory glance into my cold, damp and unfriendly cell, brought out the remarkable comment: "Very nice!"

My occupation was gumming paper bags. My performance, for a sixty-five-year-old Field-Marshal, was recognized as quite respectable. My colleagues, mostly "war criminals," were decent fellows and made the work and life more easy. When after some months I was asked how I liked the work I replied: "Well enough. In my wildest dreams I never imagined I should become a paper-bag gummer."

The next day was my last as a manual labourer, and I took up the study of history.

One fine morning, at an hour and a half's notice, we were moved to another block. The reason was kept secret; I still do not know why they moved us, but possibly they wanted us kept closer under the eye of the British, for our stable companions were British prisoners. That was a wretched time. Woe to anybody who spoke to us—even when we were visited by the chaplain a warder had to be present. On one of her visits my wife brought me a few cakes and some lozenges because the prison fare upset my stomach. She delivered the tiny parcel to a German official, who passed it to a British official, who handed it in to the office for it to be given to me. An English newspaper reporter who happened to be there witnessed this performance and concocted what one can only call a tissue of lies and sent it off to his paper. His article told the story of our receiving a constant flow of parcels and of our sharing British rations—when all we ever saw of them was their daily issue to the British prisoners, which seemed like a banquet to us who only received the nauseous and insufficient German soup—and of other pamperings. The result was that three British officials, including the governor, were transferred elsewhere.

Yet we survived even those times. A new day dawned when we were given the use of a separate floor in a rebuilt wing in which the "dining" and "recreation" rooms were decently furnished. The contributions of individual Germans to this last shows that we are capable of practical Christianity. Special recognition is due to Frau Weeck, the "Angel of Werl," the indefatigable vice-president of the Westphalian Red Cross.

On the other hand, the revision of our sentences made no progress whatever. British officialdom obstinately defended the judgments as given, heedless of the accumulation of convincing exculpatory evidence and additional testimony which could not be put forward at the time of our trial. I cannot imagine that responsible British circles can believe in the legality of the proceedings, even if Kirkpatrick's open letter to the press gives us matter for reflection. The British High Commissioner's statements are in irreconcilable contradiction to our admittedly subjective but thorough knowledge of each case. For these reasons—after obtaining the consent of the Federal Chancellor—I wanted to address a petition to the Speaker of the House of Commons that the war crimes cases should be investigated, in their general and legal aspects, by a mixed parliamentary commission on the spot, that is to say at Werl. Taking into consideration the sense of justice of independent members of Parliament, I assumed that this commission would have taken an opposite view of the court's proceedings, have taken account of the multifarious deficiencies and gaps in the documents of the trial, and certainly have proposed a way out. I was, however, forbidden to carry out my intention. A pity! [1] I realize that subordinate officials have to carry out the orders of their superiors even if they themselves question them; I do not wish to bring up the point that we Germans after 1945 were condemned to death or to heavy sentences of imprisonment for obeying orders. I have never discovered a comprehensible reason for the refusal of those in authority to reconsider our cases, but justice must prevail even in the face of a public opinion unsympathetic, ill advised and admittedly provoked. It is also difficult to understand the attempt to hide behind a Four-Power Pact as this had already lost its justification and legal validity; anyhow, a pact which is disavowed *urbi et orbi* can never be regarded as valid international law.

When the death sentence was passed upon me in 1947 I believed I had the courage to face what lay before me. I had behind me a rich life in which there could be no further peaks of experience. Today, five years later, I must confess that this life so outwardly defamed has been enriched by new springs

[1] On 15 July 1952 Field-Marshal Kesselring was given leave on parole for an operation performed by Professor Bürkle de la Camp. On 24 October he was released as an act of clemency.

of comfort. I had indeed always made a habit of meditating at
the end of every day on the day's lessons, but I had never had
the time to see myself, my surroundings and the times so clearly
in perspective. I now tried to judge objectively, to regard my
disappointments as symptomatic of the malady of the age and
to subdue revenge and hatred to understanding. Feeling as I did,
it was only natural that I should become the mediator among
my fellows in misfortune and between them and the prison
authorities. Gradually my efforts were rewarded by the awaken-
ing of a new sympathy for us as human beings and as soldiers
instead of the hostility born of propaganda. The men who were
big enough to take up the cudgels for us in spite of the prevailing atmosphere and who made the conditions of our existence
easier have already been mentioned. They did a lot more than
those who devoted themselves to "re-education." The heart
speaks more effectively than such questionable experiments.

Many things happened during my imprisonment to fascinate
someone whose place was formerly at the hub of the world.
The further one is removed from the daily carping of events,
the easier it is to see through the confusion in things. I am only
stating a truism when I say that our performance in the war was
something of an achievement, as Liddell Hart confirms. In contrast to his opinion, however, I remember different utterances
and articles written by Germans referring to the "genius," in
plain language, the "idiocy" of the German High Command,
according to which the German infantryman was a dragooned
and pitiable creature who suffered from the treatment of his
superiors and was continually bullied by them. As an old soldier
with more than forty years' active service who has the right to
claim that, despite his severity and exactingness, he all along
even enjoyed a certain popularity, I fail to understand this kind
of journalism. I readily admit that mistakes were made. But as
we succeeded in bringing every campaign in the first years of
the war to a victorious and swift conclusion, it can only be
assumed that on the Allied side still greater "ignoramuses" must
have been at the helm. The more astonishing, therefore, must
it be to any reasoning person to hear that our military training

and education was wrong all along the line and that we must revise our ideas in accordance with democratic principles—for example, those of the U.S. army. That is more than I can take.

I had the honour to have under my command a large number of the best German divisions, and I know that the victories of German soldiers in the field would have been impossible had there not been a sworn comradeship between the men and their officers. It gave me great joy on tours of inspection in the line to see this unity. I was especially proud of the generally model behaviour of the German soldier in 1945 when he surrendered. I considered then this behaviour a triumph of discipline, training and harmony of command and troops. True, there are many things we can alter, we can adapt ourselves to progress and learn new and valuable lessons; but let us keep our national character and respect our traditions. Let us beware of becoming a people without roots.

I did not lightly decide to write this book. In the end I made the decision in order from my observatory to contribute something towards a truthful record of a good piece of German history, to the raising of a monument to our magnificent soldiers and to helping the world to recognize the face of war in its grim totality. The old tale of the relativity of all events is here confirmed for those who ponder them. To the young I would say that the meaning of life lies in the endeavour to do right, and that perfection is not to be found on this earth. In the ancient saying *errare humanum est* we can hear man's cry for self-determination and a warning not to be hasty in passing judgment on other people.

Index

377